DESTROYER SQUADRON
23

DESTROYER SQUADRON
23

Combat Exploits of
Arleigh Burke's Gallant Force

KEN JONES

BLUEJACKET BOOKS

NAVAL INSTITUTE PRESS
Annapolis, Maryland

Originally published by the Chilton Company
First Bluejacket Books printing, 1997

Library of Congress Cataloging-in-Publication Data
Jones, Ken, 1903 Feb. 11–
    Destroyer Squadron 23 : combat exploits of Arleigh Burke's gallant force / Ken Jones.
        p.   cm. — (Bluejacket books)
    Originally published: Philadelphia : Chilton Co., 1959.
    Includes index.
    ISBN 1-55750-412-1 (pbk. : alk. paper)
    1. World War, 1939–1945—Naval operations, American.   2. United States. Navy.
Destroyer Squadron, 23rd.   3. Burke, Arleigh A., 1901–   . I. Title. II. Series.
D769.537 23rd.J66   1997
940.54′5973—dc21   97-26229

Printed in the United States of America on acid-free paper ∞

04   03   02   01   00   99   98   97   8   7   6   5   4   3   2   1

For my beloved wife, Iris

Foreword

by

Fleet Admiral W. F. Halsey, United States Navy (Retired)

~~~~~~

For many decades, men have searched for a magic formula for leadership. Volumes have been written in an attempt to describe those personal qualities that kindle the spark of inspiration among others in great human undertakings.

But a master equation has not yet been evolved, because leadership is a product of many variables—among them human character, individual personality, and the times and circumstances in which men live.

History has recorded many instances in which the right man was present at the right time to further a just cause and bring credit to his nation at a critical moment.

This book tells the story of such a man and such a time.

Commodore Arleigh Burke provided the fire of leadership that fused a squadron of destroyers into a superb combat organization—DESTROYER SQUADRON 23, the Gallant Squadron of this book—a real fighting outfit with that vital combat ingredient we know as "fighting spirit."

Fighting spirit, like leadership, is difficult if not well-nigh impossible to describe—yet that spirit is brought to life in these pages. Here is a narrative that captures the elusive and mysterious combination of human qualities that add up to inspiration, because here is a story of action, human action, and reaction, in the heat of battle.

But this is more than a story of ships and their tactical deployment in sea battles that will live as classics of naval warfare. Most of all, it is a story of men in action—over thirty-six hundred officers and men of the United States Navy—and how they lived and fought as a magnificent combat team.

Men of the sea have known for generations that individual ships develop qualities of personality and character all their own.

"A ship is as good as the men who man her!"

The whole-hearted effort and teamwork of every last officer and man on board are required to give a ship the capabilities so necessary to become an effective fighting unit. Each officer and man is proud of his ship and his own important part in making her an efficient weapon of war.

This story of the Gallant Squadron describes the rare phenomenon of a spirit which extended beyond the individual ship to create a sense of pride in, and loyalty to, the *entire* squadron.

Each ship was good—not only because her men were good, but also because she belonged to DesRon-23! In this, each ship contributed to a higher standard, and each ship strove to live up to the reputation earned by the whole squadron.

While the period covered by this book is relatively short, it was a crucial period in the Pacific War, and the vital part played by Destroyer Squadron 23 under the inspiring leadership of Arleigh Burke was, in a sense, only a beginning, but the vital beginning, of a steady drive forward which gained momentum and power until United States naval forces steamed victoriously into Tokyo Bay.

W.F. Halsey

FLEET ADMIRAL
UNITED STATES NAVY (RETIRED)

Preface

~~~~~~

For an author, reaching the end of a book is like reaching the end of a journey. In the case of *Destroyer Squadron 23* it has been a long journey and the most rewarding of my life. Many have accompanied me briefly along the way—Cavenagh, Lampman, Reynolds . . . Others have peeped helpfully over my shoulder—Armstrong, Gano, Hamberger, Stout. All have given generously of their mellow wisdom and, more importantly, of the inspirational spirit of the Squadron which abides in them.

In all candor, *Destroyer Squadron 23* is not a writing for those who would dwell overlong upon or cuddle the dolorous sentiment of John Donne—". . . *never send to see for whom the bell tolls; it tolls for thee*"—unless they are willing, also, to accept its rational corollary, which is that the bell can peal as well as it can toll, and that *it peals for thee*, too.

Many things are recorded of United States Destroyer Squadron 23. The one thing *never* recorded of them is that they took counsel of their fears, for they did not. They were confident in competence, strong in faith, and for them the bell never tolled and it never will. It pealed a clear signal of their courage, their conviction, and their dedication even unto death. And in pealing for them it peals also for thee and for me.

A Word of Explanation and Appreciation

This chronicle has been taken from and faithfully reflects the official records of the United States Navy. In perhaps two or three instances which the reader will have no difficulty identifying, I have found it desirable to supply names for individuals whose participation in the events recorded seemed something less than champion. With these inconsequential exceptions, however, all persons are identified by their

ix

proper names. In the matter of dialogue the words spoken may be
accepted as interpreting reliably the personality of the speaker and
the sense of the situation portrayed. All TBS transmissions are recorded word for word as they appear in the official record compiled
at the times the conversations took place. All other dialogue is substantially supported by log entries, by signed battle reports, by war
diaries, or by official memoranda, or else reported orally or in writing
to the author by the speakers. All times given are as they appear in
the officially accepted record. Interpretation of senior Japanese officers is supported by post-war interrogations of enemy nationals, in
many instances including the subjects themselves.

Together with all who write of this period of our naval history I
must acknowledge my indebtedness for guidance to the impressive
works of Samuel Eliot Morison, naval historian; and to Theodore
Roscoe whose compilation of destroyer operations in World War II
often saved me much time by indicating appropriate areas for intensive
research. I should like, also, to acknowledge my debt to Colonel Allison
Ind, Army of the United States, for the guidance derived from his
study of the intelligence network of coast watchers and secret agents,
of which he was a part, which functioned for the Allies throughout
the campaign in the Solomons.

I am, of course, indebted to a great many individuals for their kind
and unselfish assistance which has enabled me to present herein a study
with more dimensions than a mere flat projection of continuity in time.
At the top of this list I must place Admiral Arleigh Burke, the Chief
of Naval Operations, and Mrs. Burke. Both received me graciously,
answered my many questions patiently, and supplied invaluable docu-
mentary material. Next I must express my deep appreciation to the
following officers for sustained personal assistance:

Vice Admiral Bernard L. Austin, USN
Rear Admiral Robert Cavenagh, USN
Rear Admiral Roy Gano, USN
Rear Admiral Henry Jacques Armstrong, USN (Ret.)
Rear Admiral DeWitt Clinton Ellis Hamberger, USN (Ret.)
Rear Admiral Ralph Lampman, USN (Ret.)
Rear Admiral Luther Kendrick Reynolds, USN (Ret.)
Rear Admiral Herald Franklin Stout, USN (Ret.)
Commander John H. Davis, USN

Every one of these officers has contributed personally and importantly
to this study of United States Destroyer Squadron 23. Indeed, their
contributions have been so unique that without them the story could
not have been written.

For official co-operation, great courtesy and patience and expressions of confidence, I wish to record my gratitude to Rear Admiral E. M. Eller, USN (Ret.), Director of Naval History; Captain F. Kent Loomis, USN (Ret.), Assistant Director of Naval History; Commander Herb Gimpel, USN, and Commander C. R. Wilhide, USN. Finally, for unfailing encouragement and many helpful suggestions, I wish to thank three very dear friends, Mr. Edmund L. Browning, Jr., attorney; Dr. Ivor Cornman, scientist; and Mr. Alex Jackinson, of New York City.

In conclusion, in *Destroyer Squadron 23* I have made far less attempt to record deeds of heroism than I have to study and present clearly the origins of the compulsions which prompted such deeds. That, to me, is the greater challenge, and its accomplishment the more enduring achievement. It was denied me to be of their company. As second best I can only hope that in the *telling* I have been as faithful and as worthy as they were in the *doing*.

KEN JONES

Contents

DESTROYER SQUADRON
23

1

Night of the Long Lances

~~~~~~

The quartermaster on the bridge of destroyer *Waller* took an appraising look at the barrel-shaped brass clock on the bulkhead, then stepped around to the flag bridge behind and struck six sharp taps on the ship's bell affixed to the foremast, thus officially certifying the instant to be 2300 hours on the night of 5th May, 1943. *Waller*, the "flag boat" of Destroyer Division 43, swung obediently around her anchor in Havannah Channel off the island of Efate at the bottom end of the New Hebrides group, 18 degrees south of the equator.

The topside temperature was a humid 88, but a relentless sun blazing day long on the DD's steel deck plates had converted her lower compartments into a fireless cooker. Even at the late hour of 11 and with ventilating fans making top revolutions, temperatures below ranged upward to 100 degrees.

A young ensign had the deck and the vessel was dark and quiet, for *Waller* was enjoying an unaccustomed respite from her usual busy pattern of escort and battle employment. She was on 12 hours' notice— a sabbatical for a ship of her class at the time and place. She steamed one boiler which gave her available power to shift anchorage, operate her generators and turrets in the event of a surprise surface attack, or take evasive action should enemy aircraft appear. And she maintained a skeletal watch—engineroom, communications, bridge. Otherwise *Waller* slumbered.

In a below-decks cubicle screened from the wardroom and adjacent spaces by a pleated and heavy dark green curtain, a shaded bulb cast spare illumination over the tiny rectangle of a drop-leaf desk at which an officer sat writing. He was of well-knit, medium stature, blond and blue-eyed. A fresh film of perspiration covered his throat down into the V of his open-necked shirt, and droplets of moisture beaded the fine reddish hairs on the backs of his stubby hands. He was 42 years old, and in 20 years of naval service he had risen to the rank of commander, an achievement attested by the silver leaves flanking the wilted collar of his shirt.

On the Navy's roster this officer's name appeared as Arleigh A. Burke, and he was taken for an Irishman by all save his intimates. He was, however, not an Irishman but a Swede. His patronymic was Bjorkegren, which means *limb of a birch tree.* His grandfather had changed the name to Burke many years before and thus young Arleigh, upon entering the Naval Academy in 1919, had registered as Burke, and he never was known by any other name in the Navy.

Burke commanded the four ships of Destroyer Division 43. Thus he wore the designation Commodore, which is not a Navy rank but rather a title denoting command of a floating force composed of several units. In official correspondence he also carried the ideographic identification "ComDesDiv-43," which is the Navy's contraction of "Commander, Destroyer Division 43."

Twenty-two lined tablet pages covered with his bold, school-boyish calligraphy piled up at Arleigh Burke's left elbow. The document he struggled to produce was a memorandum to higher authority recommending new techniques for the employment of destroyers with cruiser task forces. With Japanese and American task forces repeatedly locking horns in the Solomons, it was a tactical subject of stature and immediacy. With an intensity reflecting two of his own dominating characteristics—audacious aggressiveness and superb technical mastery of the destroyer as a weapon—Burke concluded his doctrine:

When contact with an enemy force is made destroyers in the van should initiate a coordinated torpedo attack WITHOUT ORDERS.

Then he added (for he was fully aware of the sensitive ground upon which he intruded):

This last recommendation is the most difficult. The delegation of authority [by a task force commander] is always hard and . . . where such delegation of authority may result in disastrous consequences if a subordinate commander makes an error, it requires more than usually is meant by confidence: IT REQUIRES FAITH.

When Burke emphasized the requirement of faith he cut close to the heart of a Navy *mystique* which he personified to a greater degree than his contemporaries, and which, in 6 short months, was to set his feet on the road to greatness as commander of the Gallant Squadron— Destroyer Squadron 23. On this humid May night, however, such potent abstractions shared his thoughts with images of blazing, sinking U.S. warships and the blasted, lifeless bodies of American sailors. These images arose in dismaying array from the battle reports which Burke had been studying in preparation for drafting his own recommendations. Of these documents one had been of especial interest to and significance for Arleigh Burke. It was a report of the Battle of Tassafaronga—"The Night of the Long Lances."

At Tassafaronga a cautious United States cruiser task force commander, for 4 fatal minutes after contact with the enemy, withheld permission for his destroyers to launch torpedoes. In consequence—or at least principally in consequence, as Arleigh Burke saw it—in the ensuing 20 or 30 minutes of lurid action a resolute and skillful Japanese Rear Admiral administered to the United States Navy the most humiliating defeat in its history.

It has been said of Tassafaronga that it needn't have happened and it shouldn't have happened—but it did. The situational background was encouraging, although the immediate antecedents of the battle itself were unpropitious.

A Japanese labor force had occupied portions of Guadalcanal since June, 1942, and had constructed an air strip near Lunga Point. On 7th August, 11,000 Marines landed on Guadalcanal, captured the air strip which they named Henderson Field, and challenged the Japanese power. The Japs immediately launched a series of efforts to toss the Americans off the island, and in the next 5 months this ding-dong struggle for Guadalcanal fertilized seed which fruited in no less than six major naval engagements, culminating in the debacle of Tassafaronga.

On the Japanese side, undue confidence in the prowess of the Emperor's troops, and Admiral Isoroku Yamamoto's stubborn devotion to classic naval principles, set the stage. Instead of reinforcing their Guadalcanal garrison in overwhelming strength and sweeping the Marines into the sea, the Japs landed new forces piecemeal. Our leathernecks found it possible to deal with forces thus hesitantly committed, and at the same time extend their own perimeters.

On the strategic side afloat Yamamoto held firmly to the Mahan doctrine of seeking to bring the U.S. Pacific Fleet to battle under circumstances favorable to him. Thus naval support and supply of the Japanese troops on Guadalcanal was sporadic and often ineffective. Indeed, the Jap supply and reinforcement situation finally got so desperate that top Admiral Yamamoto dumped the whole sticky problem into the lap of one of his most astute and experienced subordinates, Rear Admiral Raizo Tanaka.

"Tenacious Tanaka" (an encomium we were forced to bestow by the time he had whipped the stuffing out of four of our heavy cruisers, one light cruiser, and six destroyers, using nothing but a handful of Jap DDs and the long lance) came up with an ingenious solution to the puzzle. He ordered food and ammunition placed in steel drums that would float and could be tossed overside from fast destroyers. The plan was simple. The Japanese DDs, carrying the supplies and some reinforcements, would steam close in along the northern coast of Guadalcanal in the vicinity of Tassafaronga at the mouth of the Bonegi River. At an appropriate point, under cover of darkness, the ammo and food would be flung overside to drift to the beach or be recovered by the shoreside garrison using small boats. Meanwhile, the few reinforcing troops would be transferred to shore boats; in an hour or so the job would be done, and Tanaka & Company would hightail back to their base.

Tanaka's intentions were not immediately fathomed by the top United States naval command. Successively Admirals Nimitz and Halsey had been forced to give Number 1 priority to the possibility that the Japanese would mount an all-out surface effort to recapture strategic Guadalcanal. This *idée fixe*, in course of time, imparted its own distortion to U.S. interpretation of reports of Japanese ship movements, and intelligence officers at Pacific Fleet headquarters tended to magnify into formidable intentions reports of many routine enemy surface operations. Thus it chanced that when, as early as 24th November, suspicious enemy ship activity was reported in the Buin–Shortlands and New Georgia–Santa Isabel areas, a major naval strike against our hard-pressed Marines on Guadalcanal was envisioned—a far cry from the modest supply mission which really was being planned.

The job of preparing a plan for a riposte in force to parry the anticipated Japanese thrust was turned over to Rear Admiral Thomas C. "Tommy" Kinkaid, just arrived to take charge of our cruiser force assembled at Espiritu Santo. By 27th November the paper work was complete. But at this decisive moment the long arm of Washington reached out and plucked Kinkaid back to Pearl for other duty. He was replaced by Rear Admiral Carleton H. "Bosco" Wright, also newly arrived in the area aboard cruiser *Minneapolis*. Wright examined Kinkaid's plan, found it good, and accepted responsibility for its execution within 24 hours of his arrival. It was an example of the exigencies of the time that a flag officer should be made answerable for a combat mission less than 2 days after assuming command, and with time for but a single brief conference with the subordinate commanders of his group, which was designated Task Force 67. How much or how little this last-minute switch in command may have had to do with our fumbling performance at Tassafaronga will long remain moot. At best the task force was a scratch team with a plan on paper but lacking the solid body of practiced doctrine which alone can impart the strengths of polished teamwork in combat. That also was a thing at which Arleigh Burke had hammered away in his memorandum.

It was a curious product of Halsey's staff's anticipation of a major Japanese strike against Guadalcanal that, at almost precisely the same time on the evening of 29th November, Tanaka weighed his anchors and stood out of Buin while Wright, with shielded lights in small boats to signal the turns through the minefield off Espiritu, sortied with Task Force 67. They had a common destination: the northern coast of Guadalcanal. But that's *all* they had in common. Tanaka led eight modern, single-stacked destroyers, each loaded with 1,000 drums of supplies and equipment and a small number of Japanese Army personnel. He was not looking for a fight. Indeed, to be sure he would avoid one he set course north through Bougainville Strait and then east toward Roncador Reef. This, he figured, should throw snooping U.S. aircraft off the scent and permit him, at the last moment, to break sharply south for Indispensable Strait, thus avoiding The Slot and, possibly, a prowling enemy. This was not the first of wily Tanaka's supply missions; he'd been running them every fourth night for some time, and such devious tactics had served him well.

For Wright the run to "Cactus," which was our code designation for Guadalcanal, was 580 miles by the most direct route passing eastward of San Cristobal and thence via Indispensable Strait into Lengo Channel and the waters our men had dubbed Ironbottom Sound because of the number of ships sunk in the area. That was the route he chose. His destroyers got under way at 2310 and his cruisers at 2335, a trifle earlier than he had thought possible. The average speed of the Task Force was 28.2 knots, and as the darkened ships plowed silently through the mellow night Admiral Wright strolled out on the starboard bridge wing of his flagship, *Minneapolis*, spread his forearms along the teak rail, relaxed, and reviewed in his mind the intelligence he had received up to that moment and the details of Operation Plan 1-42 which now was to govern the tactical evolutions of the force under his command.

The intelligence he had was confusing. Original estimate of the enemy force to be anticipated was eight destroyers and six transports. Subsequent information indicated that combatant ships might be substituted for the transports, and a still later report warned that a Japanese cruiser task force comparable to his own might be on the way. On balance, Bosco Wright had little real notion of what he might be poking his nose into.

Task Force 67 was a sturdy formation which any Rear Admiral might have been proud to command. It was composed of four 10,000-ton heavy cruisers mounting 8-inch batteries—*Minneapolis, New Orleans, Pensacola*, and *Northampton*—and one 6-inch cruiser, *Honolulu*. Wright had split this force assigning *Northampton* and *Honolulu* to his next in command, Rear Admiral Mahlon S. Tisdale, who rode in *Honolulu*, and this unit of two cruisers was designated Task Group

67.2. Only four destroyers—*Fletcher, Drayton, Maury,* and *Perkins*—
sortied from Espiritu. Two more, *Lamson* and *Lardner,* were to join
the Task Force en route. The destroyer force was designated Task
Group 67.4 and, under Commander William M. Cole, in *Fletcher,* was
assigned to lead the formation on what Wright assumed would be his
engaged bow should he meet the enemy.

The essentials of Operation Plan 1-42 were standard for the kind
of mission. Should the enemy be met at night as was expected, the plan
specified that the van destroyers, using their radar advantage (the
Japanese didn't yet possess radar) would launch a surprise torpedo
attack and then steam clear so the cruisers could open gunfire. The
cruisers were not to shoot, however, until the DDs' torpedoes had time
to run to target.

The cruiser float planes, more of an encumbrance than a help during
a night engagement, were to be flown ashore, all but two returning to
"Base Button," which was Espiritu. Two planes were to go to Tulagi,
there to await Wright's summons to rejoin and illuminate the enemy if
met. Recognition lights—green over white over white—were to be
flashed on momentarily only to check the fire of one friendly ship upon
another should the chaos of battle produce such a situation. Searchlights were forbidden as providing the enemy with too accurate a point
of aim, and to thwart the effective use of searchlights by the Japanese
the U.S. cruisers were instructed not to close the enemy under 12,000
yards (about 7 miles) unless special circumstances required it.

So far as Bosco Wright could tell, Operation Plan 1-42 was a good
enough instrument. Essentially it was. But no plan can be of much
effectiveness unless it is followed, and "1-42" was followed but loosely
and briefly at Tassafaronga. Beyond that, probably no plan could have
accommodated three of the enemy's principal strengths. The first was
the Japanese "long lance" torpedo. It has been described as "blue
murder," and it was exactly that. The second enemy strength lay in
the high skill and the cool courage of the Japanese destroyermen in
general and torpedomen in particular. For nearly 2 years, as the interrogation of Japanese officers revealed after the war, they had been
practicing at night the precise evolutions to which Wright found it
impossible to reply effectively at Tassafaronga. They could go through
the drill blindfolded, and they were as battle-hardened as wharf rats
and as self-reliant as eagles. The third factor was the very high technical competence and contempt for danger or the odds against him of
Rear Admiral Raizo Tanaka.

Tanaka was of Samurai lineage. He was of medium stature, his shoulders sloped, and his bearing was short of the pouter pigeon carriage
encouraged by some military classicists. He had a wedge-shaped face,

broad across the forehead and slanting obliquely downward from the temples to a heavy jaw and a decidedly pointed chin. His eyebrows were black and bushy and the menacing mien they imparted to his countenance was italicized by a similarly bristly black mustache. His neck was thin and his head, above an overly prominent Adam's apple, seemed to have precarious support. However, despite his unprepossessing appearance, there were other and better measures of the man.

As Tanaka approached Indispensable Strait his Chief of Staff, Captain Yasumi Toyama, stepped forward with a sheaf of messages. They were from Japanese Army headquarters on Guadalcanal and naval headquarters at Rabaul, and all sounded an urgent warning: Japanese snooper planes had "spooked" a United States cruiser task force entering the area for which Tanaka was bound. His decks were cluttered with cargo and Army personnel who would be in the way in the event of battle. The ⅜-inch steel plates and the 5-inch popguns of his 2,000-ton destroyers were fragile things with which to oppose armor-clad giants of five times his displacement hurling 8-inch salvos. A single cruiser salvo registering on one of his DDs could tear it to bits. Here, then, was ample excuse for Admiral Tanaka to "make a 180" and withdraw the way he had come. But he did not. He had consummate confidence in his own tactical skill, the technical ability of his crews, and the devastating characteristics of the long lance. He barely glanced at the warnings; then shoved the messages back at Toyama and snapped, *"Tell the men to prepare for a fight!"* Destroyer Squadron 2 of the Imperial Japanese Navy, with attached destroyer transport units, stood on course. Tanaka's was a valiant resolution.

The long lance in which Admiral Tanaka had such faith was a formidable weapon in the hands of those who knew how to employ it, and the Emperor's sailors knew precisely how. It was the Japanese Model 93 torpedo and it was superior in every respect to the 21-inch Mark XV torpedo which was the best we could offer to oppose it. The long lance took its name from the fact that it could and did run hot and true for distances up to 11 miles at the high speed of 49 knots. Oxygen-fueled, it could travel twice as far at the slower speed of 36 knots, which made it out-range an American battleship's main battery. Its payload was an incredible 1,036 pounds of high explosive, better than twice the payload of our Mark XV. It was an altogether superior piece of ordnance which we were unable to match during the entire course of the war.

Plowing north by west through the daylight hours of Monday, 30th November, Bosco Wright's task force was a picture-book formation. The sky was slightly overcast, which imparted to the waters offshore a deep blue color on top of which the wakes cast up ivory fretwork. The rollers which lifted under his bows were long, low, and lazy, and the peacefulness of the scene gave little signal of the grim night to follow. The ships of the task force, however, were pregnant with latent power— hundreds of tons of high explosive and armor-piercing projectiles, and the instruments for their efficient delivery on target. Also they were heavy with fuel. *Minneapolis* displaced 3,400 tons above her rated 10,000 "dry" tons and her engines throbbed at better than 300 revolutions to enable her to maintain 28 knots.

Aboard their respective ships, officers went methodically about preparing their units for battle. In *Northampton* the executive officer, meticulous Commander J. S. Crenshaw, made a careful inspection above and below. He found eight cans of lard and six cans of salad oil in the general mess issue-room and pondered their danger as a fire hazard. Finally he decided to let them remain where they were. He noted with satisfaction that his damage control officer had set out 100 buckets to be used either for bailing or fighting fire. Finding forty 100-pound bags of salt stacked handily against a midships bulkhead, he inquired their purpose of a grizzled chief. "I'll tell you, sir," replied the seasoned shellback. "Blood makes decks pretty slippery. If we need traction to move around that salt could come in mighty handy. Then too," he added as an afterthought, "we might could use it to smother fires." Commander Crenshaw was well pleased with the foresight of his ship's company. By 1700 hours he was back on the bridge reporting to Captain Willard A. Kitts, III, commanding, that *Northampton* was in proper posture for battle.

The tally of preparation and inspection throughout the rest of the task force was comparable. Aboard *New Orleans* Captain Clifford H. Roper, commanding, ordered that tubs of sandwiches be brought topside and served to the men along with hot coffee at 2100, when they would be at general quarters. *Minneapolis* was temporarily missing an "exec," her executive officer having been detached an hour and a half before the task force sortied. Her gunnery officer, Commander R. G. McCool, was slated to take over as Number 1, but Captain Charles E. Rosendahl, commanding, preferred to keep McCool as "guns" until after the anticipated battle, and so split the "exec's" responsibilities between himself and two other officers.

Wright catapulted his planes beginning at 1613. The pair which flew to Tulagi, there to await Wright's summons to rejoin and illuminate, carried four Mark V parachute flares each. As matters turned out, these two planes were jinxed. When the summons came their pilots shoved throttles forward and made long, furious runs across the smooth black waters of Tulagi harbor, but it was no use. The night was so absolutely flat calm at Tulagi that the float planes could not get airborne. They kept trying and eventually they did manage to stagger into the air, but by that time the battle was over.

This was one of several bits of bad luck that harassed Bosco Wright on the evening of 30th November. Another minor bit of ill fortune had to do with destroyers *Lamson* and *Lardner*, which he was forced to carry into battle at the tail end of his cruiser column. Wright picked up *Lamson* and *Lardner*, on orders from Admiral Halsey, from an east-bound convoy which he met as he entered Lengo Channel. Aboard *Lamson* was Commander Laurence A. Abercrombie, commander of Destroyer Division 9, and thus the senior destroyer officer present with the task force. However, Abercrombie had no copy of Plan 1-42 and didn't even know the proper recognition lights to display for identification if fired on by his own forces. In the circumstances, Wright had no choice but to order Abercrombie to join up in the rear. Indeed, when the battle roared to life, the senior destroyer officer present found that his main job was to keep from being sunk by his friends, and his engagement of enemy units was rather a left-handed affair.

When, at 2245, Task Force 67 entered Ironbottom Sound, Wright's silent ships were steering a bit north of west, perhaps 20 miles off the northern coast of Guadalcanal, with Henderson Field bearing broad on their port beam. The moon had not yet risen and the night was very dark, with a completely overcast sky which limited visibility to 2 miles. The wind was from the southwest at 12 knots, the sea calm and glassy. On the decks and in the turrets of destroyers and cruisers alike, men wearing steel helmets and lifejackets crouched at their weapons and waited. Many of them were new to combat—and many of them would not see the dawn of another day. As they passed moistened tongues over dry lips they shared common thoughts, although few realized it: "What shall I be called upon to do—to endure? Shall I be able to meet this challenge? What will it be like . . . ?"

In dimly lighted compartments below decks practiced eyes were riveted on radar screens, not alone to catch first glimpse of the enemy but also to check the navigator's calculations. Lights burned bright in combat information centers and officers huddled around tables and panels laden with sensitive instruments to calculate range and bearing and the score of other details, including the temperature of the powder which must be correlated for efficient modern fire control.

The skippers of most of the ships were on the bridges, but Captain Frank H. Lowe, of heavy cruiser *Pensacola*, preferred to fight his ship from sky control, above and forward of the pilot house, and had made arrangements to take that station in the event an enemy appeared. His "exec," Commander Harry Keeler, Jr., was in the pilot house; Lieutenant L. K. Taylor was officer of the deck. Aboard *Minneapolis* another officer, Marine Captain A. R. Schirman, had provided himself with a lofty perch from which to observe the festivities. Night binoculars in hand, he manned "sky aft," a station better than 60 feet above the water. Admiral Wright had reduced speed to 20 knots; Task Force 67 was on the prowl—as ready for battle as ever she would be!

"Tenacious Tanaka" rounded Savo Island at about 2245 and came left to parallel the coast. He was close inshore—only 2 miles off—and with a single exception his destroyers were in column. Destroyer *Takanami* was stationed as a picket on the port bow of the flagship, several thousand yards to seaward of the advancing column. Tanaka, in destroyer *Naganami*, led the main column and was followed by the destroyers of Transport Unit 1 under command of Captain Torajiro Sato. Their order of steaming was *Makanami, Oyashio, Kuroshio,* and *Kagero*. Following them came *Kawakaze* and *Suzukaze*, comprising Transport Unit 2 under command of Captain Giichiro Nakahara. By 2300 Tanaka had reduced speed to 12 knots preparatory to jettisoning his drums of supplies. Although expecting to meet opposition sooner or later, he did not at the moment know of the immediate presence of the United States cruiser task force only a few miles away. The two groups of fighting ships were closing on collision courses; their head-on meeting could be but a matter of minutes.

At 2306 *Minneapolis* made first radar contact with the enemy. Eight pips appeared on the screen of her "Sugar George" (search) radar, bearing 284 degrees, distant about 14 miles. The targets seemed to be on a southerly course at a speed of 15 knots. Immediately upon receiving this report Admiral Wright brought his formation into column of ships with *Fletcher* and the other three DDs of Task Group 67.4 out in front. There was a 2-mile interval between *Minneapolis* leading the cruiser line and *Drayton,* last of the four destroyers. The cruisers were steaming at a distance of 1,000 yards between ships. The U.S. and the Japanese formations were closing each other at a combined rate of speed of the order of 32 knots.

Within 8 minutes Commander Cole, leading the cruisers by several miles in *Fletcher,* had the forward elements of Tanaka's destroyer column on his radar screen bearing 285 degrees true, and a torpedo firing "solution"—the product of computations of ranges, bearings, courses, and speeds which is computed electrically or mechanically and controls effective torpedo aiming and firing—which would enable him to fire torpedoes at a range of about 7,000 yards. His means of communication with the Task Force Commander was by TBS, which is the Navy's contraction for Talk Between Ships. TBS is a radio-telephone circuit of limited range linking an ordinary telephone handset on the bridge of each ship with a standard loudspeaker on the bridge of each other ship. Through this simple network voice communication was maintained among all the ships of a formation. Code designations for ships and individuals often were used as a precaution on TBS, but despite fears to the contrary there is no solid evidence that the enemy was aware of or monitored our transmissions.

Cole had been standing with the TBS phone in his hand. Now he pressed the activating button, called Admiral Wright, and sang out, *"Request permission to fire torpedoes!"* The time was 2316.

That precise moment marked the beginning of the fatal 4 minutes during which Bosco Wright "hung in stays," not yet sufficiently sure to act himself and unwilling to relinquish the initiative to his destroyer commanders. Arleigh Burke was to put his finger unerringly on this flaw in his recommendation demanding faith in subordinate officers by task force commanders, but at Tassafaronga that sort of faith was in short supply.

Instead of granting permission for Cole to launch the surprise torpedo attack called for in Plan 1-42, Wright replied, "Range on our bogey [enemy force] is excessive; 14,000 yards." Cole was lashed to the mast; under Navy protocol there was nothing he could do but stand by until it suited the Task Force Commander to grant him permission to fire torpedoes. Meanwhile, the positions of the opposing forces relative to each other were changing fast, and not to the advantage of the destroyers of Task Force 67.

There followed 2 minutes of extraneous TBS traffic after which Wright came back to Cole and inquired, "Do you have them located?"

"Affirmative!" snapped Cole. And then, making a final effort to secure permission to go into action, he added, *"Range is all right for us!"* Again he waited hopefully; once more he was disappointed. Still temporizing, Admiral Wright merely observed, "Suspect bogies are DDs. We now have four." The flagship seems temporarily to have lost half of Tanaka's formation from her radar screens—not an unusual occurrence with some types of radar.

At this point *Northampton* broke in to report a flashing light on Tassafaronga, and it was not until 2320, his doubts finally resolved, that the Task Force Commander told Cole to "Go ahead and fire torpedoes."

For Bill Cole and the destroyermen of Division 45 the golden moment had come and gone. On opposite parallel courses the two formations were sweeping past each other by the time he was free to act. Now, instead of having a comfortable shot at ships approaching, he had to accept an "up the kilt" shot at ships going away. At the moment Cole was granted permission to fire torpedoes, his range to *Naganami*, Tanaka's leading destroyer, had opened to 9,600 yards and his "fish" would have to travel considerably farther than that to intercept the passing enemy. At best this meant a long overtaking run for his torpedoes, but *Fletcher* fired ten in two salvos anyway and *Perkins*, next in line, got off eight. *Maury* was having trouble getting a "solution" and she held her fire. *Drayton* fired two on a very wobbly "solution" and more out of desperation than hope. It was an ineffective bit of business; all twenty of the Mark XVs sailed off into the void of missed targets. Following doctrine, Cole now led his little ships northeast toward Savo Island to clear the area for the gunfire of the cruisers. He was subsequently censored for this by Admiral Halsey, who regarded his lack of offensive action after firing torpedoes as "contrary to instructions" and reported to ComSoPac [Commander, South Pacific] that "in future such actions will not be tolerated." Cole was the only officer to receive official reprimand for his part in the defeat at Tassafaronga.

Having unwittingly fumbled the surprise torpedo attack called for in Plan 1-42, which might conceivably have been successful if launched in time, Admiral Wright now practically threw the plan out of a porthole. Cole's torpedoes had scarcely buried their noses in the black offshore rollers and started their runs when, at 2321, the Task Force Commander ordered his cruisers to "Stand by to Roger," which meant stand by to open fire with guns. A moment later he gave the order, "Commence firing!", and the whole cruiser line blazed into a thundering salvo of radar-aimed 8- and 6-inch gunfire. If ever there had been hope of surprising Tanaka with the torpedo barrage, the cruiser gunfire effectively disposed of it. You can hardly be shot at by five cruisers and still be unaware of the presence of an enemy or where he is!

Their planes still grounded at Tulagi, the cruisers were forced to illuminate with star shell, which they did. However, the illumination of targets was only partially effective. The cruisers' salvos, landing around Tanaka's destroyers, kicked up such a curtain of fire and smoke that the Japanese vessels were often obscured from view. Wright continued to pump out salvos, however, with these principal results:

As we did not have flashless powder, the winking flashes from the guns of the cruisers gave the Japanese torpedomen the points of aim which Kinkaid had sought to deny them by prohibiting the use of searchlights. For this precise reason Tanaka's doctrine specified that his destroyers were *not* to open gunfire, and this order was violated by only one ship, picket destroyer *Takanami*.

As the battle opened *Takanami* was between the two opposing formations and considerably closer to the American ships than any of her fellows. She immediately fired torpedoes and reversed course, turning away to the right. Her nearness to the cruisers, however, made her a sitting duck, and she was pounded unmercifully. Aboard *Pensacola* Lieutenant Commander J. C. Landstreet, gunnery officer, observing the effect of his tracer fire, shouted to a comrade, "Boy, look at those tracers! They're penetrating that tin can—look, they leave a glowing red ring at the point of impact! That's what I call shooting!" It was shooting indeed, the only effective shooting the U.S. ships were to do in the entire battle. Pummeled into helplessness, *Takanami* finally replied with her own feeble 5-inch guns and actually managed to fire about 70 rounds before she was rendered dead in the water, on fire, and with all of her battery silenced. She finally went down at 0137, leaving few survivors.

The killing of *Takanami* was observed by hundreds of American eyes from many different points of vantage alow and aloft. Marine Captain Schirman in his sky aft aerie above *Minneapolis* saw her die and chalked her up for a cruiser. But it remained for the Task Force Commander and his staff to proliferate this single sinking beyond even a tenuous reflection of reality. In his action report after the battle, Admiral Wright wrote, "Probable Japanese losses are two light cruisers and seven destroyers." Thus, to American eyes thrown out of focus by the refractions and magnifications of battle, poor *Takanami*, the only Japanese ship to be hit, became a whole task force by herself!

With the fire from Wright's cruisers lifting solid curtains of water around his ships and garlanding them with wreaths of cordite smoke, Tanaka's stern courage did not falter and the iron discipline of his destroyermen held firm. At the first wink of a cruiser's guns Tanaka surmised that torpedoes already would be streaking toward him. Flagship *Naganami* immediately countermarched to the right and wasted no time clearing torpedo water. Meanwhile, on the bridge of *Makanami*, Captain Sato resolutely led his four transport destroyers of Unit 1 on a southerly course while their crews worked diligently to cast off the lashings and toss overboard the drums of supplies which Tanaka was determined to deliver. This accomplished, he rang up 24 knots and led the formation in a column turn to the right, which was according to doctrine. He had, meanwhile, been readying his long lances.

Captain Nakahara's two DDs of Transport Unit 2, *Kawakaze* and *Suzukaze*, followed in train behind Sato, jettisoning their deck cargoes and turning away. By 2333 Tanaka's entire force less *Takanami* was on a retirement course at 24 knots. Their doctrine had been precisely complied with. Reflecting the first part—"Make liberal use of torpedoes"— *Suzukaze* had fired a salvo of long lances at 2324, *Kuroshio* fired five a minute later, *Takanami* had fired torpedoes earlier when the U.S. cruisers first opened on her, and at 2330 *Kawakaze* launched the first

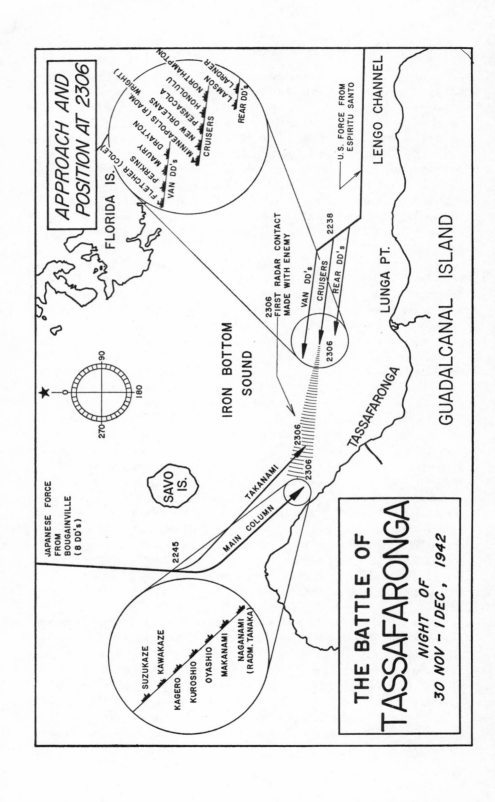

APPROACH AND POSITION AT 2306

FLORIDA IS.

FLETCHER (COLE)
PERKINS
MAURY
DRAYTON
VAN DD's

MINNEAPOLIS (RADM. WRIGHT)
NEW ORLEANS
PENSACOLA
HONOLULU
NORTHAMPTON
CRUISERS

LAMSON
LARDNER
REAR DD's

U.S. FORCE FROM ESPIRITU SANTO

LENGO CHANNEL

2238

2306
FIRST RADAR CONTACT MADE WITH ENEMY

VAN DD's
CRUISERS
2306
REAR DD's

IRON BOTTOM SOUND

2306

2306 / 2306

TASSAFARONGA

LUNGA PT.

GUADALCANAL ISLAND

90
180
270

JAPANESE FORCE FROM BOUGAINVILLE (8 DD's)

SAVO IS.

2245

TAKANAMI

MAIN COLUMN

SUZUKAZE
KAWAKAZE
KAGERO
KUROSHIO
OYASHIO
MAKANAMI
NAGANAMI
(RADM. TANAKA)

THE BATTLE OF
TASSAFARONGA
NIGHT OF
30 NOV - 1 DEC, 1942

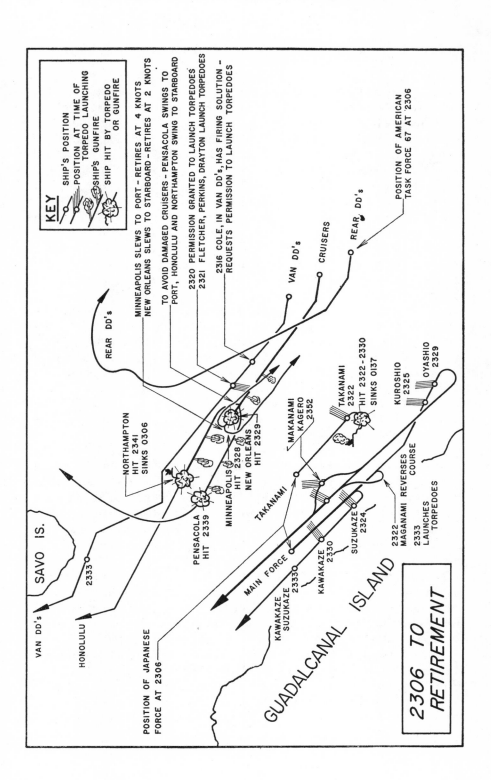

KEY

SHIP'S POSITION
POSITION AT TIME OF
TORPEDO LAUNCHING
SHIP'S GUNFIRE
SHIP HIT BY TORPEDO
OR GUNFIRE

MINNEAPOLIS SLEWS TO PORT - RETIRES AT 4 KNOTS
NEW ORLEANS SLEWS TO STARBOARD - RETIRES AT 2 KNOTS

TO AVOID DAMAGED CRUISERS - PENSACOLA SWINGS TO
PORT, HONOLULU AND NORTHAMPTON SWING TO STARBOARD

2320 PERMISSION GRANTED TO LAUNCH TORPEDOES
2321 FLETCHER, PERKINS, DRAYTON LAUNCH TORPEDOES

2316 COLE, IN VAN DD'S, HAS FIRING SOLUTION -
REQUESTS PERMISSION TO LAUNCH TORPEDOES

POSITION OF AMERICAN
TASK FORCE 67 AT 2306

REAR DD's

VAN DD's

CRUISERS

REAR, DD's

REAR DD's

SAVO IS.

2333

NORTHAMPTON
HIT 2341
SINKS 0306

MAKANAMI
KAGERO
2352

TAKANAMI
2322
HIT 2322-2330
SINKS 0137

KUROSHIO
2325

OYASHIO
2329

PENSACOLA
HIT 2339

MINNEAPOLIS
HIT 2328
NEW ORLEANS
HIT 2329

TAKANAMI

TAKANAMI

SUZUKAZE
2324

2322
MAGANAMI REVERSES
COURSE

2333
LAUNCHES
TORPEDOES

MAIN FORCE

KAWAKAZE
SUZUKAZE
2330

KAWAKAZE
2330

SUZUKAZE
2330

VAN DD's

HONOLULU

2333

POSITION OF JAPANESE
FORCE AT 2306

GUADALCANAL ISLAND

2306 TO
RETIREMENT

of eight. Thus, by the time he undertook the second phase of his doctrine—"Retire without employing guns"—Admiral Tanaka had more than twenty long lances reaching out through the black night to pierce the heart of his more powerful antagonist.

Twelve minutes earlier Bill Cole had requested permission to surprise Tanaka with a torpedo barrage. Now, at 2328, pluperfect hell descended upon the American cruisers at latitude 9°—16'—0" South; longitude 159°—15'—0" East. And it was U.S. Admiral Bosco Wright, not Japanese Admiral Raizo Tanaka, who was surprised!

The gunfire of the United States ships was dazzling in volume and shell were flying at a rate to suggest a veritable canopy of whistling steel spanning the ocean between Wright and Tanaka. Aboard *New Orleans* Lieutenant Commander J. H. Howard, gunnery officer, noted that at the range of 11,000 yards the salvo interval and time of flight of projectiles exactly coincided, so that, as each salvo landed near a target, a new salvo was leaving the gun muzzles. It was an altogether busy and boisterous scene.

By 2327½ Wright had closed the range to a point-blank 6,000 yards and in the white overhead glare from the star shell being liberally fired by all ships he looked across the water and saw three Japanese destroyers dead abeam of his cruiser formation to port. He reached out his hand for the TBS transmitter, but his intentions were arrested in mid-execution. For at that moment two long lances buried themselves in the vitals of *Minneapolis* and blasted her apart.

The first torpedo hit forward of Number 1 turret, abreast of the aviation gasoline storeroom. Within seconds a blanket of flame and fumes from mingling gasoline and fuel oil lapped the ship from bow to stern, and streamed from the fantail like the train of a comet. The second torpedo hit at Number 2 fireroom. The sledge-hammer impact of the detonation instantly snuffed out the lives of twelve men in the compartment. Inrushing water trapped and drowned twenty-four more in adjoining Firerooms 1 and 3.

Topside, two tremendous columns of water were sent skyward by the blasts, and as they fell back they deluged the stricken ship. The descending seawater swept a good bit of the flaming gasoline and fuel oil overside. It also swept away Seaman, 1st, Arthur Peltier and a mate who were in the 5-inch battery. On the bridge Captain Rosendahl and his officers struggled to remain upright against the whip of the ship and the foot of water which roiled around their feet. With a banshee scream of tortured metal 60 feet of the cruiser's bow caved downward at a 270-degree angle and in short minutes she was drawing 40 feet of water forward and her forecastle deck was awash to the roots of Number 1 turret.

Sore hurt, *Minneapolis* slewed out of line to port and limped away at 3 knots. Her first lieutenant and damage control officer, Lieutenant Commander H. W. Chanler, left his station at Battle 2 and organized parties to fight fire and jettison all movable weighty objects in a desperate attempt to maintain what little freeboard the ship still had. Powder cans and projectiles went overside and *Minneapolis* managed to remain afloat. By 2333, power had failed aboard the flagship, and with communications about to go Admiral Wright relinquished tactical command to Admiral Tisdale in *Honolulu*. The men of *Minneapolis* fought on to save their ship and in Number 4 fireroom the watch, with flooded compartments above and all around them, stood to their duty. Chief Engineer Lieutenant Commander Alston E. Parker fed seawater into the boilers of his one remaining fireroom and managed to turn the engines over for a time. Painfully *Minneapolis* started limping away toward Tulagi. The first of the long lances to arrive had torn up the flagship and knocked the task force commander out of the battle. It was very nice shooting for Tanaka & Company!

In line behind *Minneapolis* came a second armor-clad monster, heavy cruiser *New Orleans*, her guns belching out director-aimed salvos. Her skipper, Captain Clifford H. Roper, was on the bridge; her executive officer, Commander W. F. Riggs, Jr., at his station in Battle 2, aft. Captain Roper saw the flagship hit and he had but seconds in which to maneuver to keep from running her down. He hadn't even a prayer of checking the momentum of his 10,000-ton vessel within the time and distance provided, so he ordered hard right rudder in an effort to avoid a collision.

New Orleans had barely begun to swing her head away in response to the helm when a long lance grabbed her by the throat. The resultant blast shook her like a rat in the teeth of a terrier. The torpedo struck on the port side forward, in the area of the two forward magazines and the gasoline storeroom, all three of which instantly blew up. Dazed officers on the bridge, clutching wildly for support as the ship shuddered and bucked beneath them, saw a pedestal of flame and water leap upward from the bow to twice the height of the foremast. Whirling grotesquely on its periphery were the bodies of more than a score of officers and men who, an instant before, had been fighting the ship forward.

By the time the water flung up by the explosion fell back, *New Orleans* had lost 120 feet of her bow back to Number 2 turret. The bow section, with Number 1 turret intact and the guns cocked crazily skyward, floated close aboard the port side. As the ship, still with way on, plowed past it, the floating bow section tore two great gashes in her side aft, and ripped off two blades of Number 3 propeller. When she pulled free of her own bow a seaman in the fantail mistook it for *Minneapolis* and reported that they had just passed over that vessel which he insisted was sinking beneath them.

Death, mercifully swift or agonizingly tortured, peopled the below-decks compartments of the cruiser with the bodies of officers and men. A large party was trapped below in Central Station and faced certain asphyxiation from poisoned fumes. All three damage control officers— Lieutenant Commander H. M. Hayter and his two assistants, Lieu- tenant R. A. Haines and Ensign A. L. Foreman—rushed to the rescue. They finally were able to free the trapped men, but in so doing they became trapped themselves. All three perished. A check of compartments at a later time yielded the bodies of five officers and 53 enlisted men. Three more officers and 117 enlisted personnel were forever missing, either blown to bits or overside to drown.

Steering control and communications forward were lost with the deto- nations which gutted the whole front part of the ship, and within minutes *New Orleans* was down by the head, with 4 feet of water in the forward part of the wardroom. At his after station in Battle 2 Commander Riggs tested the bridge talker circuit and found it dead. He then rang the steering alarm and took the conn. Below, Chief Engi- neer Lieutenant Commander H. S. Parsons was still answering bells, and by midnight *New Orleans* too was limping off toward Tulagi. She could make but 2 knots, and her survival depended on the shoring of a forward bulkhead which had to withstand the tremendous pressures of the sea. To relieve this strain Commander Riggs endeavored to turn the ship around and back to Tulagi. However, because of the extreme distortion of her underwater plating forward, the vessel was unmanageable going astern. Riggs had to turn her once more and risk the weakening bulk- head. She finally made Tulagi at 0610 on 1st December, and, as all her ground tackle had been blown away, she was forced to tie up alongside a destroyer.

Pensacola was a shooting ship. She came thundering along behind *New Orleans* before that vessel was hit, long ribbons of flame licking from her gun tubes like the fiery tongues of mythological serpents. She hurled a greater weight of metal at Tanaka & Company than any other U.S. ship: 120 rounds of 8-inch armor-piercing, 80 rounds of 8-inch common, and 140 rounds of 5-inch illumination. Had her gun pointers been as apt at range and deflection as her gun loaders were at the speedy recharging of their breaches, the story of Tassafaronga might well have been different!

As has been noted, Captain Frank H. Lowe preferred to fight his ship from the anti-aircraft station, sky control forward, and it was from this lofty perch that he saw *New Orleans* ahead of him stagger and then sag to the right. Captain Lowe ordered his helm hard down to the left, and scraped by *New Orleans* with but feet to spare. Then he made a mistake. He brought *Pensacola* back to her base course of 300 degrees true—and at 2339 the long lance cut her down!

The thrust which took the lives of seven officers and 118 enlisted men (only 92 bodies were recovered) and sent *Pensacola* to join *Minneapolis* and *New Orleans* in a full 12 months of rebuilding before she could fight again, produced the most spectacular pyrotechnical display of the battle. The torpedo took her in the port flank and the ship whipped so violently that Captain Lowe and those with him aloft were thrown from their feet. A full oil tank just forward of Number 3 turret absorbed the major blast, with devastating results. Blazing oil was forced into the after living compartments and the after engineroom— blown into the after control station, and all over Number 3 turret and adjacent areas. It blanketed the main deck and the decks below, and coated the mainmast which blazed like a huge wick, trapping many and roasting them alive.

Lieutenant Julian D. Venter and his damage control parties strove valiantly to bring the flames under control. They flooded magazines and pumped CO_2 into compartments, but by 0145 the heat was so intense that 150 8-inch shells stored in Number 3 turret started "cooking off." Almost miraculously, the huge projectiles let go one by one with relatively low-order explosions, and, although adding greatly to the dangers of fire fighting, they did not do a great deal of additional damage. However, despite all damage control efforts the fires ravaged the vessel for a solid 7 hours after the long lance hit.

One man managed to escape from the holocaust in the after engineroom. A second tried to follow him but was trapped by the trailing wire of his telephone headset which he had neglected to remove, and perished. Power, communications, and steering control were lost temporarily, all gyros were knocked out, and for a time *Pensacola* sat dead in the water, seemingly nothing but a blazing wreck. But Captain Lowe and his officers fought disaster as stubbornly as they had fought the enemy. Correcting a 13-degree list by pumping fuel oil overside, they finally had one fireroom feeding steam to the turbines in one engineroom, and using a spare magnetic compass *Pensacola* finally crawled off toward Tulagi to join her smashed and broken sisters.

Honolulu, next in the cruiser line, was the "lucky blue goose" of the Pacific Fleet. At Tassafaronga her luck was fortified by the calm good judgment of her skipper, Captain Robert W. Hayler, and her officer of the deck, Lieutenant Commander George F. Davis.

In the early phases of the action there had been a spot of trouble aboard *Honolulu*. An ensign, new to combat and serving as turret officer, found the strain more than he could bear and had to be removed from the turret. Some of the men, too, "froze" when the guns opened up and had to be kidded out of their momentary funk by more seasoned mates. By 2339, however, all that was past and *Honolulu* was giving a good account of herself in terms of volume of fire when Lieutenant Commander Davis saw *Pensacola* burst into flame immediately ahead of him. Correctly, he swung hard right, thus placing *Honolulu* on the disengaged side of crippled *Pensacola* and *New Orleans*. The cripples were still shooting occasionally, and were as dangerous as wounded tigers, often firing on each other in the confusion of battle.

Captain Hayler now took the deck with the firm determination to get out of torpedo water pronto. He gave the engineroom "four-bells-and-a-jingle"—slang for "let me have all the revolutions you've got!"—and *Honolulu* went hightailing for Savo Island at 30 knots. When she was abeam of *Northampton*, last of the cruiser line, that vessel fired on her. Hayler immediately flashed his recognition lights for 2 seconds, and the firing ceased. As they approached Savo Island the navigator, Commander Ringle, spoke up: "Captain, you'd better come left 25 degrees to miss the island." "Won't 10 degrees do?" asked Hayler. "Captain," replied Ringle, "either you'll come left 25 degrees, or you'll take her over the island!" Hayler changed course accordingly and the "lucky blue goose" missed the mountain on Savo Island!

Although *Honolulu*, a light cruiser and thus more maneuverable than the others, had escaped, the long lances were not yet through with Task Force 67. Their final and most complete destruction was reserved for heavy cruiser *Northampton*, who now came barreling along firing methodically (she fired a total of only 132 rounds in the battle).

Captain Willard A. Kitts, III, saw *Pensacola* on fire ahead of him and called for a left turn to avoid running her down. He avoided a collision and was starting to swing back when two long lances pierced *Northampton*'s heart with a mortal thrust. They hit in the area of the after engineroom, one about 10 feet under water and the other very near the surface.

The side of the ship was blown out, parts of the second and main decks were ripped away, and the sea roared in, giving the vessel a 10-degree list almost before survivors could organize to assess the damage. As in the case of *Pensacola*, great sheets of black fuel oil were sent flying up the mainmast to coat it and the rigging aloft, cascade back over the after portions of the ship, and burst into banners of streaming flame. Men and officers looked aloft in awe to see a long finger of fire reaching skyward from the top of the mainmast, and oil-soaked halyards and stays festively outlined by dancing flame. On deck, where it did not immediately ignite, the descending oil covered surfaces to a depth of 4 inches, greatly inhibiting the work of damage control parties, which was further hindered by the cooking off of the 5-inch ready ammunition stored aft. Soon after receiving the long lances *Northampton* was a blazing pyre, dead in the water, all power and communications gone, and settling by the stern.

By 0115 the ship's list had increased to 23 degrees, and Captain Kitts, receiving fragmentary reports and surveying the scene from his post on the bridge, had grave doubts of the ship's survival. He personally picked a damage control and salvage party to remain aboard and continue the fight to save *Northampton*. Then he ordered all hands topside and placed Commander Crenshaw in charge of the *abandon ship* evolution which he ordered 15 minutes later. As nearly 800 officers and men followed life rafts and other flotation gear over the side they left fire pumps running untended below in the forlorn hope that some good might come of it.

No good came of anything for *Northampton* that night or any night thereafter. By 0230 her port list had increased to 35 degrees and Captain Kitts knew his vessel was doomed. He ordered all hands to abandon, and he followed them into the water at 0240. Within 10 minutes the lifeless cruiser achieved a crazy 45-degree list, and at 0304 on the morning of 1st December she rolled her red bottom to the empty heavens and sank. Although she was the only U.S. ship to go down, prompt rescue operations by destroyers *Fletcher* and *Drayton* minimized loss of life. Only four of *Northampton*'s officers and fifty of her men met death at Tassafaronga.

Admiral Tisdale in *Honolulu* continued to make motions of trying to find the enemy, but the night of the long lances was over. He rounded Savo Island and prowled Ironbottom Sound, but all he encountered were life rafts loaded with American sailors who sent up an eerie, keening chant into the moonless night. By 0130 Tanaka and his seven victorious destroyers had cleared the area, and by noon they were safely back in Shortland Harbor. Swapping observations, Tanaka and Toyama estimated that the U.S. force had consisted of one battleship, four cruisers, and perhaps a dozen destroyers. They were off the mark only to the extent of mistakenly identifying the fifth cruiser as a battleship, and adding to Task Force 67 a handful of destroyers who were not there. Wright's estimate of Tanaka's force was far less reliable. He put it at four cruisers, fifteen destroyers, and possible submarines. As late as 9th December he was recommending subordinate officers for decorations for "destroying all enemy vessels within range." That would be *Takanami!* Seven others were within range, but Wright just couldn't hit 'em!

Like the gallant officer he was, Bosco Wright took full responsibility for the grievous losses at Tassafaronga. Those losses were more than 400 officers and men killed, a heavy cruiser sunk, and three other heavy cruisers knocked out of the war for a year—not an inconsiderable score. In his final report Admiral Wright wrote:

I specifically absolve the commanding officers of the four heavy cruisers from any blame for the torpedoing of their ships. . . . It is my opinion that none of these commanding officers could properly have placed their vessels elsewhere but where they did.

Although ungrammatical the statement was gallant. Wright took the blame, but the record does not show any convincing explanation by him of what caused the disaster. The enemy was less reticent. Interrogated after the war, one Japanese officer who was present at Tassafaronga called attention to the woeful inaccuracy, especially in deflection, of our cruiser gunfire. Inexperienced crews may well have contributed importantly to this situation. Another Japanese officer placed the blame squarely where Arleigh Burke thought it should rest. This ranking officer wrote:

A more active use of destroyer divisions is necessary in night battles. Annihilation of our reinforcing units would not necessarily have been difficult even for a few destroyers if they had chosen to penetrate our lines and carry on a decisive battle with the support of the main force.

Obviously this referred to the early and "liberal" use of torpedoes as called for in Tanaka's doctrine. Our DDs could hardly be expected to close the enemy for a short-range gunfight, only to have their own cruisers blow them out of water with 8-inch salvos.

Arleigh Burke had considered the facts of Tassafaronga and learned the lesson: *Have faith in subordinate officers; destroyers to attack upon enemy contact WITHOUT ORDERS from the task force commander.*

He gathered his classified papers, put them in the safe, snapped off the light above his tiny desk, shucked out of his perspiration-stained clothes, and headed for a reviving shower. The time was straight up for midnight, and destroyer *Waller* continued to slumber. Working while others rested and at a task beyond the multitude of specific chores envisioned in his orders, Commodore Burke had made the first move in the development of his characteristically aggressive destroyer doctrine. A venerable Chinese proverb states it pithily:

The journey of a thousand miles starts with but a single step.

Arleigh Burke had taken that step. Although he couldn't know it, the path upon which he had set his feet was to lead him to the very apex of the Navy's pyramid; he was to become Chief of Naval Operations and win every decoration it is within the competence of the Navy to bestow. Meanwhile, in less than six months he was to pick up an extra stripe, be appointed Commodore of the Gallant Squadron, win a mandate from Rear Admiral Aaron S. "Tip" Merrill to apply his doctrine of faith at the blazing Battle of Empress Augusta Bay, and go on to fight the only "perfect" battle of World War II, at Cape St. George.

2

The Commodore Comes Aboard

~~~~~~

At 0630 hours on the moist morning of Saturday, 23rd October, 1943, Commander Luther K. Reynolds, U.S.N., Captain of *U.S.S. Charles Ausburne*—Destroyer Number 570—stood on his bridge and took a precautionary look alow and aloft. The whole Navy called him "Brute" Reynolds from the circumstance that he wouldn't have weighed 120 pounds soaking wet and with a rock in each hand. He had delicate features and an almost girlish figure, but there was nothing effeminate about the Brute or the way he fought his ship.

"Charlie" Ausburne was moored alongside *U.S.S. Dixie* in the harbor of Espiritu Santo near the top end of the New Hebrides group and only about 15 degrees below the line. Having assured himself that all preparations for getting under way had been completed, the Captain took charge and issued a succession of commands expertly cadenced by long experience:

"Cast off all lines . . . she'll fall free; let her drift . . . NOW, all ahead two-thirds . . . indicate turns for 10 knots . . . come right to course one zero six. . . ."

In smooth sequence the special underway detail, which mustered the most experienced and reliable men in the ship at key stations when docking, undocking, or engaging in other delicate maneuvering, executed their Captain's orders. The first lieutenant and the chief bosun's mate were on the fo'c'sle head; Division bosun's mates were in the waist and on the fantail. They supervised release of the heavy mooring lines which went overside with soft splashes. The chief yeoman, standing before the engineroom telegraph on the bridge, squeezed a brass spring-grip handle in each hand and pushed both levers forward until the locking lugs fell into the notches arresting the indicator at "Two Thirds." Then he twisted the gnarled knob beneath the barrel of the annunciator until the numerals "nine eight"—the shaft revolutions per minute which would deliver 10 knots of speed—appeared at the tiny glass windows of the panel in front of him.

Bells clanged below and the chief engineer, at his control station, watched hawk-like as first class machinist's mates spun their throttle wheels to the left, backed their valves open until 98 revolutions registered on their indicators, then checked the flow of steam through the trembling turbines. Astern of *Ausburne* a great dome of churning water struggled to the surface and broke in rushing, ivory-fretted foam as her bronze screws bit into the dark green depths, and the vessel surged ahead.

"Passing ninety . . . passing ninety-five . . . passing one hundred . . . steady on course one zero six," chanted the chief quartermaster on the helm as *Charlie Ausburne*'s bow swung in slow traverse of the compass points and she sheered gracefully away from *Dixie* to settle on the ordered heading toward her assigned anchorage. The destroyer had been enjoying a sorely needed "engineering availability"—time out for repairs—alongside the 16,000-ton destroyer tender and repair ship. In 48 hours of working around the clock *Dixie*'s hard-pressed engineers and artisans had tinkered up the DD's propulsion plant and coaxed it once more to concert pitch. As he moved off, Captain Reynolds thoughtfully signalled his appreciation. It was part of his philosophy of seagoing that, while the gunners usually were the ones to receive the Navy congratulation of "Well done!", the engineers who "took you there and brought you back" deserved an equal measure of praise. In his ship he saw that they got it. *Dixie*, having set up her "boarding house," never lacked for lodgers during the bitter Solomons campaign which was in full swing, and almost before *Ausburne* was well clear another destroyer moved in to take her place.

Scarcely had *Charlie Ausburne* plunged down her port anchor, veered 40 fathoms of chain, and settled into her new berth when a bronzed, blue-eyed and broad-shouldered officer boarded her, climbing nimbly up the vertical steel ladder rigged from her starboard quarter. Although he was a Captain, it was strictly a fighting, "dungaree Navy" in the Solomons; formality was dispensed with; no sideboys turned out, and no bosun piped the new Commodore of DesRon-23 over the side as he boarded his flagship.

"I'm Arleigh Burke," said the stranger as he stepped forward with outstretched hand to meet Captain Reynolds who had come aft. "You're Brute Reynolds?" Although Burke knew most of the "23" skippers, he and Reynolds had not met.

"I'm Reynolds, yes, sir. It's nice to have you aboard, Commodore. We knew you were coming, but I didn't expect you quite so soon." He fell in at the Commodore's left as they started forward toward the wardroom.

"You know, Brute," chuckled the four-striper, "I sometimes think the difference between a good officer and a poor one is about 10 seconds. It's a fine rule to get going sooner than anticipated, travel faster than expected, and arrive before you're due. You'd be surprised how many fights you can get into that way and, after all, if you're ready, you can expect to win your share." Thus informally, upon first setting foot aboard his "flag boat" did Arleigh Burke, soon to be christened "31-Knot-Burke" by no less a personage than Admiral William F. Halsey, top Pacific Commander, enunciate three of the cardinal principles which were to guide DesRon-23 under his leadership. *Speed:* move quickly while the other fellow's trying to make up his mind. *Look for fights:* if you look for 'em you'll probably find 'em. *Be prepared:* if you're ready for a fight you should win your share.

The Commodore's numbered burgee was broken at the forepeak and minutes later on his order, a hoist summoning all Squadron 23 skippers present at Espiritu to a conference aboard *Charlie Ausburne* was two-blocked at the signal yard. There was work to be done; there was no time to waste; Captain-Commodore Arleigh Albert Burke literally had arrived with battle orders in his hand!

By 1400 several captain's gigs were milling around off *Ausburne*'s quarter. They were, in fact, standard motor whaleboats with canvas tops rigged forward, but they were further distinguished as captain's gigs by the doggy symbols painted on their bows—the numerals of the ships to which they belonged, pierced by arrows. Almost, their cox'uns thought themselves jaunty yachtsmen as they tinkled their engine bells and jockeyed toward the foot of *Ausburne*'s ladder. "Bow hooks," determined to demonstrate their superior seamanship to the "old man" under the canvas dodger, grabbed and held with a tenacity which admitted of but two possible consequences: either the captain would find the bottom rung of the ladder ready to his foot, and ascend with dignity, or the bow hook would be pulled bodily into the sea. None was.

The conference had been called for 1430 and by that time four of the Squadron captains plus Commander Bernard L. Austin, Commodore of Division 46—the "off" Division of DesRon-23—sat facing Arleigh Burke around the green felt-topped table in *Charlie Ausburn*'s wardroom. Electric fans droned a polyphonic lullaby accented by an occasional muted clank or thud both heard and felt from the deck above, a small ship being such an intimate thing and such a good conductor of vibrations that sensory perception even of remote happenings often is multiple. A Negro mess boy poured coffee from glass decanters on the two-burner electric hot plate set in a recess of the built-in sideboard, and passed the cups.

"Gentlemen," began Arleigh Burke addressing his khaki-clad captains most of whom wore their garrison caps neatly folded over their belts, and drank coffee despite the perspiration pouring from their armpits, "as I believe most of you know, I have relieved 'Rosey' Gillan [Captain

Martin J. Gillan, Jr.] in command of Squadron 23. The times being what they are, I have dispensed with the formality of reading my orders. I trust you don't object?"

"Excellent idea," observed blunt, sardonic Commander Herald Franklin Stout, Captain of *U.S.S. Claxton*. "Rosey would have taken all afternoon on protocol, and we'd be here 'til midnight. Personally, I've still got 'Operation Snowstorm' to deal with this afternoon."

"Heraldo," as Stout was nicknamed, was something of an odd fish in the Squadron. He was compactly built, dark almost to the point of swarthiness, had piercing black eyes which danced with repressed merriment when he was planning one of the japes to which he was addicted, and he wore a small black mustache with points waxed to a stiffness suggesting the spurs of a fighting chicken. He was deliberate of manner and address, and smoked a sulphurous curved pipe which had stained his teeth beyond the mercy of any dentist and was both a comfort and a stage prop to his relished role of Squadron philosopher. His hobbies were printing and genealogy, and he had attested his erudition by assisting in the preparation of a physics textbook later used as standard at the United States Naval Academy.

"Well, we've no time to bother with ceremony," continued Burke crisply. "I have orders for the Squadron, and they promise to be battle orders. This will have to be a two-session conference. *Stanly* and *Spence* are at Purvis [United States Florida Island base off Guadalcanal at the gateway to The Slot] and *Converse* and *Thatcher* are en route there. You will all, I'm sure, be pleased to know that our orders are to get under way with Task Group 39.3 of Task Force 39 at 0415 tomorrow morning for Purvis, there to rendezvous with Task Group 39.2, which will include the four ships of this Squadron not here today. These orders reflect ComSoPac's [Commander, South Pacific] Op-Plan 16A-43, and while they are not specific with regard to this Squadron once we gather at Purvis, they direct that we refuel immediately and hold ourselves in readiness for—and I quote—'a forward movement against the enemy.' That I interpret as encouraging."

The announcement elicited nods and murmurs of kindled interest around the table. Heraldo turned momentarily away to dislodge the dottle from his pipe against the horny heel of his hand, and immediately began refilling the briar from an oversized rubber pouch.

"I understand," continued the Commodore, "that up until today this Squadron has had no doctrine."

"Up until today," replied "Count" Austin, "this Squadron hasn't had anything but 180's every time 'Washing-machine Charlie' came over, resulting in aborted missions and missed interceptions of the enemy!" Thus briefly and bitterly, but accurately, the Commodore of the "off"

Division expressed the Squadron's general dissatisfaction at the hesitant tactics imposed upon it by the Squadron Commander just relieved and shipped back Stateside. Bernard Lige Austin, who flew his pennant in *Foote*, was from South Carolina. He was slight of stature, with stooping shoulders and rather sparse hair. The courtly manner which he had affected as a midshipman at the Naval Academy had won him the nickname of Count, but his present colleagues seized upon the nickname to administer a bit of chiding. When Austin exhibited a marked reluctance to relinquish the TBS circuit, and kept spouting sonorous profundities while others waited impatiently to deliver urgent reports, it was merry Heraldo Stout who dubbed him *"Long* Count" Austin, and the name stuck with the adhesiveness of aptness.

"Well, you've got a doctrine now," Burke told the gathering. "There'll be copies for each of you when we break up, and I suggest that you study them. This is a hurry-up thing. As you know, I've had just about 2 hours to prepare it, and I'm sure we'll improve it as time goes on and we gain experience and confidence. Meanwhile let me read to you the five cardinal points of the doctrine which will govern this Squadron under my command."

Confident that he had their total attention, Arleigh Burke read slowly and with careful emphasis from a typewritten page on the table before him the doctrine which appeared thus on the first page of the complete document which he was to give each skipper later:

DESTROYER SQUADRON TWENTY-THREE

DOCTRINE

If it will help kill Japs—it's important.
If it will not help kill Japs—it's not important.
Keep your ship trained for battle!
Keep your material ready for battle!
Keep your boss informed concerning your readiness for battle!

"That's the heart of it, fellows," concluded the Commodore, looking up with a smile. "If you comply with these five cardinal points I promise you this Squadron will go places."

"How will the Divisions work if we make a night surface contact?" Austin wanted to know.*

* As is customary in the United States Navy, Squadron 23 was composed of two Divisions, 45 and 46, each comprised of four destroyers. In this type of organization it is traditional for the Commodore of the Squadron to serve also as Commander of the lower numbered Division. Thus Burke, in addition to having over-all command of the Squadron, retained direct command of Division 45 as well, while Austin was Commander of Division 46.

"When we're steaming in Squadron formation at night and expecting to intercept an enemy surface force," Burke replied, "the Divisions will be in column of ships, with Division 46 on a line of bearing 10 degrees abaft Division 45; interval between Divisions 4,000 to 5,000 yards.

"Upon contacting an enemy I'm going to head for him with Division 45 on a collision course. If I get to 6,000 yards of him undetected I will come approximately to the reciprocal of his course and fire torpedoes when my flag boat is 50–60 degrees on the enemy's bow."

"And what will I be doing all that time?" Austin inquired with a faint tinge of acidity.

"You'll be standing by to cover me with gunfire if the enemy wakes up, and deliver a follow-up torpedo attack after I've cleared your torpedo water. Meanwhile I'll probably try to get between the enemy and his base to cut him off if he tries to run. If he does I'll go after him, while you finish off the cripples. It's a one-two punch, Count."

"It's a one-two punch in your ever-lovin' hat, Arleigh Burke, and you know it!" stormed the outraged Austin. "I'm always 10 degrees behind you. You jump the enemy, do the fighting and have all the fun while I play Aunt Sally and probably never get into the show!"

"That, Count," replied the imperturbable Burke, "is the measure of one year's seniority in this man's Navy! I figure a year is worth a 10-degree advantage, and I'm taking it."

The assembled captains laughed. They knew the Commodore was teasing his "off"-Division commander, but they also knew that what he said had validity in the Navy scheme of things. Burke had graduated from Annapolis in 1923, Austin the following year. Now Burke had four stripes, Austin three, and, as the old Navy saying has it, "rank has its privileges." It was Arleigh Burke's Squadron and he proposed to run it the way he saw fit, although his method would be to hold a loose rein, and give fully of the tremendous inspirational resources of his own being.

There was to emerge in this Squadron a quality which, for aptness, can only be described as a *mystique.* For those who may not have explored the subject it may be explained that *mystique* is from the French and there does not seem to be a precise equivalent in English. By definition a *mystique* is a belief which forms around an idea, a sentiment, or a person. Its fundamental is faith. Under Arleigh Burke the skippers of DesRon-23 were to share a *mystique* which sprang from different roots for each one but which had a uniform expression in high courage, supreme aggressiveness, and superb technical skill. These differing interpretations—these fumbling faiths—were precipitated, as it were, by the catalytic agent of Burke's leadership genius and inspiration, and fused into a pattern of brilliant action which illuminated the whole grim story of how we stopped the Japanese at the equator and headed them back toward their home islands.

The conference droned on in the wardroom while, topside, the crew manhandled tons of supplies aboard, worked on their guns, and slaved at the half-hundred and more back-breaking and exacting harbor routines which denied the exhausted sailorman sleep even when in port. Indeed, as Arleigh Burke soon was to find out, fatigue was the greatest enemy the Squadron faced, and far more insidious than the Japs. His creation of "Condition One-Easy" was to relieve the strain considerably when the Squadron started making nightly excursions up The Slot, and officers and men alike had to stand up to constant punishment of minds, bodies, and nerves.

"Commodore," asked Roy Gano, Captain of *U.S.S. Dyson*, "what's your doctrine on cripples? Say a ship's hit and disabled, and we know damned well enemy air's going to pounce on us at dawn or before. What do we do? Stand by the cripple, or get the hell out of there?"

Roy Alexander Gano (pronounced *Gai*-no), born in the minuscule community of Pipestone, Minnesota, had the distinction of being the only prospective midshipman ever to start out looking for the United States Naval Academy at Indianapolis, Indiana, of which city he had heard, rather than at Annapolis, Maryland, where it is located but of which town he'd never heard. He was a tall, dark, ruggedly handsome Commander of 41, with a ready smile. He was essentially uncomplicated although a splendid ship handler and man-of-war's-man. For Captain Gano the *mystique*, still dormant in the Squadron, had an essentially fraternal flavor and his appreciation of it was relatively unsophisticated.

"Roy," replied Burke, "I'm glad you asked that question. You'll find the answer in detail in the doctrine I'll give you before you leave, but let's hash it over a little now to be sure that everybody understands. But first I want to make an observation that you won't find in the typed doctrine. It's simply this: If you're really *good*—and by the Lord Harry you've *got* to be good if you're going to sail with me!—you shouldn't get hurt in the first place. Men die by the things they fear. I propose that this Squadron shall be so good that it won't fear anything; then it won't get hurt!"

"But, Arleigh," bridled Austin, "illogical necessities frequently arise in battle and accidents will happen. Rarely is a fight fought by the book."

"I know, Count," replied Burke with a reassuring smile. "And the answer to Roy's question is an emphatic *NO*. We will *not* desert a cripple. Let me read you the doctrine on that:

" 'If any ship is damaged so that she must slow, she will haul out of column, report what she's doing, fire torpedoes as soon as she can get a clear shot, if she hasn't already done so, *and support our attack as long as she floats.'*

"After the battle is over and all enemy ships are sunk [no Burke doctrine ever envisioned anything but the complete annihilation of the enemy!] our undamaged ships will form screen 1500 yards around the damaged ship and repel the air attack which probably will follow. Does that answer your question, Roy?"

"It sure does, boss!"

"Very well. Now, has anybody got any ideas about all this? What I want is discussion, fellows."

The Commodore got his discussion in full measure, and it was not until the captains were standing up ready to depart that he swung back to Heraldo Stout. Burke had a good memory. He also had a keen insight into the value of relieving undue tension with an occasional laugh, and he had a hunch on this occasion that Heraldo was the boy to provide it. "What's this 'Operation Snowstorm' you were griping about, Heraldo?"

Whether his disgust was real or feigned it was convincingly evidenced by Stout's tone of voice as he replied, "It's this damned blizzard of forms to be filled out and stupid questions to be answered that we're constantly getting from Washington, Commodore. I got a new one just this morning—a monstrous 4-page thing asking a lot of fool questions about our use of dehydrated potatoes—stuff like that."

"So what do you do?" pressed Burke with a straight face although he sensed that the answer might not be dignified.

"I've got a technique," Stout told him and the still-assembled company. "If it doesn't concern beans or bullets I use the 'flush system' and," he added, pantomiming the pulling of an old-fashioned toilet chain, *"one flush usually is enough!"* The conference broke up amid laughter and the captains returned to their ships well pleased with the strong leadership promised by their new Commodore.

Two days later, on Monday, 25th October, at about 1300 in the afternoon *Charlie Ausburne* slid smoothly to a mooring alongside the *Marker Dog* fuel barge in Purvis Bay, nearly 600 miles north by west of Espiritu Santo, and the "oil king" took over. The oil king, customarily a chief petty officer of an Engineering Division, had the tremendous responsibility of superintending the refueling of a destroyer and the provision of fresh water. He reported directly to the Engineering Officer as the "Chief Engineer" is styled, and habitually the oil king and his working party were topside and ready long before the vessel made fast to the oiler.

With daily consumption running between 12,000 and 24,000 gallons depending upon the ship's employment, there rarely was an occasion in port when the destroyers of Squadron-23 couldn't accommodate any-where up to 100,000 gallons of fuel oil each and, on the eve of the Battle of Empress Augusta Bay, the captains of Division 45 had to fight what Arleigh Burke called "the battle for fuel" long before they let off a shot at the enemy.

As oil expands under heat, in the Navy the intake always is figured at the cubic volume of the oil at a temperature of 60 degrees Fahrenheit, and in a routine fueling an oil king might handle upwards of 600 tons. Occasionally in the Solomons—not often!—an oil king would get his signals crossed, the wrong valve would be closed or opened, pressure put on the wrong tank, and the decks and living spaces of the vessel flooded with fuel oil. This was a situation which no one could appreciate quite so fully as a crew bone-tired from a night at general quarters up The Slot, and fresh from the sport of repelling a dawn air raid, which more often than not was the situation in DesRon-23.

Reflecting his principle of "getting going before anticipated" Arleigh Burke two-blocked a signal for a conference of his skippers less than 15 minutes after the destroyers of Division 45 had made fast alongside the fuel barge or anchored off awaiting their turns. Probably for the first time in the history of the Squadron all eight ships were present in company. They were *Charles Ausburne, Dyson, Stanly* and *Claxton* of Division 45; *Foote, Spence, Thatcher,* and *Converse* of Division 46. However, the setting for the Purvis Bay conference to which all eight captains now were bid was pleasantly different from the humid and stuffy wardroom of *Charlie Ausburne* where the previous Division conference had been held. The skippers were directed to assemble in half an hour on the beach at the *Cloob des Slot.* (The name was thus spelled on the lettered board which hung over what might have been the entrance had the *Cloob* had any sides, which it didn't.)

Like most things in life the rating of a club can be a relative proposi-tion. Evaluated by Stateside standards the *Cloob des Slot* was a sad and sorry thing. It was, indeed, nothing but a nipa shack which had been erected at the water's edge by a woolly-headed family of natives after payment of three bags of rice. An occasional additional bag defrayed the expense of maintenance and repairs, constantly necessary. It was about 40 feet square, simply a peaked thatched roof on uprights, and its principal function was to provide some protection against the sun and the rain. Unfortunately however, the site had been selected more with an eye to its being handy to the beach than with a prudent regard for winds and tides. In consequence, when the waters of Purvis Bay made up, the *Cloob* often was flooded to a depth of several inches. On those occasions the men who used it—enlisted personnel and officers alike—sat on top of the crude tables provided, put their feet on the rough benches, and enjoyed their Acme beer. This brew, from a now defunct San Francisco brewery, came in squat throw-away bottles and was carried by the ships in spaces immediately below the refrigerated compartments for storing perishables. When a party at the *Cloob des Slot* was in order the liberty party from a ship would load a galvanized iron tub with the requisite amount of beer—two bottles per man was the basic ration although some did better because others didn't like the stuff—and take it ashore. They beached their boats, for there were no docking facilities at Purvis in the early days. Lugging the tub up under the nipa shelter the men would enjoy an hour or so of relaxation and shooting the breeze. This dull business, as many might regard it, played an important role in fortifying the morale of men whose eyes were gritty with too much waking and whose nerves were fine-drawn from unrelieved tension. In choosing the *Cloob* as the locus for the further expounding of his doctrine Arleigh Burke simply demonstrated his instinctive grasp of the appropriate.

As the warriors of "23" gathered on the beach there lurked, at the backs of all their minds, the spectre of the Battle of Savo Island, fought almost within gun range of where they sat. At Savo Island we paid a spectacular price in sunken cruisers for the foothold our Marines gained on Guadalcanal. Because of the toll exacted of the Allies in this savage engagement, which is a proper part of this history, and at Tassafaronga, the top United States command had, on occasion, been forced to employ destroyers as "little cruisers," to quote "Ham" Hamberger, the perspicacious skipper of *Converse,* and the challenges presented to DesRon-23 often were formidable.

Everybody nursed a second bottle of beer, everybody knew everybody else, and Commodore Burke had covered the ground of the preceding conference for the new arrivals when, in response to the invitation for discussion which was a root principle of Burke's philosophy of command, Alston Ramsay, Captain of *Foote,* asked a question. "Commodore, what about signals when steaming in formation? As Captain of the flag boat of Division 46 I'd like to know what to expect from you when you start maneuvering."

Ramsay, nicknamed "Governor" because of his dignified bearing, was of medium build, the son of a North Carolina physician, and the mystery man of the Squadron—the man nobody knew. While technically competent he did not seem to be able to get through to his colleagues, and he was to be tragically alone a few nights later when *Foote* took a torpedo in her stern and her decks were sown with death.

"If we make an enemy contact, Governor," Burke told him, "you may expect me to maneuver without signal. You'll have the basic doctrine and the plan for that particular operation. I shall expect you all to have your eyes open, to be alert, and to do what you're expected to do without orders from me." Arleigh Burke was applying in his own Squadron the doctrine of faith which he advocated for all the Navy.

"Let me emphasize one point," he continued. "Don't lose your ship by too late or too cautious maneuvers. If you make a mistake, for Pete's sake make it on the radical side. For instance, don't wait until a plane proves its identity by dropping bombs before you try to shoot it down. If there's any question in your mind, shoot first and ask questions afterward!"

"Any dope on torpedo settings and points of aim, Boss?" The questioner was Ralph Lampman, Captain of *Thatcher*. The son of a design draftsman and manufacturer of small components in the tiny town of Angola, Indiana, Ralph Lampman's address to life was contained in his pungent observation "All the men I know put on their trousers one leg at a time like I do. If anybody knows a better way, I'm willing to learn." Meanwhile Ralph, a square-cut man of below average height, with an unusually strong jaw and, like Stout, a pipe smoker, was content with the degree of his mastery of navigation, gunnery, seamanship, and "steam," and he had no misgivings at all concerning his ability to be a reliable member of the "23" team. That he was until that confused night when, in the smoke and roar of battle, he received only the second half of a signal and, in consequence, flung *Thatcher* into *Spence* at 30 knots, knocking himself and his ship temporarily out of the war. Lampman's comprehension of the *mystique* was tenuous. For a brief time, when he served on the Asiatic Station, he'd achieved a certain insight but later, curiously, he seemed to feel a bit ashamed of this and if you asked him he'd probably say (although he wouldn't really mean it) that he'd be just as content skippering a towboat as a destroyer of Squadron 23.

"Torpedo settings," Burke told him, "will be a 1-degree spread, intermediate speed, 6-foot depth. When targets are *not* visible and you're relying on radar the point of aim should be the middle of the enemy formation. When targets *are* visible the point of aim should be, first, undamaged enemy ships; second, enemy ships one third away from the leading enemy ships."

It was Ham Hamberger, of *Converse*, who spoke up next, framing the kind of question which naturally would suggest itself to his analytical and far-ranging mind. Hamberger who, along with "Heinie" Armstrong, Captain of *Spence*, is studied in depth in the next chapter, had the most sophisticated appreciation of any of the skippers of Squadron 23 of their *mystique* which was developing, and his question was reflective of his thoughtful approach to every facet which life presented to him. "Arleigh, for the first time this Squadron's getting an intelligible and cogent doctrine and I, for one, am damned happy to get it. Of course, for each mission, I assume we'll have an operation plan. But the thought strikes me that, no matter how careful you are in working out the details of an op-plan before battle, chances to change and improve it are likely to emerge when the guns start shooting. How do you feel about one of us changing or departing from the previously agreed upon op-plan if he thinks he sees an opportunity to do better?"

"A good question, Ham, and I've a couple or three thoughts on that," replied Burke, finishing his second bottle of beer and declining a third which someone pressed upon him. "If you have a casualty at sea—say an engineering casualty—and you're not completely ready for battle, in Heaven's name report in detail to the OTC [Officer in Tactical Command] and the Squadron Commander at once. And keep us informed of the progress of repairs not less frequently than once an hour. It's surprising how often damage to your ship will change OTC's plan, and if he has to ask you for information you're not doing your job.

"Now, about changing the operation plan, my advice would be to go slow. I want all of you to feel that you have complete flexibility, and the main thing I want you to be is aggressive. But even a poor op-plan previously conceived and well known to all ships, will give better results than changing to a wonderful op-plan in the heat of battle. During an engagement it's hard for all hands to get the word and, by and large, I'd rather see no departure from the op-plan unless it affects only your ship and does not require a report which would change the plans of others. This advice may be wrong for some future battle, fellows. I'm quite aware of that. But please remember it before you go kicking things around once a plan has been put into execution."

The discussion had been long and, at times, tense. Despite their pleasure at meeting their new Commodore and receiving his revitalizing doctrine, all of the captains labored under a nagging, half-conscious compulsion to return to their ships. There was much to be done, no time to do it in, and their hardworking "execs," sturdy characters all, as they *had* to be, simply were buried under the demands. Only two of the skippers had failed to take an active part in the discussion. One, Bob Cavenagh, Captain of *Stanly*, was a handsome, naturally reserved, intellectual type and an accomplished pianist. He was Cleveland born and, after the war, as a Rear Admiral, he was to become United States Naval Attaché at London. As a matter of fact every man present at that meeting was to achieve at least the rank of Rear Admiral, and several were to go farther. That afternoon at the *Cloob des Slot* Cavenagh absorbed all of the fighting notions being batted about, but he preserved an amiable silence.

Heinie Armstrong, of *Spence*, was the one who came up with the concluding question: "Commodore, you've given us clear battle orders—but what about *non*-battle orders?" Even in that high-gaited Squadron Heinie was a standout. It was he who shamelessly had used a crock of "Vallejo brandy" to win a wife (thus becoming a 24-carat heel, by his own admission!) and created the wondrous fantasy of "Gonzales' Miracle."

"Heinie, there's just one answer to that," replied Arleigh Burke crisply. "I'm ready to give each of you several copies of Squadron 23 Doctrine. It consists of twelve mimeographed pages, although scant text as you'll discover. So far as I am concerned there can be, and I hope there will be, changes and improvements to the first eleven pages. But I direct your attention to page twelve which states, simply, "NON-BATTLE ORDERS: *NONE.* CORRECTIONS TO THIS SECTION WILL NOT BE PERMITTED."

Thus did the Gallant Squadron come by its fighting doctrine. That, as Arleigh Burke envisioned, it was to have little or no use for a non-fighting doctrine events were to prove. Meanwhile, as the conference broke up, it was Brute Reynolds who expressed the appreciation of all. "It was a good idea, Commodore, to get together here on the beach. I dare say we could all stand a little more of this sort of thing."

"I know, Brute," replied Burke thoughtfully. "We all need a break now and then. Did any of you ever hear about the time Admiral Halsey was all set to chew me out?"

None had.

"Well," related the Commodore with a chuckle, "6 or 8 months ago, when I was ComDesDiv-43, in *Waller*, Halsey and his staff at Noumea were always giving orders direct to the boats of my Division, and I never *could* get the four of them together at one time. I swore then that if ever I got them all in one place I'd never let 'em get separated, and that's precisely how I feel about this Squadron. One day, at Espiritu, I found I had *Saufley* with me, and she hadn't yet gotten any orders from the high command. We were fresh out of beer, whiskey, and everything else, so I packed her off to Sydney before anybody knew what it was all about, to bring us the supplies we needed. Before *Saufley* got back Halsey's staff wanted her for something, but she just wasn't available. The next time I passed Noumea way the Admiral called me in and asked 'How come?' 'Admiral,' I told him, 'we needed beer and whiskey, and I sent *Saufley* to Sydney after it.'

"He studied me for about a minute. Then he growled—and Halsey can *growl*, in case you don't know it!—'Burke, that's all right. *But if you'd sent her to Sydney for repairs or anything like that, I'd have had your hide!*'"

3

The Eagles Gather

The instrument which came to Arleigh Burke's hand at Purvis Bay and on the eve of battle, had been rough-forged half a world away and while he had still been a Division Commander.

Two events transpiring within a few weeks of each other and reflecting the personalities, attitudes, talents and temperaments of two men give perceptive entry upon the painful birth of DesRon-23, the timbre of the captains, and the early days of the Squadron. Look first at "Manuel's Miracle" and the man behind it, Lieutenant Commander Henry Jacques Armstrong, USN, Captain of *U.S.S. Spence*—Destroyer Number 512:

It was mid-April, 1943. At Hunter's Point in San Francisco *Spence* pulled teasingly at the standard manila lines which held her loosely but obdurately in berth Number 3. In officer's country below decks there was a mood of troubled concern. Scarcely half the men from the last liberty party had returned to the ship on schedule; presumably the rest were scattered all over town, and this was threatening to become a way of life among the crew rather than the occasional symbol of liberated youthful spirits. The Captain was unhappy, the executive officer was unhappy; topside the officer of the deck was unhappy—even the chief master at arms—the "Jimmylegs," standing watch at the head of the gangway, was unhappy.

The one man of *Spence*'s company who definitely was *not* unhappy was Seaman, 2nd, Manuel Gonzales, and he wasn't even aboard. In terms of his own ready reference Manuel had recently become the victim of a miracle, and he was enjoying his own somewhat primitive interpretation of the four freedoms. First he had freedom from discipline; he was "on the beach" with special liberty. Second, he had freedom from loneliness; he was wrapped in the treacherous embrace of a Turk Street tart. Third, he had freedom from want; an appreciable portion of his accumulated back pay crackled comfortably in his wallet.

Fourth, he had freedom from fear; he had achieved a state of ossification only a few degrees east of the prime meridian of alcoholic helplessness, and he was running down his easting with an enthusiasm which his foxy doxy did not suffer to flag.

Manuel's miracle, so far as he knew, had been born two days previously with a summons to the Captain's cabin.

"Gonzales," said the skipper, "you've heard about the war?"

"Yes, sir."

"And you've heard about our orders . . . ?"

"No, sir."

"Well, we'll be shoving off soon for a combat zone—*and some of us won't be coming back.*"

The Captain paused to let that sink in as Seaman Gonzales mumbled a thoughtful "Yes, sir."

"Son," resumed the skipper, "how long has it been since you had liberty?"

"Oh, a very long time, Captain. Before I joined the ship yesterday I was in the brig for quite a while."

"I guessed as much," said Captain Armstrong drily. "Well, I'll look into it; that's all; you may go."

The very next day without his having said another word Gonzales was called up by the exec, given special liberty, and his back pay was pressed on him. It was indeed a miracle if ever there was one.

Although he had no notion of it, Seaman, 2nd, Manuel Gonzales was a token of what was happening to *Spence*, and his "miracle" exemplified the sagacity of her skipper. The skeletal deck and engineering drafts sent to *Spence* on her commissioning in January, 1943, had been bad enough, but the additional and replacement drafts were worse. Almost none of them ever had been to sea before; they were but remotely acquainted with naval discipline and, as the Captain summed it up bitterly to the exec after an inspection and in the privacy of his cabin, "They're the damndest bunch of swabs, slobs, and lubbers I've ever seen!"

Gonzales was the straw that broke the camel's back. When he reported aboard phlegmatic Lieutenant Commander Bill Dutton, the executive officer, took one look at his record; then Dutton went streaking to Armstrong with fire in his eyes. "Captain," he said as he stood in the doorway combing his long fingers nervously through tousled hair, "do we have to take aboard a man such as this Gonzales? He's been over the hill so often he's a ridge runner, not a sailor!"

Spence had telephone service from shoreside. The Captain flipped through Gonzales' dismal record; then he called the personnel officer on Treasure Island and tried a bluff: "I refuse to have a man of this type in my ship!" he stormed. "Fine," replied the bureaucrat. "But either you'll take him, or you'll explain to the Commandant of the Twelfth Naval District in San Francisco."

That, of course, had been that. Lieutenant Commanders skippering destroyers don't take their routine personnel problems to Rear Admirals—not if they've been around as long as Heinie Armstrong they don't. "Tell you what you do, Bill," said the skipper. "I just got word we'll be under way day after tomorrow for Pearl. Send this Gonzales to me for a talk this afternoon. Tomorrow give him special liberty and all the back pay he's got coming. If he runs true to form I've got a hunch he won't be with us when we sail."

Thus was Manuel's Miracle born of the sagacity of a destroyer captain who knew when to observe Navy protocol, but also how to do a little improvising of his own. It was a discernible characteristic of the skippers who were to form up behind the broad pennant of Arleigh Burke. They all knew when to follow the book and when to desert it to follow their own judgment. As Armstrong had anticipated, when *Spence* kicked all astern dead slow, slid smoothly from her slip, and swung her knife bow toward the Golden Gate, Seaman, 2nd, Gonzales was nowhere in evidence. They tossed his bag to the beach party, transferred his accounts to the Twelfth Naval District, and forgot him. There was serious work ahead and it called for men who could absorb training and adjust, not odd-balls like Gonzales.

Spence, steaming toward Honolulu, represented three values fundamental to the Gallant Squadron. First the ships: like *Spence* all were new and of the *Fletcher* class. Next the captains: all were professional Navy officers, and all had been contemporaneous with Heinie Armstrong at the United States Naval Academy. Finally the immediate challenge: all appreciated the transcendent need to achieve, as quickly as possible, such a high degree of operating and fighting efficiency that Admiral Halsey, soon to assume command of the Allied climb up the Solomons ladder from Noumea to Rabaul, could rely upon the Squadron not alone for the multitude of onerous chores always thrust upon the "little boys" by the disparate demands of war, but also for reliable performance of the endless patrols and tactical missions through which combat often must be sought and frequently is found.

Spence was a Bath boat, built at the Bath Iron Works, Bath, Maine, and launched 27th October, 1942. Some purists might suggest that she be called a Bath *ship*, but the purest purists—seasoned officers of the Navy with long memories—always call Bath-built DDs "Bath boats" from the circumstance that the first United States torpedo boats were Bath-built, and from them has evolved the present "torpedo boat destroyer." A Bath boat is the Stradivarius of DDs—a magnificent instrument upon which a talented captain can play a singing melody. So it was to be with *Spence* under Heinie Armstrong, *Converse* under the sensitive fingers of Ham Hamberger, *Thatcher* under Ralph Lampman, and *Foote-the-Unfortunate* under Alston Ramsay—the man nobody knew.

The *Fletcher* class, our newest at the time and some say the finest destroyers we ever laid down, were flush-deck vessels with two stacks, one 5-inch .38 battery forward of two guns and one aft of three guns; six 40-mm guns, ten 20-mm guns, and two sets of five 21-inch torpedo tubes. For their class they were well armed, hard-hitting ships although, of course, they had no armor plate and no protection save maneuverability and speed against accurate gunfire. They did everything well at speeds above 5 knots but when built were equipped with single rudders, which were too short. This made them handle sloppily when making a landing, but eventually the rudders were lengthened and the defect corrected.

Spence had a length of 376½ feet, a beam of 39¼ feet, a standard displacement of 2,050 tons—2,750 tons full load. Her propulsion plant was General Electric geared turbines on two shafts which gave her a total of 60,000 shaft horsepower and a rated speed of 35-plus knots.

If there was a soft spot in *Spence* and her sisters it was the engineering plant. There were four boilers. Since the efficiency of a heat engine depends upon the range of temperatures, to get speed and operating range increases the steam in the *Fletcher* class ships was generated at higher than average pressures. Then heat was added to the steam by passing it through superheaters. These superheaters were to prove a constant source of trouble. In some installations the superheater tubes were thin-walled, which made for efficiency in superheating the steam passing through them, but also caused them to melt if, for any reason, the flow of steam had to be shut down suddenly. In consequence in these DDs it became the practice to "rock" the ship—one third ahead, one third astern—at intervals which would permit the vessel to remain relatively stationary while the superheat was taken off gradually. This, of course, became necessary only when unexpected circumstances made it essential to shut down the propulsion plant suddenly. If, later on in the Solomons, the officer of the deck forgot to tell the engineers to take off the superheat—keep the kettle from boiling dry—as they approached harbor, it was sometimes necessary for a destroyer to cruise outside the submarine nets for an hour or more before she could enter and anchor without risk to her boilers.

Not only was this the Achilles' heel of the *Fletcher* class but, in the early days of the Squadron, a further aggravation was added by the lack of technical skill on the part of fireroom personnel. Most of these crews, if experienced at all, had come from ships employing 250 pounds of saturated steam. The superheater technique was different—newfangled—and for some time the fireroom crews were not too adept at its implementation. This resulted in the fairly frequent need of engineering availability—time out for repairs—and many, many times in the dispatch of ships of the Squadron on missions when they were capable of doing only 30 or fewer knots of their rated 35. Indeed, as will be related, it was precisely such a situation which won for the Squadron Commodore the nickname of 31-Knot-Burke, which was a gentle reproach for his going so slow, and not a tribute to his blazing speed as many have erroneously assumed.

Standing on the bridge of DD 512 as she lanced southwestward through cobalt seas her skipper, Lieutenant Commander Armstrong, had just turned 40 years, and was at the peak both of physical and intellectual vigor. He was a man of average height and weight, inclined to slouch a little when in repose but with a reputation for being "taut" in all things pertaining to duty. He had a high forehead, eyes which could twinkle with amusement or blaze with anger as the circumstances dictated, a small mustache which grace-noted ample, often smiling lips, a strong, somewhat thick nose, and a sense of humor which added cumulatively to his popularity with his colleagues.

Although born in Salt Lake City, home of American Mormons, Armstrong was not a member of the Church of Jesus Christ of Latter-Day Saints. He was an Episcopalian and inclined toward the devout side. The family was of English-Scottish-French derivation which accounted for his middle name of Jacques, and as a child he couldn't understand why his playmates didn't take this cue and call him "Jack." Instead they seized on his first name, Henry; altered it to Heinie, and caused the lad grievous distress during the First World War by this implication of German ancestry. He got over it.

The family line on the male side came down through General Sherman Armstrong who played a lusty part in the Revolutionary War, and Heinie's father, Henry Jacques Armstrong senior, was a drummer boy in the war between the States. On the male side the family had consistently tended toward the martial. After coming home from the war the elder Armstrong served for a while as Indian Agent with the Sioux tribe. Later he set up as a druggist, and his pestles seem to have led to politics for at about that time he also became an ardent and articulate Republican.

Young Armstrong's mother was born Elizabeth Green and her parents came to the United States from England. Elizabeth and Henry senior met in Montana where both were living; they married and went to Utah in 1901. Heinie, the fruit of this union, was born on 14th June, two years later.

Heinie Armstrong was the kind of kid who could grasp an idea and run with it. Between 1915 and 1923 he was a staunch Boy Scout but it was not enough for him to subscribe to the Scouting oath, go on a hike or two, and call it good as many boys did. Heinie became an Eagle Scout, then a Veteran, finally an Assistant Scout Master. It was an early reflection of the perception and thoroughness which were to make *Spence* one of the fastest shooting, smoothest operating ships of the Gallant Squadron. As a destroyer captain Lieutenant Commander (soon to be Commander) Armstrong had a simple code of performance: "I expect all hands to work as hard as I do, and I shall see to it that I work hard enough to do my job as thoroughly and as well as I possibly can do it." The code and its fulfillment were to elicit an accolade from Arleigh Burke: "*Spence* is one of the best ships in the Squadron."

While comfortably situated the Armstrong family was not wealthy and Heinie found it convenient to take an odd job now and again to fortify his personal funds. The most sustained enterprise in this connection was two years spent as a part-time messenger with the Union Pacific Railroad. In the course of this employment he met and talked with the father of three boys who had graduated from the Academy at Annapolis and entered upon careers as naval officers. Naturally inclined toward the military, conversations with this gentleman finally determined young Armstrong upon a career in the service of his country, but he did not put all his eggs in the Navy basket at first. He secured a principal appointment to the United States Military Academy at West Point, and only a first alternate appointment to Annapolis. The principal Annapolis appointment bilged out, however; Armstrong took the examination, passed it, and entered the Academy on 3rd June, 1923, less than two weeks before his twentieth birthday.

As a child Armstrong had penetrated into, grasped, and effectively applied the idea as well as the practices of Scouting. As a youth he now penetrated with equal grasp and enthusiasm into the abstraction of patriotism and mastered with equal facility the necessary practices which constitute the working tools of the Navy officer who will be successful in his profession. In any study of the Navy spectrum Heinie Armstrong and those like him must loom large. He was a good man; he was a good officer; he was a good symbol. More than most he absorbed the peculiar *mystique* of the Navy as distinct from the broader, deeper and more fundamental *mystique* of the sea which his colleague

DeWitt Clinton Ellis "Cut-of-his-jib" Hamberger, also of the Gallant Squadron, was to perceive, ponder, and convert to a scale for the measurement of men and events.

For Henry Jacques Armstrong the United States Naval Academy provided entrance upon a new and exuberant way of life. By temperament adjustable, he had little difficulty accommodating the highly systematized routines of the Academy. He took the customary hazing in his stride and, in his senior year, dished it out to his sorrow. The plebe (freshman) in First (senior) Classman Armstrong's room had just recited *"How doth the little busy bee improve each shining hour"* with appropriate buzzes and gestures and, bent over, was exposing his stern to a strophe of the broom wielded by Mr. Armstrong when the door was flung open and the Duty Officer stood revealed. "Gentlemen," he inquired of the assembled midshipmen, "exactly what goes on here?"

"Sir," said Heinie, "I was just entertaining this plebe in a friendly fashion!"

"I see," said the OD. "Well, the way you're going about it looks suspiciously like a Class A offense to me. We shall take this matter up in detail later."

As a consequence of "entertaining this plebe in a friendly fashion" First Classman Armstrong carried his gear aboard the *Riena Mercedes* —the Academy "brig"—for a full 7 days of lost privileges and closely supervised conduct. He also lost a hundred numbers which, it being his senior year, was more penalizing than it might have been had his offense happened earlier in his Academy career. A midshipman's class standing and thus his "number" upon graduation is the product of a complex computation involving scholastic marks, rating for aptitude and leadership qualities, deportment, adjustment to the Navy and other comprehensive considerations. The number emerging from this calculation as he is about to leave the Academy becomes his for life and determines his seniority in the service. To lose a hundred numbers then —to be dropped back a hundred points as he was about to enter upon his career and with no time to overcome the loss by superior marks— was to be handicapped appreciably in the tedious climb up the ladder of promotion toward senior rank in the Navy hierarchy.

At the time this more permanent implication of his "Class A" did not impress young Armstrong as forcibly as the more immediate consequence that he almost missed June Week. June Week, an interlude of formal exhibitions by the Corps of Midshipmen and social functions featuring the first classmen whose graduation climaxes the festivities is THE major event of the Academy year. Honor swords are received by exemplary midshipmen, pretty girls present new colors to crack units, hopeful debutantes and their duennas swarm Carval Hall and other Annapolis hostelries as well as private mansions thrown open for the occasion, and "flirtation walk" gets a heavy play. To have missed June Week would have been to pay a dear price indeed for a momentary departure from the paths of academic rectitude, and Heinie Armstrong was fortunate enough not to have to pay this final forfeit. He lashed his hammock and came ashore from the *Riena* just as the celebrations were entering their accelerated early phase.

With the resilience of youth it would have been understandable had Armstrong simply shrugged the whole matter off as a painful memory at best. He did no such thing. Instead he reflected perceptively upon the basic lesson to be derived from his crime and punishment. Caught in the act of infraction of rules, still he had been offered the opportunity to make a free statement in his own defense. Justice had been swift and stern but also it had been open, above-board, and fair. Those making the determination of guilt and meting out punishment had exhibited no concern with personalities or values tangential to the base line of the offense. While he guessed he wouldn't recommend getting a Class A as the best approach to understanding the mechanics of Navy discipline and justice, still there were valuable lessons to be learned through the experience and he took them to heart. "That kind of thing," young Armstrong told himself, "when you look at it right, helps to stiffen the moral fiber of the officer, remind him of his duty to set an example, and fortifies his respect for the traditions of the service." When it came his time to sit in judgment and dispense punishment he remembered this lesson and was meticulous in seeing to it that the process was swift but thorough, uninfluenced by extraneous considerations, the verdict openly arrived at, and the punishment realistically related to the nature and degree of the offense. The lesson had not been a superficial one; its roots struck deep and tapped rich sources for the building of the strong morale which was to become epitomatic of *Spence*.

For young Henry Jacques the Academy was not all work and no play. He found many subjects hard and their mastery demanding, but he also found time to play class and company football, to be a member of the Stage Gang, and to participate in dramatic and musical clubs. The Stage Gang was a select few midshipmen who had responsibility for class shows and other presentations and during Armstrong's affiliation they labored lovingly over productions of "Bulldog Drummond," "The Bat," and "Clarence," acquitting themselves with distinction by undergraduate standards.

Perhaps the net of Heinie Armstrong's legacy from the Academy may be summed up in the phrase "dedication to service" although it would be prudent hastily to add the clarifying qualification "service to country." As he went forth to become a watch and junior division

officer aboard *U.S.S. Medusa* and *U.S.S. Colorado* and later Assistant
Engineer Officer of *U.S.S. Renshaw* his appreciation of the Navy as a
way of life with patriotic service as its ultimate goal broadened and
strengthened. For this junior officer service to country became the
heart of that abstraction which we recognize as the Navy *mystique*.
In this appreciation he was to differ from some of his colleagues, but
for Heinie Armstrong this dedication was no mere lip service to a
nebulous principle gaudily labeled "patriotism." It was a living philosophy of specific although not limited service often demanding rigorous
self-discipline, the denial of easy indulgences, and the unhesitating assumption of responsibility often under circumstances which made such
responsibility a dangerous and awkward burden.

Having learned to work a running fix, to figure the precise number of
turns required to catch high tide at White Water Bay, Alaska, from
a designated point at sea within a specified time, to curb his temper,
to regard the Deity with awe, to be a reliable member of the team—
to follow as well as to lead—Henry Jacques Armstrong went forth and,
by his own admission, became a simon-pure, 24-carat gold heel!

It was a star-powdered night in San Diego and Lieutenant Armstrong had the evening off from the Naval Air Station on North Island
where he was undergoing flight training. Alone and lonesome he wandered into the rococo del Coronado Hotel locally known simply as "the
del," took a table at the edge of the dance floor, ordered a set-up which
he spiked sparingly from a flask of Vallejo brandy (the year was 1930
and the nation was in the grip of prohibition) and sat contemplating
his drink and his unwelcome solitude. The afternoon had been marked
by nothing more notable than the ordering of some shirts from "Jake-
the-Naval-Tailor" who was deferentially solicitous of the officer custom,
and the evening ahead promised little more by way of diversion or
excitement.

Ten minutes later young Armstrong's morose musings were suddenly arrested, his pulse skipped a beat, and his listlessness vanished
with a celerity which he would not have thought possible had he reflected upon it—which he didn't. He'd looked up to observe a classmate
swinging out on the floor. In the classmate's arms was a vision of such
compelling loveliness that Heinie's jaw flopped open in incredulity and
he was momentarily bereft of initiative. But not for long! When the
music stopped Mr. Armstrong waited barely a decent interval before
presenting himself at his colleague's table and being introduced to Miss
Virginia Vincent of Los Angeles, who was all floating chiffon, sparkling
eyes, and ethereal radiance.

During the next couple of hours Armstrong acted shamelessly and without thought of regret. He absented himself only long enough to replenish his supply of Vallejo brandy—a skull-popping elixir popular with the young fry of the officer corps at the time and place—and this powerful potation he pressed upon his mellowing fellow officer in frequent and liberal doses. The campaign was successful; the results somewhat comparable to a surprise torpedo salvo from DesRon-23; the classmate was "sunk." Having deftly disposed of her original escort Armstrong then proceeded to escort Miss Vincent to her doorstep by the longest route he could discover short of an excursion into Mexico. They were married in August of the following year; a daughter, Jan, was born at Annapolis in 1935, and a son, Derik, at Santa Ana, California, in 1937. Considering its volatile foundation on Vallejo brandy the union proved singularly fruitful and enduring.

As a lieutenant commander, Heinie's deep devotion to his family almost made him miss his own boat when the time came for him to accept delivery of *Spence* on behalf of the Navy and assume command of her at Bath. He had been skippering *U.S.S. Waters*, Destroyer Number 112, in the Aleutians. The *Waters*, of but 1,200 tons, was one of the old four-pipers left over from World War I, and Armstrong was understandably excited to be getting command of a brand new 2,000 tonner. Even so he did not let this eagerness interfere with an opportunity for a brief visit with his family then resident in Long Beach. Heinie proceeded from Dutch Harbor to Bath via California, and he arrived at Bath so tardily that he inspected and accepted *Spence* one day and sailed with her toward Boston three days later. It was a crash program not recommended by Navy custom.

Somehow Captain Armstrong and his officers, most of whom were reserves, managed to get *Spence* pulled together, out to the West coast, and pointed for Pearl Harbor. They were not, however, the least bit happy about the state of fitness of the ship's company and some were discouraged almost to the point of disgust. In keeping with his strong convictions, however, the Captain accepted the challenge and set patiently about the double job of discharging ordered convoy and other war missions while at the same time converting his heterogeneous mob of a crew into a ship's company that could be relied upon to fight and, if necessary, to die at their posts. Never was a crew worked harder than the men of *Spence* as she plowed the placid Pacific. But when she reached Espiritu Santo in the New Hebrides on Saturday, 18th September, 1943, and at precisely 1009 in the morning tied up alongside the tanker *Western Sun* to refuel, she had on board at least the makings of a crew who knew fore from aft, port from starboard, and had a glimmering of pride in their ship and in their Navy. Captain Armstrong, reporting

to the Commodore of DesRon-23, was well on his way to war; his men
were ready to follow him; soon they would be able as well. One of the
eagles had come to roost on a lofty perch.

At about the time Seaman Gonzales was enjoying his miracle and
living it up on the beach at San Francisco, Destroyer Number 509—
U.S.S. Converse—was standing out through the crowded traffic of
Boston harbor preparatory to doubling the hook of Cape Cod and
heading south through the offshore rollers of a sullen winter Atlantic.
She was majestic in her long low grace with its implicit promise of
greyhound speed. Wisps of smoke from her two raking stacks gave
token of throbbing power below, controlled by watchful eyes and steady,
competent hands. Her guns and torpedo tubes, trained in, spoke mutely
of her might when angered. Outwardly *Converse* was a solid symbol of
the implacable determination of the American people to exact retribution for Pearl Harbor. Unfortunately the impression of strength and
competence which this fine vessel gave was illusory. She was about the
most confused and frantic one warship ever to wear the national ensign,
and had her Captain himself not been on the helm other vessels would
have been well advised to steer clear for fear of being cut in twain.

In the process of undocking two hawsers had been parted. This was
an unheard-of happening under normal circumstances and shrieked of
butterfingers on deck. In the first minutes away from the dock the
officer of the deck had shown himself dangerously irresolute and far too
jittery to be trusted with the responsibilities of command in crowded
waters. With an easygoing, "I'll take her; you go grab a bit of lunch,"
the Old Man had assumed the duties of officer of the deck in addition to
his own responsibilities. Next it had been the man on the wheel. He
was the ship's chief quartermaster as befitted a member of the special
underway detail and he was, indeed, technically competent enough.
But he was an ancient shellback recalled to active duty from honorable
years of soft retirement, and he simply did not have the physical
stamina to meet the demands of the job.

"Captain, sir," he said, "my legs are killing me!" He paused a moment and then added desperately, "I'm just not able to stand this wheel
watch any longer."

"Very well," replied the skipper, keeping a sharp lookout all around
for the multiple dangers that threatened, "put one of your mates on
the helm."

"But, Captain," explained the wretched oldtimer, "not one of my
men has learned to steer yet! I'm the only one who can handle the
wheel!"

The Captain stifled what started out to be an audible gulp. Almost
every man on the bridge, he realized, was in a state of jitters reflecting

lack of confidence which adequate training and experience would have given them. His job was not to increase their confusion and lack of reliance on themselves, but rather to try to bolster their courage. At the same time the safety of the ship was paramount.

"Very well," said the Captain, "I'll take the wheel. Go somewhere and sit down until you feel better."

As he stepped up on the low grating and slid his fingers into the inside notches of the mahogany-rimmed wheel the Captain nudged a seaman away from his station in front of the engineroom telegraph with its bright brass barrel and spring-grip handles. "Stand aside, son," he said, not unkindly. "I might as well take that thing too, and run the whole shootin' match!"

Thus, possibly for the first time in the history of the United States Navy, a skipper took a 2,000-ton warship to sea through dangerous waters virtually single-handed. He was Commander DeWitt Clinton Ellis Hamberger—Ham Hamberger to his colleagues—and he was by all odds one of the most compelling and complex characters in the bright galaxy of DesRon-23 skippers.

As Armstrong had found it aboard *Spence*, so Hamberger found the situation aboard *Converse* grim. Of her 350 officers and men not 5 per cent were experienced hands. The crew, with few exceptions, were just out of the naval training station where they had received their inoculations, a partial "bag" apiece—one set of blues; two sets of whites—and little else. The possession of bell-bottomed trousers was about the only claim most of them could make on the mysteries of seamanship. Indeed they were so green that several forthrightly admitted they hadn't known which end of the ship went out of the harbor first, and despite the posting of special signs to guide them below decks it was two weeks before many could find the compartments where they lived or worked without a Cook's tour of the ship including the engineroom and forepeak. For a month or more *Converse* was to remain a very confused ship beneath the outward seeming of Navy spit, polish, and efficiency. The seasoned members of her company lived on coffee and largely dispensed with sitting or sleeping. This was excellent conditioning for the role ahead of them in the Solomons and later, at the *Cloob des Slot* they were to tell hilarious tales of their harassments during this shakedown period which would seem trivial in terms of the pressures of the fighting war.

At 40 years Captain Hamberger was sturdily built, a trifle on the tall side. He had an oval face, strikingly green eyes, and a strong jaw. Already his hair was beginning to recede at the temples, and he exhibited a deceptively placid manner which a few foolish people erroneously interpreted as indicative of a slow mind. The fact was that Ham

Hamberger had a mind which worked with the precision of a camera shutter—one of the most comprehensive intellects in the Squadron. While others were brushing a problem superficially and sometimes reaching shaky conclusions, Hamberger was thinking through it and all around it as well. He spoke little, but that was but an inverse reflection of his thinking which could be profound. He knew precisely what he wanted at all times; he was patient in seeing to it that others knew what he wanted and why, and usually he got what he wanted, which was the reason he stood on the bridge of *Converse*. Previously he'd been skipper of *U.S.S. Decatur*, the Navy's oldest living four-piper. She was a flush-deck vessel and Hamberger wanted to stay in a ship of that design, considering that it contributed to more efficient handling. However, he'd also wanted to get to the Pacific where he could shoot his guns and his torpedoes, and had mounted a quiet little campaign which finally brought him to the bridge of *Converse*, headed for the kind of fighting that would make one of his big jobs finding enough shell and torpedoes to implement his opportunities.

DeWitt Clinton Ellis Hamberger, a study in the tradition of the sea as well as the more parochial tradition of the United States Navy, was born at Fredericksburg, in the Old Dominion, on 2nd April, 1903. His father, William Francis Hamberger, was a naval officer from New Jersey and of Alsatian descent in the male line; Scottish on the distaff side. His mother, the former Elizabeth Martin Ellis, was of New York Dutch and Huguenot extraction, resident in Virginia at the time of her marriage.

The senior Hamberger was a man of parts—part soaring dreams and part iron will—and he transmitted both of these valuable characteristics to his son. There were seagoing and military men aplenty in the long lines of both families and the famous clipper ship Captain George Wendell, whose memorabilia are now preserved at Mystic, Connecticut, was an illustrious forebear.

As a youth questing after his dreams William Francis Hamberger ran away from home three times. Twice he was fetched back with scant ceremony but the third time, applying the lessons of previous unsuccessful attempts, he eluded pursuit, enlisted in the Navy as an apprentice, and eventually realized his dreams of studying at first hand the mysteries of blue water below and wheeling constellations overhead. He adapted readily to the Navy pattern—much more severe then than now—and rose to the rank of warrant officer. He participated in the relief expedition to Peking during the crisis of the Boxer Rebellion in China, and was awarded his country's highest decoration, the Congressional Medal of Honor, for leading a charge stark naked. He and some mates were bathing in a canal when they looked up to discover that the

Chinese had driven in their pickets and were about to overrun the position. Grabbing their weapons they rushed to reinforce the pickets, and the situation was saved by the timely arrival of a train mounting a Gatling gun.

While not unaware of the stature of the tribute to his valor which the Congressional Medal represented, William Francis probably set more store by one of his less spectacular achievements. Deeply interested in helping enlisted men associated with him to advance and qualify for officer rank, he formed a class of a dozen lads young in naval service and fired with ambition. They bought courses from the early International Correspondence School and under his voluntary tutelage spent their very few spare hours delving into the abstruse principles of navigation, gunnery, and what then passed for engineering. All twelve eventually took the examination for warrant officer and all twelve passed it. But there was to be an even greater gratification in this experiment for William Francis Hamberger: the whole dozen of his newly minted warrant officers went on to attain commissioned rank. There was at that time no formal Navy educational program and the elder Hamberger came close to pioneering it in a very real sense. Thus he left his impress upon the naval service and as a junior officer the son, DeWitt Clinton, came into contact with many senior officers who had observed and admired his father's dedication to the improvement of the seagoing breed. The roots sank uncommonly deep.

Temperament, philosophical discernment, and physical circumstances all three combined to set DeWitt Clinton Hamberger somewhat apart from his fellows, and it was a circumstance which he did not regard with disfavor. Because of the service demands upon his father the family was largely itinerant. At an early age the boy achieved an awareness of major concepts more appropriately associated with maturity, but this wider knowledge was come by at considerable sacrifice in scholastic continuity. One result, curiously, was the germination in young Hamberger of a command characteristic often acquired with the greatest difficulty even by talented and versatile officers, and never achieved by some. In a word it may be described as "aloneness." During the crucial hours and minutes and moments of decision the Commander—he who exercises total authority at the price of total responsibility—always must be alone. Although surrounded by a multitude many of whom may recognize it, none properly may share their commander's loneliness of ultimate responsibility and accountability. In the naval service which is forced by ever-present dangers to be especially orthodox, acceptance of emotional isolation is a command requirement which has brought many a sturdy and technically competent officer face to face with failure in his chosen profession.

Although in no sense unsocial, Ham Hamberger never sought the
artificial stimulus and support of the mob. While he lacked Arleigh
Burke's bright inspirational talents—his ability to speak to men's
emotions and their hearts—even as a young officer Hamberger had
threaded through the warp and woof of his fiber the cardinal command
characteristics of a readiness to accept full responsibility even for the
lives and honor of himself and others, and the ability to welcome and
enjoy the isolation such acceptance demanded. All of the skippers of
"23" had command characteristics of a very superior order but among
them Hamberger would have to be rated very close to the top in this
particular quality.

Improvisation intrigued Hamberger. Under him *Decatur* was organized along non-reg lines a year before the Department officially adopted
the patterns which he had pioneered. Aboard *Converse* he introduced
non-regulation features, two of which later became type alterations and
were incorporated in all ships of the *Fletcher* class. As a naval officer
he exercised a restless, probing, assimilating and often daring intelligence and imagination much of the time cloaked by an instinctive mod-
esty which often took the form of undue reticence. His colleagues in
DesRon-23 were not fooled. They came quickly to expect wise and considered counsel of him and effective innovations as well. In the Solomons
campaign at one point Count Austin broke his Division-46 pennant in
Converse in tribute to that ship's superior organization and equipment
for gathering and interpreting vital data at the threshold or in the
heat of battle. These were the products of Hamberger's analytical approach to whatever problem confronted him and his unceasing quest
for improvement.

It was a gangling young man who arrived at Crabtown—midshipman
slang for Annapolis, Maryland—on 16th June, 1922, and began his
Navy career under the formidable name of DeWitt Clinton Ellis Hamberger. He was two months and a few days over his nineteenth birthday,
and he had reached the Academy over the hard route. Because of their
frequent changes of domicile the Hamberger family had no claim upon
a senator or a congressman for an appointment to the Naval Academy.
DeWitt Clinton had, perforce, sought a Presidential appointment of
which there were ten each year, awarded to the top ten survivors in a
competitive examination. Even as he took these tests young Hamberger
regarded them as archaic although that did not mean that they were
not difficult. The academic requirements were established by law and
thus realistically stultified in a rapidly expanding body of general and
scientific knowledge. He had, however, taken the precaution of being
well prepared through a cram course at Columbia Preparatory School
in the nation's capital. At that time Columbia Prep specialized in

grooming young men for the entrance examinations to West Point as well as Annapolis, and however unrealistic the set questions may have been, the relation of the Columbia curriculum to them was precise and apt. When the final scores were tabulated DeWitt Clinton Ellis Hamberger was well up among the top ten and had taken the first step toward the rank of Rear Admiral which he eventually attained along with every other skipper of DesRon-23.

Academy years were fleeting, rewarding, and puzzling. Ham became a class athlete, a member of the class swimming and fencing teams and the class crew. He picked a mandolin in a musical club, sang in the choir, and a fathomless depth crept into his green eyes when he came to the words

> *Eternal Father, strong to save,*
> *Whose hand hath bound the restless wave*

but it vanished with the certitude of clearly perceived intention when he added

> *O hear us when we cry to Thee*
> *For those in peril on the sea.*

That last sentiment and supplication he could completely understand. Nominally an Episcopalian, a regular church goer which he has remained throughout his life, and with a firm belief and faith in God, still he bridled at theology as a man-made technicality and sat resentfully beneath sermons burdened with theologic interpretation. The concept of an all-wise, all-powerful, all-merciful and all-loving God who could and would smooth the raging billows and succor honest sailormen in distress—that was something else again. It was a notion which Ham Hamberger could and did grasp, and he carried it with him when he went down to the sea in ships. Nor was he alone in this. Sailors are often short on theology but long on faith which emerged as a necessary conclusion from the contemplation and experience of the elemental forces of nature. If Jesus Christ had not introduced faith as the imperative of human moral striving, some sailor would have.

Hamberger was not the first youth to find numbers the bugaboo of his days and nights at the Naval Academy. In a year and a half he had to dash through math from college algebra to integral calculus. Two weeks were allotted for the mastery of solid geometry, and a month for analytical geometry, and so it went. Always—and this was the thing upon which he reflected bitterly during many a long night when the lights were out and he was supposed to be getting the rest he needed for a demanding next day—*always* his instructors wanted a number for an answer. It was as though the very secret of existence were wrapped up in a number. It might be a fat, round number like 2080, or a weaselly little insidious fragment like $2^{12}\!\!/_{32}$—but always a number! Ham Hamberger's preoccupation lay not in primary products—2 plus 2 equals 4 —but in the theory behind: *why* does 2 plus 2 equal 4—and does it always? And for that kind of fundamental approach there was little time in the schedule of instruction at Annapolis. He realized, with a perception alien to his years, that the academic gait had a double purpose—to teach the apt and to eliminate the slow learners. He determined to fool them. He did what he could with the courses which required numbers for answers, and he squeaked by. But in the classes in seamanship he came into his own; his long heritage of the sea asserted itself, and he got marks. Hard driven in math, he relaxed behind the bulge of a filling sail, read the leech and the luff as others might a printed page, and became one of the first in his class to qualify as skipper in the sailing boats used at the Academy to train midshipmen in the vagaries of wind, wave, and weather.

Toward his instructors Midshipman Hamberger exhibited the same questioning attitude which was his usual address to life. Most of them he ended by regarding with little favor, but "Red" McGruder and "Sock" McMorris were exceptions. McGruder, in a complex personality, managed to accommodate the somewhat antithetical characteristics of fanatically high standards of devotion to duty while at the same time indulging a sense of humor of classic proportions. The combination confused most people. Red lived by the regulations and he gave the Navy, which he dearly loved, every break but, on occasion, even he was moved to leniency. When so impelled, however, it was his habit to swear the subject of his mercy to secrecy and thus his "good deeds" were known to but few. So far as his quick wit and sharp sense of humor are concerned, the following anecdote is now a part of living Academy legend:

A midshipman officer having charge of a dormitory floor or "deck" as the Navy would have it, went to the foot of the stairs (read "ladder" in Navyese) one evening and, cupping his hands to his mouth, hailed his corresponding number on the deck above sotto voce: "Watch out for that old son-of-a-bitch Red McGruder! He's around here somewhere!" Whereupon Commander McGruder tapped the startled midshipman on the back and, as he spun around in a state of stiff dismay suggesting rigor mortis said, simply, "Son, don't EVER call me RED!" And with that the terror strode off leaving a midshipman officer wiping his brow in thankful amazement.

McGruder went on to become Chief of Staff to Admiral Nimitz in the Pacific, was generally credited with being one of the top brains formulating our policy in that area, and fully vindicated Hamberger's perception that he was an officer several cuts above average.

Sock McMorris was a totally different personality. His name was Charles H. McMorris, and he was to retire a Rear Admiral. When not called Sock, McMorris was known to the midshipmen as "The Phantom of the Opera." This nickname reflected the unthinking cruelty of youth. An unhappy accident had left McMorris with facial scars suggestive of the grotesque makeup employed by Lon Chaney, the movie actor, then starring in the popular film "The Phantom of the Opera." Also there were those who attributed to McMorris a penchant for emerging out of nowhere in the best cloak-and-dagger tradition, to the consternation of midshipmen who were not minding their muttons. Actually, Sock was an instructor in seamanship in which Hamberger excelled, and this divined sympathy of one sea-man for another sea-man was the basis of their rapport. In practice McMorris concerned himself but little with disciplinary matters.

While he was battling his way through the tough third and fourth year courses at Annapolis, seeking to multiply his opportunities for piling up good marks through theoretical rather than manifest erudition, Midshipman Hamberger's dreams inched over onto the incalescent side. In his days at Columbia Prep he had met slight, vivacious brunette Henrietta Albers, whose family were Washingtonians. Henrietta and Ham corresponded and continued to see each other during his leaves and on those infrequent occasions when midshipmen were allowed to "drag" their dates to Academy dances. It was in keeping with Hamberger's character that romance was not something into which he dashed at flank speed and with superheaters cut in. He took his increasing emotional involvement in stride, examined it critically, weighed it appraisingly, and allowed it to mature slowly and reliably. He had, indeed, been an ensign serving on *U.S.S. Omaha* for 11 months before he and Henrietta married in May, 1927.

The way of *Converse* to Noumea, New Caledonia, and what Captain Hamberger called "the more tangible war in the Pacific" lay via Guantanamo Bay, Cuba, and Pearl Harbor, and it took nearly 6 months. In that time magic was accomplished on board. To those uninitiated into the challenges of naval command this magic may not seem to have been of great stature, but its fruits were substantial. Commander Hamberger adroitly used a single disciplinary case as an object lesson for his green and restless crew. Eschewing savage severity as quite the improper tactic, he employed public shame to drive home his lesson. The subject for punishment was a hardened offender against Navy rules and regulations who had found his way aboard *Converse* because somebody wanted to get rid of him as Heinie Armstrong had gotten rid of Gonzales. When this man reverted to his accustomed patterns of insubordination he was haled to Captain's Mast with stern promptitude. Although other and seemingly more appropriate

places were available, the Captain ordered the clearing out of a storeroom located on the berth deck and immediately in the path of the crew
going about their daily concerns. He had the word B-R-I-G painted
on the door in large letters. Then he popped the malefactor in for a
term of days of solitary confinement. As anticipated, young and im-
pressionable seamen passing this improvised but well-advertised brig
and listening to the lonely pace-pace-pace of the caged culprit, were
struck with the undesirability of changing places with him. More,
through the example as well as the explanations of their officers, they
were brought to the conviction that the man had let the *ship* down—
not just broken a rule. Gradually they began to perceive the common
sense origins of many aspects of discipline which they found superficially galling, and out of their teaching and reflection there emerged
a state of morale built around pride of ship and pride of service which
proved proof against the most insidious temptations.

The supreme test came when, after a year of fighting, *Converse* made
a liberty in Sydney, Australia, at Christmas time. Orders for the ship's
next mission required that liberty be terminated at an early hour on
Christmas Eve. The men of *Converse* were ashore with money in their
pockets, nostalgia in their hearts, and the narcotic chime of Christmas
carols in their ears, and only the merciless demands of war and the
promise of death to lure them back aboard their vessel. But back they
came when the time was up; there was not a single AOL [absent over
leave] from *Converse*'s company; she sailed on schedule and she sailed
proudly. In those formative months when things seemed chaotic and
uncertain the work of Commander Hamberger and his officers was well
done. *Converse* was a sound ship and she was to become a lucky ship as
well—a nautical state of grace much to be admired and envied.

The planting of the fragile seeds of morale and the solicitous hus-
banding of their tender blossoms was a natural compulsion for such a
perceptive officer as Ham Hamberger. At the same time he did not
neglect concrete challenges. On the way to the Pacific theater, and in
company with three other ships, *Converse* escorted *H.M.S. Victorious*.
The carrier had been converted to U.S. type landing gear for the
handling of U.S. planes, and she was a veteran of the war in the Medi-
terranean, having flown her planes against both the German and the
Italian air forces. Hamberger boarded *Victorious* and talked earnestly
and exhaustively with her officers and technicians. A result was the
creation in the destroyer of an air tracking station to give early warning of the approach of enemy aircraft. The men of *Converse* used such
equipment as they had or could scrounge, and quietly constituted themselves the first "air fighter director" group in the Pacific. Their competence was proven later when, in a big raid, a special group sent out

from Stateside for the purpose of rendering fighter-director service, lost contact and control, and *Converse* stepped effectively into the breach. The final extension of Hamberger's pioneering, along with the work of Heinie Armstrong, was the creation of a combat information center for destroyers. Previously such a luxury was reserved for cruisers and larger ships, but eventually every DD of DesRon-23 was to boast a CIC.

The junior officers sailing in *Converse* were given no glimpse of the soul-searching which often lay behind the hard decisions the whiplash of necessity drove their Commander to deliver, but which always were announced to them with the casualness one might exhibit upon addressing a breakfast egg. The case of the gunner is revelatory both of the nature of the problems the Captain faced and the resolution with which he tackled them even while fighting back the doubts which rasped his heart.

What should be the gunnery officer's talents and capabilities? A professional and a perfectionist, Ham Hamberger knew very well. "Guns" should be able to start from scratch, align, set up, and adjust every element of the battery, repair and adjust the computers, test the powder for deterioration, and perform a score more intricate technical tasks while at the same time training his inexperienced crews and developing them into sharpshooters. With the possible exception of his executive officer, and he couldn't be spared, there wasn't a man in the ship other than the Captain who could begin to do the job in its full dimensions. Yet the responsibility had to be given to somebody; *Converse* needed a gunnery officer and that's all there was to it.

Viewing the problem through the prism of his own philosophy of the Navy, Commander Hamberger had resented its implications basically, but his resentment was tempered by convictions equally strong and tending oppositely. His initial resentment was born of his abiding obligation which he felt to fight for his ship and his men. Naval gunnery is a sensitive science in which a well-meant mistake or a bit of thoughtlessness can kill a lot of the wrong people. To have to demand that an inadequately trained officer assume the great responsibilities implicit in the job of "guns" rubbed the Old Man the wrong way; somehow it just didn't seem quite cricket. But on the other side there was this: as dedicated as he was to fighting for his ship and his men, he was equally if not more strongly impelled to fight for his Navy. That meant doing everything and anything to improve the Navy (as had his father before him) and assist in the discharge of its missions. Along that line of reasoning, then, it was the Captain's conviction that it was the plain duty of every officer to accept without quibble all of the responsibilities which came his way in his naval service. Nor did it matter one whit that such acceptance might place his career in jeopardy; his prime obligation to the Navy still was to shoulder the burden and do his best. Thus reasoning, Ham Hamberger made up his mind.

Reserve Lieutenant P. E. Hurley had no notion of the introspective theorizing which lay behind the Captain's summons and the calm, almost casual order "Hurley, from now on you're the gunnery officer of this ship."

Hurley was a well-set-up lad with a conscientious approach to whatever job he was given, and a willingness to try under those desperate circumstances when trying alone is a mark of merit regardless of the success attained. He had been a former Eastern collegiate tennis champion and had quickness coupled with instinctive coordination. Adducing negative values when forced to choose among the few candidates available, the Captain had decided that Hurley, who seemed to have all-around ability, was the least likely to do anything importantly stupid, and there was the possible plus that his quick eye and lightning reflexes might make him a really superlative gunner.

"Captain," said Lieutenant Hurley slowly, torn between pride and dark misgivings, "of course it's an honor, sir. But I'm afraid you're putting too much responsibility on us reserves. If I make a mistake in a job like that it will hang over me for the rest of my life."

"Don't let it bother you too much," the Captain replied. "I'm an old gunner myself, and I think I recognize talents in you that you don't even know you have. Just do a careful job, and I'll keep an eye on you to see that you don't make any serious mistakes."

Although he had tried to reassure his new gunnery officer by a show of confidence, Hamberger was fully aware of the imbalance between experience and responsibility which the appointment represented. While he could do nothing to avoid the necessity of designating a gunnery officer, there *was* something he could do to promote the favorable development of the appointee in the job—or so he conceived. Which was why, less than a week later, a very bewildered and somewhat chagrined Mr. Hurley once more found himself facing his Captain and heard the pronouncement:

"Hurley, from now on you'll take over as first lieutenant as well as 'guns.' "

The young man all but collapsed. Wasn't being gunnery officer of a new destroyer enough of a job for one frightened reserve officer with strong misgivings as to his own knowledge of the science? It was, and more. But Commander Hamberger, thinking the problem through as was his wont, was playing as deep a game as had his colleague Armstrong when he marooned Seaman Gonzales on the beach in San Francisco. In his mind, *Converse*'s skipper had cast up the problem thus for equation:

If Hurley was to whip his inexperienced gun crews into shape he'd have to drill them day and night, and sometimes all day and all night. There was no other course through which they could approach competence.

BUT . . .

Responsibility for painting and hull maintenance was the first lieutenant's. Every first lieutenant worth his salt dearly loved to order a "field day" as frequently as possible. *On a field day all hands were turned out with chipping hammers and paint pots, while the rest of the ship's business waited. Any such interference would be sure to wreck Hurley's schedule of vitally necessary gun drills.*

The skipper's solution of the problem was obvious and effective. By making Hurley first lieutenant while retaining him as "guns," the young man was given additional responsibilities, true. But at the same time he was given the authority necessary to dovetail the two jobs so that conflict could be eliminated and progress permitted.

The Captain's cuteness bore prime fruit. Under Lieutenant Hurley in the Solomons *Converse* achieved a salvo interval of 3 seconds, which is slick shooting if you're hitting anything, and she was. But the first lieutenant appointment also turned out to have a small hook in it. During a fierce night engagement when *Converse* was jumped by fifteen *"Bettys"*—Mitsubishi Zero 1 two engined bombers employing dive tactics—gunnery officer Hurley caught one plane with a direct hit when it was half way through a screaming dive from high off the starboard bow. Trailing a brilliant plume of blazing gasoline the *Betty* barely skimmed over the destroyer's fo'c'sle head before exploding. The next morning first lieutenant Hurley was inspecting the damage topside. When he came to the fo'c'sle's head his expression registered complete disgust. "Dammit, Captain!" he exploded, "the burning gasoline from that bomber we got last night has taken off all our chain paint—*and that's the last chain paint in the Solomons!*"

"Well, son," said the skipper, "you'll just have to start shooting them down before they get to us. And do you know," the Commander added with a touch of awe when he came to tell the story later in the senior officer's Ironbottom Bay Club at Port Purvis, "since then Hurley has been knocking them down all over the place, but we haven't had a single plane bounced aboard us!"

As *Converse* bowed with stately grace to the undulating billows of the Pacific, scending rhythmically with the sea and occasionally flirting her propellers saucily in the air astern, her Captain sat in his own special chair on a bridge wing, sunk in reflection. It has been noted that DeWitt Clinton Ellis Hamberger probably had the most sophisticated philosophy and the most cogent formulization of his ideas of any of the skippers of the Gallant Squadron. This was not accidental but, rather, the product of a lifetime habit of leisurely contemplation and analysis of all of those values which touched his existence. In realistic terms Commander Hamberger had little notion of what lay ahead for himself or his ship, nor did he know with what kind of people he would be called upon to work. This was the point which preoccupied him at the moment. "I just hope," he reflected, "that they'll be *sea-men* (in his thinking he hyphenated the word) and *sea-men* I can recognize by the cut of their jibs!" He needn't have concerned himself on that score; he was well on the way to finding his *sea-men!*

IN DesRon-23 Hamberger was to encounter a compelling *mystique* which had a different point of origin and impinged differently on the consciousness of each of the skippers who recognized it (and not all of them did) but which had a uniform and transcendent impact when precipitated through the catalytic agent of Arleigh Burke's leadership reflecting his doctrine of faith.

TO DesRon-23 the Captain of *Converse* was taking an understanding and visualization of the *mystique* of the sea in which the true *sea-man* is caught up; which is basic and eternal; which treats of the ways of men with ships and the ways of ships with men; and which provides within its scope a deep-rooted foundation out of which has grown the more circumscribed *mystique* of the Navy, and many another. DeWitt Clinton Ellis Hamberger pondered the problem as he rolled slowly southeastward, and these were the stages of inference through which he approached its resolution:

Seagoing is nearly as ancient as the human race. Down through the centuries the art of seagoing has absorbed and amalgamated the sea ways of all peoples, including their practical inventions along with their legends and superstitions. Thus ships, their organizations and the customs and traditions embodied in their design, building, and sailing are truly empirical creations. Perforce the false has been battered down and destroyed along with the lives of countless thousands of sailors by the implacable might of the killer sea against which they sought to stand. What survives is the true—the true design, the true fabrication, the true organization, the true practices of seagoing; most of all, the true men. For the false cannot long survive at sea.

A sailor's ways and his very thinking are colored by these ancient sea conventions which themselves derive from the natural laws of the sea. At its fullest comprehension this constitutes a pantheism in which the sailor, *no matter what his race, creed, or era*, recognizes the sea and its customs as one with God. It is a stern creed which must withstand and has withstood the caprices of nature, but it favors the "good sailor." And *mystique* has its origin right here. These inherent laws and customs of the sea are a discipline of the sea as well. Your true sailor is a disciple in the original sense. Not that he could explain this to you; probably he couldn't. But he is aware of it, and although his rational reference to this force emerging from the laws and customs of the sea may be oblique, his actions in accommodating it are direct *and may be uniformly forecast.* Thus "by the cut of their jibs," i.e., "by the way they act and react," can you identify those who share in the *mystique* of the sea. But . . .

It is not to be supposed that every man who goes to sea experiences an intellectual or sensory perception of the *mystique.* It requires, as does every system of discipline, some self-giving. Those who are unable or unwilling to give are barred. Thus it is one thing to go to sea; quite another to be a *sea-man.*

Thus did Captain Hamberger formulate in his thoughts the *mystique* of the sea. He turned his thoughts next to an examination of the more limited and specialized *mystique* of the naval service, which he cast up in this fashion:

Both faiths, before being precipitated and translated into the different dimension of the actions which they condition and govern are, fundamentally, attitudes and they have common roots as well as many points of similarity. In both, the crew exists for the ship, and the ship exists for a purpose. While in the naval *mystique* the ultimate purpose of the ship may be to fight, its first and fundamental purpose must be to survive the rigors of the sea, which makes its disciples one with the basic faith of the sea. There are other values common to both *mystiques* which the Captain expressed in military terms thus:

Movement: The seaman must always be on the move. To stay in port is death for a ship—economic death for the merchantman; literal death for the man-of-war. The French under Napoleon savored this fully when, after weary months of stopping in port they finally sortied against the British who had continually kept the sea. The French discovered that they had forgotten how to sail *or* shoot! Worse, they had lost their *élan.*

Initiative: The sailor, whether merchant or man-of-war, is proverbially forehanded. Along with the farmer with whom he has much in common, he invented weather forecasting. He always plans for contingencies and drills to perfect preparations against future needs.

Logistics: This is just a newfangled word for what Old Man Noah invented and sailors always have practiced. A ship on a voyage is a perfect example of planned logistics, whether merchantman or man-of-war.

From these and other considerations it follows, reasoned the Captain, that a naval seaman must first partake to some extent of the sea *mystique* and then, by extension into naval discipline, penetrate the narrowed faith of the man-of-war's-man. The requirements of this peculiar attitude and capability may be roughly compared with the problem faced by a musician upon approaching an instrument for the first time. Certainly he must master the instrument as a first requirement. But this is only a beginning. Only when he has acquired an insight and virtuosity which will permit him to grasp the composer's meaning, and render that meaning with the authenticity of his own sure understanding can he be said to have achieved the *mystique* of music. The naval officer faces much the same challenge save that he contends with a more volatile medium, the sea, which introduces the pantheistic pattern. Only when he has become such a complete master of his ship and his science that he can interpret with sure virtuosity the most subtle intention of his commanding officer in battle, can he be said to have penetrated the *mystique* of the Navy as it emerges from the more comprehensive *mystique* of the sea.

"By the cut of their jibs I shall know them!" That's the way Ham Hamberger summed it up as he looked ahead to his coming battle employment, and speculated upon those with whom he would be called upon to serve—not knowing. And by the cut of their jibs he *did* know them when the time came, and they him, for in the skippers of DesRon-23 he found not only a group of colleagues but the near-perfect expression of the Navy *mystique* which he had now resolved to his own satisfaction.

Dusk was drawing on when the Captain climbed stiffly down from his tall chair and gratefully accepted a cup of coffee which a thoughtful watch officer had ordered. The electrician's mate of the watch tested the lights and checked the connections in the red master switchbox on the bridge bulkhead. *Converse*, a busy but a quiet little ship and a happy one, steamed along on the flank of her ward *Victorious* a few points off the red path of the setting sun. At exactly 1300 hours on the afternoon of Monday, 17th May, 1943, a light heaving line trailing from a balled "monkey fist" arced upward and outward from her fo'c'sle head and was caught by a dockside sailor at Noumea. Standard manila mooring lines followed and were made fast over bollards. Fourteen days out of Pearl a second eagle settled onto her perch, waiting . . .

Like Arleigh Burke and Heinie Armstrong, Ham Hamberger had taken the first step on the journey of a thousand miles.

4

Requiem over Ironbottom Bay

~~~~~~

Lieutenant Commander G. A. Sinclair, Captain of Destroyer *Bagley*, stood ramrod straight on the fantail of his vessel. Every man of his crew who could be spared from his station was mustered about the Captain. *Bagley*'s way through the water was of the order of 2 knots—about the minimum to steer by. The saffron sun burned down upon the assembled ship's company through a light haze. It was the afternoon of 9th August, 1942, and *Bagley* was only a few degrees below the equator. A collective, group empathy impelled voices to become muted and quickly subside after the initial rustle and murmur of assembly, and soon all sound save the hum of the hull, felt rather than heard, seemed to evaporate into the soggy atmosphere as if sponged up by a blotter.

After a glance around the Captain uncovered, tucking his stiff visored cap beneath his left arm. Then, in a voice hesitant at first with the uncertainty of experienced precept, but strengthening as the majestic cadences asserted their own rhythm, he began to read from a small black book:

> *I am the resurrection and the life, saith the Lord: he that believeth in me, though he were dead, yet shall he live: and whosoever liveth and believeth in me, shall never die. . . .*
>
> *I know that my redeemer liveth, and that he shall stand at the latter day . . . and though this body may be destroyed, yet shall I see God: whom I shall see for myself, and mine eyes shall behold, and not as a stranger . . .*

"Let us pray . . ."

Some in the assembled company blessed themselves with the sign of the cross. Others dropped on one or both knees to the deck.

"*Lord have mercy upon us,*" led the Captain.

"*Christ have mercy upon us,*" responded those few who were familiar with the liturgy.

"Lord have mercy upon us."

The prayer was short. Upon its completion Captain Sinclair signed to the burial detail in whose charge were the bodies of eight of their comrades sewn in canvas shrouds, each weighted to sink at once. One by one the corpses slid from beneath the national ensign and plunged to the depths of Ironbottom Bay as the Captain completed reading the service:

> *Unto Almighty God we commend the souls of our comrades departed, and we commit their bodies to the deep; in sure and certain hope of the Resurrection unto eternal life, through our Lord Jesus Christ; at whose coming in glorious majesty to judge the world, the sea shall give up her dead; and the corruptible bodies of those who sleep in Him shall be changed and made like unto His glorious body . . .*

With a final splash the last body was committed to the sea and to God. A moment longer the company remained listening to the melancholy measures of taps blown by a bugler in stately tempo. Then the Captain closed his book and put his cap back on; the formation was dismissed; 25 knots were rung up, and *Bagley* stood southeast toward Espiritu Santo to quench her ever-present thirst for fuel. Although Sinclair had read the service for the burial of the dead over but eight bodies, the requiem chanted by the wind through the struts and stays of the hurrying destroyer sighed for the souls of nearly 1,500 sailormen and the torn and fire-gutted carcasses of four fine 8-inch cruisers just wiped forever from the face of the earth by Japanese guns and torpedoes at the savage battle of Savo Island.

As on the night of the long lances, while sinking our ships and killing our sailors, the enemy himself suffered relatively little inconvenience at Savo—a total of 58 dead, fewer than that wounded, inconsequential damage to his ships. And, together with the battle of Tassafaronga, the grim naval fight on the night of 8–9th August, 1942, helped dress the stage and create the need for the hard demands which were to be presented scarcely a year later to Destroyer Squadron 23. For Allied strategy at the time was fiercely focused on winning the sea war in the Atlantic. Until that could be accomplished the naval campaign in the Solomons had a high priority on what those prosecuting it called the list of "Haven't gots, and won't gets." If, therefore, we were unfortunate or inept enough (which we were) to lose good and irreplaceable cruisers among King Solomon's Isles—not to speak of trained and experienced cruisermen—well, the "little boys" would just have to do the job. The Jap, who thought he was headed for Sydney, had to be stopped and turned back with whatever weapons we could find.

When, at about 1600 on the afternoon of 7th August, 1942, Vice

Admiral Gunichi Mikawa broke his flag in heavy cruiser *Chokai* at Rabaul, and assumed command of a formidable force of five heavy cruisers, two light cruisers, and a destroyer, he had a man-sized job cut out for him. That very morning, behind a naval bombardment of the beach, a determined force of United States Marines had stormed ashore on inhospitable Guadalcanal Island and by late afternoon had achieved a lodgment of about 11,000 men between Lunga and Koli Points. Simultaneously another force, meeting and smothering somewhat stiffer opposition, had staked out and were clinging to claims on Tulagi and Gavutu Islands, northeastward across Ironbottom Sound, in the Florida group. The landings, spearheading Operation Watchtower, had been made from eighteen transports which now were pressing every facility and device to unload the thousands of tons of supplies and materiel needed to support the beachheads.

The enemy had not been slow to react, but his early countermeasures attained only indifferent success. In the afternoon of the 7th some thirty-two Japanese bombers flew down from Rabaul and tried to work over the transports but were driven off with losses by the carrier-based aircraft of the Allied screening force. About noon of the next day a stronger force of torpedo bombers came winging south over Savo, but they, too, were driven off. However, destroyer *Jarvis* sustained a hit which, although it did not sink her at the time, resulted later in her loss with all hands—247 officers and men—while she was trying to limp away from the battle of Savo Island. Also, a mortally stricken bomber crashed on transport *George F. Elliot* and left that vessel a blazing wreck beached on the Tulagi side. There, flaming, she was to serve as a sure beacon to orient the Japanese surface strike which was fast taking form.

Mikawa's sortie from St. George's Channel was observed and reported by picket submarine *S-38*, Lieutenant Commander H. G. Munson. The Japanese Admiral, an austere man with almost a square face, heavy lidded eyes, and a fold or two of flesh at the jowls, had accepted unhesitatingly the basic challenge which was to meet and wipe out the Allied force, both warships and transports, so audacious as to place a foot on the bottom rung of the Solomons ladder. He shaped his course to pass north of Buka Island, which would then permit him to haul southeast for almost a straight shot down The Slot. Mikawa bent on 24 knots and by midafternoon of the 8th was entering New Georgia Sound, south of Choiseul.

In his flagship, heavy cruiser *Chokai*, the Vice Admiral headed a formation composed of heavy cruisers *Aoba, Kako, Kinugasa*, and *Furutaka;* light cruisers *Tenryu* and *Yubari;* and destroyer *Yunagi*, which steamed in that order in a column of ships. On the hot, sticky night of 8th August, at 1840 hours which was still some time before local sunset, Mikawa, with typical Japanese bravura, invoked the spirit of bushido in a message to all ships: "Let us attack with the expectation of certain victory in the traditional night attack of the Imperial Navy. May each one calmly do his utmost."

The Allied screening force waiting to receive Gunichi Mikawa about matched his weight of metal and was superior in number of ships. But the seeds of disaster were latent in its formations and the lack of a battle plan coordinated and understood by all commanders. To begin with, the dispositions of the Allied surface formations were awkward. The ships were split into three separate units operating more or less autonomously. Off the northern coast of Guadalcanal was the "*Australia* Group"—cruisers *Australia*, *Canberra*, and *Chicago*, steaming in that order and screening south of a line of bearing 125 degrees true from the center of Savo Island to intersect longitude 160°, 04′ East. Northeast, at about the middle of Ironbottom Bay, was the "*Vincennes* Group"—cruisers *Vincennes*, *Quincy*, and *Astoria*, steaming in that order and conducting a box patrol in the sector northeast of the 125-degree line of bearing. This box was around grid position V-77-29 on Allied charts each leg being approximately 5 miles long and the courses steered being 315°, 045°, 135°, and 225°, at 10 knots. The northwest corner of this box where course was changed from 315° to 045° was about 2¾ miles from Savo Island. Further to the eastward of the 160°, 04′ longitudinal line was the "*San Juan* Group"—cruisers *San Juan* and *Hobart*, steaming in that order, and held fairly close in around the transports unloading on the Tulagi side.

The disposition of destroyers was "by the book" for the job in hand. *Patterson* and *Bagley* flanked the *Australia* Group to port and starboard respectively; *Helm* and *Wilson* rendered the same service to the *Vincennes* Group; *Buchanan* and *Monssen* shepherded the *San Juan* Group. In addition destroyers *Blue* (to the westward) and *Ralph Talbot* (to the eastward), both equipped with the new and highly thought-of Sugar George radar, maintained patrols north of Savo Island, each steaming back and forth on a 6-mile line athwart the expected course of an approaching enemy. It was confidently hoped that one or the other of these vessels would give early warning of an approaching surface raid on the transports.

Pugnacious, bushy-browed and salty-tongued Rear Admiral Richmond Kelly Turner had tactical command of the ships on the Guadalcanal side and flew his flag in transport *McCawley*, lying off Lunga Point. And at 2000 hours on the night of 8th August he was one unhappy sailor. His distress was caused primarily by the previous adamant refusal of Vice Admiral Frank J. Fletcher, who flew his flag in *Saratoga* and had command of the carriers which had supported the landings, to remain in the area once the Marines were ashore. Although he did not immediately receive the permission to retire which he sought of higher authority, Fletcher's carriers were, in fact, fast clearing the area long before the battle broke leaving Turner, as he pungently phrased it, "bare arse."

So concerned was Turner with being jumped by Japanese air (because of misinformation transmitted by one of our planes which had "spooked" Mikawa's formation but reported that it contained seaplane tenders which would seem to indicate an air strike) that, at 2032 on the night of the 8th he convened a conference aboard his flagship. To it he summoned Rear Admiral V. A. C. Crutchley, RN, who commanded the *Australia* screening force, and when the Admiral went to the conference he took his cruiser with him! This was the first of an astonishing number of inadvertencies which was to plague the Allied naval forces that night. When he left his group Admiral Crutchley directed Captain Howard D. Bode, commanding *Chicago*, to assume command of the *Australia* Group. The Admiral also advised that he did not know whether he would or would not return. When the conference finally broke up Crutchley took time out for a courteous gesture—in his barge he set Marine Corps General A. A. Vandergrift aboard minesweeper *Southard*. Concluding that it was then too late to rejoin his Group Admiral Crutchley directed *Australia* to patrol 7 miles west of the Guadalcanal transport area until dawn. Mikawa was to play merry hell with that pleasant scheme, the net of which was that when *Australia* was desperately needed in the van, she was out of position, and never took any effective part in the battle.

Although they were not to know it until much, much later, the men of destroyer *Blue* probably were as close to shaking hands with death as any of them ever had been at 0054 on the morning of 9th August. At that moment heavy cruiser *Chokai*, leading the Japanese formation and tearing southwest at 26 knots, made visual contact on *Blue*. At breakneck speed Mikawa's heavyweights were steaming in column with a distance between ships of 1,300 yards. The Japanese Admiral actually already knew the disposition of the Allied forces. One of his cruiser float planes already had been over our formations and had reported. In another of the inadvertencies which marked this strange night, destroyer *Ralph Talbot* had spotted this snooper, but her warning never reached Admiral Turner, within easy radio hail, and either was disregarded or misinterpreted by those who did get it.

In the circumstances Gunichi Mikawa was not interested in killing a destroyer if he could possibly help it, for he was after far more important game. His battle plan, which had been communicated to all ships of

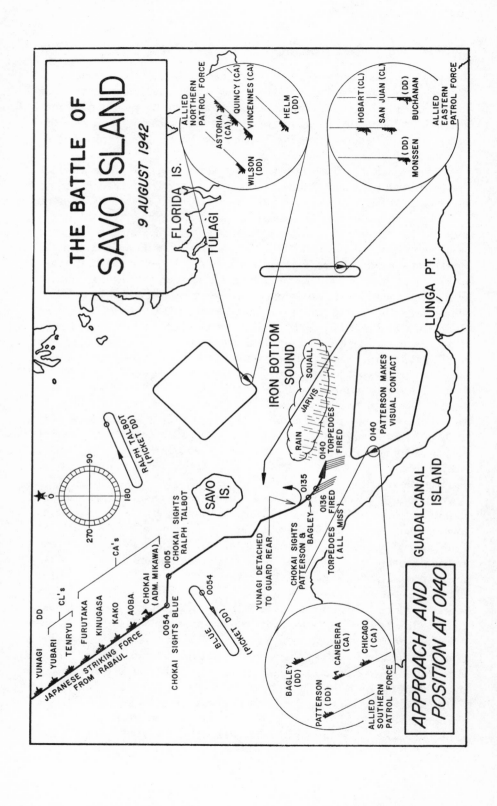

THE BATTLE OF SAVO ISLAND

9 AUGUST 1942

FLORIDA IS.

TULAGI

ALLIED NORTHERN PATROL FORCE

ASTORIA (CA)
QUINCY (CA)
VINCENNES (CA)
HELM (DD)
WILSON (DD)

HOBART (CL)
SAN JUAN (CL)
BUCHANAN (DD)
MONSSEN (DD)
ALLIED EASTERN PATROL FORCE

IRON BOTTOM SOUND

LUNGA PT.

RALPH TALBOT (PICKET DD)

SAVO IS.

CHOKAI SIGHTS RALPH TALBOT

90
270
180
0

YUNAGI DD
YUBARI CL's
TENRYU
FURUTAKA CA's
KINUGASA
KAKO
AOBA
CHOKAI (ADM. MIKAWA)

0105 CHOKAI SIGHTS BLUE

JAPANESE STRIKING FORCE FROM RABAUL

0054 CHOKAI SIGHTS BLUE

BLUE (PICKET DD)

0054

YUNAGI DETACHED TO GUARD REAR

0135

0136 BAGLEY

CHOKAI SIGHTS PATTERSON & BAGLEY

TORPEDOES FIRED (ALL MISS)

SQUALL
RAIN
JARVIS
0140 TORPEDOES FIRED

0140 PATTERSON MAKES VISUAL CONTACT

GUADALCANAL ISLAND

BAGLEY (DD)
CANBERRA (CA)
CHICAGO (CA)
PATTERSON (DD)
ALLIED SOUTHERN PATROL FORCE

APPROACH AND POSITION AT 0140

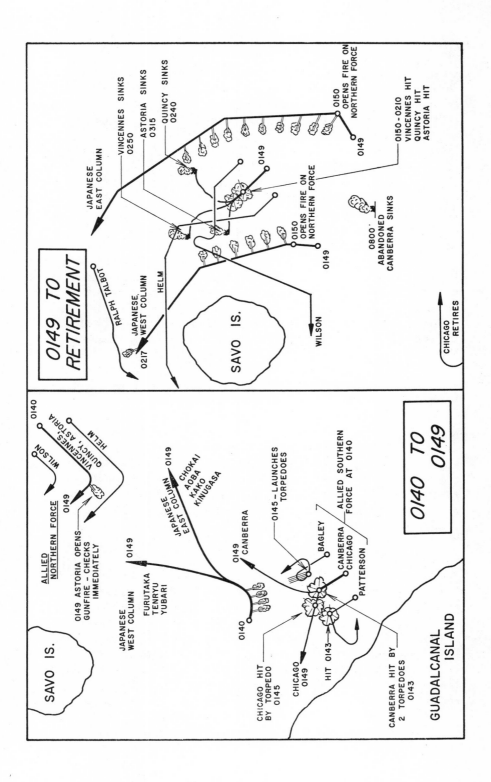

his formation, was to tackle the *Chicago* force nearest Guadalcanal first; then swing east to blast the *Vincennes* Group; then dash for the bulging and defenseless transports and stage a carnival of destruction. And the God of Battle must have ridden at Mikawa's trucks that night! One by one, their 8- and 6-inch batteries trained on *Blue*, Mikawa's whole battle line tore astern of that complacent little ship. *Blue's* lookouts were looking everywhere but behind them; they never even suspected the presence of the strong enemy force which now lanced into the vitals of the Allied dispositions. Guns manned and torpedo tubes primed (some of ours were not, at the battle which ensued, with the result that a destroyer had to swing full 360 degrees before she could bring primed tubes to bear), the slit-eyed Mikawa led his formation into the Sound about midway between Savo and Cape Esperance, hauled a trifle to the eastward, and prepared to administer to the United States Navy what has since been accepted as the most disastrous defeat in its history—*although it was not to be decisive.*

The sneak punch with which the battle opened gave little earnest of the complete confusion and devastation which were to lie at its core. Pursuing his cat-and-mouse strategy of waiting until he was fairly among his targets before revealing his presence, Mikawa spared yet another U.S. destroyer. As early as 0132 the guns of his cruisers were trained on crippled destroyer *Jarvis*, limping haltingly away from the transport concentration near Lunga Point. She was allowed to withdraw, unsuspecting, and when, a few minutes later, Mikawa made visual contact with DDs *Patterson* and *Bagley*, screening *Canberra* and *Chicago*, and making a turn which brought them virtually broadside to his cruisers, he ordered a torpedo attack on the Allied cruisers but, conforming to well-established Japanese torpedo doctrine, he held his gunfire to give his "fish" time to run to target.

This first thrust failed when the torpedoes missed. Four minutes later Mikawa gave permission for his captains to fire torpedoes independently. This resulted in a well-aimed barrage of torpedoes from *Chokai, Aoba,* and *Kako,* the van Japanese cruisers, streaking toward the *Australia* Group, and these "fish" were running hot and true when, moments later, destroyer *Patterson* (Commander Frank R. Walker) finally made first contact, which was visual, with the enemy, distant 5,000 yards.

A word of elaboration here would seem useful. In his battle report filed subsequently Captain Walker said that heavy rain squalls were sweeping the area for some time both before and after this contact; that they were accompanied by thunder and lightning; that the sea was choppy, and that he estimated visibility at less than one mile. There is, moreover, reason to believe that, at least during this preface to the battle, a heavy rain squall had drawn a scrim curtain between *Canberra* and *Chicago*, and the *Vincennes* Group north of them, thus emphasizing the factors of isolation and compartmentation which were undesirable if necessary concomitants of the patrol plan and pattern. Finally, the almost phenomenal superiority of the Japanese optics cannot be over-stressed. Predisposed as many Americans are to put extravagant confidence in new and "scientific" gadgets it was to be some time before we learned, through brittle experience, what the practical limitations of radar really were, and developed sound technics for the employment of this new and promising but not wholly trustworthy instrument. Mean-while—and time after time—the Japanese, with their huge, tremen-dously effective night glasses tripod-mounted at points of vantage aboard their warships, sighted our formations and, in documented in-stances, tracked them for very appreciable periods without themselves being discovered. All of these considerations and one other—the fright-ening malaise of cumulative fatigue so long borne and grown so crushing as to be no longer supportable—were startlingly reflected in the events which immediately followed.

WARNING! WARNING! STRANGE SHIPS APPROACHING!

Hardly had *Patterson* flashed the alarm when Mikawa's cruiser float planes dropped flares over the Guadalcanal transport area thus sil-houetting *Canberra* and *Chicago*. The leading Japanese ships opened gunfire instantly at ranges which shortened to 5,000 yards.

Canberra was caught flatfooted, all guns trained in and *empty!* She was "closed up" as the Australians phrase it "in the second degree of readiness," which meant that her gunners were sleeping in the vicinity of their stations, with a full communications watch awake. At 0143, while the clangor of the general alarm still sounded through the ship, Japanese torpedoes leaped at *Canberra* from both flanks. Her starboard side forward was grievously slashed and torn, and the great column of water flung up by the torpedo detonation still was poised on its pedestal when the first of an estimated twenty-four shells which were to tear her to pieces arrived on board.

While she struggled futilely to load and train her guns "on vague silhouettes ahead," *Canberra* was methodically knocked to kindling in a matter of minutes. An early hit in the plotting office mortally wounded Captain F. E. Getting, RAN, commanding, instantly killed the gunnery officer, and snuffed out additional lives. Hearing that his Captain was stricken, Commander J. A. Walsh, RAN, the executive officer, managed to fight his way to the bridge and assumed command.

In rapid succession heavy caliber Japanese shell wiped out *Canberra*'s sick bay, killing all in that area; blasted both of her boiler rooms to death traps of live steam; made a shambles of her forward engineroom; robbed her of all light, power, and communications, and left her dead in the water, a blazing wreck. The devastation had required approximately 6 minutes and although *Canberra* floated until after daylight when she was sunk by friendly torpedoes, her lingering survival served only the good purpose of permitting rescue of her wounded and unwounded personnel. She lost 84 dead, including Captain Getting, and counted 55 wounded. In the course of the battle *Canberra* actually did fire torpedoes, but not at the enemy. With bucket brigades rhythmically but ineffectually pouring water on the fires which ranged throughout her length, and ammunition cooking off fore and aft, Commander Walsh ordered the torpedoes fired simply to rid her decks of an additional danger in the path of the spreading flames. The "torps" whooshed into the dark sea, harmless of the destruction they were intended to inflict upon the enemy.

Chicago, following behind *Canberra*, was lucky in two particulars at the Battle of Savo Island. First, although she suffered a torpedo hit which damaged her bow and killed two men, she absorbed little punishment from Japanese shell hits. Second, although the powerful Nipponese formation could well have smashed her to splinters, by the time he'd finished with *Canberra* Mikawa was in visual contact with the *Vincennes* Group and ordered his cruisers to head for this new and more promising target at best speed. Thus *Chicago* never came to the party. She maneuvered radically to escape torpedoes, fired three four-gun salvos of star shell all of which failed to function, and pumped out a few salvos from her port 5-inch battery while her main battery was trying to get a set-up on an enemy the gunners couldn't see. Before they got a solution the whole battle had swept to the northeast, leaving *Chicago* crippled and fighting a couple of small fires. At 0154, while the battle raged and the angel of death soared over *Vincennes*, *Quincy*, and *Astoria*, the communications officer of *Chicago* received and decoded a signal ordering withdrawal to Lengo Channel, whereupon Captain Bode bent on knots and complied. *Chicago* never re-entered the fighting.

Not the least curious of the several phenomena exhibited at the Battle of Savo Island was the fact that a powerful group of warships—*Vincennes*, *Quincy*, and *Astoria*—continued patiently on patrol, with their escorting destroyers, seemingly not effectively alerted while the superior Japanese cruiser force battered *Canberra* into helplessness not far away, and wounded and routed *Chicago*.

In the "Aunt Sally" position at the after end of the three cruiser formation *Astoria* had Boilers 3, 4, 7, and 8 on the line, with steam pressure of 150 pounds on her remaining boilers. This gave her power for 24 knots, with possibly a 2-knot reserve. Her bridge was fully manned. The officer of the deck was Lieutenant (jg) N. A. Burkey, USNR; junior OOD, Lieutenant (jg) J. J. Mullen, USNR; quartermaster, R. A. Radke, QM2; helmsman, D. F. Liefur, QM3; and four talkers. Lieutenant Commander J. R. Topper, damage control officer, was supervisor of the bridge watch. *Astoria*'s commanding officer, Captain William G. Greenman, even more desperately fatigued than his subordinate officers, had turned in "all standing" [fully clothed] in his emergency cabin off the pilot house and was asleep.

The appearance of the flares dropped over Lunga Point by Mikawa's float planes a moment before he opened with guns on *Canberra* and *Chicago* did not go unnoticed on *Astoria*'s bridge, but the sudden illumination was by no means understood. Reports were confusing, and as he stood on a bridge wing contemplating the lights over Guadalcanal Lieutenant Commander Topper tried to put the puzzle together. In the first place, there had been reports of enemy air overhead, although *Astoria* had seen nothing. In the second place, how about submarines? They too had been reported, and not 2 minutes before Topper and his colleagues had felt, or thought they had felt, the vibrations from an underwater explosion. Were the DDs dropping depth charges on a submarine contact? Or was everybody getting a bit jumpy and imagining things? Actually, the men of *Astoria* had felt underwater detonations which released the powerful effect of the "water hammer" against their hull, although the ship was remote from the event. The shocks were occasioned by the detonations of the torpedoes fired by Mikawa at *Canberra* and *Chicago* which, having missed, destroyed themselves at the ends of their runs. These and other mysteries each potent enough to constitute the margin between the quick and the dead, Commander Topper stood pondering, when a familiar concussion and drumbeat of sound smote his senses. *His main battery had fired to port!*

At the Battle of Savo Island it was given only to *Astoria* to anticipate the enemy and engage him before he announced his presence with the impact of 8-inch shell arriving on target. The man who uncorked the main battery was Lieutenant Commander W. H. Truesdell, USN, the *Astoria*'s "guns." His main battery spotter had picked up enemy cruisers on the port quarter; searchlights hit the ship from the same direction shortly thereafter; bow lookouts reported shell splashes "ahead and short." What was everybody waiting for?

Almost precisely as the main battery thundered out its interrogatory, bulbous ribbons of orange flame flicking from the gun tubes, Lieutenant Mullen stood beside his Captain's bunk and plucked respectfully at his sleeve. If evidence of the Captain's exhaustion was needed it was amply supplied by the fact that the brittle, ear-shattering bang of the main battery didn't disturb him a mite, but he was instantly alert to the gentle tug of the Lieutenant on his sleeve.

Mercifully, counting knots along the tenuous thread of naval history, not many captains have been impiously summoned from the narcosis of sleep to find their ships fully engaged with an overwhelmingly powerful enemy. But that was Captain Greenman's unfortunate fate. Mikawa, upon disposing of *Canberra* and *Chicago*, did a curious, possibly even a daring thing: he split his force.

The basic reasons (many subsidiary reasons were turned up later by an official Navy inquiry) for the signal defeat of the Allied naval forces at Savo were two: first, the enemy achieved complete surprise—a fundamental to be sought in most punitive expeditions; second, while his force was concentrated, tightly closed up in line of battle and under effective command, he was fortunate enough to find the Allied defensive forces split into three units, considerably separated, and with no commonly understood or accepted plan of battle. In such circumstances certainly it was not surprising that Mikawa's seven cruisers and one destroyer had no difficulty in disposing of *Canberra* and *Chicago* hung, as they were, like gifts on a Christmas tree. We had neglected to put Mikawa's name on them, but he claimed them nonetheless, and with a resolution permitting no challenge.

Approaching the *Vincennes* group Mikawa adopted a chancy tactic. He divided his force, sending *Yubari*, *Tenryu*, and *Furutaka* on a northerly course which brought them to the west of *Vincennes*, *Quincy*, and *Astoria*. In *Chokai* he led *Aoba*, *Kako*, and *Kinugasa* more to the southeast. Thus between the two Japanese columns, three cruisers to one side, four to the other, the *Vincennes* Group found themselves between the jaws of a crushing nutcracker. Mikawa previously had detached destroyer *Yunagi* to protect his rear as best she could, and that harassed DD was hurrying hither and thither trying to figure out what was going on.

From the moment *Astoria* opened with her main battery on the Japanese column led by *Chokai*, at 0149, all times must be approximate. The precise records were lost with the men and the ships. Stumbling onto his bridge, and with the disposition of the United States cruisers fresh in his memory, Captain Greenman first concluded that his ship was firing on friendlies. "Cease firing!" he ordered. "Let's not get excited. Who ordered all this . . . ?" His gunnery officer, Lieutenant Commander Truesdell, did not share his Commander's confusion. "Sir," he messaged, "I'm sure I have Japs in my sights. For God's sake give the order to commence firing!" "Very well," replied Greenman. "Japs or no Japs those ships out there have got to be stopped. You may commence firing."

Captain Greenman rang up flank speed and swung to his left. The maneuver was no good. *Chokai*, *Aoba*, and *Kako* found the range almost instantly, and *Astoria* was a sitting duck. The story of her death is soon told. First, an 8-inch salvo crashed aboard forward, ripping super-structure and decks to jagged lances of spiked steel. Another landed on Number 1 turret knocking it out of action, and in seconds planes were burning bright on both port and starboard catapults. Had the Japanese previously needed points of aim they now had them. Although Captain Greenman zigzagged frantically he could not evade the annihilating enemy salvos. A hit at the break of the gun deck started fires which were to sweep out of control. A salvo, finding its mark on the starboard side of the bridge, killed the navigator and chief quartermaster and knocked every man present to the deck. For a time there was nobody at *Astoria*'s helm, and she slewed incontinently through the arc of the maneuver in which she had been engaged. Finally Bosun's Mate W. J. Brower, although grievously wounded, managed to gain his feet, took the wheel, and brought the ship to a northerly heading.

As *Astoria*'s speed fell off Captain Greenman initiated a call to his engineering officer, Lieutenant Commander John D. Hayes, USN, inquiring why. The answer was less than welcome. Hayes replied that he was being forced to abandon the after engineroom which had been rendered untenable by the smoke and heat from the fires above, and that the best speed the ship was capable of was 8 knots.

After standing to his duty as long as he possibly could Bosun Brower, fainting from weakness occasioned by pain and loss of blood, announced that he could no longer keep the wheel. He was relieved by a quarter-master who quickly realized that steering control had been lost. An attempt was made to shift steering to central station, but before that could be effected the forward engineroom was abandoned and all power was lost. The ship was fiercely ablaze from her foremast aft; there was no water or pressure to fight fires, and ammunition was cooking off on all sides. Captain Greenman ordered the magazines flooded. Then, at approximately 0215, he ordered all wounded and survivors to be gathered on the fo'c'sle head and himself took command station forward of Number 2 turret. Not for a moment forgetting or forsaking the traditions of the sea and the service of which he was a senior officer, the Captain then ordered that all dead be assembled on the after deck, and the sailmaker and his mates were set the task of sewing the 118 bodies which were found, into canvas shrouds and weighting them for the mass burial which Captain Greenman planned to conduct. Fate, however, had a different end planned for the gallant dead of *Astoria* than the one the Captain would have chosen. Holed by 8-inch hits below the waterline and listing 15 degrees to port, the cruiser suddenly was shaken throughout her length by a heavy explosion below, and the first lieutenant reported bubbles of yellow gas streaming to the surface of the sea on the port side abreast the forward magazines. Perhaps bitterly recalling the rollicking chantey from the days of wind ships, Captain Greenman knew that the time had come to "leave her, Johnny, *leave* her!"

Destroyer *Bagley* already had taken off the wounded and all personnel not included in the large damage control party which the skipper had retained aboard in his unremitting fight to save his ship. These remaining officers and men now were collected in the stern and ordered into the sea where their Captain followed them. When *Astoria* finally capsized and sank, which she did at approximately 0225, she was manned only by a crew of the dead, sewed in shrouds, weighted, and in every way accoutered for their voyage to Valhalla.

At the Battle of Savo Island it would seem a reasonable conclusion, from the official reports, that neither cruiser *Quincy* nor cruiser *Vincennes* knew what hit her until she was pounded into junk. The story of *Quincy* is a tale of unrelieved frightfulness. The middle ship between *Vincennes* ahead and *Astoria* astern, the first warning she had of the doom stalking her was when *Aoba* snapped open her searchlight shutters and illuminated. What Admiral Mikawa saw revealed by this probing pencil of white light must have afforded him a chuckle of satisfaction. On his side of *Quincy* the guns of *Chokai*, *Aoba*, and *Kako* were accurately trained on the United States cruiser. On her other side the guns of *Yubari*, *Tenryu*, and *Furutaka* followed her every movement. But the guns of *U.S.S. Quincy* weren't even trained out, nor was her battery completely manned! It may seem a worn cliché to say that *Quincy* was like a clay target in a shooting gallery, but it would be difficult to find a more apt or precise description of her situation. With one reservation: The shooting gallery target is hit only from one side. *Quincy* was to be hit from both sides, and with such a bewildering smother of fire that her officers and men were stupefied by concussion and the shock of the impossible happening all about them.

At the moment when searchlights illuminated *Quincy* she was, within the limits implied by employment on a task which always postulated battle as a likely possibility, a quiescent ship. Like his opposite numbers Captain Samuel N. Moore, commanding, had turned in fully dressed in his emergency cabin. The navigator was in the chart house, and the bridge was fully manned. Lieutenant Commander Harry B. Heneberger, gunnery officer, was alert—a state of grace italicized by the fact that he managed to get off one nine-gun salvo before *Quincy* was blasted out of the battle.

Boilers 5 and 6 were not on the line when the fight engulfed *Quincy*. The engineer of the watch gave immediate attention to that. Torches at the ends of long and stiff twisted wire handles were doused in diesel oil, set alight, and thrust through holes in the face plates of the boilers. The fuel, already at flash point, roared into flame, the tubes became cherry red; *Quincy* soon had full propulsion power.

Called to the bridge Captain Moore spent the very few remaining moments of his life trying to fight his ship. He estimated the nearest enemy to be distant about 8,000 yards, and he called for fire on the Japanese cruiser illuminating him with searchlights. The searchlights were snapped off by the enemy himself, however, for within 15 seconds they were no longer necessary. The first Japanese salvo to register on *Quincy* struck Number 3 turret and jammed it in train. Immediately thereafter, and continuously, she was battered from bow to stern by armor-piercing projectiles.

Planes blazing on her catapults afforded the Japanese gunners every assistance they needed to lay their guns with deadly accuracy. Number 2 turret took a direct hit, exploded, and burned out. Number 1 turret was silenced, battle 2 torn to pieces and set ablaze, and sky aft abandoned. The forestay was shot away and the flailing end of the wire tangled around the radar antenna and rendered that equipment useless.

For *Quincy* the battle was but short seconds old when a brace of shell burst on her bridge virtually wiping out all personnel there. Captain Moore did not die instantly but lay stunned, bleeding and smashed on the deck beside the wheel. Burning flag bags filled the area with heavy, acrid smoke laced with the searing rasp of cordite fumes, and steering control was lost. A freak hit on the port 5-inch anti-aircraft battery inflicted agony on the gunners and exacted all of their lives. Conforming to the immutable laws of physics a Japanese shell neatly cut away the cartridge case bases of the 5-inch ammunition in the fuse pots, and the propellant powder in the 5-inch shell transformed them instantly into Roman candles which first seared and then roasted alive the gunners of the battery. Guns 1, 5, and 7 of the starboard 5-inch battery took direct hits, and the ammo on Guns 1 and 5 exploded. A ruptured line at Number 1 stack released a roaring Kyrie eleison of escaping steam— *Lord have mercy upon us; Christ have mercy upon us*—which cut through even the din of bursting enemy shell and ammunition cooking off, and thundered a diapason of doom over the stricken ship

Things were as bad below decks as above. All but two men were killed at the forward repair station which was abandoned when water flooded over the door coaming. Direct hits in Number 1 fireroom put out all fires, and fuel suction was lost. Tubes in Number 2 boiler burst filling the space with live steam; the blowers were smashed; partially parboiled firemen fought their way to the deck above and collapsed in writhing pain. A tremendous explosion, believed to be from a torpedo although this never could be demonstrated, wiped out all personnel in Firerooms 3 and 4. One man in Number 1 engineroom was lucky: he was sent to the bridge as a messenger to inform the Captain that the engines would have to be shut down because of excessive vibration. He never returned to the engineroom but the mates he left behind him were trapped and died to a man when *Quincy* finally capsized and sank.

Lying on the bridge of the ship nearer death than life Captain Moore mumbled to the helmsman to try to beach *Quincy* on Savo Island. The quartermaster, however, soon discovered that he was spinning a useless wheel; there was no connection between it and the cruiser's twin rudders. With communications out, gunnery officer Heneberger sent his assistant, Lieutenant Commander John D. Andrew, USN, to the bridge for instructions. Andrew found the pilot house "thick with bodies" and the helmsman dazedly trying to bring the ship under control with the useless wheel. As Andrew stepped into the pilot house Captain Moore rose spasmodically to a sitting position; then without a word collapsed back to the deck in death.

When Andrew made his report about 0237 Commander Heneberger, the senior surviving officer, ordered those in forward control where he had established a command station, to abandon. The evolution could not be completed however, for at 0240 *Quincy* rolled over to port, lifted her stern high in a twisting motion, and slid beneath the sea. She took with her the bodies of 370 officers and men. More than 150 wounded later were picked up by destroyers *Ellet* and *Wilson*, along with several hundred non-wounded who were without shoes or other clothing save underwear.

Cruiser *Vincennes*—the *"Vinny Maru"* as she was affectionately known to her crew—leading the U.S. formation next ahead of *Quincy*, never knew what hit her when Mikawa's flanking files of cruisers bared their teeth and started chewing her to pieces. In earnest of this fact she was to stage one of the most amazing performances ever to grace-note a naval engagement.

At midnight of the 8–9th Captain Frederick L. Riefkohl, commanding both *Vincennes* and the patrol group which she led, was relieved on the bridge by his executive officer, Commander W. E. A. Mullan, USN. Lieutenant Commander C. D. Miller relieved the navigator, Commander A. M. Loker, as officer of the deck. In his night order book, before retiring to his emergency cabin at 0050, the Captain left special instructions to be alert for an air attack followed by a surface raid. That was the order of enemy reply which he expected to issue from the evocative challenge of our landings. The ship was in condition of readiness II— all guns loaded, two guns manned in each turret, anti-aircraft battery fully manned.

At about 0145, when he observed the flares dropped over Guadalcanal by Mikawa's cruiser float planes, Commander Mullan called the Captain, and the ship was at general quarters by the time he stepped onto the bridge. Captain Riefkohl immediately rang up 15 knots, but he maintained his course while he and his officers tried to interpret the flares, and the gunfire which now was observable to the southward. The Captain surmised that the *Australia* Group had made an enemy contact, but he definitely was not going to let himself be foxed. It would be just like Mikawa, he reasoned, to send a sacrificial destroyer barreling in as bait to draw *Vincennes, Quincy,* and *Astoria* off station so the Japanese main force could get through and jump the transports. Riefkohl was to be taken in by no such hanky-panky. He stayed on course hoping for some orders or at least some clarifying reports, and waiting for the situation to unravel itself.

At approximately 0150 the Captain's fear of a decoy destroyer vanished in the glare of searchlights from *Chokai, Kako,* and *Kinugasa* which fastened upon *Vincennes* and held her transfixed by lances of white light. Captain Riefkohl immediately ordered all guns to fire on the searchlights and targets of opportunity. His 5-inch battery managed to fire star shell, and he got off two 8-inch salvos against *Kinugasa* before the Japanese gunners got their solution and set about the grim but now familiar business of blasting yet another United States heavy cruiser to meaningless scrap.

An early 5-inch hit on the forward port side of the bridge killed the communications officer and knocked out the TBS leaving the Captain without effective means for communicating with the other ships of his formation. As had been the fate of other Allied cruisers, enemy salvos quickly found the planes on the catapults and the aviation gasoline storeroom, and with towering sheets of flame streaming from these points the enemy extinguished his searchlights and settled down to the turkey shoot. Captain Riefkohl went to 20 knots, then to 25, and took violent evasive action, but the Japanese gun pointers stayed with him, and their salvos arrived aboard with sickening precision and devastating consequences.

When the Captain called for flank speed his request was not answered. The ship service telephone in the pilot house still seemed to be operative, but he could get no response from the engineroom, central station, or main battery. *Helm* and *Wilson* were maneuvering out ahead, and *Quincy* could be seen astern on the port side, blazing. *Astoria* was nowhere in sight. Riefkohl's 5-inch pyrotechnics failed him as these same mark shells had failed others before, and save for an indistinct silhouette glimpsed once by the gunnery officer, the men of *Vincennes* never did see the enemy who was pounding them to pieces.

Repeatedly pummeled by 8- and 5-inch salvos, the Captain ordered the magazines flooded at 0155, and sent messengers to find out what the situation was in the engineroom and at the battery. The messenger found both enginerooms peopled only by darkness and death. A direct hit had carried away the exhaust steam line in the forward engineroom and ruptured the flange on the main steam line. Those not cooked by the scalding steam were driven out. Steam pressure was gone in the after engineroom and the space was deserted. A torpedo hit at Number 1 fireroom had blasted that compartment and killed all personnel present. Number 3 fireroom had been abandoned after the torpedo hit, and smoke and flames were being sucked in by the still operating blowers. One man, chief watertender E. E. Clothier, had escaped from Number 2 fireroom and another, chief watertender M. S. Iwanicki, got out of Number 4 fireroom; all others in both spaces died. By 0200 *Vincennes* was an inferno below decks, all power, steering and communications gone. Topside not a gun fired, and the ship couldn't even make smoke to attempt to hide her pitiable condition.

At 0207 on that fateful and lightning-laced night, at approximately 9°—6'—40" of south latitude; 159°—52'—10" of east longitude, what surely must have been one of the strangest fragments in the naval history of the world took place. As shell and torpedoes continued to plunge into *Vincennes* from both sides and out of an impenetrable darkness, Captain Riefkohl arrived at the firm conviction that his own ships must be firing on him. Lacking information, in no other way could he explain the rain of shell hitting him from all directions—or so it seemed. Unable to communicate with other Allied ships the Captain ordered a large American flag, rove by its brass grommets to the snap hooks of the one remaining halyard on the starboard signal yard, sent aloft, *and illuminated by spotlights!*

There is no record of whether the Japanese accepted this as a gesture of defiance, which well they might have, but it is known that the enemy's reaction was to unleash a final annihilating storm of fire before deciding that *Vincennes* was finished and sweeping off after other targets. And the *"Vinny Maru"* had indeed had it! With the ship listing dangerously Captain Riefkohl gave the order to abandon at 0230. Life jackets were placed on the wounded and they were assisted over the side. At 0240 the Captain left the bridge with his orderly, Marine Corporal J. J. Patrick, and his yeoman, chief yeoman L. E. Stucker, and literally swam off *Vincennes* when the water reached the place where he was standing. With her colors still flying defiantly from her last signal halyard the ship capsized and sank at about 0250, the swimming Captain being barely clear of the long reach of the foremast as it slapped the water close behind him when the ship turned over. Later the Captain estimated that his ship had been hit by between 75 and 100 heavy caliber shell, and at least two torpedoes. Three hundred and thirty-two men lost their lives in *Vincennes,* and 258 were wounded.

With this sinking of the third of the four Allied cruisers to be lost (*Canberra* didn't die until later in the morning) the effective battle of Savo Island was over. Although he had staged a magnificent attack and taught the Allies lessons both in tactics and gunnery, Admiral Mikawa did not press on to claim the complete victory which might have been his. With his powerful striking force intact and poised, and only cruisers *San Juan* and *Hobart* between him and a whole shoal of juicy transports, instead of attacking this final and fragmentary force the Japanese commander gave orders to withdraw northward. Two reasons have been given for this decision: one, his ships were separated and time would be required to gather them into battle formation again; two, he feared an attack by Allied air at dawn, and wanted to put as much ocean as possible between himself and Savo Island before that time. Undoubtedly both considerations entered into his calculations. He could well afford to withdraw, leaving to haggard and shaken United States sailors and their British and Australian mates the gnawing pain of the requiem their hearts were forced to sing over Ironbottom Bay.

5

"Across the Ocean Wild and Wide . . ."

At 1125 on the balmy May morning of Tuesday, 11th May, 1943, the sharp ring of a bugle sounded along the decks of United States Destroyer *Charles Ausburne* (DD-570) and went lifting out over the sun-dappled waters of Boston harbor. *Ausburne* was moored alongside Pier 5, West, Navy Yard Annex, South Boston. Warships of both ancient and modern vintage surrounded her. Nearby was the old frigate *U.S.S. Constitution,* flying the flag of the senior officer present afloat. Distributed about the harbor were United States ships *Charlotte, Connor, Hall, Hudson, Wakefield, Baltimore, Spenser, Clemson, Foote,* and *Spence.* Present, too, were His Britannic Majesty's ships *Guinvere* and *Pleiades,* and the Free French warships *Le Terrible* and *Fantasque.*

Curiosity piqued by the attention-arresting timbre of the bugle tone, watch officers here and there about the basin trained their long glasses on *Ausburne* and examined with interest the unaccustomed activity taking place aboard. On the foredeck *Ausburne*'s crew, in spotless blues, was drawn up in string-straight ranks and standing at attention. Evenly distributed to either side of the center line of the ship between the rows of sailors facing each other, and themselves facing aft, stood the company of *Ausburne*'s officers augmented by the officers of *Spence* and *Foote.*

As the bugle sounded a corpulent little man, pausing only long enough to render the traditional salutes, hurried over *Ausburne*'s rail, was greeted by her skipper, Lieutenant Commander Luther K. Reynolds, and made his way forward to take his place facing the assembled officers and crew. In a deliberate voice which was amplified by loud-speakers he started reading his orders:

"*Hereby detached . . . proceed to Boston . . . assume command of Destroyer Squadron 23 . . .*" Then Commodore Martin J. Gillan, Jr., whose rank was that of Captain, USN, put his orders away and talked informally to the assembled company. Gillan was Irish and like many of that derivation he was slow of speech but full of words. He forecast a happy time for all in the Squadron if they would but do their duty. He wouldn't, he warned, stand for any nonsense. He regretted the absence of the other five ships of the Squadron "but that's war, men, and it can't be helped. Those other ships are widely scattered but, I believe, they are all engaged on war missions and I expect that we shall be too, and that very shortly." Commodore Gillan wandered on for a little time more, finally ran out of words, the formation was dismissed, and leaving his numbered pennant flying at the peak the Commodore hurried back ashore to attend upon other duties. As he crossed the rail the second time the absentee pennant fluttered up to the starboard yardarm.

Thus the birth of United States Destroyer Squadron 23. Although the Squadron had been formed on paper in the Bureau of Navigation some time before, it came to life as a palpable Navy integral only when it achieved a Commodore. From that time forward orders could be and were addressed to the Squadron as a whole with a responsible officer in command.

What manner of man was this first Commodore of the Gallant Squadron? That is not an easy question to answer, for not a great deal is known about Martin J. Gillan, Jr. In 30 years of naval service he moved up through the customary spectrum of diversified duties to the rank of Captain, in which rank he was retired 1st January, 1947. But he left few crystals of his own personality imbedded in the receptive matrix of the Navy. He was a controversial figure to the senior officers who served under him in the Squadron. "A martinet and a tyrant!" said one bitterly. Undoubtedly this impression was heightened by Gillan's maintenance of a big staff (Burke cut it in half when he took over) and his practice of dining in solitary state in his own cabin and his insistence upon the observance of "old Navy" punctilio under conditions in which many thought it could be dispensed with. "More sinned against than sinning," said another, taking a long, hard look at the crude state of readiness of the Squadron when Gillan came to command. "He offered the men no inspiration," said a third, "and destroyermen didn't have confidence in his knowledge of DDs. He never gave us a Squadron doctrine, and he never encouraged informal examination of Squadron problems."

It is probable that this last observation cut closer to the heart of the problem than either of the others. There is no reason to believe that Captain Gillan, at least so far as the record shows, was anything but a competent and conscientious naval officer. But—and this theme was iterated repeatedly by a majority of the senior officers who sailed with him during his brief term in the South Pacific—he simply wasn't a destroyerman, and he wasn't apt to become one.

The destroyerman, to employ a Navy idiom, exhibits a distinctive and rakish silhouette. An official Navy publication puts it this way: "To qualify successfully in destroyers requires superior abilities and superior determination, both of which are indispensable in war. The destroyer characteristic is 'No matter what the job or what the odds may be, we will not be defeated.' " Such requirements were meat and drink to Arleigh Burke, but they simply weren't Rosey Gillan's dish of tea.

Martin J. Gillan, Jr. (he had an ardent complexion and during his Navy career was known both as Rosey and Red) was born in the tiny community of Whitestone, a Long Island suburb of New York City, on 6th February, 1899, the son of Martin J. and Rose (Murphy) Gillan. He graduated from the United States Naval Academy in 1919, and was the only officer of the Gallant Squadron to see service in the first two world wars. In 1926 he married Miss Mary Carr, of Philadelphia, and fathered one son who was christened Martin J. Gillan, third. Thus the Gillan line was fortified by an unbroken succession of three Martin J's.

At the end of the Second World War Captain Gillan was the holder of various broadly inclusive decorations—"Victory," "Campaign," and "American Defense" medals—but the record fails to show the award of any decoration for personal merit, achievement, or gallantry. Following his abrupt relief as ComDesRon-23 during the heart of the campaign in the central Solomons he engaged principally in staff and training duties, and responsibilities in connection with courts martial. He never returned to destroyers. This, then, on a thumbnail, is a sketch of the man to whom the destinies of "23" first were entrusted.

On the bright Tuesday morning when Rosey Gillan was reading his orders aboard *Ausburne* in Boston, Captain Roy Gano was having his own troubles aboard *Dyson* at "Base How," which was Norfolk. Flanked by his executive officer, Lieutenant J. B. Morland, USN, and his chief master at arms, the Captain stood at mast prepared to mete out punishment. A somewhat sullen sailor stood before him cap in hand, and both listened as the charge was read:

"Seaman, 2nd, Wizowsky, B.: Absent over leave 6 hours. Drunk."

"What have you got to say for yourself, Wizowsky?" asked the skipper.

"Nothing," muttered the seaman and, reminded by a glare from the "Jimmylegs," tardily added, "Sir!"

"What were the circumstances in this matter, Chief?" asked Gano.

"Sir, we picked him up out of a gutter dead drunk. His uniform was filthy, and he couldn't talk coherently. That was night before last. He's been sobering up since. He was just out of boot camp when he joined us two months ago, sir," the chief added as if by way of extenuation. "He hasn't been in the Navy long."

"And still you have nothing to say?" the Captain asked a second time. Wizowsky remained silent.

Leaning over the lectern, braced by a powerful hand gripping the edge of the small desk, Roy Gano gave himself over to momentary reflection. As he did so a slow heat spread upward from the pit of his stomach until he feared his face must be a fiery mirror of the resentment which burned deep within him. Commander Gano could understand a seaman, second class taking a drink. He could understand his getting drunk. And he could understand his being 6 hours over leave. But what he could *not* understand was any man's casting discredit upon the uniform of the United States Navy by wearing it while lying pig-drunk in a gutter. For the United States Navy was very dear to the heart of Roy Alexander Gano. Always and throughout, in his own life and conduct, he had honored its symbols. Relaxing his tense grip at last the Captain stood erect and pronounced sentence:

"For being 6 hours over leave, the loss of four liberties and 2 hours extra duty. *For casting discredit upon the uniform of the United States Navy, 5 days solitary confinement on bread and water in the Marine barracks ashore!* Next case!"

With Ralph Lampman, Roy Gano shared the honor of being one of the most technically competent and at the same time one of the least psychologically complex of the Squadron-23 captains. His father, Harry A., was of Normandy French extraction and the name originally was Gunieux. In 1650 the family had migrated from Normandy to the Jersey Islands and in time Gunieux was Anglicized to Gano. His mother, the former Myrtle Adell Hitchcox, was British. Among the boy's birthrights were a quick sense of humor, a lively and light touch in his routine dealings with others, and a very mellow "humanness" which had little trouble shining through even the stern façade demanded by senior command. He was one of several of the "23" skippers who were destined to see service as Rear Admiral or Vice Admiral after the war.

Certainly as a child no one would have forecast a naval career for Roy Gano. Just before reaching his teens he fell victim to inflammatory rheumatism, his weight dropped to a mere 79 pounds, and he was given but two weeks to live. After considerable ineffective treatment a kindly and understanding physician was found who massaged and manipulated the child's joints and limbs several times daily, and finally restored them to full use. Roy's weight did not show a gratifying increase, however, and when first examined for admission to the United States Naval Academy he was turned down for being underweight. He sought and obtained permission to have a second physical examination, and ate bananas with dedicated determination right up to "H" hour of "D" day. He squeaked **through.**

Roy's path to Annapolis was not direct as was Ham Hamberger's. After graduating from high school in his home town of Pipestone, Minnesota, young Gano went to work in a bank and he stayed with the job for two years. But a disquieting uneasiness was gnawing at the boy. Ever since the two of them were about eight years old he had been smitten with a pretty little girl who lived around the corner, and who had followed him through high school. Her name was Harriet Pauline Howard. Harriet's father, an attorney, had pioneered from Michigan to South Dakota where he served a term as Speaker of the State Legislature. He then moved on to Red Falls, Minnesota, where he met and married Harriet's mother whose maiden name was Beecher. Harriet was born in Red Falls, and eventually the family moved on to Pipestone where the senior Howard became a District judge for Southwestern Minnesota. One of Harriet's uncles, Lieutenant Albert Morrison Beecher, USN, was killed aboard the battleship *Maine*. Her brother, Paul E. Howard, graduated from Annapolis with the class of 1921. Thus there was a strong lacing of Navy in the family pattern.

Harriet Howard was to become (*a*) a talented artist especially favoring pastels ; and (*b*) Mrs. Roy Alexander Gano. While Roy was working in the bank, however, this latter eventuality was no foregone conclusion. Specifically, the boy began to feel that he needed a bit of a boost to make the grade with his light of love—and what better boost than a trim blue uniform picked out in gold, and the romantic aura of a naval officer, or at least a potential one? After all, he had a case in point very close at hand for study. At the time Paul Howard was a Midshipman, and it was to be observed that when he came home on leave many of the young feminine hearts of Pipestone were set aflutter.

Thus it eventuated that Roy renounced the bank and journeyed to Minneapolis where, having secured a principal appointment to the Naval Academy, he sought assistance in preparing for the admittedly difficult entrance examinations. Chance led him to the door of a West Point graduate and retired Army officer who told him:

"Here's what I'll do : I'll give you a cram course, and I'll work as hard as you will. If you pass the examination my fee will be $150 ; if you don't pass, the fee will be only $100."

That sounded like a bit of all right to young Gano. He entered upon his cram course with both enthusiasm and determination, and when he took the exam he had no difficulty. Although he hadn't even known where the Academy was when first he made up his mind to enter he now discovered, with chop-chop speed and disconcerting certitude that he was a plebe Midshipman in the Sixth Company of the Third Battalion of the Corps of Midshipmen at Annapolis. It was a sobering and final reality which brought him up all standing, although he tried to conceal his temporary confusion from his classmates who seemed to be getting on with things pretty handsomely. In the same battalion with him were two men he was to come to know much better and with whom he was to forge the bond which emerges only from shared danger in combat and the teamwork and competence which defies that danger. Their names were Herald Franklin Stout and Luther Kendrick Reynolds, but at the time their propinquity meant nothing to any of them.

Probably because of his inherent ingenuousness his four years at the Academy made more of an impress upon Roy Gano than a like experience was to make on most of his future colleagues in DesRon-23. He was manager of the varsity basketball team and won his letter. He participated in Class track and Company lacrosse. He was a slender, dark, volatile lad—the type that would be classified as "outgiving"—and he took with good grace and never a protest the extra work which went with his assignment to an upper bunk and its care according to strict midshipman standards.

Like many before and after him young Gano found the academic work at Annapolis hard, and math especially difficult. Conversely, unlike many others, he drew a considerable inspiration from aspects of Academy life which were, in the main, a backdrop to the more immediate program of learning *things*—acquiring specific knowledge of concrete facts and the immutable laws of physics. This backdrop was a tapestry woven principally of naval history, customs, traditions and regulations, and its pith was imparted to the boy through a number of channels. Ubiquitous and strong was the influence of his Company officer, a naval Lieutenant named Russell M. Irig. Irig was taut, but Irig was fair. He set a splendid example in his own conduct and bearing; he emphasized leadership qualities, and he placed the Navy next under God in his order of worship. Basic, too, were Roy's classes in history, naturally oriented toward naval values. But on top of his preparations to meet the recurring classroom challenges of the history curriculum he soon discovered that as a plebe, if he was to keep out of constant trouble with upperclassmen, he'd better study considerably more U.S. naval history than might be required to get even a 4.0—a perfect mark under the grading system used at the Academy—in his formal examinations. An upperclassman might demand at any time that Midshipman Gano deliver a factual dissertation on this or that obscure figure in United States or world naval history. If Plebe Gano couldn't do it he might be given until the next day to seek out the required information, but he knew it would be prudent to have accurate and comprehensive data at the second asking. Otherwise trouble was sure to follow.

While this was a wholly informal influence it had a strong conditioning impact upon Roy Gano. The more he learned of the United States

Navy and its heroes, the more he related these values to himself and the cavalcade in which he moved. He accepted as proper the strong emphasis upon loyalty to the Navy as a foremost institution guarding the cherished freedoms of an invincible democracy, and he considered himself fortunate to be an acolyte of so splendid a company. There and then he vowed that, upon being admitted to the priesthood of this order upon graduation and commissioning as an ensign in the United States Navy, he would never betray his trust. He never did. Of course, at the Battle of Cape St. George he "fired his torpedoes at too much altitude," as Arleigh Burke twitted him, and racing to another battle he almost broke up the formation with his TBS crack "Just a minute; Major Smith is studying the order." But Roy Gano was in there pitching every second of every minute of every hour, and in the history of the Gallant Squadron no ship bears a prouder name than *U.S.S. Dyson*.

Commander Gano fully shared the fundamental *mystique* of technical competence and faith which was to characterize DesRon-23 but for him, unlike Armstrong and unlike Hamberger, the overtones of the *mystique* were to have a fraternal flavor—the fraternity of the Navy rather than of the sea. An incident in which he participated while serving in *U.S.S. John D. Edwards* on the Asiatic Station in 1930 pointed up his personal perception with cameo clarity. The vessel was lying to her anchor in the turgid waters of the Yangtze, and Lieutenant Gano was topside. So was Lou Casowitz, an engineering chief full of years and faithful Navy service.

"Chief," said the young lieutenant, "I hear your time's about up."

"That's right, sir."

"And I hear you plan to ship over . . ." .

"That is my intention, sir."

"Well, we'll miss you while you're away."

"Away? I don't understand, sir."

"Oh, certainly you plan to go home for a bit of relaxation before starting another hitch?"

"Home, sir?" asked the old chief, his brow furrowed in puzzlement. *"This is my home,* Lieutenant. I'm not going anywhere."

As the years passed Roy Gano was to come to feel much the same way. The Navy was his home, and he was not going anywhere the Navy didn't go.

It took the constructors and workmen of the Consolidated Steel Corporation, at Orange, Texas, a shade under 10 months to complete and launch the hull of *U.S.S. Dyson* and another 7½ months to complete her for delivery to the United States Navy. However, 9 days might have been lopped off this not inconsiderable achievement had Commander Gano been willing to settle for something less than perfection. He was not, and in consequence, when the vessel was first offered to the Navy on 21st December, 1942, he declined to accept her.

When tapped for command of *Dyson* in October, 1942, Gano was serving as Material Officer on the staff of Commander, Task Force Eight, operating in Alaskan waters. He had behind him an officially acknowledged meritorious career in engineering and staff work, but had not previously exercised command of a Navy vessel. Immediately prior to his detachment in the north he wired his wife; she met him in Seattle, and they drove the Gano Ford to Texas by way of San Diego, arriving in mid-November. In those days the booming little city of Orange, having burgeoned from 7,000 to 35,000 population almost overnight, had scant time and less inclination to concern itself with the creature comforts of a Navy Commander and his wife looking for some sort of roof over their heads and an occasional meal. The one hotel was bulging with resident guests, and had it not been for a family named Tieman who had a home at Vinton, Louisiana, about seven miles from Orange, Commander and Mrs. Gano might have had some rough sailing. Instead, however, the Tiemans took the Ganos in, gave them comfortable accommodations and breakfast each morning, and Roy saw in it a lucky omen for his upcoming command.

Daily the captain-to-be haunted his ship in which, for the time being at least, he had no authority whatever. He watched the dockside "mateys," in their headlong plunge to complete the job, ignore every rite of sentiment and service that a proper sea-man might have observed in his ministrations to a new and splendid vessel, and his sensibilities were affronted. Finally, on the morning of 21st December, a top official of the Corporation told him "Captain, she's ready for you! Just sign here!"

"I'll sign nowhere," Gano retorted, "until I've made a thorough inspection above and below." And when he'd made his inspection the Commander said, simply, "I can't accept her."

"In Heaven's name why not?" demanded the exasperated shipyard boss.

"Two reasons," Gano told him quietly. "One, there are no spare parts. We're headed for a war, and I mean to have my spare parts while the having's good; otherwise I may never get them. Two, the lagging on the steam lines is not complete. With the Christmas holidays at hand your workmen are bound to want to take time off, which means that they won't get to work completing that insulation until after the new year. But by that time I'll be trying to break in a crew and get the ship ready for sea. I can't do that with your men working below. No, I'm afraid you'll have to complete the job before I can accept *Dyson*."

The Consolidated executive grimaced but he capitulated when he saw the Commander was not to be moved. Workmen toiled below decks on *Dyson* through the solemn night hours of Christmas Eve, the joyous span of Christmas Day, and on until 30th December when the job was completed to Roy Gano's satisfaction and he accepted *Dyson* for the United States Navy. In a sentimental gesture the metal shop of the shipyard presented *Dyson* with a set of handsome silver goblets, one for each officer. Subsequently these goblets disappeared; Captain Gano never was able to learn what happened to them.

Powerful *Dyson*, sleek and smooth, raced and cavorted through the sparkling waters of the Gulf, having freed herself from the taint of land by a brief passage down the Sabine River from Orange. Captain Gano, his mind alert to the test maneuvers through which he was putting his vessel, stood on the bridge observing. A Negro mess boy approached with coffee, and the Captain accepted a cup. "What's your name, son?" he asked pleasantly. "Name's Brown, sah," was the reply. A few hours later the little episode was repeated, only this time it was a different mess boy. "What's your name, son?" asked the Captain. "Name's Brown, sah," replied the attendant.

That night the Captain spoke in some perplexity to his executive officer. "Do we have all the Browns in the fleet in this vessel?" he wanted to know.

"I guess the personnel people just dealt 'em right off the top of the pile, Captain," Lieutenant Morland told him. "Out of our eight mess attendants, five are named Brown! We'll just have to start calling 'em 'Jim' and 'Joe' and 'Bill'—all except one. His name is Jubilee; I don't guess we'll forget him."

Morland, an imperturbable fellow, was to prove an assistant of inestimable value to Roy Gano. He was about 32, quiet and tall, with fair, wavy hair. Before coming to *Dyson* he had been in a DD on the North Atlantic patrol; he was a good leader and an especially fine navigator. On one occasion he was to take *Dyson* into New York harbor at 25 knots through thick fog. Standing beside him on the bridge the Captain was extremely apprehensive, but Morland's voice was soothing and reassuring. "In just two minutes, Captain," he said, "we're going to pick up the first buoy, and it'll be dead ahead." They did, and after that Gano trusted Morland completely as the ship's eyes in the dark. He was thoroughly reliable in small as well as large things and, of course, eventually went on to command, relieving Bob Cavenagh as skipper of *Stanly* in 1944. Rather late in life Morland married a girl from Key West, who was as voluble as he was reticent, but the marriage proved a happy union of opposite temperaments.

Although Roy Gano was gently amused at having a complement of five mess boys named Brown (they later furnished the nucleus for a colored choir which did much to enrich the somewhat sporadic attempts at formal divine services under combat conditions in the Solomons) he was genuinely puzzled by another of the mess-boy fraternity named Canada Carter. As the time drew on for *Dyson* to sail forth toward battle the Captain determined on a gracious gesture. He'd give them a proper farewell party. One morning all the wives and relatives of the crew present in the area were invited aboard. To do the thing up really brown (and because he couldn't resist the temptation to show off his beloved ship) the Captain announced that he was going to take them all to sea for a little spin. But, while preparations for getting under way were in progress, Lieutenant (jg) Hollis F. Garrard, USNR (MC), the ship's doctor, reported to the bridge. He was a breezy type, immensely popular throughout the ship, and it was not his way to stand on formality. "We've got a boy down below, Captain—Birmingham darkey named Carter. He's out cold. I think he should go ashore and I think I should go with him."

"Whatever you say, Doc," replied the Captain. Canada Carter was set ashore and the doctor with him; *Dyson* sailed for her short jaunt in the Gulf, and in a few hours she was back at the dock and cleared of the encumbrance of civilians. Division officers busied themselves with the realistic chores of a final departure, and the Captain was preoccupied with terminal paper work and reports when Garrard tapped smartly on the door jamb of his cabin and, in response to the Captain's, "Come in," pulled the heavy green curtain aside and stood in the doorway.

"Oh, yes," said Gano remembering. "What's with that boy Carter?"

"I'm sorry, Captain, but we're going to have to leave him ashore when we sail."

"M-m-m-m! That's too bad. What's the matter with him?"

"It's a bit unusual, Captain, but he's absolutely no good. *He's scared to death.*"

"Scared to death? Of bullets . . . ?" Gano groped in his mind to get a grip on this news. So far as he knew, Carter had never yet heard a naval gun fired, and for him to get the wind up while still so remote from combat seemed surprising.

"No, Sir, not of bullets," the doctor told him. "Of *sharks.*"

"I don't get it, Doc," said the skipper laying his fountain pen down and squaring away from his littered desk. "Suppose you tell me the story."

"It's a doozy, Skipper!" chuckled the breezy medic. "Sort of primitive as a matter of fact, but none the less real. Everybody knows we're bound for the Pacific sooner or later, and from the chiefs down they've been telling this boy that, should the occasion ever arise where we had to abandon ship, the first thing done is to throw a Negro mess boy overside to find out whether the sharks are biting! He believes it absolutely; he fully expects to be fed to the sharks, and he's terrified. Believe me, Captain, he'll be no good to us. We're much better off leaving him on the beach."

"I'm sure you're right," said the Captain reflectively. "Report it to the exec, will you, Hollis, and the two of you take care of it."

Dr. Garrard departed to complete his mission with something of a puckish smile claiming his handsome face. It was, indeed, his habitual expression. The doctor was one of those rare characters who not infrequently fetch up in ships and, despite their obvious lack of nautical know-how very quickly have a ship's company charmed beyond caring. At the outbreak of the war Garrard had been physician-in-residence at a swank hotel in a top southern resort. He enjoyed a lucrative practice and commanded ample means. Standing a swarthy 6 feet and weighing better than 200 pounds, he had been a semi-pro athlete. At 32 he was married and the father of two children. Before *Dyson* pulled away from the dock on her final departure Lieutenant Garrard knew every man in the ship by his first name. Subsequently he would pass among them at all hours of the day and night, telling humorous stories to relieve tension. During battle he helped pass around sandwiches and hot coffee. In the wearing months to come he kept a special eye on the Captain, and instead of feeding him "wake-up pills" to offset the corrosive cerebral impairments of insupportable fatigue, Garrard trotted out an endless procession of amusing stories to divert Gano's mind from its preoccupation with the need for rest. The "Doc" was an exceptional tennis player and a born gambler who would bet on anything. Both of these attributes were to make him a chum of Ensign Roger E. Spreen, USN, a young watchkeeping officer of handy talents. Spreen, who was 24, was very tall and a top-ranking tennis and basketball player. From Sidney, Ohio, he was assistant gunnery officer in *Dyson* and a reliable leader of men. Like Garrard he would bet on anything, and the two racked up some of the wackiest wagers in the South Pacific when *Dyson* finally got to the wars.

Dyson's officers, her crew, and the seemingly erratic manner in which she made her way toward what Hamberger called "the more realistic war" were quite typical of her sister ships in DesRon-23. On Tuesday, 12th January, 1943, Ensign Fred Fuld, USNR, supply officer, came over *Dyson*'s rail carrying $50,000 in crisp, new bills from the Orange National Bank. With a nucleus crew of experienced hands stiffening some 120 raw recruits fresh from Great Lakes Training Center the destroyer sailed the following day toward Guantánamo Bay, Cuba.

Almost immediately young Fuld found himself in trouble. A slight young man, in civilian life Fuld had been a certified public accountant in the Los Angeles office of Price-Waterhouse. He thoroughly understood his duties, and he discharged them efficiently, but *Dyson* had been on her passage only two days when Fuld sought and obtained permission from the "exec" to speak to the Captain, whom he found in his cabin below.

"Captain, Sir," began the troubled young ensign, "I've got a hideous problem."

"I'm sorry to hear that, Fuld. What's the trouble?"

"I get seasick, sir, and I *stay* seasick! I've been deathly sick every minute since we left Sabine Pass, and I'm sick now!"

"You've seen the doctor, of course?"

"Yes, sir. He gave me some pills, but they don't make any difference. I'm still sick."

The Captain sighed. It was a real enough problem; one present in virtually every Navy ship afloat. Some people are seasick-prone, and no reliable remedy has been found for their relief. "What do you have in mind, Fred?" asked the skipper.

"Where do we go from Guantánamo, Captain?"

"I haven't the remotest notion; maybe back Stateside—maybe to the South Pacific."

"Well, Sir, if I could be transferred to shore duty the next time we *do* make a Stateside port, I'd be mighty obliged—and relieved!"

Roy Gano considered a moment before replying. Then he said, "Fred, I'd like to make a little deal with you. I think I have some understanding of how miserable you feel, and I know it's tough. But I also know that the morale that Morland and I are trying to build in this ship will be shot all to hell the moment I start making the kind of transfers you request. I've seen it happen before; it never fails."

"Well," said the sick ensign miserably, "what can I do, Sir?"

"This, Fred. If you'll load yourself with those pills of Doc's, grit your teeth, and fight this thing until we've had a little combat experience—it only takes a *little* combat to crystallize morale in a ship, Fred— then I'll be glad to transfer you ashore at the first opportunity. That way the ship will be protected and, after all, we live for the ship, don't we?"

"I suppose we do, Sir," said Ensign Fuld with resignation. "I'll try, Captain."

Roy Gano permitted himself the warm gesture of rising and shaking hands with his Supply Corps ensign. Fuld stuck it out until *Dyson* reached the Solomons and engaged in combat. Then the Captain, faithful to his promise, transferred the former CPA to shore duty for, by that time, *Dyson*'s morale was higher than a flag on the Fourth of July.

As *Dyson* slid alongside the fuel dock at Guantánamo and the oil king took over to load 49,611 gallons of fuel, Lieutenant Leland W. Devereaux, USNR, relieved Lieutenant Carl Sanders, USN, the ship's "gun boss," as officer of the deck. Captain Gano had been studying Devereaux intently for some time but had not been able to reach any definite conclusion concerning the real merits of the man. Devereaux was 29, had thinning dark hair, a ruddy complexion, stood 6 feet, weighed about 185, and wore glasses. He was a "Ninety Day Wonder" —product of one of the Navy's quick "refresher" courses given junior officers before they went to sea. Before reporting aboard *Dyson* Devereaux had served about a year in another DD, so that he'd had time to gain some experience. He managed to convey the impression that he knew all the answers, but the Captain's analytic scrutiny led him to the conclusion that this was largely bluff. Discussing officer "problem children" (every ship had at least one such, and most had several) with a fellow captain at Noumea, Roy Gano summed it up this way: "Devereaux has an answer for everything, but usually it's the wrong answer. He vacillates, and I'm really afraid to trust him to take any necessary decisive action in time. He's a soldier-of-fortune type, and to listen to him you'd think there wasn't anything he couldn't do. I just don't know how to classify this man. He's either damned good, or he's a frightful fraud."

Good or not, Lieutenant Devereaux made the Captain eat at least some of his caustic skepticism at precisely 1704 hours on the afternoon of Monday, 27th September, 1943. At 0330 that morning *Dyson* had returned to Tulagi from maneuvers with Task Group 39.2. Her engineering plant was on 15 minutes standby, and at noon the ship went to general quarters when Condition Red was proclaimed at the anchorage. The ships present, having fought off a minor air attack, secured from general quarters at 1432, and at 1550 *Dyson*'s log showed the usual entry "Made all preparations for getting under way." But it was *not* followed by the customary "Under way" entry. Instead, despite the presence of the "Captain at the conn; navigator on the bridge" and the special underway detail at their stations, *Dyson* managed to foul her starboard anchor in the anti-submarine net at the harbor entrance. Worse, the wind spun her around until the vessel herself became entangled in the net. On *Dyson*'s bridge it was an exasperated Captain Gano who stormed, "Isn't *this* a fine damned kettle of fish! What do we do now—just sit here corking up the harbor until the Japs find time to come over and knock us all off?"

It was then that Leland Devereaux stepped forward. "I believe I might be able to help, Captain."

"You, huh?" snapped Gano. "And just how, may I ask?"

"Well, sir, if we can find a rig somewhere, I'm a deep-sea diver, and I could go down and clear that anchor."

"Th' *hell* you are!" exploded the worried Skipper. "Well, I thought I'd seen everything, but this should be one for the book. Morland," he added turning to the "exec," "message the beach and see if they can send us out a diver's rig. Lieutenant Devereaux might just as well have a try at it."

Not only did Leland Devereaux have a try at it; by 1638 he had cleared the fouled anchor, and at 1704 *Dyson* stood out of the harbor and bent on 32 knots in pursuit of Task Unit 39.2.2 with which she was supposed to be operating.

Unfortunately, although he had scored a thumping vindication of his previously questioned virtuosity, the sweets of fulfillment soon were to turn to ashes in the mouth of Lieutenant Leland Devereaux. By his own admission, shortly prior to having joined *Dyson*, the Lieutenant had married a dark and reportedly ravishingly beautiful San Francisco girl. Certainly her picture in his cabin justified the claim that she was breathtakingly exquisite. But a few days after the episode of the fouled anchor his mates came upon Devereaux sitting disconsolately in the *Cloob des Slot*, nor did he raise his head to acknowledge their greeting.

It was Ensign Bob Keil, USNR, the communications officer, who sensed that there was something seriously amiss, placed a hand on the grieving officer's shoulder, and spoke what he hoped were words of comfort. "Anything we can do to help, Leland? Want to get something off your chest?"

"There's nothing to do," moaned Devereaux. "I've already done it—and so has she!"

"Done what, old boy?"

"Well, for a long time there I got almost no mail from my wife, Leticia . . ."

"And . . . ?"

"And you know what you fellows always say when you don't get mail from your wives—'Cut off their allotments . . .' "

"But, Leland—we're just kidding . . ."

"*Kidding?*" Lieutenant Devereaux looked up as though jerked erect by hidden wires. "Hell, I thought you were serious, so I *did* it!"

"You cut off your wife's allotment because she didn't write often enough?"

"I sure did," said the desperate Devereaux.

"Oh, my achin' back!" groaned Keil. "So what happened?"

"Read this," said the victim, handing him a typed note. It was brief and told the story succinctly. Mrs. Leland Devereaux was no longer

Mrs. Leland Devereaux, thank you. She had secured a divorce alleging non-support, had resumed her maiden name and, as she concluded her letter transmitting this devastating intelligence, "I now have a wonderful job in San Francisco as a secretary, and my boss is a duck!"

"Sic transit gloria," muttered Ensign Keil with a sympathetic sigh as he moved off toward a small knot of *Dyson* officers nearby. Remembering Devereaux's all too recent heroship, it was the most appropriate observation he could think of.

While lying at Guantánamo *Dyson's* crew turned in a tolerable performance at fire drill, getting the first stream of water overside in 4 minutes. There was plenty of room for improvement in that, the Captain knew, but at least it showed progress since their last effort when they had required 6 minutes, 30 seconds to perform the same evolution. The men were showing some signs of working up into a crew.

In March DD-572 escorted transports *Alcoyne*, *Betelgeuse*, and *Bellatrix* to the Charleston Navy Yard, and at the start of the passage Lieutenant Sanders was officer of the deck. Along with John Morland, Captain Gano considered Carl Sanders a sheet anchor to windward. For one thing he was regular Navy, having graduated from Annapolis with the class of '40. For another, he was a combat veteran and the only officer in the ship who had seen service in the South Pacific in this war. At the Battle of Savo Island he had been a gunnery spotter aboard cruiser *Vincennes*, had managed to survive when the beloved *"Vinny-Maru"* capsized and sank, and had come to *Dyson* almost direct from that toughest sort of seasoning. At 26 Carl was a very positive type, and as a concomitant of his natural temperament and combat experience he exerted a very steadying influence on all in the ship. He was from Cumberland, Maryland; a good-looking blond of medium stature, and married to a San Francisco girl whose allowance he had *not* cut off. Even so, this San Francisco girl, too, found her way to the divorce courts before the war was out. To his job as gunnery officer Sanders brought extreme aggressiveness and an especial aptitude for the maintenance of fire-control equipment at concert pitch; the Captain was well pleased to have such a steady and reliable gun boss in his ship.

Delivering her charges at Charleston *Dyson* took aboard 80,000 gallons of fuel oil and lay a few days recuperating before leaving for the Naval Air Station, Trinidad, British West Indies. The days at Charleston were busy ones for several of her junior officers, and tantalizing days for one in particular, Ensign Keil. A reserve officer of about 24, Keil did the coding and decoding in the communications department, and took care of the classified publications. But aside from the efficient performance of these duties he had other claims to fame. He stood a solid 6 feet, weighed 180, was darkly handsome, and hailed from Chicago. He had unusual stamina, and was the regular pitcher on the ship's softball team. But Bob Keil's principal forte was romance. During those hectic days when officers and men were busy at the Consolidated yards back in Texas readying *Dyson* for sea, a ship's sweetheart was chosen. She was a beautiful young girl named Betsy, the daughter of one of the naval constructors who had worked on *Dyson* and other *Fletcher* class DDs. Young Mr. Keil had proceeded to woo, win, and marry Mistress Betsy in the teeth of panting competition. It was a feat carried out with such éclat, speed, and singleness of purpose as to compel the admiration of Ensign Keil's several disappointed rivals. Now, with the ship only a few hundred airline miles from his sweetheart-wife, he eyed maps and air schedules hopefully although he knew in his heart it couldn't be—and it wasn't. Early in April *Dyson* swung ship to correct her compasses, and pulled out for Trinidad, which she reached a mighty thirsty destroyer. Perhaps the most relieved man aboard was Lieutenant Frank V. Andrews, USNR, *Dyson*'s engineering officer. He had been watching his fuel consumption with approaching panic, and sighed in thankful relief when the ordeal was over.

Frank Andrews was not a marine engineer. A balding little blue-eyed blond of indeterminate age, he had absorbed his seagoing yen principally by osmosis: he was married to the daughter of a Supply Corps Admiral. Before coming to *Dyson* he had been a textile engineer in California, had virtually no experience in the engine spaces of a DD, and needed all the help Roy Gano could give him. Somewhat surprisingly *Dyson*'s assistant engineer, although a graduate of the United States Merchant Marine Academy and knowledgeable in his department, played little forceful part in the engineroom. He was a young easterner of German extraction, and displayed a timidity which earned his Captain's conclusion that the degree or effectiveness of his leadership in an emergency might be a matter of question.

Wednesday, 5th May, found *Dyson* at Base How and racing to sea to investigate a reported submarine contact. The "submarine contact" turned out to be contact with a semi-submerged wreck which was disposed of. *Dyson*'s next duty sent her escorting convoy *Nan King* 539 from Norfolk to Cristobal, Canal Zone. The mission completed, *Dyson* moved slowly toward her berth at Pier 16-C and Captain Gano, glass in hand, got a pleasurable surprise. A destroyer already was tied up at the pier and he read her number—571—in the foot-high numerals on her bow. His "exec," Morland, standing at his side, already had identified the vessel. "That would be *Claxton*, Captain," he ventured.

"*Claxton* my foot!" retorted the skipper. "*That would be old Heraldo Stout, th' rascal,* and I'm going aboard him the minute we tie up! I'll bet he's got every joint in this town pegged. If anybody knows where to go for a bit of quiet relaxation it'll be Heraldo, mustache and all!"

The incident was not without relevance. In the grueling days ahead, when one or another of the little ships of the Gallant Squadron would come slamming or creeping into Espiritu or Tulagi or Hathorn or Purvis as the case might be, watch officers aboard ships already present might identify her as *Claxton* or *Stanly* or *Spence* or *Thatcher* and make appropriate log entries: *1106: Thatcher stood in.* But that's not the way the skippers interpreted it. To them, once the craft was identified, it was "Here comes Heraldo!" or "Where's Heinie Armstrong been, do you suppose?," or "I want to talk with Ralph Lampman as soon as he ties up." For this Squadron was a superior fraternity—of ships, yes, but also of individual leaders all caught and held fast in the steel web of the Navy's traditions, customs, practices and mores. Heinie Armstrong might be in one ship today and in another ship tomorrow. But for the skippers of DesRon-23 Heinie, no matter what ship he was in, would always be the lad who caught a "Class A" at the Academy, snatched a bride from under the nose of a too-trusting colleague and who, when refueling at sea, invariably came up beside the oiler at a smart clip, cut to one third the speed of the tanker just before steadying up, and went to the speed of the tanker the moment the quartermaster reported that the pitometer log was dropping off. Watching such an evolution thus performed Armstrong's colleagues wouldn't need to know the identity of the ship; they'd simply say "There's Heinie"—and they'd be right. In the Solomons and in combat this characteristic of Destroyer Squadron 23 was to exert a measurable force. Each skipper knew what each other skipper would do in any given circumstances, *and how he would do it.* This freed all from one of the most corroding worries of naval combat command—what will the other guy do next?

Early in June, 1943, in company with *Claxton* and escorting another convoy, *Dyson* sailed toward Point Jig, which was nothing but a foam-flecked billow at 26°—15'—00" South; 172°—54'—00" East. At Point Jig other ships were to join the formation for final delivery at Noumea. Upon completion of that mission *Claxton* and *Dyson* would, at long last, be in the active theater of the South Pacific war. From that area they were not to return until their fighting was done.

On the passage (in the tradition of the sea the word "voyage" signifies a round trip, the word "passage" denotes a journey from one point to another), Captain Gano made a final inventory of his assets and perplexities as reflected by his officers and crew. They represented, he guessed rightly, a pretty good sample of the run-of-ship personnel to be found in the other new *Fletcher* class DDs and on balance he decided that they would meet the test when it came. Happily, the Navy's system of slow peacetime promotion now was exerting a beneficent influence upon the challenging and all-important job of making fighting sailors out of "the butcher, the baker, and the candlestick maker." Many long-service men fully qualified for the rating and responsibility of "Chief" had been denied that advancement simply because there wasn't room for more chiefs. Now, with an expanding Navy, these seasoned men were being moved up into the chiefs' jobs for which they were fitted by training and service, and the impact of these skilled and indoctrinated old-timers upon the raw material of the training stations was a sight to hearten any captain worthy of command and capable of exercising it wisely by not interfering with the job which only the chiefs could do. From Texas *Dyson* had started out with an aggregation of "deck apes." She arrived Point Jig with a complement of sailors, gunners, engineers, and communications experts.

As assistant gunnery officer under Carl Sanders *Dyson* had Ensign H. H. Ballard, USNR, from Long Beach, Mississippi. As a "rebel type," at least in the terms of reference popularly employed in the North and East, Ballard might have served as a matrix for the turning out of an endless file of simon-pure "Johnny Rebs." At 24 he was a dark 6 feet, 1 inch, and weighed a shade under 200. He was not very voluble, and when he did speak it was often to inform his hearers of the sterling virtues of his wife Doris. He had a very strong character which registered both on wardroom and turret.

Another southerner, Ensign J. B. Collins, USNR, from middle Texas, was the senior communications officer and a thoroughly reliable one. He, too, was over 6 feet, thin as a wire, and played first base on the softball team. "He drinks more than is strictly necessary," Gano told a fellow skipper, but "JB" as he was known to all on board developed so steadily that, when expecting battle, the Captain preferred to have this Texan as his officer of the deck.

Dyson's first lieutenant and damage control officer was something of an anomaly, and Captain Gano never could reconcile his obvious talents with the quite different requirements of a competent sea-going officer. He was another "90 day wonder" from the Chicago plant of Northwestern University, and in civilian life he had been a furniture salesman in Kansas City, Missouri. He had a smooth knack for getting along with people and was popular in the wardroom. However, the Captain noted that this officer lacked resolution when required to make a decision, and he was assigned several jobs about the ship during his term of service, all of them of such character as to permit pretty constant observation either by the skipper or the exec. The assistant first lieutenant and later assistant torpedo officer, Lieutenant Charles "Chuck" Dozark, USNR, was a chunky, dark Mittel-europa type, destined for death. He was detached from *Dyson* after spending some time in the

Solomons, returned to the States, was assigned to another DD, and was lost when that vessel was sunk in combat.

At 1500 hours on the afternoon of Saturday, 12th June, 1943, *U.S.S. Dyson* moored starboard to port alongside *U.S.S. Warrington* in the harbor of Noumea, New Caledonia. Another member of the Gallant Squadron had come to the wars. Two typical events followed shortly— typical in that they were reflective of *Dyson*'s habit of being combat-ready, and the faith of the officers and men who sailed in her. First, she took a great big drink—108,729 gallons of fuel oil. Thus being rendered fully ready for instant duty her main engines were placed on 15 minutes' notice.

The next day being Sunday, the ship's bell was tolled at 1000 hours and the word passed "Quiet about the decks; church service in progress." Standing forward, informally surrounded by a numerous company of uncovered officers and men, Ensign Jack Murray, USNR, prepared to conduct divine worship. *Dyson* was one of the relatively few small ships in which religious services were held with fair regularity. The cruisers had chaplains and the ritual of worship was routine. But in the "cans" it was largely a matter of the Captain's or some other officer's predilection toward things spiritual. As a youth Roy Gano had been accepted into the Methodist communion but on the eve of marriage, led by his bride-to-be, he entered upon the Episcopal faith. In *Dyson* he made it a practice to conduct services with reasonable frequency, being "spelled" in this duty by Jack Murray.

Murray was a young man of commanding talents. He came from Chicago, and was a quietly pious graduate of a Catholic college. He had very high ideals, and showed precision and accuracy in his work which soon won the Captain's admiration and trust. He wrote up the logs and ship's war diaries—no responsibility to be entrusted to a sloppy worker—and during combat or expected combat he worked in CIC. He was a tall, thin chap with fair hair and was almost never seen without his glasses.

Murray opened the service with a short prayer of thanksgiving for the safe arrival of the ship at her destination. Following this the mess-boy choir, singing without accompaniment, of course, for *Dyson* sailed under a strip-ship bill and there wasn't even a ukulele in the living spaces, led the gathering in the Navy hymn "Eternal Father Strong to Save." As the last of the simple harmony floated out over the harbor Jack Murray opened his Bible but without the necessity of glancing at it recited his text: *"Fight the good fight of faith; lay hold on eternal life."* In simple words he elaborated briefly on the thought. Fight the good fight they could and would, fortified by the faith which they must have and did have. Some might be killed. But mortal life was transitory at best. At the end, for each one who kept the faith, lay a greater glory and life eternal. It was a sincere preachment uncomplicated by ponderous theology and it was received and understood by those officers and men who were to fight *Dyson* through a score of bitter battles. The service was concluded with a gospel hymn which had proved very popular with the men on similar occasions: "What a Friend We Have in Jesus," and the reciting of the Lord's Prayer by the assembled company. A sacerdotal pedant might have curled a lip at the spectacle of a devout Roman Catholic leading a heterogeneous collection of Protestants and Jews in a service opening with the stately measures of the Navy hymn and ending with the musically and philosophically unsophisticated asseveration of the gospel idiom. But that's the way things were in the South Pacific. Men's emotions were very near the surface and any impromptu religious service, whether attended by many or few, was apt to reflect little liturgy but a broad spectrum of emotional interpretation.

At a later regular formation that day some of the Articles for the Governance of the Navy were read in accordance with regulations, and *Dyson* settled down to await whatever duty she might be called upon to perform. Looking across the waters of the harbor, briefly rose-tinted by a setting sun, Roy Gano noted that *Stanly* was present. That would mean Bob Cavenagh. He didn't know Cavenagh very well, reflected Gano, even though they'd been classmates at the Academy. But then, at that time, *Stanly* wasn't even a part of DesRon-23. She flew the broad pennant of ComDesRon-4, and only later was she to replace *Aulick*, an original member of the Gallant Squadron although she never actually served with it in the Solomons. Well, he'd pay a courtesy call on Bob in the morning if he could find the time. Meanwhile some sleep was indicated. The Captain turned in; *Dyson* slumbered. Around the harbor signal lights winked silently at the end of signal yardarms, and blinker tubes, aimed for more private reception, flashed messages of consequence and otherwise. On *Dyson*'s bridge Lieutenant Carl Sanders, who had the duty, paced slowly port to starboard and back again, lost in melancholy musings. Here he was back, within spitting distance of Ironbottom Bay where lay the rusting bones of his last ship, old *"Vinny-Maru."* What would it be like this time around? Of all the men in the ship he was one of the very few who, on the basis of experience, had any notion. It would be tough! Therefore the thing to do was to relax while circumstances still permitted such luxury. He stopped his pacing, spread his arms along the rail of the starboard bridge wing, gazed unseeing at the black water 35 feet below, and sang softly to himself:

I'll take you home again, Kathleen . . .

If anyone had asked, he couldn't have explained why he chose that ballad. It just seemed to fit his mood. Slowly the moon rose over the darkly peaceful scene, beautiful but portentous with the latent threat of sudden death for any and all of those present . . .

Across the ocean wild and wide . . .

Maybe that was it, thought Sanders. They'd crossed the ocean wild and wide. What would be next?

6

Commander Burke Goes to War

~~~~~~

"No, Burke! NO!"

The Assistant Chief of the Bureau of Ordnance spoke with the gritty inflection of irritation he might have used in saying "Down, boy! DOWN!" to an incorrigible St. Bernard.

It was December, 1942, in Washington, D. C. At the Admiral's upraised thumb a taxicab had pulled to the curb in front of the Main Navy Building on Constitution Avenue, and as he spoke the Assistant Chief reached out a gloved hand, opened the door, ducked his head for he was a tall man, and started to climb in.

"But, Admiral . . . don't you see, sir . . ." The opposite door of the taxi opened and an earnest young Commander whose name was Arleigh Albert Burke started to climb in from the off side. He, too, was tall, a fraction of an inch under 6 feet; he, too, ducked his head; only a miracle prevented Admiral and Commander from butting their noggins together in the taxicab version of a low-comedy prattfall.

The Admiral took his seat. Having done so he fixed upon the still poised Commander a stare which glittered with anger and outrage. Then he roared in a voice which would have matched that of a bucko mate of a Cape Horner screaming "Hell or Melbourne in 60 days!" "Dammit, Burke! *God* damn it, sir! If you don't get out of this taxicab and let me alone I'll exile you to Siberia! I'll have your stripes, sir!"

Commander Burke backed carefully out of the cab, closed the door carefully, and rendered a sober salute which was not acknowledged by the Admiral as the vehicle swept off into the freshet of noonday traffic flowing eastward through the majestic canyon of Constitution Avenue. Standing disconsolate in the street and watching the taxi vanish, the Commander figured he'd just lost one more battle in his year-long and perfervid campaign to wrest from his superiors permission to go to sea and thus get into the war at the fighting level. Actually, as he was to learn later, he'd won a point. The moment when the Admiral blew his stack was the oiled hinge—the precious balance—upon which fate turned to speed Arleigh Burke on to glory and greatness.

Burke's way to the war had its hilarious aspects not the least titillating of which was the fact that it was a woman who got him there. Her name was Delores. She was a lithe brunette secretary of about 25, attached to the office of the Assistant Chief of the Bureau of Ordnance. She had a quick, throaty laugh, dancing hazel eyes, and a mischievous little smile. Like many other smart government girls Delores knew her way around backstage in high places. For something like 11 months naive Commander Burke had been butting his head against the granite walls of seemingly insensible officialdom, and he hadn't gotten anywhere. Then Delores took him in hand, and in 2 weeks he was headed for the South Pacific.

When war came on 7th December, 1941, Arleigh Burke was on duty at the Naval Gun Factory in Washington as an inspector of anti-aircraft and broadside gunmounts. He had special qualifications for this exacting duty, having taken a Master of Science degree in engineering from the University of Michigan after graduating from the Naval Academy. Now that he had reached senior rank he and his wife "Bobbie" had bought a house in Northwest Washington and their two great danes "Faffin" and "Schatz" managed to keep the premises in a livable state of disorder. But Burke was a destroyerman at heart, and he was to remain a destroyer buff even after becoming Chief of Naval Operations. Rising through the ranks he viewed with suspicion and distaste any duty which took him away from "those lovely destroyers," and certainly in December, 1941, his notion of his proper place in a shooting war was on the bridge of a DD, not poking around an ordnance plant.

Burke's desperate battle to get aboard a destroyer and sail for where the guns were shooting was characterized principally by comedy—soul lacerating comedy for him, but comedy nonetheless. The production chief at the gun factory and Arleigh's immediate superior was a Navy Captain. He was a man with a dry, edged sense of humor, and when inspector Burke first applied for release so he could seek sea duty the Captain merely said, "Well, why don't you train a relief first?" That sounded encouraging to the Commander who immediately set about training someone to take his place in the shortest possible time. Then he renewed his request.

"Sorry, Arleigh," said the Captain, "but I need that man you've trained for other duty. Train somebody else."

This see-saw went on for 10 months during which time Burke trained three men to take over his job only to see them snatched away and assigned elsewhere while he remained tied to the gun factory. Finally he taxed the Captain with having a ghoulish sense of humor.

The lanky Captain pushed his chair back from his blueprint-littered desk, fixed Burke with a contemplative gaze, stroked his chin thoughtfully for a moment, and then delivered his answer: "Arleigh, you're just too good; I can't spare you. But I'll tell you what I *will* do; you may have a standing appointment with me at 1600 every Friday afternoon to renew your request. How's that for handsome?"

Commander Burke gritted his teeth and bespoke the Captain's permission to take his request direct to the Assistant Chief of the Bureau of Ordnance. Permission was granted and that's when the Commander met Delores. At first, however, she had bad news for him when he called to get the Admiral's decision. The Admiral was not in his office but had left word for Burke with Delores. "The Admiral has no objection to releasing you," she told him, "if the Captain agrees. But the Captain won't agree."

Probably it was the expression of utter frustration which possessed him when Delores delivered this dictum which won her sympathy. "Commander," she continued, "if you will give me a telephone number through which I can reach you at any time, and if you'll promise to do exactly as I tell you, I'll get you to sea."

The effect on Burke was electric. True to her word, it was only a few days later when Delores called and said she'd made an appointment for Commander Burke to see the Admiral personally. But, again, frustration! The appointment was for 1000 on a Tuesday morning in December. From that time until 1215 Burke cooled his heels in the Admiral's outer office and chatted with Delores. The Admiral was in a meeting. Finally he sent out word that he wouldn't be able to see the Commander after all; he had to deliver a speech at a luncheon.

"Th' hell he won't see me!" exploded Burke. In desperation he barged straight into the Admiral's office and started talking. The Admiral continued his preparations to leave for the luncheon, and Arleigh Burke continued to talk. He trotted down the passageway at the Admiral's side still talking, and he continued to press his request as the Admiral signaled for a cab. It was then that the Admiral blew his stack and drove off in high dudgeon leaving Burke finally crushed.

For once in his life Arleigh Burke had too little faith—too little faith in a girl named Delores. How she managed it he never had time to ask and she never told him, but 2 days later Burke received a peremptory summons to the Admiral's office. Almost, the Assistant Chief of BuOrd was contrite! He apologized to Burke for his bad manners in the taxicab incident, and he granted the Commander's request for release from the gun factory.

Arleigh Albert Burke emerged from the sanctum sanctorum in a roseate glow but it was crisply dispelled by the practical Delores.

"Look, Commander, if you don't move fast you're going to be a dead duck! When news of the Admiral's softheartedness—or softheadedness as some will consider it—gets around, a lot of people are going to try to change his mind."

"What do you suggest?"

"Three things: First, get your assignment to sea duty."

"I've already got it. I'm being given command of a destroyer Division, Number 43, in the Pacific."

"Good! Next, your orders. Can you operate a typewriter?"

"Sure, but what's that got to do with it?"

"Just this. It takes the people in the Bureau of Navigation an average of 4 days to cut and process a set of orders. And if you hang around Washington 4 days longer, you're going to end up right back at the gun factory where you started."

"Sounds reasonable."

"Now," continued Delores, "if you can run a typewriter you can cut the stencils for your own orders. So point Number 2: Get over to BuNav and if you can't get somebody to cut your orders at once, do it yourself."

"That adds up. What's the third point?"

"*Get lost!* As soon as your orders are processed get out of town, and don't leave a forwarding address, because they're going to be looking for you!"

"Honey, I'm on my way, and I don't know how to tell you how much I appreciate . . ."

"Skip it, Commander. You've got a job to do."

As Burke bolted through the door she called after him, "I'll try to hold the home front meanwhile." And then, softly, "And a fair breeze to you, Arleigh!" She'd never dare call him Arleigh to his face but then—what th' hell—maybe she'd earned the right to, just this once.

The last thing Arleigh Burke did before grabbing commercial air for San Francisco was to order two dozen long-stemmed roses sent to a certain young lady—a government-girl type name of Delores. Then the Commander, a latter-day combination of Lochinvar, Sir Lancelot, and Eric the Red, took off for the wars.

What manner of man was this officer who yearned with all his soul to be let at the enemy? He was different things to different men. Simplicity and humbleness—not humbleness before men, but humbleness before God and the great events in which he was about to participate— were observable characteristics. Yet, too, he was many-faceted. Much later, when the Ironbottom Bay Club had been built by the Sea-Bees at Purvis Bay, several of the senior officers of DesRon-23 sat in "Tip's Tavern" engaged in a colloquy the subject of which was the Squadron

Commodore. It was in no sense a gossip session, but simply a sympathetic exploration of a subject in which each was legitimately interested because of his membership in the Squadron.

For senior officers, to which it was restricted, the Ironbottom Bay Club eventually took the place of the *Cloob des Slot*. The black Bishop of the Solomons granted permission for the building of the Ironbottom Bay Club on church property with the understanding that, when the war swept away from the area, the structure would revert to him for sacerdotal uses. Dues in the Club were $5 per stripe—$15 for a Commander, $20 for a Captain. Its principal features were Tip's Tavern named for Rear Admiral "Tip" Merrill, and "Pug's Pub" named for Rear Admiral "Pug" Ainsworth. Beer and brandy usually were available in quantity, but bourbon, scotch, and rye were in short supply although in principal demand. The problem was met by opening one bottle of bourbon, scotch or rye every hour. When that happened everyone had a drink around. Then it was beer or brandy for the next 60 minutes.

Coldly precise and weighing his words, Count Austin gave the group his own summary of their Commodore: "Arleigh is a great leader. As we all know, he's vigilant and alert, and he exudes enthusiasm. He has a happy combination of humor and seriousness, and he sets an excellent example."

"He also eats raw carrots!" observed Brute Reynolds drily. The Brute's observation reflected more than was apparent on the surface. It was true that Arleigh Burke had become something of a fanatic in his belief that eating raw carrots improved night vision. He was not one to overlook a single point, however small, that might add to his efficiency as a fighting man, and he often appeared on *Charlie Ausburne*'s bridge munching on a pale pink root. But the real difference between Burke and Reynolds was more fundamental. Burke was a pizza man, whereas Reynolds favored ham sandwiches. The Commodore rarely got his pizza aboard *Ausburne*. After all, Reynolds was skipper, so they ate ham sandwiches.

"He's certainly all business," contributed Ralph Lampman lighting his pipe and settling himself comfortably to nurse the one and only bourbon-and-soda he expected to enjoy that afternoon. "When I first brought *Thatcher* in to Espiritu he boarded me and congratulated me on the state of the vessel. Now, I'm telling you fellows, at that time *Thatcher* was as sad and sorry a one DD as anybody would ever hope to see. We'd painted all our brightwork, there were streaks of rust and patches here and there below, and Irish pennants aloft. I thought he was kidding me. But he wasn't! What he was talking about was the guns, and I must confess that our battery really was in good shape."

"Trying to analyze Arleigh Burke," said Ham Hamberger in his characteristically thoughtful and deliberate manner, "is like trying to analyze a natural phenomenon. His is a fortuitous concourse of all the talents required of a naval officer."

"And he excels in each one," observed Austin, methodically making perpendicular stripes with his forefinger through the beads which studded his cold beer bottle in the humid atmosphere of the Club. There were nods of agreement around the table.

"Obviously," continued Hamberger, "the Commodore is a man of great physical, mental, and spiritual power."

"I probably see more of him than the rest of you fellows do," said Reynolds, mopping the perspiration from his brow with an already limp handkerchief. "Remembering Rosey Gillan, I'd say Burke has few if any eccentricities."

"I don't think he has any," replied Lampman. "After all, he puts his pants on one leg at a time, just as we do."

"Maybe Rosey jumped into them both feet at once, all standing!" contributed Austin with a tinge of acidity.

"The Commodore's standards are the highest—we all know that," said Hamberger.

"But, somehow, he makes it easy for us," interjected Reynolds.

"That he does, Brute," replied Hamberger. "And I think I know how he does it. He has a good sense of humor, and a deep understanding of the human touch and the human tools he has to work with."

Heraldo Stout, detained aboard *Claxton*, was late joining the group. As Hamberger spoke, Stout came charging up, a cloud of smoke trailing from his glowing pipe which he smoked with his right hand. In his left he held a pony of brandy.

"Brief me, gentlemen," he requested seating himself.

"We were just trying to figure out what makes Arleigh tick," Austin told him.

"Seek no further! Seek no further!" pontificated the irrepressible Heraldo. "It is my pleasure to give you the answer in one word: *simplicity*. Our beloved Commodore has honesty of purpose, clarity of thought, and simplicity of action. Therein lies his greatness. All honest men either perceive this intellectually or sense it emotionally, and all respond."

"What about dishonest men?" asked Lampman.

"Dishonest men, my dear Ralph, simply don't stay long around Arleigh Burke."

The talk drifted on only for a short while longer. These were busy officers and they could not afford to be long away from their ships. Indeed, a brief interlude of relaxation such as they were now enjoying was as great a rarity as it was a necessity and, usually, 20 or 30 minutes were the dimension of it.

The Captains of "23" had indeed put their fingers on some of the salient points of Arleigh Burke's admittedly inspired leadership quali-ties. However, they so completely took for granted another Burke characteristic that they hadn't even mentioned it. That was his aggres-siveness. Standing out sharp and clear above all other values which influenced the career of Arleigh Burke were his complete and uncom-promising devotion to the United States Navy, and his extreme aggres-siveness in preparing to meet, seeking out, and attacking its enemies. Nor is this aggressiveness wholly to be charged to indoctrination at the United States Naval Academy, or to the simple abstractions of patriotism and service which fed a similarly steady if somewhat less spectacular flame in Heinie Armstrong. Its roots must be sought in blood—Viking blood. That's where Arleigh Burke started. From thence came his love of ships, the sea, and sea-men; from thence came his instinctive determination always to dare; from thence came his faith. Once he said:

"We are destroyermen! A big-ship man would have trouble filling our shoes. We like to think that we would have no trouble filling his. We have learned the lesson of self-reliance, of not being afraid of a little rough living or any other tough assignment. We are real sailor-men, the destroyermen of the fleet. When things are getting too hard for anyone else, they're getting just right for us!" And he meant it. He meant it, too, when he took a quotation ascribed to an Episcopal Antiphon, and exhorted his men:

> *Arm yourselves and be ye men of valor,*
> *And be in readiness for the conflict;*
> *For it is better to perish in battle*
> *Than to look upon the outrage of our altars and our nation.*

Heraldo had said that the key to Burke's genius was simplicity. It was a simplicity arising, refined and pure, from a profound complexity, and certainly it was shot through with the drumbeat and elemental savagery of his Viking ancestors. Arleigh Burke might have agreed that there is no glory in the devastation of war, as so many have pointed out, but he never would have agreed that there is no glory in the individual battle. He dearly loved to do battle; he inspired the love of battle in others; supreme aggressiveness was one of the principal elements which composed the *mystique* of the Gallant Squadron, and it flowed to them in a strong stream from Arleigh Burke, straight out of his Eighth Century Viking heritage.

Arleigh Albert Burke was born and raised about as far away from blue water as one may conveniently get within the borders of continental United States. His father, Oscar Burke, owned and operated a 170-acre ranch near Boulder, Colorado, and Arleigh, the eldest of six children, was born on the ranch 19th October, 1901. The lad's youth was marked by the Spartan routines incident upon farming and "running cattle" at high altitudes and in remote places. The patronymic Bjorkegren means "limb of a birch tree," and the young Burke was a sturdy pioneer reflecting, in his taciturnity and in his uncompromising integrity the tree symbol which the name implied. This is not to say that he was inarticulate. He was alert and fully aware of the milieu in which he lived but circumstances as well as natural inclination fostered in him a predilection for keeping his own counsel save where the expression of an opinion was patently called for. When it was he gave it, and it always was a considered reflection. Arleigh's mother, Claire Mokler before she married, was of Pennsylvania Dutch stock. Thus the boy had a sturdy heritage in both blood lines.

Arleigh was an average Western boy, which means that he was all boy. He had his pony, he had his gun, and he had dogs. Knowing nothing else, he took as a matter of course the severe winter temperatures and considerable distances which were the conditions of the family setting, but he had a sharp curiosity which leaped far beyond his father's ranch, and which was fired by two of his schoolteachers. One was Miss Maude Morgan; the other a Mrs. Cockerell. Neither of these prim schoolmarms, so far as Arleigh ever knew, had any direct contact with the sea which indeed was remote from their scheme of things. Yet both fed him tales of the sea—"Miss Maude" in the elementary grades, Mrs. Cockerell in high school—and these tales found an answering pulse in the boy's emotions. He reacted intensely to books about the sea loaned to him by both teachers, and he considered thoughtfully when Mrs. Cockerell told him what little she knew about the United States Naval Academy, and indicated that a career as a Navy officer might offer satisfying rewards not necessarily monetary.

There came the time inevitably when Oscar Burke saddled up, rode away, and sought a conference with his Congressman, Charles B. Timberlake. The result was Arleigh's appointment to the Naval Academy.

On a humid morning in June, 1919, blond and blue-eyed Burke climbed off the Washington, Baltimore and Annapolis Railway, an electrified line now defunct but known to many generations of midshipmen as the "Weary, Belated and Annoyed," and entered upon four resinous years at the United States Naval Academy at Annapolis, Maryland. Midshipman Burke was no scholastic hot-shot. His academic training in the Colorado hinterland had been sketchy, to describe it generously, and the boy found it all he could manage through constant application to keep from "bilging out." His associates made half-hearted efforts to hang a nickname on him—"Billy" and "Whitey" were tried—but none stuck and his colleagues soon reverted to calling him Arleigh. He spent his first three years at the Academy with his nose buried in text books, and came close to qualifying as a proper "greasy grind," although his basic temperament was not studious in the accepted academic sense. He was not a "striper," i.e., a midshipman officer, and taken all in all his four years at the Academy must be considered adequate but undistinguished. A little wrestling was the sum of his athletic prowess. However, during his plebe year, one of the most important things ever to happen to Arleigh Burke took place. He met 5-foot, 2-inch, 95-pound Roberta Gorsuch.

At the time the significance of the event went unrecognized on both sides. "Bobbie" Gorsuch journeyed down to the Academy from Baltimore with her older sister, Annanora Gorsuch, at the invitation of Burke's roommate, Bernard Duncan, who was from Pennsylvania. Burke was drafted to help squire the sisters on an inspection of the Academy and its grounds. From such a simple beginning was to spring a love story of the greatest tenderness, steadfastness, and faith.

Roberta Gorsuch was a tiny creature almost bird-like in bone structure, although with a figure pleasingly proportioned. She had a symmetrically round face and notably balanced features. Her eyes were arresting. They were almost Oriental in shape, with long creases which, through the years, eroded more deeply and extended a fine line considerably beyond the outer corner of each eye. Firm lines framed her mouth, and her carriage was unusually erect for a woman. As a young girl she was thoughtful and deliberate of mien and this reserve was to combine with a natural grace of address to make her an admirable Admiral's lady when Arleigh picked up his fourth star, and they both faced heavy social responsibilities. These were considerably more numerous than either of them considered the optimum.

The Gorsuch family was talented throughout. Roberta's father, Emerson Benjamin Gorsuch, was of British ancestry. Her mother's maiden name was Moore, and she brought a rich Irish heritage to the union. Emerson Benjamin's family owned farm property near Westminster, Maryland, and for a time he endeavored to work these acres. However, a disagreement with the senior Gorsuch over the introduction of modern methods, which he opposed, resulted in a father-son disagreement. Emerson Benjamin went West, settled at Lawrence, Kansas, as a fruit buyer, met and married, and it was at Lawrence that

Roberta was born. He later turned his talents to the operation of a grain business, but the family returned East while Roberta still was quite young.

There were three daughters and all inherited musical talent from their mother who was an accomplished pianist. It was her caprice, at the end of the day when work was done, twilight shadows lengthening, and she awaited the return of her husband from business, to group the children around her in the front parlor and play softly the sad, nostalgic melodies she loved so dearly. Studying with private teachers as she grew up, Roberta learned to play the violin, later the harp. She was a pleasing performer although far from professional. One of her sisters also performed on the harp; the other became a skilled flutist. This predilection of Bobbie's for the dulcet, soft tones and rippling cadenzas of the Irish national instrument was to have amusing impact later when she became Mrs. Arleigh Burke. She very quickly discovered that her forthright and martially minded husband, while not entirely unappreciative of the ballads of a bygone minstrelsy, far preferred stirring marches of the John Philip Sousa sort. So she put up the harp, bought an accordion, and in due time was squeezing out energetic if not precisely subtle "Anchors Aweigh," "Under the Double Eagle," and other robust favorites. Arleigh himself, inspired by this staunch effort on Bobbie's part to please him, decided to take his place musically beside his wife. He purchased a guitar and fell seriously to the study of chords and notation, but little came of it. During the early days of their marriage he was forever having to go to sea, and every time he went to sea he gave his guitar away. However, he achieved greater success in another department of the social graces. Although not blessed with a strong sense of rhythm or physical coordination he studied dancing, overcame his deficiencies, and became the master of intricate rhythmic patterns on the ballroom floor.

When Arleigh Burke and Bobbie Gorsuch first met there was no sudden sunburst of love at first sight, as experienced by Heinie Armstrong. Indeed, Bobbie did not think the somewhat diffident midshipman was much impressed with her, although she welcomed and enjoyed the correspondence which sprang up between them and which tended to be superficial until his youngster year at the Academy. On her part, she contemplated the young midshipman thoughtfully and decided that she liked what she saw. Although not herself an ambitious person, Roberta Gorsuch decided that Arleigh Burke exhibited an unusual capacity to change and mold himself in terms of higher values and broader perspectives. He showed no smugness or self-satisfaction, but was interested in everything around him. All in all, Roberta concluded, the tall, serious midshipman was a pretty nice young man and she responded readily to his gestures of friendship which ripened into a warm love.

The Gorsuch family moved to Washington and Arleigh soon developed the habit of spending his September leaves there. September leave was the only extended holiday granted midshipmen. In Washington Arleigh changed to civilian clothes and long after they were married Bobbie preserved two efflorescent cravats of which he was especially fond and which he would leave in her custody on returning to Annapolis. Always a meticulous dresser, Burke sometimes was inclined to deplore the paucity of his wardrobe during his days as a young officer, and one of his satisfactions upon attaining senior rank was to provide himself with what he considered an adequacy of suits and accessories, both uniform and civilian.

In Washington young Arleigh and Bobbie dined, danced, and took long walks. He was an earnest student which she knew he had to be to make the grade at the Academy, and she sensed that he had problems. At that time, indeed, and for some time afterward, Burke was the victim of recurrent fits of melancholia. But these were his personal problem and he did his best to conceal them from Bobbie. It was never his way to weep on her shoulder or inflict his burdens on her.

Matters finally came to a head during Arleigh's youngster year, and in the romantic setting of an Academy dance. He gave Bobbie his class pin "and," she told her friends upon returning to Washington although slight puzzlement puckered her brow, "I guess we're engaged!" A score of midshipmen would have set her mind at rest about that! For months Burke had been making a nuisance of himself to his intimates. A dozen times a day he'd stop whatever he was doing, an expression of noncomprehending vacuity would steal over his face, and with a heartfelt sigh he'd observe, "Lord, but that girl of mine's a wonder!"

Although Arleigh Burke never was to get over his slight bafflement at winning Bobbie Gorsuch, it simply was not in him to be hypocritical and occasionally during their early life together they approached the verge of slight strain. If she liked something and he happened not to, he was likely to state as much in blunt terms. For a time Bobbie, always quiet and saying little, was inclined to resent this as reflecting a lack of consideration on Arleigh's part. As they matured however, she grew thankful for her husband's undeviating, almost aggressive honesty. It established a firm basis of friendship and comradeship in their relations.

Arleigh and Roberta walked beneath the sword arch of an Annapolis wedding on the day of his graduation, 7th June, 1923—but he almost didn't make it! The antecedents were these:

Until his senior year Midshipman Burke's conduct record at the Academy was exemplary. As he explained, "I had to work like hell; I found languages especially tough; I just didn't have time to misbehave." But during his first class cruise in battleship *Michigan* he relaxed momentarily and ended by getting mixed up in some mischief with a lighthearted character known as "Tweet-Tweet" Bird. Midshipman Bird got away with it; Midshipman Burke didn't. As Heinie Armstrong was to do after him, he caught a "Class A." Official punishment for his infraction stopped short of his dismissal from the Academy, but it cost him a long sequence of numbers. He was to catch these up impressively, but it would take him 30 years. In August, 1955, having received every decoration it is within the competence of the Navy to award, Arleigh Burke was appointed Chief of Naval Operations over the heads of 92 senior Admirals. His vindication may have been delayed, but when it arrived it left no room for refutation! As it was, despite his "Class A," Midshipman Burke passed out seventieth in a class of 414—certainly a creditable performance for a lad who laid no claim to brilliance—and on the same day acquired the single stripe of an Ensign in the United States Navy, and a wife.

Ensign Burke's first duty was aboard battleship *Arizona*, based on Seattle, Washington, and he and Bobbie went West. There was wealth in neither family, yet, over the years, the Burkes developed a saying "We never had more money than when Arleigh was an Ensign." Those were days of careful budgeting, modest entertaining, and close association with and reliance on other junior officer families. Bobbie learned to shop economically, establish credit for the lean times just before payday, and they managed to keep out of debt. Neither was particularly ambitious for wealth, and they regarded the Navy with its relatively low pay and slow peacetime promotion escalator as a wholly adequate and satisfying career. As *Arizona* changed base Bobbie followed her up and down the West coast. She knew that Arleigh liked to live ashore but near the ship, and when she learned where *Arizona* was going to dock, Bobbie would "start walking." Usually she was able to find quarters they could afford in the vicinity of the dock.

Although wholly green to the Navy, Bobbie's natural reticence and good manners interposed between her and the frictions which sometimes spring up between ambitious Navy wives. In this particular she was greatly helped by the guidance of the wife of a senior officer on the same station who set an example which could not be ignored. From the very beginning Ensign Burke and Bobbie—later to become plain "Bob"— worked out a pattern of living and loving which was richly rewarding to both of them over the span of the years.

An amusing anecdote illustrating Bobbie's penetrating perception of and concern for "her man" occurred when Arleigh was serving in Washington as CNO. Their home, then, was the handsome Victorian mansion known as Admiral's House, set in the beautifully landscaped grounds of the Naval Observatory on Massachusetts Avenue, above Washington's impressive Embassy Row. Here duty demanded that they be hosts at many brilliant social functions, and in the evening the mansion often was a'glitter with the exotic uniforms of visiting naval and military functionaries and diplomats of top rank.

The social pattern showed no great abatement when the Chief of Naval Operations and his wife were forced to visit naval installations about the country save that they were guests rather than hosts. It was at one such soiree at Newport, Rhode Island, that a Navy Captain, apparently fortified by the general atmosphere of friendliness and informality, cornered the CNO and loosed a vehement attack upon one of Burke's pet projects. The Admiral kept his temper in deference to the social occasion but when he retired he still was in a seething rage which was a storm signal to Bobbie. Knowing her husband's impatience with incompetence, his insistence upon loyalty and personal responsibility in the chain of command, and his penchant for direct and immediate action, there was no doubt in her mind that the Captain was due for a wigging the next morning. She knew also that Arleigh could be impetuous and when angered sometimes needed abrupt measures to restore his habitual perspective. Finally, she felt sorry for the Captain, and there settled upon her a sense of responsibility for restoring objectivity to the situation—if she could.

The next day Bobbie Burke was up long before her husband. For a good many minutes she sat at her writing desk puckering her brows, writing short lines, crossing them out, then writing new ones. Finally she had a brief note composed to her satisfaction. She folded it into a small square and placed it in the pocket of the Admiral's jacket where he kept his pipe. Then she crept back to bed.

Arleigh Burke had an official breakfast conference scheduled that morning but he had not forgotten the Captain and was fully resolved to have him on the carpet the moment a break in the morning schedule permitted. Breakfast over, the Admiral reached for his pipe to enjoy the first smoke of the day. With the pipe he drew out Bobbie's note, regarded it with a puckered frown for a moment, then opened it and read:

> *Please take a look*
> *Before you leap,*
> *For "Hell am wide*
> *An' Hell am deep!"*

Count fifty first
Or you'll regret
That temper burst
Ne'er solved it yet!

Whatever's planned,
The man needs help,
So give a hand
And not a yelp!

Arleigh Burke, always quick to laugh, flung back his head and whooped! More, he perceived the lesson and took it to heart. He never did get around to ticking off the disagreeing Captain.

Burke's rise through the ranks was not spectacular. He made junior grade lieutenant in 1926, got his second full stripe in 1930, and served as executive officer of destroyer *Craven* in 1937. By 1939 he had risen to the rank of lieutenant commander and was given his first command, *U.S.S. Mugford*, a 1,500-ton destroyer. As destroyers are popularly thought of—sleek greyhound racers of the deep—*Mugford* could hardly be described as a living doll. She was a bunchy affair with one thick and heavily rooted stack, seemingly all head and shoulders with precious little tail. But she was fast, and with war clouds gathering in Europe, and professional prognosis promising their spread to the United States, Lieutenant Commander Burke fully subscribed to the plea of John Paul Jones: "*Give me a fast ship, for I mean to go in harm's way!*" Burke meant to go in harm's way too, if he could get there, and he fell in love with *Mugford* at first sight.

Unremitting, meticulous work was a Burke characteristic. He lived by certain truisms among which was the conviction that stagnation springs from the lack of adequate employment. He phrased his doctrine this way: "Boredom comes from lack of work. Outline for yourself work to do each day. Make sure that you achieve something in your career each day. Never let a day go by when you don't do something good— not for yourself but for somebody else and, more importantly, for your Navy and your country." It surprised few, then, that the same year Burke became Captain of *Mugford* that vessel won the fleet gunnery trophy with the highest score chalked up in many years. Had Ralph Lampman remembered that, which he probably didn't, when Burke boarded *Thatcher* at Espiritu and congratulated him on the condition of the ship, meaning the guns, he need not have been surprised. Arleigh was a fanatic on guns and gunnery for, after all, without good guns and good gunners, how can a ship fight? The year she won the fleet gunnery trophy *Mugford* also placed third in the engineering competition and was well to the fore in the communications competition. All of this contributed to an extreme degree of cockiness among the crew, and a diverting sequel.

Mugford had been at Pearl Harbor less than a week when a somewhat dour four-striper started up over her gangway. An alert officer of the deck turned out the prescribed sideboys, notified Burke, and met the four-striper as he stepped aboard. They had the traditional coffee in the Lieutenant Commander's cabin, and the Captain inquired politely into the state of things on board. "Well," Burke told him, "I guess we could all benefit from a little more hard work, but by and large things seem satisfactory to me, sir."

"How's morale?"

"Oh, morale's quite good, sir; I couldn't ask for higher morale."

"Humph!" humphed the Captain. "That's what I want to speak with you about. There's such a thing as having too much morale, you know."

"I'm afraid I don't quite understand, sir," said the junior officer in honest puzzlement.

"Burke," the Captain told him with an inflection freighted with reproof, "it has been reported to me that your men are making nuisances of themselves on the beach. They're bragging and boasting in a manner which is unseemly in the United States Navy. They're *too* cocky!"

Lieutenant Commander Arleigh Burke gulped. Here was a ranking officer chewing him out for something he'd always thought a matter for congratulation and praise. But when he got over his surprise he was prepared to exhibit a proper degree of contrition before the majesty of senior rank. "I'm indeed sorry to hear that, sir. This is the first I've known of it. Just what are my men doing—what are they saying?"

"Well, in the first place," snorted the Captain, "they're not showing much respect for you and your officers. Your POs are bragging all over the base and all over Honolulu that they don't *need* any officers. They're offering to lay bets they can take *Mugford* to sea and put her through her paces without the help or supervision of a single commissioned officer!"

"But, sir . . . ," stammered Burke.

The Captain threw up a fat hand in an imperious gesture demanding silence. "And your communications people," he continued, "they're challenging every ship at this base to competition. I'm afraid your crew's getting a bit out of hand, Captain."

By this time Arleigh Burke was beginning to enjoy the whole thing hugely. He got a warm inner glow from this official evidence of the faith his crew had in their training and their own competence. Too, loyalty *downward* was a religion with Burke. He frequently repeated to associates his conviction that "an officer's service reputation is made among those who serve under him, not those above." Finally, his deep-running sense of humor was irresistibly tickled by the Captain's lugubrious concern.

"Captain," said the Lieutenant Commander solemnly, "my men aren't boasting!"

A four-striped eyebrow shot skyward and the Captain snorted, "What do you mean, not boasting?"

"They can do it, sir," said Burke earnestly. "They can do precisely what they say."

"*Preposterous!* Burke, you've made your bed; now you may lie in it! I'm tied up tomorrow, but the day after, at 1100, I'll be aboard this vessel. I'll take care that you receive the proper orders. You will then turn *Mugford* over to your petty officers and enlisted personnel. They will take her to sea and put her through exercises which I shall prescribe—and they will receive no help from you or your officers. And by God, sir, they'd better not foul this vessel up, because if they do, she'll be your last command in *this* man's Navy!" After which the Captain thumped ashore honored once more by the appropriate number of sideboys.*

Whether the Captain had anything to do with it or not Arleigh Burke never knew, but the day after his visit *Mugford* was ordered away from her comfortable dockside berth and assigned a new berth as middle ship in a nest of three destroyers. This is a tricky position from which to withdraw a ship of any length and weight, and an even trickier one to put her back into. Almost never is the latter maneuver necessary. There are many seasoned DD skippers who don't relish either job.

At the appointed time the Captain was on *Mugford*'s bridge. Burke and the "exec" stood beside him; the other officers were in plain view forward where they could take no part in handling the ship. A barnacled Chief Bosun's Mate was in command, and he looked at the Captain

---

* "Sideboys" are a traditional element in the system of Navy honors. They are sailors, the number varying with the rank of the visitor, who line up at either side of the gangway to receive a senior officer as he comes aboard and the same ceremony is repeated when he leaves the ship. The higher the rank of the visitor, the larger the number of sideboys. Usually the visitor is "piped" aboard by a bosun's mate.

The custom had its origin, which was a humorous although eminently practicable one, in the days of sailing ships. When they met in the remote harbors of the Antarctic or the South Seas the captains would visit back and forth, and the rum was apt to flow freely. Lacking docks, the ships were always "anchored off," and not infrequently when the Old Man returned to his vessel in his gig, he was in no condition to negotiate the Jacob's ladder slung from the ship's waist. When that happened the bosun piped enough hands of the watch to swing the Old Man aboard at the end of a whip, and deposit him gently on the deck. Against this emergency a lighted "lanthorn" always was placed on the hatch opposite the ladder to light the Captain to his cabin. Although the lanthorn has disappeared in modern days, the sideboys and the bosun's pipe remain in the guise of naval courtesy. It is not officially recorded that any senior officer of the United States Navy ever returned to his ship in such condition as to need hoisting aboard in a sling.

expectantly. "All right," said the Captain, "you may take her out."

The first order the bosun gave just about scared the fur off both the Captain and Arleigh Burke. It was a two part order, but he allowed virtually no time between the parts. *"Cast off all lines!"* boomed the bosun in an authoritative diapason which had about it the hoarse cachet of faithful and protracted communion at the altars of grog shops from the Asiatic Station to Brooklyn's Sands Street. And then, scarcely a decent moment later he roared *"Back 'r down full!"*

The Captain winced. Lieutenant Commander Burke smiled broadly. He would have been keel-hauled rather than exhibit any outward sign of apprehension, although he was fully aware of the values involved. Only a superb ship handler with the utmost confidence in his own skill and his knowledge of the characteristics of the ship under him would have dared apply full power in the circumstances. But the seasoned old chief was unconcerned. He knew certain basic things. One of them was that he could have his engines going from full astern to full ahead in precisely 90 seconds. Another was that he could have the vessel herself moving from astern to ahead in 3 minutes. And a third was that the wash of his backing propellers would tend to free his vessel from those on either side of her, pushing them away. He'd observed the water clear behind him, and he now proceeded to apply these statistics. *Mugford* shuddered and bucked, rammed her transom stern deep in the water in response to the powerful rearward pull of the heavy screws, and slid smartly out of the nest at a speed rapidly approaching knots.

"All ahead two thirds; indicate turns for ten knots," ordered the bosun. "Right standard rudder, an' check her on course zero-zero-six!" *

Slowly the reversed screws overcame *Mugford*'s sternway, the helmsman found his course and reported that he was on it; she went to sea.

For an hour the Captain put the ship through her paces and they were intricate. There was never a moment's hesitation either below, on deck, or in the battery. Finally he ordered her back to harbor, and after she had secured he stood at the rail taking leave of her skipper. "I'm sorry, Burke," he said. "You were right; your men weren't boasting; they *can* do what they say! And I hope this teaches me a lesson to find out a few things before I open my big fat mouth!"

It was not the last time Arleigh Burke was to be tripped up by the cockiness of his crews. Morale of a magnificent order was a wholly natural concomitant of his brand of leadership. The next time it happened

---

* "Standard" rudder is that degree of rudder which will cause the ship to turn in a circle the diameter of which is 1,000 yards. In the *Fletcher* class destroyers standard rudder was 17½ degrees. In *Mugford* it was less. If pressed, a *Fletcher* class DD, under "hard" rudder, could reverse course in an arc with a diameter of only 400 yards. This great flexibility of maneuver is one of the destroyer's greatest assets in battle.

he was Commodore of the Gallant Squadron in the Solomons. In the nature of things the cruisers had to spend much time in harbor. The attrition of battle had reduced their numbers, and they had to be employed with a certain diffidence, usually for major strikes only. Conversely, the little ships of DesRon-23 were perpetually engaged on combat missions up The Slot, and the cruisermen had a song about "23" which included the lines:

> *Each Sunday morn at the break of dawn*
> *In the OD's log you'll see*
> *"Under way at the break of day; DesRon-23!"*

There was some poetic license here. A vast majority of the Squadron's missions were mounted at night. The DDs would get going in the late afternoon, raid Japanese supply and reinforcement shipping up The Slot during the hours of darkness, and then "gallop for the barn" with the hope of getting out from under Japanese air which was sure to show up in strength at dawn. They didn't always make it and they drove off innumerable air attacks, but when all went well they usually were steaming back into Purvis or Hathorn sometime between 1000 and noon. Thus, while in all truth they were "under way at the break of day," they were not just starting out as the cruisermen's jingle implied.

It often happened that the men aboard the ships in harbor learned about the exploits of the DDs on various voice circuits considerably ahead of the return of the little vessels to port. It was not unusual for the cruisermen to cheer this or that DD of the Squadron upon her return from a particularly successful or action-packed mission. But these tributes had an effect not anticipated and certainly not desirable. The destroyermen eventually got so cocky that they started taunting their comrades aboard the cruisers for spending so much time in port, and there even were fist fights on the beach.

When Arleigh Burke heard about this he blew a gasket! It was one thing for his men to maintain proudly that they could do a certain thing, and then proceed to demonstrate that they could, as in *Mugford*. It was quite another thing for them to taunt the cruisermen who were equally brave, but whose ordered duty kept them out of constant combat employment. The Commodore issued a stern order in which he said, *"Stop picking on the cruisers! They're bigger than we are and, anyway, they're on OUR side!"* The problem disappeared.

When Arleigh Burke was made Commodore of Division 43 in Washington upon his detachment from the gun factory, two courses of action were open to him. A couple of ships of the Division, *Waller* and *Saufley*, already were in the South Pacific area. The other two ships, *Renshaw* and *Philip*, were still on the east coast of the United States, with green crews needing training and working up. The Commodore could either join these last two, supervise their training, and take them to the Pacific when they were ready, or he could proceed at once to Noumea, assume command of the half-Division there, and await the arrival of *Renshaw* and *Philip*. Impelled both by natural inclination and the knowledgeable advice of Delores he chose the latter course, and got out of Washington with a nimbleness born of fear that his orders might be changed. At the time he felt that he was in the position of a batter trying to beat out a bunt down the first-base line; whether or not he'd make it was anybody's guess.

Arriving San Francisco Commander Burke reported to the Twelfth Naval District and inquired about transportation to Noumea, New Caledonia. The yeoman who received his query regarded him with detached amusement. Was the Commander, perhaps, making little jokes? No, the Commander was *not* making little jokes; he wanted to get to the war. Didn't the Commander know that there was no transportation either surface or air toward Noumea; there had not been for a long time; it was doubtful that there would be in the immediate future? No, the Commander knew nothing about that. What priority did the Commander have? Oh, he had *no* priority! Well, *c'est la guerre!* It was time for the yeoman to go to lunch anyway.

The Commodore of DesDiv-43 walked back out into Market Street with its four-ply trolley tracks, and considered. Unlike Mr. Micawber, Burke was not the lad to sit around waiting for something to turn up. He started hustling, and within 2 hours he'd dug up the information that the *President Monroe* was due to sail toward Noumea via San Diego the next morning. She was a transport and reported fully loaded, but to Burke this was a mere bagatelle. He returned to Twelfth Naval District Headquarters and laid siege to a Captain for permission to sail in *President Monroe*.

"There are an awful lot of people trying to get out there," he was told. "We can't take all of you."

"No, sir. But in a big ship like *President Monroe* there must be room for just one more."

The Captain considered a moment before reaching a decision. "Commander, I'll make a little deal with you. As you know, *Monroe* is a troop transport. Thus far we haven't designated a troop commander. If you'll sail as troop commander you have my permission to go."

"I haven't the slightest idea what the duties of a troop commander are, sir—but you are now looking at the troop commander for *President Monroe!*"

The Captain gave a grunt which seemed to Burke to express vast cynicism. "Well, you'll soon find out what the duties of a troop commander are—and I wish you joy of it! It's one of those nice little jobs where you can't win, no matter what you do. If you'll step into the next office they'll process your orders."

That same afternoon Burke reported aboard. He found that there were two thousand troops already in the ship but that, as troop commander, at least he had a bunk. Neither the quartermaster nor the mate of the watch nor anyone else he could find had any notion of the responsibilities of the troop commander, so Arleigh Burke turned in. Vague warning signals flew in his mind, but he was adept at meeting trouble when it arrived, but not anticipating it to his distress.

Troop commander Burke was wakened from delicious, dreamless sleep about 11 o'clock that night by a most unpious uproar on deck and—what was that?—the word was being passed for the troop commander! That was Arleigh Burke, he reflected. He dressed quickly, hurried out on deck, and reported to the quartermaster of the watch. "I'm the troop commander; what's the problem?"

"Well, sir," said the quartermaster pointing shoreward, "those 400 bluejackets on the dock there have got to come aboard. They go with us, but nobody knows where to put them; that's your job." Troop commander Burke's duties had started with a rush.

Commander Burke got the bluejackets stowed somehow, and *President Monroe* got under way. He now knew that as troop commander he was responsible for the wellbeing of the troops, and that seemed fair enough. But on the way to San Diego he made an alarming discovery. No provision had been made aboard the vessel for handling the large number of men being transported. There were no "heads," no buckets, no brooms, and no way for the men to keep clean. There were no facilities for recreation—no games, nothing for the men to do during the long hours at sea. And there was a critical shortage of cooks.

Burke tackled the galley problem first. "How many of you men were cooks in civilian life?" he asked. Two men responded. "Well," pressed the troop commander, "how many of you ever cooked on camping trips?" He got a few more. Finally, in desperation he shot out, "How many of you ever watched your mothers cook?" A few more naive souls raised their hands, and Burke filled out his watch bill for cooks.

When *President Monroe* reached San Diego Burke was over the side almost before the lines were made fast. He knew what he needed—hundreds of buckets, brooms, cleaning gear, shaving gear, personal toilet articles, and games. But he was completely without guidance as to where to find these necessary articles in quantity, and his time was limited to the few hours it would take to embark the Tenth Marine Replacement Battalion which completed *Monroe*'s troop complement. At long last and by great good luck he ran down a young chaplain who seemed interested. Between them they managed to scrounge several hundred buckets, some brooms, the necessary cleaning gear, money to buy shaving kits and toilet articles and, not least important, a few score card, board, and dart games.

Back aboard, and as they sailed, Burke discovered that nobody in the troop space ever had been to sea before. However, he found four officers who had previously been ocean voyaging and these he assigned on a watch-and-watch basis to exercise supervision over the troops. The men were organized into sections, and the officers undertook to teach them what they must do for personal cleanliness and sanitation in the primitive conditions obtaining. Over-all, the effort was successful and *President Monroe*, with her "workaway" troop commander and his charges, arrived at Noumea early in February, 1943, without further untoward incident.

7

The Seasoning of 31-Knot-Burke

~~~~~~

Burke found Noumea an unimposing town of weathered and un-
painted shacks in a grotesque state of disrepair, but there were compen-
sating beauties in nature. The daytime temperature was a steady 86, the
nights were cool, the trade winds blew fresh and reliably, and the coast
presented inviting vistas of brilliant coral sand. Upon reporting to
ComSoPac he was informed that his flagship, *Waller*, was presently
with Task Force 18 (Rear Admiral R. C. "Ike" Giffen) and was at the
moment returning to Havannah Harbor, Island of Efate, from a roaring battle up Guadalcanal way in which six Japanese torps had sunk
cruiser *Chicago*. Burke was ordered to proceed to Efate in cruiser
Denver, there to report to ComTaskForce 19, and await the arrival of
Waller and *Saufley*.

The basic and broad strategic situation in the South and Central
Pacific at the time of Burke's arrival in early February, 1943, was
crystal clear. The Japanese, driving south from the Philippines, knew
that they must do one of two things if their phantasy of the Greater
East Asia Co-Prosperity Sphere was not to come unglued at the seams.
Australia was the threat and must be secured one way or another. The
United States could land awesomely powerful concentrations of men,
munitions and shipping at Australian ports—Darwin, Townsville, Brisbane—and from these and other bases, in her own good time, launch
tremendous blows north against the Japanese strongholds of Rabaul,
New Guinea, and the Philippines, rolling them up in succession. Hinging
in the Philippines the Allied offensive would then swing northeast against
the Home Islands. That, substantially, was the way the Japanese had
come and that, substantially, was the way they would have to be swept
back. At the time, of course, there was no forecast of the atomic bomb
which was to smash Nippon to her knees in two devastating blows. It
was envisioned that the Home Islands would have to be secured by as-
saulting the beaches one by one and taking major cities in like manner.

The basic Japanese problem, then, was (*a*) to storm and occupy Australia—a most uninviting chore in the extant state of Japanese resources or, (*b*) to screen Australia effectively to the eastward so that the continent could not realistically be reinforced and used as a staging area for thrusts northward by the Allies. The basic Allied strategy was to check the Japanese drive south and turn the enemy back, sweeping him out of the lower and central Solomons and driving him implacably until he was effectively penned up in the Home Islands. In its early phases this Allied campaign was given the code designation "Operation Watchtower" and it was approved by the heads of state at the Casablanca Conference.

In the strategy of creating a *cordon sanitaire* northeastward of Australia, which recommended itself strongly to Japanese naval and military commands, New Guinea, the central and lower Solomons, the New Hebrides, and New Caledonia were the keys. Streaming northwestward from New Caledonia and the New Hebrides, the lower and central Solomons and New Guinea, properly invested with men, aircraft, submarines and surface warships, offered a well-nigh impenetrable screen to bar decisive Allied military use of Australia. This, then, was the Japanese goal and, having gotten as far south as Guadalcanal, they had made appreciable progress toward its fulfillment. But the U.S. Marines had stemmed the tide. Masked by the bloody Battle of Savo Island they had achieved a lodgment on Guadalcanal in mid-1942 and, in February of 1943, the Nipponese staged "Operation KE." This was the evacuation of their troops from the island and, by 8th February, which was about when Arleigh Burke reached Noumea, the Japs had gotten nearly 12,000 of their half-starved and disease-ridden soldiers safely away from "Guadal." They estimated they had lost nearly 15,000 troops killed or missing, 9,000 dead from disease, and 1,000 prisoners in their efforts to hold the island. They were decisively licked and despite the bold threats of Tokyo Rose they never returned to "Guadal" which was the high water mark of their southern drive.

The enemy position in New Guinea was still strong although there and on New Britain he was being driven to impotent frenzy by the teams of coast watchers coordinated and supplied by the Allied Intelligence Bureau back in Brisbane and rendering a reporting service beyond price to the predominantly U.S. forces in the area.

Considerably prior to World War II American interests had a foothold on New Guinea. Commerce marched ahead of the flag and the powerful firm of Lever Brothers, manufacturers of soaps and cosmetics, had established a coconut plantation at Gili Gili at the head of Milne Bay, which cuts deeply into the tapering tail of the New Guinea peninsula. In mid-1942 a pickup team of Americans and Australians dug themselves in at this plantation for a time, and were supplied by the able little ships of the Dutch *Koninklijke Paket Vaart-Maaschappij*. In this supply mission the tiny ships of other lines eventually took a hand, but by February, 1943, the Japanese were operating at will in New Guinea. They had an air strip at Madang, one at Lae on Huon Gulf, one at Wewak, in the far North, and one at Port Moresby. However, a curious naval and air intelligence phenomenon had emerged out of the Japanese invasion of the area.

The planters, mostly Australian, a few British, and a sprinkling of Dutch who later were joined by Americans specifically trained for the job, "went bush" and set up well-concealed coastal observation posts from which they observed and reported all movements of Japanese shipping, military formations, and aircraft. Whenever possible these OPs were established in tall trees on or near headlands, and reports were made via wireless sets especially adapted for the purpose and either parachute-dropped or landed by submarine. Thus, eventually, was formed a complex radio network. In February, 1943, for instance, there was Stavermann watching the north coast of New Guinea, Ashton toward the middle, Ross keeping an eye on Japanese doings off the Rai Coast, Smith overseeing the Finishafen area, Bridge at Cape Ward Hunt, and Noakes at the mouth of the Mambare River. On New Guinea, New Britain, Bougainville and, later, in the Philippines as Operation Watchtower drove north leap-frogging and by-passing Japanese garrisons which were left to starve in their isolated and sterile strongholds, these courageous men were greatly aided by friendly natives who, having had a taste of Japanese "friendship," wanted nothing further to do with the ruthless little men from the land of the rising sun.

The Japanese were quick to realize that the coast watchers were observing and reporting their every movement, and they made frantic efforts to liquidate the watchers. On occasion Nip troops in Division strength swept an island end-for-end poking into every cave, scrutinizing every tree. They killed some coast watchers, of course; they captured and tortured others; but new teams and equipment were landed by submarine (*Nautilus, Thresher, Dace*, and *Guardfish* played conspicuous roles in this tricky service) and the coast watchers continued to elude and defy the Japanese to the very end.

In an appreciable number of instances the Allied coast watchers, predominantly Australian through 1943 and into early 1944, were at the far ends of the tenuous threads which moved the ships and men of Squadron 23 as though they were marionettes. It was not unusual for a coast watcher's faint radio signal to be picked up first by high capacity Navy listening equipment in San Francisco. Amplified, the coded message would be sent booming back across the Pacific to Brisbane.

Decoded there, the gist of the report would be once more encoded and sent on to ComSoPac at Noumea. And here it would condition appropriate action. On the ships and men of DesRon-23 this process usually had its impact between 1400 and 1500 in the afternoon. A message would be received: *"Destroyer Squadron 23: under way up The Slot at 2000; further orders later."* Or it might be *"Destroyer Squadron 23, under way for Point Uncle at 1900; further orders later."* Thus reacting instantly to the first coast-watcher report, Halsey's staff would set forces in motion to counter whatever Japanese activity might be afoot. As additional reports came in and the enemy's intentions became clearer, the necessary information would be radioed to Commodore Burke, and his specific orders for the desired action of the Squadron firmed up. Thus the tiny intelligence impulse loosed by a coast watcher from the site of his lonely and concealed point of vigil in the bush, surged along intelligence channels and the chains of command gathering momentum and power until it had the impact of action and, frequently, thundering guns from destroyers and even cruisers.

One of the first things Commodore Burke did upon arriving at Efate where he was to await *Waller* and assume command of Division 43, was to show how green he was with reference to the war in the Pacific. He wrote a letter to ComSoPac requesting that all four ships of his Division be assembled in one place. This request caused some amusement at headquarters. For a long time destroyers had been so scarce and the insistent demands for their services as escorts for carriers, tankers and transports and as raiders of Japanese reinforcement and supply formations had been so pressing, that the useful little vessels were snatched one by one whenever they turned up without immediate missions, and set directly to work. The notion of gathering all four DDs of a Division in the same place at the same time was considered hilariously funny by Halsey's staff. In due time the earnest but inexperienced Commander Burke was placed in possession of the "facts of life," and was expected to subside. He didn't. He had firmly in mind that, sooner or later, the time would come when a destroyer formation trained as a team would be urgently needed, and he planned to make Division 43 that formation. In this objective he was to be frustrated, but his convictions were to be applied with outstanding success in Squadron 23. True, they were to have little enough time for team training, but the skippers of "23" were such able technicians and such competent craftsmen that, given the inspiration of Arleigh Burke's leadership and the concrete values of his doctrine, they developed their own technique and ran with the ball. Burke summed it up in four words when he said "They played good piano!"

In due time *Waller* returned to Efate, Burke went aboard and met her skipper, Lieutenant Commander Laurence H. ("Jack") Frost, and inspected the vessel. He was favorably impressed. Larry or Jack Frost, as he was variously known, was a keen officer although of somewhat homely appearance. He had a narrow, wedge-shaped chin with a notice-able knob at the point, ears that suggested a fore-and-aft vessel sailing "wing-and-wing" before a spanking breeze, a veritable column of a nose, and level and lively light eyes which gave earnest of an alert in-telligence. *Waller* herself was in good shape as was *Saufley* who arrived from Guadal somewhat later, and the Commodore was content when he moved his scanty gear aboard his flagship and settled down to the job of making DesDiv-43 the best destroyer Division in the Navy. Char-acteristically, Burke visualized nothing less.

In later years when he had attained four-star rank and faced the exacting responsibilities which attached to the job of Chief of Naval Operations, Arleigh Burke was to entertain the belief that his famous destroyer doctrine of faith sprang from DesRon-23—the Gallant Squadron. This is only partially the fact. It is true that the basic doctrine was honed to a razor edge by the keen minds of the "23" skippers, and that many tactical problems were faced, analyzed, and resolved by daring innovations of technique. The basic doctrine, how-ever, was Burke's. He took it to the Squadron when he became Com-modore, and he started to formulate it in *Waller* when he was still Com-DesDiv-43. Curiously, for a man of Arleigh Burke's temperament, the compulsion behind his initiation of the doctrine was partly fear. He was new to the South Pacific. He was new to destroyer Division com-mand, and he was still a bit scared of his job. He figured the best way he could get his teeth into things was to study the action reports of previous battles, isolate what seemed to him to be the mistakes made on both sides, and be very sure that he didn't repeat them. That's why, with *Waller* usually on 2-hours' notice or underway, *Saufley* ranging far afield on direct orders from ComSoPac, and *Renshaw* and *Philip* not yet joined at Espiritu, Arleigh Burke spent every moment he could spare from demanded administrative work poring over such action reports as "The Night of the Long Lances" and the Battle of Savo Island. In both battles we'd lost—lost heavily. Commodore Burke wanted to know why. Reports of victories might have made pleasanter reading, but reports of losses were apt to be more instructive.

The Commodore of DesDiv-43 got some of the answers for which he quested on his first combat mission—the bombardment of the Japanese airfield at Vila Plantation on the Island of Kolombangara at the head of Kula Gulf, early in March, 1943. *Waller* was one half of the forward screen of Task Force 68, Rear Admiral Aaron S. (Tip) Merrill, who flew his flag in cruiser *Montpelier*, with cruisers *Cleveland* and *Denver* steaming behind him in that order.

Tip Merrill was a staunch little fellow. He was inclined to be a natty dresser, preferred the soft garrison cap to the more formal visored cap of the Navy, had heavy dark eyebrows with a decided cleft between them above his strong nose, and this cleft was matched by a deep dimple in his chin. He was a Mississippian, having been born at Brandon Hall, Stanton, Mississippi, on 26th March, 1890. He was short of stature, and by the time he arrived in the South Pacific as a Rear Admiral he was well over 50 years of age; perhaps a trifle old for combat, some thought. However, Tip Merrill was extremely alert, had a flexible mind, and he was not above listening thoughtfully to his juniors—especially a destroyer Division commander named Burke. The measure of his listening and understanding was to be proved up at the slashing Battle of Empress Augusta Bay somewhat later.

The bombardment of Vila Plantation was a routine gun strike implementing Admiral Halsey's basic tactical dictum "Keep pushing the Japanese around." The action was not notable save that it taught Arleigh Burke a lesson which he pondered and learned well. At midnight, while *Waller* was 6,000 yards ahead of the cruiser formation, the U.S. ships rounded Visuvisu Point on New Georgia Island and entered the Gulf. There was a flat calm on the sea, the night was pitch black, and there were uneasy minds on *Waller*'s bridge. The Admiral's plan was for *Waller* to lead the formation to the head of the Gulf, turn right, and start zig-zagging on either side of the cruiser track, both to screen against submarines and to give ample warning of any enemy surface craft which might be found inside. Burke was new to bombardment as were his officers. None ever had been in Kula Gulf before. It was enemy territory and they knew that if an enemy reception committee was awaiting them, *Waller* would be the first to get it.

At 0057, only 10 minutes before the formation was due to come to the bombardment course, *Waller*'s radar operator picked up what he thought was a ship moving slowly near the Kolombangara shore. He so reported, but Arleigh Burke was skeptical. "Are you sure it's a ship—not just a rock?" he asked. "We've got to be dead certain, you know." "I'm sure, sir. It's a ship all right." But still Arleigh Burke fussed and refused to be convinced. He wasted perhaps 90 seconds before giving the order to fire a five-torpedo salvo. The torps had hardly left the tubes before *Montpelier* picked up the target, Japanese destroyer *Murasame*, and the cruisers opened with gunfire. At that precise instant Arleigh Burke knew that he had muffed the ball!

The bombardment was successful. *Murasame* and another Japanese destroyer, *Minegumo*, were sunk; Task Force 68 suffered no casualties. But Burke had learned two basic lessons. The first and most fundamental was the value of time in battle. Had he accepted the radar operator's report when it was first made and immediately fired torpedoes while reporting to Merrill, he might well have wiped out the enemy target without the cruisers having had to disclose their presence by gunfire. Under other circumstances this could have been decisive. For, had there been a powerful enemy force lurking at the head of Kula Gulf instead of just two destroyers, the position-revealing gunfire of the cruisers could have been the prelude to their destruction in a trap. It took Commodore Burke some little while to bring himself to face up to the unpleasant fact that he couldn't blame the radar operator. The boy had made his report. It reflected his technical training and his best judgment. It was then up to Arleigh Burke to *accept* the report—not waste time trying to check its accuracy—and make an instant decision on what action to take. He had done neither of these things and, he told himself, his indecision might have imperiled the whole cruiser line. He resolved grimly never to make that mistake again.

The other lesson the Commodore learned from this little engagement was the importance of training. At a later time, expounding his theories about training to his colleagues in Squadron 23 he said: "In the heat of battle you don't remember very much. You don't think very fast; you act by instinct which is actually training. In battle, if you're trained for it, you won't change. You won't do better and you won't do worse; you'll do just about what you do in actual training. Consequently both you and your people have got to be trained. You've got to know what *you're* going to do in any circumstances without stopping to think about it, and you've got to know what *they're* going to do. You've got to expect exactly the performance in battle you'd get on a drill—no better; no worse. So train your men and yourselves. *That's what wins battles!*"

The combat seasoning of Arleigh Burke was an intensive experience covering some 9 months and highlighted by every type of destroyer action and duty. Upon returning to Tulagi from the Vila Plantation bombardment Burke found *Saufley* awaiting him. He also found what he considered a disturbing condition morale-wise. When at the primitive bases they were using, there was nothing for the men to do on those very infrequent occasions when they did have a few hours free for relaxation. They could seldom get on the beach, and even when they could there was nowhere for them to go. There weren't even games to give them temporary release from the tension and tedium of constant work.

As ComDesDiv-43 Arleigh Burke had an impressive staff. It consisted of one man, an ensign named Merriam. But young Merriam, in his own quiet, intense way, was the kind of powerhouse the Commodore could understand and admire. The lad was a reserve officer and had been a certified public accountant in civilian life. He was a "quick study" and had an endless capacity for taking on additional chores. With the exec, Lieutenant Commander Tom Fleck, he spent much time in CIC, and without formal training made himself a competent air controller. He became watchdog over all recreation funds, mess treasurer, assistant training officer, assistant navigator, and even found time to learn some engineering under Commander John Arrington, the engineering officer. Burke made good use of this precious find.

One thing that troubled the Commodore was the difficulty of getting an enemy-contact report off promptly when the decision had been made to send it. Somehow time always was lost phrasing and writing the vital message. So on orders from Burke, Ensign Merriam was free to challenge the Commodore at any time of the night or day, and demand the information on which to send an imaginary contact report *now*. And if Burke flubbed—didn't give the information in proper order so that first things came first, or gave incomplete data—Merriam would whip out "the book" and read chapter and verse to his embarrassed commander. Burke's chagrin disappeared in about a fortnight. At the end of that time he could rattle off contact reports in his sleep, and the drill by which he acquired this facility, which was typical of his constant striving for perfection in battle, paid dividends. His contact reports became outstanding for promptness, completeness, and clarity.

In the latter part of May, 1943, Commander Burke was transferred from ComDesDiv-43 to ComDesDiv-44, and shifted his broad command pennant to *Conway* (Commander N. S. Prime). He found the employment of the Division boring; so boring, indeed, that one day he fell asleep on a bridge wing of his flagship, and was almost blown overside by a Japanese bomb.

For the most part the ships of the Division, rarely all four together, more often singly or in pairs, were employed escorting supply convoys to Guadal. After about 3 weeks of this the Japanese began mounting frequent air strikes on Allied shipping south of Guadalcanal and east of San Cristobal Island. Our shore-based aircraft could not reach the area effectively, and it became necessary to keep small carriers constantly in the zone to repel enemy attacks upon Allied surface formations. The Division drew the unexciting duty of escorting these carriers, and it was on such a mission that Burke corked off while sitting on a wing of the bridge. He was jerked to horrified wakefulness by the blast of an enemy bomb close aboard.

More exciting and more demanding duty was just around the corner. On 10th July, Arleigh Burke was appointed ComDesSlot, i.e., to command the destroyers which now started operating regularly in The Slot.

The Slot is the body of water 12 to 15 miles wide, between Choiseul, Santa Isabel, and Malaita Islands to the northeast, and New Georgia, Guadalcanal, and San Cristobal to the southwest. It is deep water permitting transit by large ships. Burke's official title was Commander, Task Group 31.2, and the situational picture at the time was this:

The Allied drive into the Central Solomons had begun in mid-February with the occupation, without a fight, of the Russells—a flyspeck complex of tiny islands some 30 miles northward of Guadalcanal. The next Allied objective was the small island of Rendova, only a little south of the larger island of New Georgia which was the tactical key to the operation. By 5th July the Rendova landing had been stabilized, and Carlson's famous Marine Raiders fought their way ashore at Rice Anchorage on the northwest coast of New Georgia. Their mission was to work their way down the island's shoreline to Enogai and Bairoko, positions from which they could inhibit Japanese supply from Vila to Munda. For obvious reasons the situation was excessively explosive afloat. Concentrated in a relatively small area Japanese garrisons and Allied challenging units faced each other. Both sides had to supply their troops, and the only way to supply them was by surface convoy. In addition, the Japanese were not the least content to allow the Allied thrusts to go uncontested, and twice powerful formations of the Tokyo Express came swooping down from Rabaul bent upon punishing the interlopers and throwing them out. Rear Admiral Teru Akiyama led the first of these punitive expeditions. On the night of 5–6th July, at the Battle of Kula Gulf, he was met, taken on, and whipped by Rear Admiral W. L. (Pug) Ainsworth commanding Task Group 36.1. Akiyama lost his life in this battle.

The second Japanese thrust fared somewhat better, although it was not successful in its mission. Commanded by Rear Admiral Shunji Izaki, a force of one light cruiser and nine destroyers headed down from Rabaul on 13th July. Their mission was primarily to reinforce and supply the Japanese garrison at Vila Stanmore, on Kolombangara. The Battle of Kolombangara was fought that night when Ainsworth once more raced to meet the enemy. Izaki's flagship, light cruiser *Jinjsu*, was sunk in the battle and once again the top Japanese commander, this time Izaki, was killed. Ainsworth suffered one DD sunk, three cruisers severely damaged by shell and torpedoes, and two more DDs badly bruised in collision. It was a stiff price to pay, but the Japanese supply and reinforcement mission was thwarted.

Although Arleigh Burke did not participate either in the Battle of Kula Gulf or the Battle of Kolombangara, both engagements were bright threads in the fabric of combat employment upon which he now entered. His first and most distressing discovery was that sustained duty up The Slot meant duty with virtually no sleep. The enemy was reinforcing and supplying his garrisons both by barge and destroyer. The barges were the *Daihatsu* type—metal-hulled, 41 to 49 feet long, weighing about 8 tons, diesel-powered for 8 knots, and capable of carrying up to 150 men or 15 tons of cargo. Their organic armament was two machine guns although, in combat zones, the Japanese frequently improvised additional armament even including light Army field pieces. The barges traveled at night and, by day, sheltered camouflaged in coves. They were duck soup for destroyers, and Arleigh Burke and his DD men chased down not a few and dispatched their human cargoes to join their honorable ancestors. But there was a fly even in that seemingly satisfying ointment, and it was the Japanese air.

For some reason which seems never to have been satisfactorily explained, at night the Japanese controlled the air above The Slot, right up to and through the days of the Gallant Squadron. The Allies put up a few Black Cats now and again to coordinate with the surface missions, but Allied aircraft in combat strength simply were not to be found in The Slot area after sunset. This was one of the root factors contributing to the incapacitating fatigue which cast a numbing palsy over The Slot operations of DD formations.

As ComDesSlot, Burke's destroyers, a hodge-podge lot of differing types drawn from various Divisions and never trained in operations together, were based on Tulagi. The run from this base to the then-active Slot area between Santa Isabel and New Georgia took a bit of steaming, and to conduct their night missions the DDs had to be under way often before dusk. Once in the combat zone they never failed to receive the professional attentions of Japanese aircraft. In terms of concrete damage inflicted these brushes were largely a stand-off: The DDs tried to hit the planes and couldn't; the planes tried to hit the DDs but didn't. But secondary honors—and they were important—went to the sons of Nippon. As Burke himself summed it up:

"There was no possibility of getting any sleep at night while we were under air attack, and there wasn't very much chance of getting sleep during the daytime because of the necessity for reading dispatches, getting into harbor, refueling fast, getting provisions, making plans, relieving ships, attending to a multitude of incidental chores, and getting going again in time to take maximum advantage of the hours of darkness on the 'happy hunting grounds.' "

This abrasive routine soon had the destroyermen worn to a dangerous state of nervous exhaustion and Commodore Burke welcomed with considerable relief a new kind of mission which promised at least a change of pace. Carlson's Marine Raiders, having reached the enemy positions at Bairoko, found themselves in deep trouble. Their supplies were running out and they had adequate supplies neither of food nor ammunition. They had a considerable number of wounded for whom they could not care, nor could they get the wounded out. Perhaps more important, they had not been able to make contact with the Marine units in the Munda area as had originally been visualized. The Japanese, overwhelmingly superior in numbers, had put up a fantastic resistance and the Marines needed supplies desperately.

Rear Admiral T. S. "Ping" Wilkinson, ComTaskForce 31, studied the situation. Our code designation for New Georgia was "Aperient." All code designations were made at Halsey's headquarters and whoever dreamed up the code words tended occasionally toward the pungent. Espiritu was "Base Button," Munda was "Jacodet," Rendova was "Dowser," and Viru Harbor was "Catsmeat"! It was wistfully hoped that these code designations were secret but everybody knew them and it is probable that the enemy did too.

New Georgia is an island about 45 miles long, bulging at the top, narrow at the shank, and lying roughly in a northwest-southeast line forming part of the southwestern margin of The Slot. On The Slot side an unbroken offshore coral reef extends the length of the island and between this reef and the shore a series of deep blue lagoons gives promise of a tropic paradise. Broken coral formations fringe the southwestern side and there is deep water, 600 fathoms having been sounded in Blanche Channel less than 1,500 yards from shore. The slow rollers of the Pacific lave the reefs and beaches, wild orchids abound, bird-size butterflies embroider colorful patterns in their erratic flight among a profusion of fragrant blossoms, and save when men and war intrude the setting suggests a true tropical idyll.

Ping Wilkinson's preoccupation was not with poems; it was with the brutal realities of no-quarter war. He decided to run up into Kula Gulf at night with four APDs [destroyers converted for troop or supply transport] escorted by six of Burke's destroyers. The APDs would stand as far inshore as was safe off Enogai Inlet, deliver their groceries, and embark Carlson's seriously wounded. While that was going on they would be screened on the seaward or Kolombangara side by DDs *Conway*, *Patterson*, *Maury*, *Gridley*, *Taylor*, and *Ellet*. However, before the little task force got under way *Maury* and *Gridley* had to be detached for other duty, leaving but four DDs to escort four APDs.

The approach through Kula Gulf was auspiciously made by moonlight but about midnight, as the formation neared its objective, complications arose. Because she was radar-equipped [the APDs were not] Burke's flagship, *Conway*, led the group. On the chart there were two points which looked pretty much alike: Bairoko Point and Enogai Point. On the radar screens there were ten or a dozen other points which looked the same. But at one point—Enogai—the Marines were waiting; at the other point—Bairoko—were the Japanese. From their charts and radar screens the officers of *Conway* had no idea which point was which. In the circumstances Arleigh Burke fell back upon the old sailing ship technique of deduced reckoning, frequently corrupted to "dead reckoning" by latterday mariners. This is a process of establishing one's probable position by a computation starting with the last reliably known position and making allowance for the speed of the vessel, the time run, the set and force of tide, currents, the wind, and any other known factors which might facilitate an accurate calculation. In the circumstances Burke knew little or nothing about the currents and their speed and set, but he ran a time check against his own course and speed and when his figures indicated that he should be off Enogai Point he turned boldly shoreward and started praying. Before too long a small boat was seen approaching, and it was manned by U.S. Marines. "We were really looked after that time," the Commodore admitted.

Burke estimated that about 3 hours would be required to unload the supplies and get the Marine wounded aboard the APDs. By that time, he was sure, the enemy would have become well aware of their presence. Why not, then, take advantage of the situation to bombard Bairoko? *Taylor* and *Ellet* were detailed for the bombardment mission, and all hands waited impatiently while the APDs continued to unload and embark wounded. At 0230 reports indicated that this operation would be completed in 20 or 30 minutes, and the Commodore headed his four escort DDs on a northerly course to make a final anti-submarine sweep into Kula Gulf thus clearing the way for the emergence of the APDs.

At 0245 a small-caliber Japanese battery on the eastern shore of Kolombangara opened on the formation. Although their shell fell short, Burke cheerfully accepted this notification that the enemy knew he was there. Accordingly he turned his formation by ship movements to a southwesterly course and detached *Taylor* and *Ellet* to undertake their bombardment, *Conway* and *Patterson*, meanwhile, being positioned to cover their sister ships should fire be drawn from the beach.

With *Taylor* and *Ellet* standing in toward the neck of Kula Gulf where they would be in range of shore batteries both on New Georgia and on Kolombangara, *Conway* and *Patterson* were taken under fire by several enemy batteries up to 6-inch. These batteries were to seaward of them and distant about 1,000 yards. At first this fire was not accurate and Burke assumed that the enemy was probing for him but hadn't yet found him. He decided not to reply unless forced to, but instead to use the enemy's muzzle flashes to pinpoint the location of his batteries so that all four DDs could hammer them on the way out of the Gulf. The Japanese, however, refused to play their part in this pleasant pastime. In a very short while *Conway* and *Patterson* were taking 6-inch bullets through their rigging, hits were registered on unimportant parts of the ships, and Commodore Burke was forced to fire counter-battery. The duel went on for about 15 minutes; some of the shore batteries were silenced; the destroyers suffered no personnel casualties. At the end of that time *Taylor* and *Ellet* began their bombardment of Bairoko, successfully silencing the enemy's counter-battery there.

While the guns were still hammering all around, the four APDs, having completed their job, came roaring out into Kula Gulf really making knots. From 23 their speed was boosted to 26 and finally 27 knots, and a chuckling Arleigh Burke, never so happy as when stimulated by the heady wine of speed and battle, had a hard time catching up with them. With his four escort destroyers he continued to plaster the enemy shore installations, primarily to draw the Japanese fire and distract them from the retiring APDs. In this design he was successful; the APDs escaped unscratched; by the time Burke pulled out the enemy fire had ceased although he was not fool enough to think that he had silenced all the Japanese guns. Undoubtedly he blasted some; the rest probably quit on the theory that they were just wasting ammunition and giving the Americans a useful "fix" for having a second go at another time. Overall, the mission was smartly performed, and Arleigh Burke had demonstrated his ability to think fast, act promptly, and shoot straight. While a tiny action in the vast complex of the South Pacific war, it was a significant event in the seasoning of "31-Knot-Burke."

As *Conway* and her consorts stood down toward Tulagi, Burke strolled out on a bridge wing and looked astern at his formation. The night was almost luminous, and he immediately noted one DD considerably out of formation and to Arleigh Burke it seemed that she was frisking about like a young colt. He immediately called the erring skipper on TBS and admonished him, "Mister, that's a destroyer you've got there; not a yo-yo!" Having watched the DD whip back into position the Commodore left the bridge, entered the emergency sea cabin immediately behind the pilot house, and fell to work on the mass of reports and forms which demanded completion after every action in which a gun was fired. Here he was found by the communications officer who stepped into the room and extended a decoded message from Ping Wilkinson: "*You will be prepared to lead a force of eight DDs up The Slot for a dawn bombardment of Munda tomorrow. The circumstances will be such that your bombardment must be delivered precisely at dawn, and your fire must register exactly on target.*"

Well, reflected the Commodore pushing back from the desk, locking his fingers at the back of his neck, and stretching a few of the kinks out of his arms and back, here's a pretty pickle! I don't know the thing before the first thing about Munda, and they want a pinpoint bombardment! The boss'll just have to tell me more! So he scribbled a message requesting permission to divert *Conway* to Koli Point on Guadalcanal for a personal conference with Admiral Wilkinson whose headquarters were there. Permission was granted and at the appropriate time *Conway* peeled off from the formation and in due course Commander Burke presented himself before his boss. Liaison officers of the Marines and the aviators were there, and at the meeting which ensued Arleigh Burke was placed in this picture:

For some time the Marines had been stalled in their efforts to capture Munda. The Japanese were dug in in depth, using both concrete pillboxes and underground defenses, and any determined effort by ground troops to dislodge them would be certain to produce frightful casualties to U.S. forces. Without some such effort however, the situation gave every promise of degenerating into an unacceptable stalemate. It had therefore been decided to stage a naval bombardment of the Japanese positions followed without interval by an intensive plastering by dive bombers. It was hoped thus to neutralize the enemy defenses long enough to permit the Marines to roll over them. However, as the Marine positions were within yards of the enemy positions, the most precise kind of shooting was called for. In addition, as the destroyer fire would have to be high trajectory and as the dive bombers would be prepared to swoop down the moment it ceased, exact timing was demanded to insure that the aircraft didn't fly down into the fire of the DDs. On a 45-degree elevation the maximum range of the 5-inch .38 was about 16,000 yards, but the effective range was only about 12,000. Lacking specific points of aim, and working with unreliable charts, the fire of the destroyers would have to be indirect, which meant high trajectory.

"What do you think, Arleigh? Can you take this one on?" asked the Admiral.

"Without question, sir, but I have one request. If it's all right with you I'd like to make a dummy run up there this afternoon and sort of case the situation. As you know, sir, our charts aren't much good, and I don't know anything about Munda."

"It's all right with me, Arleigh," the Admiral replied at once. "Do whatever you think necessary. But how long has it been since you've had any sleep, man? If you go back up there now you'll be up all night. You're just returning from one mission that's kept you on your feet far too long. Your task group will have to be under way for this one soon after midnight tonight. What're you going to do for rest? Pills'll only do it so long, you know. After that they're a hazard."

"I'll manage, sir. I figure if I start up there at once I can make some rough but realistic charts and maybe pick a few shoreside points for fire control. Then, instead of coming all the way back down to Tulagi, I'll meet the other fellows as they come up, give them the dope, and we can all take a steady strain." What Arleigh Burke did not tell the Admiral was that he had already been awake and working for close to 24 consecutive hours. While he might snatch a short nap as *Conway* dashed north again, it would likely be the only sleep he'd get in an otherwise solid 48 hours of critical tension and sustained pressure. It was the kind of beating that nerves, muscles and brain simply could not tolerate for long, and Burke was to find this out.

"Well, I guess that about wraps it up, gentlemen," said the Admiral concluding the conference. "Tell the Marines to 'saddle up,' and we'll blast a path for them—and good hunting to all of you!"

Burke made his maps and drew up his plans. The bombardment was successful and the Marines eventually captured Munda. But while this was being accomplished other decisions far from Arleigh Burke's liking were being taken at Headquarters, ComSoPac. Division 44 had now been operating up The Slot for 3 consecutive weeks. That was considerably longer than individual ships or ship formations had found it possible to stand the pressure and still perform efficiently. Admiral Halsey, a seasoned and far-sighted Commander, labored under no illusions in this matter. He knew that his ships and men must be rested before one or both cracked up. In consequence, when Commodore Burke returned from the Munda bombardment he found awaiting him at Tulagi an order for DesDiv-44 to return to Espiritu for rest, recreation and, possibly, refit.

This order did not jibe with Burke's notions. Having once gotten into the area of major combat, he wasn't to be dug out so easily. So he sought and received permission from Wilkinson to change over to destroyer *Maury*, and when DesDiv-44 sailed toward Espiritu they left the Division Commodore behind. Perhaps, too, it was only coincidence that nobody got around to the obvious duty of notifying headquarters of what had happened.

Through this bit of hanky-panky Burke managed to stay in the forward area for a few more days. Then came a peremptory ukase by despatch from the "Big Admiral" himself: *"Commander Burke will return to Espiritu on or before 5th August—period!"*

Complying with this unequivocal order, Wilkinson detached Burke on 3rd August and ordered him to Espiritu. Afterward even Burke admitted that Halsey took him out of the game just in time. While waiting at Henderson Field on Guadalcanal for air transportation to Espiritu the Commodore of Division 44 was so exhausted that he fell asleep sitting bolt upright, and slept for 8 hours in that position. Climbing stiffly aboard a plane when one finally made room for him, he instantly fell asleep once more, stretched out uncomfortably on top of a hard and knobby gas tank, and had to be awakened when the plane set down. The enemy couldn't lick Arleigh Burke, but physical and nervous exhaustion did—temporarily.

Three pleasant things happened to Burke during his brief stay at Espiritu and at Noumea where he went to join his new flagship. First, he picked up his fourth stripe and became *Captain* Arleigh Burke. Second, he was appointed ComDesRon-12, which brought a formation of eight DDs under his direct command. And third, he received the good news of the Battle of Vella Gulf.

The hero of the Battle of Vella Gulf—and very properly so—was Commander Frederick Moosebrugger, who had arrived at Tulagi as ComDesDiv-12 shortly before Burke's departure therefrom and who, at the battle, commanded a formation composed of three ships of Des-Div-12 and three of DesDiv-15. Some of these vessels had been in Burke's formations when he was ComDesSlot. The plan which Moosebrugger followed in fighting the Battle of Vella Gulf was Arleigh Burke's. Before he left the area Burke had developed the doctrine of the one-two punch—surprise torpedo attack backed up by gunfire covering a second torpedo attack—and this plan was specifically aimed at dealing with the "Tokyo Express" formations which the Japanese were sending down The Slot to reinforce and supply their troops in the Central Solomons. With three cruisers critically damaged at the Battle of Kolombangara, Wilkinson had to fall back on DDs for operations of a magnitude beyond their usually accepted capacity. In his absence Burke's plan was handed to Moosebrugger for study. That officer recognized its essential simplicity and strength, and after making appropriate geographical and navigational changes he adopted it in detail when, on 5th August, he was ordered by Admiral Wilkinson to lead his formation via Gizo Strait to Vella Gulf, there to intercept and destroy a high speed "Tokyo Express" formation of four of the most modern destroyers in the Imperial Japanese Navy. The fact that Moosebrugger studied, analyzed, and finally adopted Arleigh Burke's plan does not mean that "Moose" Moosebrugger was incapable of developing a plan of his own, and a good one too. It simply meant that Moose, having been handed what he considered to be a good plan, was big enough to adopt it without quibble, and go in and do a job.

The resultant battle, which was a lurid affair, went surprisingly nearly as planned by Burke and Moosebrugger. Enemy destroyers *Hagikaze*, *Arashi*, and *Kawakaze*, leading the Japanese formation, were blasted to the bottom primarily by the surprise torpedo attacks which were the salient features of the plan. With them went some 1,500 sailors and their soldier passengers. Only the guard destroyer, *Shigure*, crammed full of ammunition, survived to scamper back to Bougainville and report the debacle to the Japanese high command. There were no U.S. casualties, not even slightly wounded. Although regretting his own absence from the Battle of Vella Gulf, Arleigh Burke was greatly heartened by this demonstration of the application of his doctrine, and he wrote of Moosebrugger's performance "It was one of the most beautiful attacks that anybody has made in the whole war." Burke's own opportunity to apply his doctrine against an exactly matching enemy force was only months away, but when that opportunity came he even eclipsed Moosebrugger's champion performance. At Cape St. George, employing exactly the same one-two punch doctrine, Burke not only swept the enemy from the sea, but fought the "perfect battle"—an accolade hard indeed to win from crusty Admirals and Vice Admirals who sit in judgment at the Naval War College, and approach the whole thing on the premise that "it can't be done"! After all, as they could point out in justification of this attitude, it hadn't been done since Trafalgar.

As ComDesRon-12 Captain Burke flew his numbered burgee in destroyer *Farenholt* (Commander E. T. Seaward, USN), and he did not find the duty greatly to his liking although he continued to experiment and, perhaps, added a cubit to the sum of combat seasoning which he was to take to the blue-ribbon Squadron short months later. The Commodore asked once more for duty up The Slot and his request was granted, but the operational pattern proved frustrating. The thing that infuriated Arleigh Burke and sent morale plummeting was that they could never find anything really worthwhile to hit. The Japs were playing it very close to the vest. Now and then DesRon-12 would come upon a few loaded barges making their way down from Choiseul to Kolombangara, or a small group of empty barges returning over the same route. These, of course, were sunk, but it was the kind of chore hardly worth the mettle of high-spirited destroyermen, and not calculated to keep them keen.

In their nightly excursions up The Slot, whether or not they found targets, the Squadron always could count on an all-night heckling by Japanese air. A little later on this was made more onerous by an addition to the Squadron's duty. They were assigned to escort supply and reinforcement convoys to Vella La Vella, Rendova, and Munda. That's when they discovered that the Japs were running their own stuff down The Slot on the same nights that Squadron 12 was realistically immobilized by the duty of escorting Allied convoys in the opposite direction. More, they soon discovered that despite the consistently helpful tips from the coast watchers, the Japanese were handling their operations with amazing speed. Upon receipt of information which might permit an interception, unless Squadron 12 was already in a position and a condition of readiness permitting a high-speed dash toward the target instantly, it was an even-money bet that the target would be gone by the time they got there. This led to a constant struggle to refuel faster and get under way more quickly, and these pressures and tensions took their toll.

Arleigh Burke never gave up trying to lick the problem. Heckled by enemy air at night, jumped by strong Nipponese air formations in the daytime, and with the brief hours spent in port a wild scramble of "all hands" to refuel, load stores and ammo, and get going again in the shortest possible time, one of the Commodore's most pressing problems was to find a condition of readiness which would protect the ships from disaster and still permit the weary crews to get the rest they must have if they were to fight. His first answer to this was "Condition Easy" in which the battery was only partially manned permitting some of the men to sleep. But Condition Easy soon went by the board when a strong Japanese air attack developed in just 2 minutes. Radar warning was tardy, and some of the ships were not quite ready when the enemy planes came in. Burke immediately decided that he couldn't afford to take such a chance. He tried an alternate system of allowing whole ships to stand easy and rest while the remaining ships of the formation stood guard on the alert. But this was not an adequate solution of the terrible problem of fatigue and exhaustion and, indeed, none ever was found. Later on, in DesRon-23, Burke was to come up with "Condition One-Easy" which was about as close as anyone ever came to resolving this problem of mixing oil and water, but even Condition One-Easy was a tongue-in-cheek compromise of values, laced with a large hunk of hope that the enemy's intentions would be accurately defined and his movements reliably forecast.

As for bringing the Japanese to battle, DesRon-12 just simply couldn't manage it. They tried. They tried everything in the book— by going around Vella La Vella, by going around Kolombangara— they even tried the old mousetrap trick, sending a small decoy force to the south as bait, and holding a stronger force to the north to jump the Japs when they should start chasing the decoys. But Mr. Tojo's little boys weren't playing honorable games, thank you too much! and nary an engagement of any stature could Arleigh Burke set up.

Along about this time, although he certainly didn't know it nor did Arleigh Burke, time was beginning to run out for Rosey Gillan as Commodore of DesRon-23. Near the end of September Captain Burke and DesRon-12 had been on Slot duty close to 5 successive weeks. It was more than flesh and blood could take, and the Squadron was ordered back to Espiritu for overhaul and rest. This was to be followed by a few weeks of training after which the whole Squadron was to go to

Sydney for further rest. When those orders became known there was
much justified jubilation in the little ships, and at many boisterous
sessions below decks plans were conceived for an order of shoreside
recreation the magnitude of which was colossal but was bounded principally north, east, south, and west by—*women.*

As part of Task Force 39 *Farenholt* arrived Sydney on 19th October. As soon as the special underway detail was secured Arleigh
Burke called his small staff into conference. At the time the staff consisted of three young officers.

"Boys," he told them, "I've got some orders for you. I want you to
go ashore, and I want you to *stay* ashore—with one reservation: I
want one of you—it doesn't make any difference which one, and it
doesn't always have to be the same one—to be back aboard by 0800
every morning to read dispatches and be available for anything that
might need doing. I expect, myself, to be on board from 0800 until
early afternoon each day. You all understand?"

"Yes, *sir!*"

"One more thing, then. I'll probably be ashore myself most evenings.
But get this, you guys: *when I'm ashore I don't want to be disturbed
about anything*—not *anything*—unless it's really vital. Now get going
and have fun, but try to stay out of trouble!"

That evening Captain Burke spruced himself up a bit and, at an
appropriate hour, presented himself at a party which Tip Merrill was
giving for senior officers. The affair was quiet and relaxing. Along
about 1930 Burke sat chatting with Merrill, sipping a whisky-soda,
and well on the way to unwinding some of the springs which had been
wound much too tight during the preceding 6 months. But as he talked
the Captain had the uneasy feeling that someone was staring at him
intently. He looked around and saw no one, but a glance over his
shoulder provided the answer. One of his young staff officers stood at
his elbow, holding a dispatch. The Commodore was mildly annoyed,
and made an impatient gesture. "I thought I told you fellows not to
bother me with ship's business when I was on the beach!" he snapped.

"Sir," said the staffer, "you said not to bother you unless it was
important. I think you'll find this dispatch important, sir."

Burke took the message and read it. It was important. Rosey Gillan
had been relieved as Commodore of Destroyer Squadron 23. Captain
Arleigh Burke was hereby detached as ComDesRon-12. He would get
the earliest available air transportation to Espiritu, there to take command of DesRon-23 and, with Cruiser Division 12, proceed to Guadalcanal prepared for action.

Captain Burke's pulse leaped and his nerves tingled as he handed
the dispatch to Admiral Merrill. This meant *big* action! They weren't

sending a covey of cruisers and destroyers up The Slot for a college regatta. Tip Merrill handed the dispatch back with a smile. He'd known what was in the wind for quite some time, and he knew that he and his Task Force 39 were to play major roles in the upcoming action. As for Burke's appointment as ComDesRon-23, Tip Merrill had played a more active part in that selection than any other man. It was Merrill who gave Arleigh his big break and in so doing he showed himself an A-Number-One gentleman and an astute naval officer.

Burke rose and excused himself to go off and hunt air transportation to Espiritu. Merrill wished him a fair breeze and said, "I'll be seeing you, Arleigh." At 5 o'clock the next morning Arleigh Burke was in the air, once more headed north. His rest and recreation at Sydney had lasted about 12 hours, but that was the least of his concerns. He felt in his heart that this time the *blue* chips were going down for one big Swede named Bjorkegren, and although he now sailed as Burke he sailed, and he sailed toward battle. That was the important thing.

8

Mosaic in Fatigue and Frustration

~~~~~~

The delicate young man wearing the uniform and insignia of a Commander in the United States Navy stood patiently before the wicketed window of a ticket seller in the railroad station at Miami, and waited quietly until it should please that functionary to notice him. Long exposure to the Caribbean sun had left the officer deeply tanned. Although slight of figure his carriage was erect without giving an impression of tautness; he wore a small black mustache carefully trimmed; he created a feeling of neat precision.

"Yes, sir, what can I do for you?" After a minutes-long interval the ticket seller was back in business.

"I'd like a ticket and a lower berth to Orange, Texas, if it's available," the Commander told him.

The ticket seller turned to a well-pawed book of schedules and tables which he examined with bored impatience before announcing, "No sleepers on that run. No chair cars, neither. But I can sell you a ticket. Round trip?"

"One way, please. Incidentally," added the officer as the railroad man tore a segment from a long bellows of mottled green ticket and thumped it through his date stamp, "just where is Orange? I haven't been able to find anyone who knows."

"Sonny," said the man inclining his head forward and looking with martyred resignation over the tops of his thick-lensed spectacles, "don't ask me that! Th' things people come up here and ask me all day, you'd think I was a swami 'r somethin'! All I know, it's on th' railroad. An' if you get behind th' right engine, this ticket'll get you there. Now let's see . . . that'll be twelve-forty-six plus two-thirty-two, plus sixty-one . . . an' th' tax'll be . . ." His voice trailed off as he computed the total fare upon completion of which computation Commander Luther K. "Brute" Reynolds paid the demanded tariff, put the ticket carefully away in a compartment of his wallet, and sought the information booth to learn how many hours or minutes he might have until train time, and pick up any other available information about Orange. In a crabwise sort of fashion the Brute was off to the wars.

Other of his colleagues had "fit the Battle of Orange" before Reynolds, but none had brought to it the incandescence of hope which burned in his breast, and none had met with more infuriating frustrations than awaited him. Commander Reynolds, a product of the Deep South, had what seemed to him a few perfectly normal desires. After a 20-month tour of duty he had been detached from command of *U.S.S. Barry* (DD-248), one of the old World War I 1,200-ton four-pipers working on the Caribbean and Panama Sea Frontier. He was finally being given command of a brand new and powerful 2,000-tonner— *U.S.S. Charles Ausburne* (DD 511), now awaiting him at the Consolidated yards. That was fine; he was happy for the recognition which this new command implied. Indeed, it was an *occasion* in his plodding progress over the Navy's shallow and long chord of advancement from low to high degree. As such he wanted to make it memorable, graceful indeed. For one thing, after his extended tour afloat, he'd like to be comfortable ashore while he attended to the business of commissioning and assuming command of his new vessel. For another, he would like to have Mrs. Reynolds join him and share in the tingling experience of accepting a ship in the name of the United States Navy, and readying her to play a part in the defeat of the nation's enemies at sea. Visions such as these, like the sugarplums of Christmas fantasy, danced in the head of Commander Luther Kendrick Reynolds, USN, as his cinder-whipped train clanked and clunked toward Orange, Texas early in October, 1942.

Although he couldn't be sure, the nearer he drew to Orange the more reflection led him to suspect that his visions of comfort and a few weeks of gracious living ashore with his wife might have even less substance than the legendary goodies of the Yuletide.

The Brute's long ordeal by day coach ended at 6 o'clock on a Saturday night when he descended stiffly to the station platform at Orange and, carrying a suitcase in either hand, trudged off in search of a taxi. He soon discovered that no disengaged cab was to be had, so he planted himself defiantly in front of one already occupied and demanded to be taken aboard.

The occupant was a jovial Texas type who stood on no ceremony. He stuck his hand out as the Commander climbed into the cab and boomed, "Name's Josh Bunting. Work at th' shipyard."

"I'm Reynolds," the Brute told him. "I'd appreciate it if you'd drop me off at the hotel."

"Th' *New Holland?* Why?" demanded the stranger bluntly.

"To get a room, of course," Brute told him with a flick of barbed asperity. "I've come to take command of *Charles Ausburne* when she's ready. Naturally I've got to have a place to stay . . ."

"No kiddin'!" rejoined his companion with heightened interest. "Say, I'm working on that ship myself. But you don't want to waste time going to th' *New Holland*. It's Saturday night. You'll never get a room."

"Well, some other hotel then," suggested Reynolds.

"*Ain't* no other hotel," said Mr. Bunting laconically. "Tell ya' what cha' do: My missus is away for th' week end. You come home and bunk with me 'til Monday; then maybe one of th' big shots at th' Yard can get y' into th' *New Holland*."

Brute accepted the invitation; there seemed no other course. On Monday he reported in, and actually did manage to get a room at the *New Holland*. As he surveyed his quarters he decided that his memory wasn't nearly long enough to embrace the golden past when this haven for the tired traveler had won the proud qualifying adjective of "New." The lobby especially fascinated him. It was peopled principally by rangy, white-whiskered Texans who seemed to have nothing to do, all day to do it in, and preferred to do it at the *New Holland* and to the accompaniment of their ringing shots of tobacco juice registering on the numerous, magnum-sized brass cuspidors liberally distributed around the premises. Their accuracy of range and deflection caught the Brute's professional eye and he wondered whether they ever practiced firing salvos. But his next thought shrank still further the dream of fleeting luxury which he had entertained on his way to Orange. What a hell of a place into which to bring Dot, he moaned inwardly. Dot was his wife. However, reflection fortified his conviction that they'd be happier together no matter how primitive the accommodations, so he arranged for her to come on at her convenience.

In a way it might be said that the postmaster of the small but thriving community of Water Valley, Mississippi (population 6,000) put a stamp on young Luther Kendrick Reynolds and mailed him off to the United States Naval Academy. And none too soon, for the postmaster had another stamp which might have taken Reynolds to West Point, had he dawdled in making up his mind.

In 1905 when Brute Reynolds was born, Water Valley was a microcosm lying at the marge of the Illinois Central Railroad. In its shops all the rolling stock of the road including the locomotives was completely overhauled and rebuilt, and virtually every phase of the economic and social structures of the town reflected the I.C. one way or another. The boy's father, Luther Christian Reynolds, was a locomotive engineer on "the Central" and a veteran of the Spanish American

War. His mother, Frances Pauline Kendrick before her marriage, had been a schoolteacher. Luther Christian was a Methodist of English-French extraction. His wife, of predominantly British ancestry, held to the Christian church and was active in church work. Her son followed in her doctrinal trend, but his religious compulsions were not sufficiently strong to impel him to conduct divine services as Captain of *Charlie Ausburne*. He attended, but left the direction of services in other hands.

Prior to entering the Naval Academy the boy's life followed the pleasantly somnolent pattern of pastoral Mississippi. He hunted and fished with his father, visited grandparents on both paternal and maternal sides of the family living on remote farms, and at age 10 managed to fall out of a peach tree achieving a permanently if only slightly crooked left arm in consequence. The Navy medics didn't catch up with it until long after he'd achieved such rank that a stiff arm no longer mattered.

The turning point in the life of Luther K. Reynolds came one soft afternoon in spring, 1921. On his way home from school he stopped by the Post Office to collect the family mail, and fell to chatting with the postmaster, a former locomotive engineer and close friend of his father's.

"Luther, you're a likely looking young sprout. What are your plans for the future?"

"Gee, I don't know, exactly . . . I've been thinking about Mississippi State and a course in electrical engineering . . ."

"Have you ever thought about Annapolis . . . ?"

"Gee, yes, I guess so . . . but . . ."

"Or West Point?" pressed the postmaster. "I happen to know that there are appointments open for both, and either one would be a fine career . . ."

"That's what my uncle's always telling me . . . Dad too . . ."

"When do you graduate from high school, son?"

"June, 1923."

"M-m-m-m! Well, that would rule out th' Navy. The Naval Academy appointment is for 1922—next year. The West Point one's for 1923 . . ."

"I sort of like the Navy, though," said the boy thoughtfully. "I've been following their football team. They're tops."

"But how could you make it—th' time, I mean?"

"Well, sir, I could take extra classes—maybe cover two years' work in one . . ."

"Luther, you're a smart boy! An' by golly, I've got faith in you! If you can graduate from high school next year, I'll see to it that you get an appointment to the United States Naval Academy. Is it a deal?"

"Yes, sir—I'll try . . ."

Young Reynolds entered Annapolis in 1922 and graduated 3rd June, 1926. Unlike some of his future colleagues he had no trouble with math nor, indeed, any of the rest of the Annapolis curriculum. He was studious and reserved by nature, and his primary regret at the Academy was that his weight of only 120 pounds kept him on the side-lines of the more rugged sports. His academic performance was so meritorious that, in 1938, he was selected to return to Annapolis as an Instructor in Fundamental Seamanship and Navigation. Yet one would have had to burrow deep to discover the measure of the mark which the Naval Academy or, for that matter, the Navy itself made on Brute Reynolds. In time, through study and practice, he became a smooth technician in the naval art. He subscribed to the fundamental tenets of the Navy belief and doctrine, and he observed the outward forms of the service. But he was always slow to reveal his inner thinking; always reserved; never "pushy." At times, even, he seemed reluctant to his colleagues. In any case, whatever the deep psychological springs, the Brute kept them to himself. As skipper of Arleigh Burke's flag boat he turned in a performance which left nothing to be desired. Nothing, that is, if you're graceful about accepting ham sandwiches as a sub-stitute for pizza. But what he thought and felt about fundamental values remained locked in his own breast. Although not timid in action, and demonstrably ready to exchange sizzling verbal salvos with both Commodores Burke and Gillan when he disagreed with them, there was a certain over-all patina of diffidence upon the man. Outwardly he did not manifest the pugnacity which often is a concomitant of small stature in the male, an overcompensation for the physical derelictions of nature. He was to share fully in the *mystique* of DesRon-23, enter-ing it at the threshold of professional competence, which was its least common denominator. Whether his comprehension of the *mystique* was, in fact, more profound, none was to know. For the Brute had about him a touch of the ivory tower, and he vastly preferred to keep his own counsel.

Mrs. Reynolds, the former Dorothy Hopkins, of Alexandria, Vir-ginia, arrived at Orange in due season. Her fastidious husband escorted her, with marked impatience, through the *New Holland*'s spittoon-decorated lobby which he had christened "The Hall of the Ringing Gaboons," and up to the Presidential Suite which he had been for-tunate enough to engage for the occasion. Other than its elegant name, the Presidential Suite's principal boast was that it contained a private bath. The suite was on a corner. The vista from the windows on one side presented the enchanting prospect of an extensive and dank coal yard. From the other side were to be observed the adjacent railroad tracks, and Commander and Mrs. Reynolds soon discovered that un- molested rest was to be a stranger to them for some time. Most of the railroad switching was done beneath their windows at night. It would have required only the addition of "Moanin' Maggie," the bellowing San Francisco fog signal, to top off the tintinnabulation of the switch- engine bells, and render the nights completely hideous instead of only three quarters so. The Reynoldses stuck it out, however, and stood in line each evening hoping to get dinner at the Mary Anne Restaurant, which they found the only acceptable eating establishment in Orange. The joker in *that* little woodpile was that a great many other people in this boom town had made the same discovery, and as often as not Mary Anne ran out of food while numerous hopeful patrons including Commander and Mrs. Reynolds remained unfed. The Brute had just about reached the conclusion that the situation was intolerable and that his wife should return home, when their more annoying problems were solved by the finding of an available furnished apartment. It was on the second floor over a garage, but it was quiet at night and they could prepare meals to suit their individual tastes. They were content and, indeed, came to look upon an occasional trip over the Sabine into Louisiana for an especially succulent meal or a spot of sportive gambling as all the recreation needed to mitigate the considerable physical and nervous tension under which the prospective Captain of *Charlie Ausburne* was functioning.

On the afternoon of Tuesday, 24th November, 1942, *U.S.S. Charles Ausburne* was placed in commission as a fighting ship of the United States Navy by Captain J. M. Schelling, USN, retired. She was moored with her starboard side to the City Dock at Orange. At 1513 that same afternoon Commander Reynolds read his orders and assumed command. Exactly 3 minutes later the watch was posted and *Charlie Ausburne* was in business—the dimly disturbing business of killing or being killed.

In the luck of the draw for rated and enlisted personnel Brute Rey- nolds was a bit more fortunate than some of his colleagues in DesRon- 23. *Ausburne*'s crew was assembled at the Navy Receiving Station in New Orleans, and did not come aboard until the night before commis- sioning. While the majority of the men were green and just out of boot camp, there was among them a leavening of veterans from the battles of Midway, the Coral Sea, Tassafaronga, and the Java Sea. This core of seasoned men exerted both a cohesive and a steadying influence which enabled *Ausburne* to "shake down" somewhat more expeditiously than otherwise might have been possible. This necessary evolution was accomplished in Guantánamo Bay and adjacent waters, where conditions permitted working around the clock.

In terms of experience at sea *Ausburne*'s officer roster was not too impressive, and until she arrived at Guantánamo where other officers could be qualified for OOD duty, the Captain, "exec," and gunnery officer stood OOO watches. The "exec" was a tireless lieutenant commander named Joseph W. Koenig. He was an officer of the regular Navy, Academy class of 1933, and was liked by the crew despite the fact that he worked them 24 hours a day every day. He was a "can do" type and remained with *Ausburne* until July, 1943 when, like so many of his kind in those days when the Navy was desperately in need of qualified command personnel, he was detached to become Captain of a DD of his own. The command escalator had been sharply speeded up, and a competent "exec" rarely stayed long in a DD in the Number 2 spot.

The gunnery officer was Lieutenant Henry J. Ereckson, Jr., USN. "Ereck," a Texan with all the stigmata of tranquil nerves, unhurried movement and deliberate drawl, was to move up to "exec" and navigator on Joe Koenig's detachment. As navigator he was to distinguish himself by leading the Squadron by night and at boiling speed through the tricky waters of The Slot and contiguous island straits. He was a gifted night radar navigator, and chalked up many a "well done" from a relieved Commodore at the safe end of a perilous night passage. Burke paid tribute to Ereckson's skill in one of his battle reports.

Lieutenant Otis Parker, USN, the engineering officer was another Texan and a "mustang." He was an ex-chief machinist, and although not required to be qualified as OOD he was deeply interested in what went on at the bridge end of the ship. At his own request he was taught to keep station, work a maneuvering board, and the other arts needed for OOD qualification which he achieved. His assistant, who took over as Chief on Parker's detachment, was still another Texan—Lieutenant (jg) Joseph H. Gray, USNR, from Houston. Despite constant high-speed running and gunfire with consequent steam leaks and minor engineering casualties, they kept *Charlie Ausburne*'s propulsion plant always ready and able to answer bells. She was the only vessel in the Squadron never to miss a sortie through the inability of her engineering department to respond to the call for steam.

Upon Ereck's elevation Lieutenant (jg) John F. Briggs, Jr., USN, from White Plains, New York, moved into the gun boss spot. Assisting him were Lieutenant (jg) Vincent M. Dickerson, USNR, from Piedmont, Oklahoma; and Lieutenant (jg) Earl B. Shaw, USNR, in charge of the 90-mm and 20-mm batteries, respectively. Ensign Rodney W. Smith, USNR, from Rochester, New York, was a calm torpedo officer. Lieutenant Bob Grayson, USNR, from Fremont, Ohio, had worked in the Texas oil fields prior to the war, and this experience helped him considerably in his duties as first lieutenant and damage control officer. Communications officer and OOD during general quarters was Lieutenant Corwin R. Lockwood, USNR, an efficient and hard working young man from Toledo, Ohio.

The ship's doctor, Lieutenant (jg) William H. Harris, USNR, (MC), from New Orleans, very nearly caused *Ausburne* to breach the rules of war. He became fascinated by the mysterious rites which went forward in CIC, and one night in the Solomons a horrified Captain Reynolds walked into CIC to find "Doc" Harris happily helping with the current chore of plotting the positions of enemy targets.

"What th' hell are *you* doing here?" demanded the Skipper.

"Nothing, Captain—just helping the boys with a bit of plotting."

"Doc," said the Captain, "I'm surprised at you, and I'm not at all pleased! Don't you know that, as Medical Officer, your activities are restricted to the medical department by the international rules of war?"

"I hadn't known it, sir."

"Well, you know it now, so get out of here and *stay* out!"

The Doc departed to weep on the shoulder of Ensign Jack Cameron, USNR, the supply officer from Detroit. The two had at least one thing in common: they both wanted to fight, but their jobs wouldn't let them.

Thus the officers of *Charles Ausburne*. They were no better, and certainly they were no worse than their counterparts in the other ships of the Squadron. The thing that was to set them apart from their opposite numbers in other Squadrons was simply this: with all their inexperience they had the capacity to respond to inspired leadership. Until that leadership was given them at Squadron level they were an average bunch of run-of-mine destroyer officers, and *Ausburne* was an average DD of her class. But once that leadership appeared in the person of 31-Knot-Burke its catalytic action precipitated all of the talents latent but unobserved in these men, and they became a hard-hitting, professional team. This mysterious and, upon contemplation, somewhat awesome transformation was to take place in every ship of Destroyer Squadron 23 in the crucible of the South Pacific. Leadership and battle were the triphammers which pounded well-meaning but groping amateurs into keen professionals.

New Year's Day, 1943, found *Ausburne* at New Orleans, and effervescent Ensign Shaw writing up the deck log at 1 o'clock in the morning. Looking out over the tranquil harbor of the Crescent City his youthful imagination was stirred to emotions of patriotism and visions of derring-do afloat which he was sure awaited his gallant ship. Swept upward upon the crest of his soaring spirit he achieved such inspiration (and disregard for Navy protocol) that he proceeded to write up the whole log in his own approximation of iambic pentameter ending with the stirring asseveration

We're small in number and in size
But our fighting spirit never dies!

Ah, quake, you fighting men of Nippon! For *Charlie Ausburne*'s on the way to war, and her young men are strumming the lute of David and singing songs of defiance!

At 1451 hours on the tranquil afternoon of Monday, 6th June, 1943, *U.S.S. Foote,* turning 139.97 revolutions, on one boiler, two generators, plant cross-connected, using 850 degrees superheat and electric auxiliaries with no duplication, bisected the equator at longitude 87°—29'—00" West. There was a reason why she steamed as she did. Commodore Gillan had run careful tests, and had discovered this to be the most economical engineering combination so far as fuel consumption was concerned. In this and other engineering matters Rosey Gillan made his contribution to the United States Navy.

Foote's captain, Lieutenant Commander Alston Ramsay, had time only for a fleeting look across the sparkling sea at tanker *White Plains* which they were escorting toward Noumea, and the other escort destroyer, *Charles Ausburne.* Then his attention was drawn back aboard his own vessel as *Neptunus Rex* came aboard over the bow and presented the skipper with a royal protest for bringing so many pollywogs into the King's watery domain. The skipper apologized but reminded the seaweed-festooned monarch that the war was making everything difficult, and suggested that he get on with the business of initiation which would transform the green and frightened pollywogs into fearless shellbacks of the seven seas. The suggestion was welcomed, and the initiation proceeded amid much horseplay and hilarity. Looking down from the bridge was a plethora of brass, for Commodore Gillan was riding in *Foote* as was her original skipper, Commander Bernard L. (Count) Austin.

Austin had assumed command of *Foote* at 1510 hours on the bitterly cold afternoon of Tuesday, 22nd December, 1942, and 2 minutes later the watch was set. On the occasion *Foote,* a Bath boat, was moored port side to Pier 1 West, Boston Navy Yard where she had been delivered by civilian Captain George C. Stacey and a contractor's crew augmented by a Navy armed guard. The Count had remained in command but briefly. At 2045 on Thursday, 20th May, 1943, with *Foote* moored at Norfolk, there was a double ceremony. Commander Austin read his dispatch orders making him ComDesDiv-46 of DesRon-23, after which Lieutenant Commander Ramsay read his dispatch orders making him Captain of *Foote* in Austin's place. Eventually *Foote* came to Balboa, Canal Zone, where she joined *Ausburne,* picked up *White Plains,* and on 4th June the three ships got under way for the hot war in the Solomons.

The voyage toward Noumea was without spectacular incident. On 10th June, at 0800, *Foote* started fueling from the tanker. At 1000 both hose and hawser parted, and the operation was delayed until the following day when 66,000 gallons of fuel were transferred safely to the DD. The cause of the original failure was that *White Plains* was not properly fitted for this evolution. On the 12th *Ausburne* bore up alongside the oiler and took 82,500 gallons successfully, and steady steaming brought Amadee Light visible at 1000 hours on the morning of Tuesday, 28th June. In another hour they had entered Bulari Passage and stood in toward Noumea, New Caledonia. At 1430 both DDs tied up alongside *U.S.S. Whitney,* destroyer repair vessel, and *Ausburne* was granted a 2-day availability for incidental repairs. Looking around the harbor Brute Reynolds noted that *Dyson* was present, and he was planning a session with Roy Gano when, almost while his back was turned, it seemed, *Dyson* stood out to join Task Group 36.9. Aboard *Foote* Lieutenant Commander M. S. Schmidling, USN, her "exec," had the harbor routines firmly in hand. Captain Ramsay ducked below to his quarters and took time out for a brief letter to his wife back in the pleasant city of Charlotte, North Carolina:

Dear Hazel:

I can't tell you much but, at last, here we are where maybe we can do some good. The ship performed beautifully. I am well . . .

First the ship; then the Captain. It's the Navy way—the way of the sea. By the time darkness settled all at Noumea knew that two more eagles and their boss (pro tem) had tumbled into the tropic nest.

When Commodore Gillan reached Noumea several vessels of his Squadron, among them *Claxton* and *Stanly,* already were in the area and actively engaged up around Espiritu. In a way *Stanly* (DD-478) was the bastard of the Squadron, which was no reflection upon the ship, her Captain, or her crew. The other seven ships of "23" had been built either at the Bath Iron Works, in Maine, or Consolidated Steel, in Texas. Built at the Navy Yard, Charleston, South Carolina, and commissioned on 15th October, 1942, *Stanly* differed from her sisters in that she was one of a small experimental group of aircraft-carrying destroyers. She had a plane catapult abaft her stacks and stowage space for bombs and gasoline. In tests during shakedown the innovations did not prove practicable, and during her post-shakedown yard availability the catapult was removed and replaced by two additional 5-inch guns. Also she got another set of torpedo tubes on the fantail, which made her the most potent ship in the Squadron armament-wise. Unfortunately, however, temperamental boilers sent her frequently in quest of engineering availability, and while she was to fight the Battle of Empress Augusta Bay she was out of a good many other actions and missed the Squadron's crowning performance at the Battle of Cape St. George.

Stanly's skipper, tall and handsome Commander Robert Cavenagh, married to the former Mabel M. Goodyear, of Cleveland, was the only one of the Squadron's ranking officers to have exercised command in submarines. During 1936, 1937, and 1938 he served consecutively in *U.S.S. S-39*, and *U.S.S. S-37* of Submarine Division 10, Squadron 5 of the Asiatic Fleet, finally coming to command in March, 1938, as Captain of *U.S.S. S-41*. Thus, after service in *Stanly*, he had experience both of the stealthy stalkers of the ocean depths, and their arch enemies, the hunter-killer destroyers on the surface.

Bob Cavenagh was a personally charming officer who exhibited diplomatic talents which were to win him special recognition in his assignment as Rear Admiral to be U.S. Naval Attaché at London. He had a medium-slim figure, wavy dark brown hair, attention-compelling shaggy eyebrows, and his straight carriage was italicized by his over-6-foot height. Although he was in the Annapolis class of 1926 with other future skippers of Squadron 23, he neither sought nor achieved a great closeness to these comrades. Scholastically he stood near the top of his class and graduated with a sufficient numerical lead over his fellows to make him senior skipper of "23" and, eventually, ComDes-Div-46 upon Austin's detachment. Commander Cavenagh smiled easily and warmly. He was never heard to make a derogatory remark about a fellow officer. When he was critical—and he was, on occasion—he kept it to himself. He was a technically competent Captain and a good leader, although a long way from the forceful and dashing pattern of Arleigh Burke.

Stanly came to the wars without fuss or fanfare. Thirteenth May, 1943, found her getting under way from Pearl toward Noumea at 1217 hours, escorting *S.S. Robin Wentley* and *H.M.S. Leander*. At 1753 on 26th May she tied up at journey's end, fueled, and settled down to the monotonous escort duty which was to be her lot until the tocsin sounded "up north" and her shotted guns found targets worthy of her gunners' mettle.

U.S.S. Claxton (DD-571) with the somewhat quixotic Heraldo Stout pacing her bridge and erupting orders in a happy stream, was the first destroyer of DesRon-23 to reach the South Pacific. She beat *Converse*, the next one in, by several weeks, arriving Noumea in April, 1943.

Named for Midshipman Thomas Claxton, who lost his life and won glory while serving in *U.S.S. Lawrence* at the Battle of Lake Erie, the vessel was the second in the United States Navy to bear that name, and she was one of the Texas-built group.

The breezy Stout left the indelible mark of his personality and own special genius both on his ship and on the Squadron without noticeable delay. When *Claxton* stood in to any port in the South Pacific, if her identifying numbers were obscured, she still could be recognized by her own heraldic device approved by her skipper and prominently displayed on her bridge. It was a pair of dice rampant beneath which were emblazoned the proud motto *Click with the Claxton.* And under Stout *Claxton* did click. One reason she did was that he was even cuter than Heinie Armstrong in getting rid of undesirable personnel.

Stout had his problems. With a meticulousness which belied his superficially light touch, he took the trouble to check every single member of his new crew. He found that he had only 30 regular Navy people, and a total of only 60 men in his crew had even *seen* salt water, let alone sailed on it. And he found one man, mess attendant, Joe Breen, who had a General Classification Test mark of .4, which indicated a state of intelligence dangerously close to imbecility. Captain Stout immediately went into action. His technique was perhaps a bit laborious for him, but it was to pay golden dividends.

Soon after commissioning, *Claxton* lay at New Orleans. The Captain went over to the Algiers Receiving Station where he examined the service records of about 200 men who had bilged out of radio or radar school. Of this number he collected the records of 40, and requested their transfer to his ship *in excess of her standard complement.*

"Captain," said the personnel officer at the Station, "I suppose you know what you're doing. But I think I should warn you. Most of those men have been dropped from training for going AWOL or other offenses. Do you think they'll be a very stable element in your ship?"

"Doesn't bother me a bit," said Stout puffing on his ever-present briar. *"Where I'm going there's no place to go AWOL!* Beyond that, I have no trained radar or sound people, and if I wait to be supplied through channels the war'll be over before I get 'em. Finally, I fully expect to have to transfer some incompetents after our shakedown. When I do, the first thing the boys on the beach'll do is try to transfer an equal number of incompetents back to me. But I'll fool 'em, my friend! With these 40 men *over complement* I can set an equal number on the beach and still not have to ask for replacements. So they can't send me back a bunch of bums to take the places of the bums I send ashore!"

Aboard *Claxton* matters worked out precisely as the bouncy little skipper had anticipated. After shakedown at Guantánamo she returned to Charleston, where Heraldo sent 40 men ashore and told the personnel people he didn't want them. The scream that went up might have been heard at Pearl Harbor, and the general theme was "You can't do this to us!"

"Oh, yes I can!" replied the imperturbable Heraldo, whereupon he fished out his Navy Regulations and pointed to the specification—an ancient one from a by-gone day, but still on the books—that, after commissioning, a captain could take such action, although only once. But once was enough for the Captain of *Claxton*. He got rid of his incompetents, and eventually he was able to rate 38 of the 40 "replacements" he'd taken aboard in advance.

It remained only to get rid of Joe Breen, who had turned out to be a troublemaker of talent. Captain Stout handled this little chore with seeming forthrightness, but Joe was to find a hook in it. The Captain handed Joe an undesirable discharge, which was entirely wonderful so far as Joe was concerned. He disappeared below, reappeared in minutes decked out in a cheap civilian suit, and swaggered off the ship vowing that he was "through with the wah."

"I guess he is, too," said the "exec" bitterly. "That type always seem to get out of their responsibilities."

"I don't think Joe will," said the Captain quietly. "I've arranged a little reception party for him. A master-at-arms will escort him to the Navy Yard gate. As Joe passes through he'll be presented with 'greetings'—and the guy making the presentation will be a Southern sheriff. I don't think Joe will go far after that. Ah, well," he concluded turning away from the rail where they'd been watching their ex-mess attendant depart, "our loss is the Army's gain!" When *Claxton* finally sailed toward Noumea she was a happy ship.

In true Horatio Alger tradition it can literally be said that Herald Franklin Stout was born of poor but honest parents. The stock on both sides was good but there just wasn't much money lying around, and as a youth he had none of the advantages enjoyed by Austin, Cavenagh, and some of the others. The paternal side was unspectacularly Pennsylvania Dutch dating back to 1737 when Johann Peter Stout immigrated from the Palatinate to Cherry Hill and Oley Valley, in Pennsylvania.

Most of the numerous sons of old Johann fought in the Revolutionary War and some were killed. Down through the generations they divided their time about equally between fighting and farming, and in 1814 Heraldo's great-great-grandfather took out a license for one of the first taverns in northern Ohio. Rumor had it that he was one of his own best customers but that didn't prevent him from accumulating a considerable estate. Its fruits, however, did not flow to Herald's grandfather, who was the first college graduate in the line. He became a school principal in northern Ohio, and lived a full life being partial to wine, women, and song, although not necessarily in that order.

Herald's father, Franklin Lee Stout, eschewed the temptations of the flesh. He would have nothing to do with wine, didn't smoke, and limited his interest in women to his wife. He served in the Philippine Insurrection but hated soldiering and was a machinist by trade. He was eventually employed as assistant master mechanic of a blast furnace at Dover, Ohio.

The boy's ancestry on his mother's side was not sufficiently more distinguished to cause any lifting of eyebrows. She was descended from a William Tong or Tongue, a Revolutionary War soldier of the Maryland Militia and Continental Line, whose principal distinction was that he fathered twenty-six children. The other side of the family came down from the New England Putnams, of Ashburnham.

When Heraldo was a child of five his father, Franklin Lee, was killed in an explosion at the blast furnace. His mother took the family back to northern Ohio near Findlay, where she struggled to keep her little brood together, turning to newspaper reporting and office work, and not being too proud to take in washing when funds failed. Understandably young Herald Franklin started working at an early age. He peddled newspapers and magazines, graduated to store clerk, and when he was twelve entered the printing trade. Like his namesake, Franklin, he was never to divorce himself from printer's ink completely, although the salt sea tried hard to wash it away.

Young Heraldo was valedictorian of his high school class, which gave him somewhat inflated notions of his proclivities as a scholar. When he got to the Naval Academy he found he was in competition with real scholars, some of whom actually had degrees before they reached Annapolis. The class of '26 was rather hard hit by the first naval disarmament treaty, the effects of which were felt almost immediately upon their entrance at the Academy. On the semi-annual examinations they made history by losing 30 per cent of their number to academics and those who were left, unless they were brilliant, faced a grim grind to graduate.

Stout's personality was marked by a bubbling sense of humor exceeded, in the Gallant Squadron, only by Roy Gano. This tended somewhat to obscure the serious academic interest which was his. Actually, he was a bit of an egghead. After graduation he was twice brought back to the Academy as an Instructor in the Department of Electrical Engineering and Physics, and his work on the Academy's official physics textbook was recognized as notable.

Herald Stout's first command was *U.S.S. Breese*, a minelayer, and he was in *Breese* at Pearl Harbor when the Japanese struck on 7th December, 1941. Thus he was in the shooting war from the very beginning. At Pearl, under a rain of bombs and strafing, *Breese* managed to shoot down one enemy airplane. She then got under way and played an able part in depth-charging and destroying the several midget submarines which the enemy had concentrated in the area.

Looking back upon his four years at the United States Naval Academy, Heraldo evidenced a lucid appreciation of the institution's purposes and procedures. In advising the father of a prospective midshipman to enter his son at Annapolis, Stout said:

"Contrary to popular opinion the Academy does not brainwash its graduates. Rather, it provides the solid cake of necessary knowledge and information, over which the icing of each individual's personality is spread. Bite through the icing and, fundamentally, it is the same pastry."

The wisdom of this appraisal was to be evidenced by the uniformly high technical competence of the skippers of DesRon-23. Reflecting vastly different backgrounds, temperaments and talents, each of them still had that "solid cake of necessary knowledge" which enabled him to function as a reliable member of the team.

When Rosey Gillan arrived in the Solomons, Stout studied his Commodore thoughtfully for several weeks before forming an opinion about his superior. Finally he made up his mind, and his considered appraisal gave the Commodore the benefit of considerable insight. Stout summed Gillan up this way:

"Captain Gillan is in many ways a victim of circumstances over which he has no control. Right at this time he's hampered by the cumbersome machinery of a Navy which has not yet trimmed the fat of 20 years of peace-time stuffiness down to the lean competence necessary for war-time operations.

"Look at the Squadron! Not three of us have operated together before. In terms of practical evolutions we hardly know each other. These bad boilers are keeping ships tied up so that others have to carry a double load. In consequence we're all worked too hard and beyond the limits of human capability. That's not the Commodore's fault; he's got to do the best he can with what he's got, and it seems to me that he's giving it the old high school try."

Having delivered himself of this summation Heraldo bounced bravely off, his large curved pipe belching smoke, and his course set to deal summarily with some such official nonsense as Operation Snow-storm. However, right or wrong, he was soon to discover that Arleigh Burke would devise effective means of dealing with many of the more irritating and important problems the solution of which seemed to elude Commodore Gillan.

When, at noon on Monday, 27th September, 1943, "the man who puts his pants on one leg at a time" reached the New Hebrides and *Thatcher* plunged down her starboard anchor in 30 fathoms of water at Berth Four, Espiritu, Ralph Lampman's future colleagues already were doing business up The Slot. Division 45 had been attached to Task Force 31 and, based on Purvis, had operated in support of our occupation of Vella La Vella and Kolombangara. Now the available ships of the Squadron were gathered to support Task Group 39.2 in-cluding cruisers *Cleveland, Columbia,* and *Kankakee* in their mission to intercept and destroy enemy units coming down from Rabaul. *Thatcher* was to join this company at Tulagi in due course and, for the first time in history, the Squadron was to be complete in the area although all eight ships were not to operate together until the eve of the Battle of Empress Augusta Bay.

Leland Ralph Lampman had a way of seeing things straight and level like the plains of his native Illinois. Outwardly at least, he was the least emotional of the skippers of DesRon-23. A few generations back the family had been New York Dutch. Ralph's maternal grand-mother, finding herself widowed while still relatively a young woman, had loaded her crop of children in a covered wagon and struck out for the West. She unhitched for the last time in the vicinity of Rockford, Illinois, where Ralph was born to Herman W. and Lulu Bingham Lampman in February, 1905. Several removals finally brought the family to the tiny hamlet of Angola, Indiana, where the senior Lamp-man set up in business and the boy completed grade and high school.

If Heinie Armstrong won a wife through duplicity, it may be said that Ralph Lampman won his mate through persistence. It all started when he was a very young child in Angola. He saw a little girl running down the street, and he was fascinated by the flash of her black sateen bloomers, revealed by her short skirts and flying legs. Her name was Sarah Barron, and the two went through high school together. Even before they graduated Ralph started asking Sarah to become his wife some day. After 19 years of saying "no" she finally tried saying "yes" to break the monotony. They were married in 1933 upon his return from a tour of duty aboard *U.S.S. Guam*, on the Yangtze Patrol.

As was the case with several of his colleagues, environment had a great deal to do with pointing Lampman toward the United States Naval Academy. Near neighbors in Angola had two sons at the Academy, and Congressman Fairfield of the Twelfth Indiana District lived across the street. Talks with the neighbors furnished the impulse, and the Congressman the enabling appointment. Ralph entered the Academy in June, 1923 and, despite a hard tussle with his studies which found him frequently ineligible for sports because of unsatisfactory scholastic performance, he managed to graduate in 1927 in the top third of his class. He found formal math tough and Spanish, which he called "Dago," all but unconquerable. Engineering, ordnance, and seamanship were congenial subjects in which he did well.

Looking unemotionally at his Academy years, Ralph Lampman was unable to isolate any one factor which made an especial impression upon him. In this he agreed with Roy Gano and some of the others. A realist strongly inclined to de-emphasize the glamorous trappings of the Navy, he consistently referred to the Academy as "the trade school." This was an indulgence which not all Annapolis old grads permitted themselves in public. He knew both The Phantom of the Opera and "Red" McGruder. The latter he regarded as a somewhat kindly Scot but, unlike Ham Hamberger, he was impressed by neither. He perceived a certain cohesion in the Academy pattern—strict discipline, emphasis on honor, strong sports program, uniform living conditions, association with officer Instructors, and the over-all curriculum. These factors, he felt, combined to promote both competence and uniformity, in which he fully shared, adequate to his needs as a naval officer.

When tapped for command of *Thatcher*, Lieutenant Commander Lampman was skipper of one of the old World War I 1200-tonners— *U.S.S. Ellis*. He left *Ellis* at Trinidad and flew to Bath via Guantánamo, Bermuda, and New York, reporting in at the Bath B.O.Q. on 1st February, 1943. At 1500 on Wednesday, 10th February, he read his orders, assumed command, and the watch was posted. The thing that impressed him about his new command, other than her firepower, was the commodiousness of his own quarters. After *Ellis*, these seemed palatial. His anticipation of luxury, however, was to go a'glimmering. By the time *Thatcher* reached the South Pacific her Captain's quarters were so cluttered with extra electronics gear that, if anything, he had less room than he'd enjoyed in *Ellis*.

Ralph Lampman was not a person given to apprehensions. He was phlegmatic of temperament, succinct of expression, and had high standards of technical performance. He was not, as some officers have confessed themselves to have been, depressed by the constant necessity to live "under orders" in the tight framework of individual accountability which marks the Navy system, nor haunted by the spectre of being "passed over" when the promotion lists were circulated for selection of those to be moved up a step. He accepted whatever conclusions the day brought and remained undisturbed. When he assumed command of *Thatcher*, only two of his subordinate officers were commissioned in the regular Navy, the others being reservists. His crew was largely green like the crews of the other Squadron DDs which had gone before *Thatcher*. "My only worry," he told Ham Hamberger, "was whether I could get a completely inexperienced crew into some kind of shape before we started shooting for keeps."

"Well, did you?"

"I was only partially successful," admitted the Captain of *Thatcher*, sucking noisily on his pipe. "We took a convoy to Casablanca less than 2 months after the ship was put in commission. We came out here via the Fijis. I guess, in the circumstances, I should be satisfied that the old bucket's still floating and in one piece. At least we didn't put her on a reef! Come on, let's have another bottle of beer; I'm so dry I'm spitting gun cotton!"

Despite his seeming lack of emotion and almost, it would seem, his not caring overmuch about the contemporary scene, there was a key and a very basic one to the enigma which was Ralph Lampman. It emerged, as so often those deeper things did in the theaters of combat, during a casual conversation at the Ironbottom Bay Club. Sitting in Tip's Tavern and sipping their beer while waiting for the opening of the next bottle of bourbon, Captains Lampman and Armstrong talked desultorily about their ships and their problems. Eventually the conversation got around to religion and the matter of conducting divine services aboard ship.

"Personally, I'm strong for religion," said Heinie. "But the Japs know all about the practices of Christianity, and you've got to fool 'em. Up at Dutch Harbor we used to conduct our Sunday services on Monday just because of that. They never seemed to catch on. How do you handle things, Ralph?"

"M-m-m-m, well," said Captain Lampman thoughtfully, "we manage. When they can be spared while we're in harbor, those who want to, go aboard the cruisers for formal religious observation. Then, too, I've got a young ensign who occasionally gets the Jewish group together."

"How about you?" asked Armstrong. "Do you ever conduct services yourself?"

"Almost never," replied Lampman. "I'm not much of a Bible thumper, Heinie. My religious affiliation is Methodist, but my persuasion is—well, *I guess you might call it Abou ben Adhem, may his tribe increase!*"

Armstrong remembered the lines, and recited part of the poem very softly:

. . . Exceeding peace had made ben Adhem bold,
And to the presence in the room he said
"What writest thou?" The vision turned its head,
And with a look made all of sweet accord
Answered "The names of those who love the Lord."
"And is mine one?" said Abou. "Nay, not so,"
Replied the angel. Abou spoke more low,
But cheerily still; and said "I pray thee, then,
Write me as one that loves his fellow men."

There, indeed, lay key and clue to Ralph Lampman, the last of the "23" skippers to reach the South Pacific. His was a solid if rough-hewn integrity. He had the kind of instinctive honesty which, a little later on, was to be shown in his instant acceptance of full responsibility for damage to his ship in circumstances where his actual culpability might have been moot. And he had the kind of built-in respect for his fellow men that had characterized his pioneer ancestors. If one had spoken to Ralph Lampman about the *mystique* of the Gallant Squadron under Burke he would have scorned it as "fancy Dan stuff" although he participated in it whether he perceived it or not. But, too, he had his own *mystique;* that of Abou ben Adhem. It served him well.

Captain Martin J. Gillan, Jr., served in the South Pacific as Commodore of Destroyer Squadron 23 from 28th June, 1943, the date of his arrival in *Foote*, until 21st October, the date of his detachment by despatch orders. During those 115 wearing days and nights the operational pattern of the Squadron was a mosaic of fatigue and frustration. The Squadron was never together as a complete unit, but the impairment of morale and efficiency was uniform in its component parts. Fatigue was the great enemy. They could neither run nor hide from the stern demands of duty. Officers and sailors grew blear-eyed with the loss of sleep. From 3 to 4 consecutive hours in the sack was a bounteous dispensation for any man. The black stubble of prickly beards framed their hollow, grey cheeks and fringed their chins. In the interest of appearance most of the skippers frowned on beards, but in the circumstances the matter was under but haphazard control. There were dirt and oil on their dungarees, and from the Captain down they all had "the crud." The crud, which was the crew's name for it, was a loathsome fungus growth that formed in the armpits, around the groin, and the belt line. Fostered by the high temperatures and humidity of the area it was encouraged by repeatedly delayed opportunities to shower and change, and it did little for a man's peace of mind. They used alcohol and whatever other medicaments they could lay their hands on to fight the epidemic but even so a good many of the men were physically uncomfortable a great deal of the time.

Their bodies ached for rest. Upon awakening they could feel every twanging tendon, which seemed to have a direct connection with the brain. But there seemed to be no link between their muscles and the volition to move. Normally strong men rolled out of their bunks, and had to grab something solid to keep from falling until they could regain full muscular control.

The racking pattern of their duty is clearly revealed in the deck logs of the ships. Here, spelled out hour by hour, day by day, and harsh night by harsh night is the fundamental agony of DesRon-23. True, it was an agony which forged the Squadron into a rough but reliable blade of steel. Arleigh Burke was to temper and polish that blade into a flicking rapier which plunged repeatedly into the vitals of the Imperial Japanese Navy. Nevertheless, it was still agony. Details and summaries from the log of *Dyson* accurately reflect the employment of all eight ships.

On Monday, 28th June, when Joe Gillan stood in to Noumea in *Foote*, *Dyson* stood out at 1605 to join Task Force 36. Her Captain was at the conn, her navigator on the bridge. They rounded Amadee Light 1,000 yards abeam to starboard, and bore up for "Point Dog" where they were to rendezvous with the Task Force. They made contact at 0703 on the morning of Wednesday, 30th June, and from that time forward the log tells its own story:

Wednesday, 30th June to Saturday, 31st July

Converse in company. Operating general area 15°—58′—00″ South; 157°—56′—00″ East. Undertook evolutions with Task Units 36.2.9 and 36.3.9. Fueled from *U.S.S. Tappahanoc*. Maneuvers designed as an intensive working up for all ships. Drill at general quarters, firing of guns, and launching and recovery of planes by carriers executed night and day. Returned to berth Able-5, Port Noumea, at 1640. *U.S.S. Claxton* alongside.

Sunday, 1st August

0957: Under way with Task Group 36.3 consisting of *U.S.S. Saratoga*, *U.S.S. North Carolina*, *U.S.S. Massachusetts*, *U.S.S. San Diego*, *U.S.S. San Juan*, and DDs of Third U.S. Fleet and Pacific Fleet. Flag in *Saratoga*.

Monday, 2nd August

Noon position 17°—56′—00″ South; 160°—48′—00″ East. On anti-submarine and plane guard duty. Boilers 2 and 4 on the line. Condition of readiness Two Mike; material condition Baker.* Zig-zagging according to plan Number 6.

---

* Conditions Two Mike and Baker imposed a sustained strain on the crew. All guns had to be fully manned and, although complete compartmentation was not in force, only a few access doors were undogged, and very limited habitability features were available.

Thursday, 5th August to Tuesday, 10th August

Anchored berth 24, Pekoa Channel, Espiritu Santo.
Took 111,312 gallons fuel at 60° F.
U.S.S. Charles Ausburne present; *U.S.S. Converse* alongside.
Underway escorting *U.S.S. Monongahela* (tanker) to Guadalcanal. At general quarters most of the time.

Friday, 13th August

0800: Moored Port Purvis
0807: Started loading Mark 17 torpedo warheads.
1903: Under way with convoy including oiler *U.S.S. Patuxent* toward Espiritu.

Monday, 16th August, to Thursday, 2nd September

The Captain has given permission for the men to keep a parrot purchased by the chief gunner's mate from some LST sailors at Purvis. Parrot named Pablo, which was this ship's code designation some time back. All hands start teaching Pablo to talk.
Training exercises with *Ausburne, Claxton,* and *Foote.*
Escorting convoys to and from Guadalcanal. Fighting off numerous enemy air attacks.

Friday, 3rd September to Sunday, 26th September

Dyson and *Pringle* sink three Jap barges loaded with men and fuel. Gunner reports Pablo screams every time guns fire. Ship at general quarters or condition of readiness Two Mike, material condition Baker most of the time. Much high speed running; constant refueling.

Monday, 27th September *

1550: Under way to join Task Unit 39.2.2.
      Anchor fouled in anti-submarine net.
1704: Anchor cleared. Bent on 32 knots.
1910: Joined Task Unit 39.2.2; *Foote* in company.

---

* The operational pattern revealed in this sortie was typical under Commodore Gillan, and was a principal contributing factor to the low morale experienced by many of the captains of DesRon-23 at this time. The unidentified plane in question was, actually, the equivalent of "Washingmachine Charlie" or "Louie-the-Louse"— a nuisance, perhaps, but at no time a serious threat. Extremely cautious, Gillan ordered frequent course reversals in the face of this primarily pyrotechnical display by the Jap flier with the result that units of the Squadron often arrived too late to accomplish their missions to intercept and destroy Japanese surface traffic, and found only stragglers or no enemy at all. Yet they paid a terrible price for these futile evolutions in the deadening fatigue which was their legacy from constant high-speed steaming and maneuvering, and sustained alertness at general quarters. It is true that the Squadron was not fully trained and that Commodore Gillan so reported to higher authority. Many of the captains, however, felt that more aggressive tactics might have been employed.

2217: Unidentified aircraft at 13 miles.
Laid down light smoke to cover wake.
2245: Reversed course to the right.
2300: Back to base course.
2322: Sighted float lights ahead. Reversed course to the left.
2326: Back to base course.
2354: Unidentified plane continues to drop flares in accordance with the movements of this ship.
2356: *Spence* opened fire on plane.

Tuesday, 28th September

"Louie-the-Louse" continued to drop flares throughout the twelve-to-four watch. He offered no combative challenge, and *Spence* didn't hit him. The progress of the unit was further delayed by course reversals.
0148: Opened fire on surface target.
Fired 161 rounds of 5-inch .38 caliber.
Target, a barge, hit and seen to burn to the water's edge.
0913: Secured from general quarters.

At 1857 on Sunday, 3rd October, *Dyson* moored starboard side to *Spence* in berth 27, Espiritu, and for her there followed a 3-day period to get caught up in ship's work. After a brief sortie with *Montpelier, Cleveland,* and *Denver* she returned to Espiritu and was granted an engineering availability. She took aboard four Mark XV torpedoes from *U.S.S. Whitney,* and did not sortie again until Wednesday, 20th October, when she put to sea for training exercises. Thus *Dyson* was at sea when Commodore Gillan was detached, but at 1228 hours on Monday, 25th October, she moored alongside YO-164 at Purvis Bay, and commenced fueling. Leaving the supervision of that operation to the oil king and the chief engineer, Captain Gano dropped lightly into his gig and went ashore. He was looking for his new boss, Arleigh Burke. When he found him he also found a new way of life for Destroyer Squadron 23. And, had he but known it, even then tremendous events were peeking over the horizon.

In the story of the Gallant Squadron the log of *U.S.S. Dyson* is significant. It presents an almost unrelieved picture of high-speed steaming, general quarters, combat missions of questionable achievement, sustained physical and psychological strain, and debilitating discomfort. Behind every entry of "underway" there lies the work of building up fires below, handling heavy hawsers, or the backbreaking 30 minutes it takes a DD to get her anchor, every link hosed down overside as it comes in. Behind every entry of "commenced fueling" there lies dogged, time-consuming work by the engineering department. Behind every entry of "moored" there lies exhausting work by the special under way detail. Behind every entry of "took aboard ammunition" there lies the tedious job of manhandling ammo over the side, and walking it to appropriate stowage.

It was a court martial offense for a skipper not to have his full ammunition allowance if it was available. While the amount to be carried was specified by higher authority, in practice the captains tried to get all they could whenever they could. About 200 rounds per gun was considered a heartening supply at the time and place, although they'd a lot rather have had 500 rounds per gun.

Groceries had to be brought aboard, usually from a 26-foot workboat lying alongside. The supply officer was the scrounger for the ship, and he was over the side quicker than a "pier head jump" whenever he smelled the possibility of obtaining variety or delicacies ashore. Fifteen tons or better of supplies were required for a month's replenishment, and it all had to be manhandled. Guns and engines needed constant and careful maintenance. Each ship of the Squadron was to steam a third of a million miles or better, and the guns were to fire thousands of rounds. Such a record is achieved only through the most meticulous maintenance.

Finally there was the psychological depressant which operated strongly in the early days of the Squadron. If they got there at all, often they got there too late. At night, unless the Navy furnished it (and an occasional Black Cat was about all that could be managed) they had no air cover. The Japanese consistently flew at night; we did not. The claims of Army air for their daytime strikes were fantastically over-optimistic and the Navy learned to regard them as unreliable. On one occasion an Army plane reported sinking an enemy cruiser, and added that the cruiser "sank in just 14 seconds." Investigation showed that the Army plane, instead of sinking an enemy cruiser, had bombed our own submarine, *Grayling*, which had crash-dived thus convincing the Army pilot that his target had sunk in 14 seconds.

All of this was discouraging to the officers and crew of one ship, *U.S.S. Dyson*. Add seven other ships who suffered the same galling routines and the same frustrations, and there emerges an approximation of the physical condition and morale obtaining in Destroyer Squadron 23 when Arleigh Burke climbed over *Charlie Ausburne*'s rail and casually informed Brute Reynolds that he was there to take over.

9

Sortie Against the Enemy

~~~~~~

Hige Kallejian, torpedoman 2nd, emerged from an after hatch aboard *U.S.S. Dyson*, lying to her anchor at Port Purvis. In one hand he lugged a tall wooden stool, its circular seat polished to a high gloss by repeated contact with the posteriors of uncounted hundreds of petty officers and sailors. The stool was an awkward burden to fetch up the steep ladder leading to the ship's interior, and when he barked his shins, as he did more than once, Hige mumbled a few pungent Armenian phrases under his breath. There would have been no point in his speaking out, for none present could have comprehended a syllable.

The time was afternoon and the date Monday, 25th October, 1943. The rains had not yet come but the excessively high humidity gave earnest promise of their early advent. With the red column in the Fahrenheit thermometer seemingly painted to within a hair's breadth below the calibration for 90 degrees, everybody was feeling the heat.

Hige—some called him "Hike," some called him "Mike," it made no difference to him—set his stool down at the center of the open space abaft the after 5-inch battery and forward of the 20-mm mounts. From the capacious pockets of his dungarees he took comb, clippers, and scissors, and from a back pocket he drew an ample but wadded-up white cloth which he flicked expertly in the air to shake out the wrinkles as he announced "Next!" The enlisted men's barber shop aboard *Dyson* was open and ready for business.

Hige Kallejian, a slender lad of medium height with black, wavy hair, dark brows, and a somewhat pointed chin was a talkative, mercurial type in the Armenian tradition. He was an "operator" who never had less than three private projects cooking simultaneously. They might range from making small loans on the short term at high interest, to acting as go-between in the constant pattern of barter and swapping which was a characteristic of enlisted life aboard. He was popular in the ship, and his deft chatter which was invariably the obbligato of his combing and snipping brought him an incredible store of informational trivia which he filed away in a sharp mind against the implementation of future projects. When digging for information from his clients Hige turned off both sarcasm and scorn with bland refusal to recognize either.

As the barber shouted, "Next!," a seaman 1st, who had been waiting, stepped forward and was about to climb onto the stool when Hige whisked it away. "R-H-I-P, friend," he explained. The startled seaman, looking around, immediately perceived the reason for his disappointment in the person of the stocky, redheaded chief gunner's mate who had acquired Pablo the parrot with the Captain's permission several weeks back, and who now approached in quest of a haircut. In Navy slang R-H-I-P translates "Rank Has Its Privileges" and indeed it does in every ship from bridge to bilges. The seaman stepped aside, the gunner mounted the stool, Hige pinned the covering cloth around his client's neck, and the dry snick of the scissors soon was beating an irregular tattoo on the heavy air.

"So, chief," asked Hige after what might have seemed hardly a decent interval to preface cozy conversation, "what's with Pablo th' parrot?"

Snip . . . snip . . . snip . . .

"Unn-n-n-n-*ah!*"

"Yeah? I'd never a' guessed it!"

Snip . . . snip . . . snip . . .

"Okeh, wise guy! Knock it off! *You* know th' Godam parrot's dead!"

"Gee, chief, honest I didn't." *Snip . . . snip . . . snip . . .* "Dead, huh? An' me just gettin' on what you might call intimate terms with th' bird."

"You're in'na ship, aint'cha?" snapped the brittle-tempered chief.

"Sure I'm in'na ship!" Hige stepped back, wrists on hips, cocked his head to one side, closed an eye, and took a ranging sight on the chief's starboard sideburn. "I'm in'na ship, but don't nobody tell me nothin'. We get under way, I'm up to my arse in torpedo juice 'r sitting up with a sick warhead, 'r something. Believe me, chief, I got my troubles and that's a fact!"

Snip . . . snip . . . snip . . .

"Well, th' parrot's gone, so what th' hell!"

"He used t' scream so cute when them 5-inch guns fired . . . remember . . . ?"

"I remember."

"An' th' time you brought him back for me t' clip his wings . . . remember . . . ?"

"I remember."

"I done a good job on that, chief. Them wings was more gracefuller than a falcon's when I got through."

"What th' hell *you* know about falcons?"

"I seen some in'na movies oncet . . . an' th' man held out their wings, and I remember how pretty they was."

Hige pocketed the scissors and started the clippers over the back of the chief's neck.

"Well, th' damn bird's gone, so pipe down!"

"He get killed 'r just die . . . ?"

"He died of a broke heart!"

"No kiddin'! Geez—imagine that! How come, gunner?"

Hige Kallejian was genuinely interested now, and he moved in. The deferential "Chief" was all very well for casual chit-chat but from long experience in landing on his feet in this man's Navy Hige was very sure of himself. In the circumstances "gunner" about equated to the French "tu," and he didn't hesitate a moment to adopt it. The gunner had his rank, but Hige had his talents and they were sufficiently impressive and acknowledged to give him a special cachet which permitted regarding even a chief as an equal.

"How come, gunner?" repeated the barber.

"Some fool stuffed th' bird into th' breach of Number 1 5-inch," explained the chief.

"S-o-o-o-o-o . . . ?"

"Well, he got half way up th' tube, and th' only way we could rescue 'im was t' coax 'im out through th' muzzle."

"No kiddin'! That kill 'im?"

"Hell, no! But you remember how pretty he used to be—all them green an' gold an' red colors 'n stuff?"

"He sure was. Prettiest bird I ever saw. Why, geez, when them deck apes come aboard from other ships they used t' stand around an' crack about how beautiful Pablo was. They couldn't get over it."

"Well, that's what kilt him!"

"How y'a mean, gunner?"

"Lissen'! After goin' through th' gun tube nat'chally he was full a' oil an' gunk; his feathers, they're plastered down around him like th' skin on a hot dog. An' there don't seem t' be no color left, neither."

"You try t' get th' gunk off?"

"Did I try t' get th' gunk off!" The chief's outraged sarcasm was devastative, but it did not bother Kallejian. "Of *course* I tried t' get th' gunk off!"

"Turps . . . ?"

"Turps!"

"Ammonia . . . ?"

"Ammonia!"

"Alcohol . . . ?"

"*Alcohol!*"

"No dice . . . ?"

"*No dice!*"

"M-m-m-m-m! That's rough! So what happened?"

"So, after that, anybody come on board, they see Pablo, they start laughin'. They couldn't help it; he looked just that funny even *I* got'ta laugh, God forgive me, on account'a I loved that bird!"

"An' . . . ?"

"An' he died of a broke heart, stupid! How would you like people laughin' at you all th' time? Th' bird was sensitive, is all."

"I gott'a friend, gunner . . . I might could make a deal t' have th' bird stuffed. Then you could keep 'im around."

"Too late. We buried 'im off th' fantail last night."

Hige permitted himself a sibilant sigh which might have signified sympathy or merely frustration at the disappearance of what he had been carefully building up as a possibly profitable and intriguing project. He unpinned the cloth, whirled it away, and stepped back. "Gee, that's too bad, gunner. Well, there y' are—as good a haircut as you'd get from Benny-th'-barber at Dago! You interested in findin' another bird, chief?"

"Bird, smird!" The chief ran a finger around the inside of his collar to dislodge loose hair. "Th' next thing I get me'll be a fish, an' t' hell with it!"

As the gunner got down from the stool Hige detained him with the slight pressure of two fingers on his arm, and pointed with the other hand. "Ain't that our gig off there, gunner?"

The gunner shaded his eyes against the glare of the tropic sun and took a long look at the far-off boat. "Yep," he said finally, "but how'd you know? You sure as hell can't read her number at this distance."

"Don't have to," said the perspicacious Hige. "Witherspoon's coxun of th' Captain's gig, and I can spot him every time from th' way he stands at th' tiller. He stands up straight an' sort of bounces back an' forth on th' balls of his feet. You suppose th' Captain's bringing good news, gunner—maybe like we're goin' t' Sydney, 'r somethin'?"

"I got news for you, Junior! F'r th' first time since I been in *Dyson*— an' I put her in commission, remember—this whole Squadron of eight cans is all gathered together in one place. On top of that, th' brass has been conferrin' an' yackin' ever since we been here. In an old chief's book that adds up to just one thing: We're goin' places, all right, and we're goin' t' do things. But it ain't goin' t' be to Sydney t' get drunk, kid! So shake th' lead out an' rattle your scissors, on account of I don't think you're goin' t' be cuttin' much hair after th' Old Man comes aboard!" The gunner hitched up his dungaree trousers, bellowed *"Next!"* with authoritative emphasis, and rolled off forward. The seaman who had been waiting patiently since being squeezed out by R-H-I-P climbed aboard the stool and once more the snick of the scissors sounded as Hige Kallejian, instinctively sniffing for the scent of a new project, began the last haircut he was to dispense for a considerable number of days.

Captain Gano came aboard forward and was met by his executive officer. In token of enlisted personnel within earshot the Captain addressed the exec with big ship formality. "Mr. Morland, please make a careful check to be sure we're quite ready for sea and for battle. We'll sortie soon, and it may be only a matter of hours."

"Aye, sir," said the calm, competent Morland. With his habitual dispatch he had set about this new duty even before the Captain disappeared below to seize a last minute opportunity for a letter to his wife that might have some chance of getting off the ship before they sailed.

That same morning the top naval command in the South Pacific including ComSoPac himself, Admiral Halsey, had gathered in conference at Koli Point. It was the last big meeting before the kickoff of the exceedingly bold bid of the Allies to roll the Jap right up out of the Central Solomons and bring heavy and constant pressure to bear on his major concentrations at Rabaul and Truk. Rear Admirals Wilkinson, George H. Fort, and Frederick C. Sherman were present with their chiefs of staff and aides. So was Rear Admiral Merrill commanding Task Force 39, and his DD Commodore, Captain Arleigh Burke.

The room was crowded and hot. The assembled officers, wearing clean khakis with shirt collars open and no ties, sat facing a small platform at one side of which stood a portable speaker's lectern. A lamination of large-scale mounted maps and charts, each swiveled so that it could be swung out of the way to disclose the one below, lay flat against the wall behind the platform. As the meeting progressed these exhibits were referred to as they became pertinent. Most of the officers held heavy manila envelopes stamped *Top Secret*, and all had materials for notetaking. Admiral Halsey opened the meeting with a few incisive words in his clipped style which was sparing of prolixity. He then turned matters over to a staff officer who addressed the gathering.

"Gentlemen, each of you has received his orders and details of the respective parts your formations are expected to play in the campaign about to start. Actually, of course, I know that most of you have been working on one or another phase of this operation for some time now. I will, therefore, confine my remarks to sketching the evolution of this plan and its objectives, and the primary steps through which those objectives are to be attained. Please feel free to interrupt to ask questions."

The speaker then went on to develop a complex but clear picture. As early as July, he told his audience, ComSoPac had decided that an assault on Bougainville must be a key integer in the final Solomons campaign. The enemy had enjoyed two relatively unmolested years to fortify and garrison Bougainville and the adjacent area, and to build air strips. His present estimated ground strength there was approximately 100,000 men. In Japanese hands Bougainville inhibited the final Allied drive to the north and west. Conversely, Allied air strips in that locus would provide convenient points of departure for powerful strikes against enemy targets of major stature and importance. The immediate objective, then, was a limited one. It was not, necessarily, to exterminate all the Japs on Bougainville and invest the island but, rather, to seize and hold sufficient ground for the development and operation of air strips.

"Any questions?" There was none.

"Well, let us proceed to the plan itself."

After a considerable evolution accommodating many modifications, the plan of 12th October had been adopted, and that was the plan they were to implement. So far as the actual landings were concerned, two sites had been considered and both had been reconnoitered by parties put ashore from submarines. The first site considered was at Kieta Harbor, on the northeast coast. This was declined when it became apparent that its effective use would require the neutralization of Choiseul Island immediately to the southeast. The remaining possible site was at Empress Augusta Bay on the southwest coast of the Island, in the vicinity of Cape Torokina. This had the advantage of being on the inside or shorter route to the enemy stronghold at Rabaul, and had been selected.

"Any questions?"

A Marine Corps Major accepted the invitation. "It might help us all to know a little about Bougainville and especially the characteristics of the Torokina area."

The briefing officer fished a paper from the pile on the desk before him, and swung the wall maps apart to disclose a large-scale representation of Empress Augusta Bay, which was about midway up the southwest coast of Bougainville.

"Bougainville," he began, "is some 130 miles long by 30 miles wide, and lies in a northwest-southeast direction. A mountain spine runs down the middle and rises to 10,000 feet. Like all of these islands it is, of course, of volcanic origin. The jungle growth on Bougainville is denser than it is on Guadalcanal. Before World War I the island was German. After that war it became an Australian mandate. It is populated by about 43,000 natives speaking nearly a score of languages and dialects. And by a handful of our dedicated coast watchers!

"As for the Torokina area, I can't encourage you to expect the situation to be promising. There is no really suitable anchorage for big ships at Torokina. The land behind the beach is low, swampy, and timbered. It is traversed by but few usable trails, and natives known to be friendly to the Japanese are in the area. However, according to our latest intelligence, if we can achieve surprise which we have every intention of trying our best to do, the initial enemy opposition to our landings, while severe, should not be intolerable."

The speaker picked up his pointer, crossed to the map, and tapped the several locations as he mentioned them. "Here, right at Cape Torokina, we believe the enemy has only an outpost with an estimated strength of not more than a hundred men and possibly some anti-aircraft machine guns. Here, hard by the Laruma River, you will find an observation post. Small forces are known to be in this vicinity around Mawareka, and there are reserves over here at Mosigetta. These include artillery, but are believed to number less than 1,000 men. On the other hand, large forces are known to be in the Buka, Kieta, and Kahili areas, which is one reason we're hitting at Torokina. The enemy seems weakest there. Any further questions?"

"Thanks," said the Major.

After looking around for a moment the speaker resumed. In the unemotional cadences of a college professor reciting a lecture he's delivered hundreds of times before, he blocked in a broad picture for the steaming group of senior officers before him. Under command of Marine Corps Brigadier General Field Harris, intensive air attacks already were being mounted against enemy air facilities in the area. This would continue right up to and through D-Day for the Bougainville landings, which was 1st November at dawn. On D-minus-5, diversionary landings would be made in the Treasury group and at Voza, on Choiseul. These landings, which would be the responsibility of Admiral Fort commanding the Southern Force, were expected to divert the enemy's attention from the impending major strike at Cape Torokina, and would be protected against enemy surface intervention by Task Group 39.3, which included DesDiv-45 as well as cruisers *Cleveland* and *Denver*.

"In essence," said the speaker, "what we plan here is a series of short right jabs designed to throw the enemy off balance and conceal the real power of our left hook to his midriff at Empress Augusta Bay. The Treasury landings will be made at Blanche Harbor, between the Saveke River and Falami Point on Mono Island, and on Stirling Island. The troops will be the 8th Brigade Group of the 3rd New Zealand Division. They are seasoned soldiers who have fought on Crete and in North Africa, and they may be relied on to be tough. We plan to pull them out, however, and also those on Choiseul when our positions on Bougainville have been secured."

Before continuing, the speaker consulted his wrist watch and then said "As a matter of fact, gentlemen, some of these troops already are en route to their rendezvous. There are five groups of them collected from Guadalcanal, Rendova, and Lambu Lambu. The second Guadalcanal group shoved off at 0400 this morning, so you can see that we're already well into this operation."

The rounding out of the picture was quickly completed. Task Force 39 under Tip Merrill and composed of CruDiv-12—*Montpelier, Cleveland, Columbia*, and *Denver*—screened by the eight DDs of DesRon-23 under Arleigh Burke, was given the assignment of making the Jap keep his head down, at least temporarily. This was to be accomplished by an intensive surface bombardment of enemy air installations at Buka and Bonis, at the northern tip of Bougainville, and starting at 0021 on the morning of D-Day. The task force would then race south to mount a gunstrike against enemy positions in the Shortland Islands, just below Bougainville, timed to begin at 0631, when the troops would be starting in at Cape Torokina. This bombardment at Skunk Hollow would be the first surface daylight bombardment undertaken by the Allies in the Solomons. The Shortlands area long had been known as Skunk Hollow because it was quite productive of "skunks" or unidentified surface radar targets when visited by U.S. surface formations.

"And that, gentlemen," said the staff officer collecting his papers, "about concludes the briefing unless, of course, there are further questions."

There were no further questions and the meeting broke up, although little knots of officers gathered here and there for last-minute discussions of their intentions and capabilities. Arleigh Burke sought out Admiral Merrill. "Tip," he said, "I'd like to have a chance to talk with you about my doctrine before we get too deep in this damned thing."

"What's your schedule, Arleigh?"

"Well, tomorrow's the 26th. Shep [Captain Andrew G. Shepard, commanding *Cleveland* and also acting as ComTaskGroup 39.3] has called a final conference for 0900, and I understand we get under way right after that to look out for any enemy surface which might try to bust up our Treasury and Choiseul landings."

"How about when you get back? I'll be here, and I want to talk with you, too, Arleigh. Frankly, I can see some rough problems ahead of us and I'm a mite worried. When you return from tomorrow's mission, come aboard and we'll make time to thresh out some kinks."

It was mid-afternoon when Commodore Burke got back to Purvis. He had a tremendous number of things that he wanted to do and that he knew needed doing. One of them was to take a look at *Claxton*. She'd been the last ship of DesRon-23 to reach the Solomons and she was one of the ships of the Squadron Burke had not yet had an opportunity to board. He had flown to the Koli Point conference in a plane from *Denver*. Now, instead of having a boat set him aboard his flagship, *Charlie Ausburne*, he directed that he be put aboard *Claxton*. It was Arleigh Burke's rule not only to go to people but to seek out problems. A duller man might have looked about him, found the ships of the Squadron seemingly in good order, and concluded that nothing further was needed. That was not Burke's way. His sight habitually refracted over the horizon of today to contemplate and study the problems of tomorrow. While he could be very taut and very stiff when the occasion warranted, and while he had a temper quick to blaze when he sensed ineptitude or disloyalty, he also had a gentling human touch which often turned tears to laughter. This quality was especially noticeable in his tender relationships with Bobbie and because of it they'd many times found themselves smiling appreciatively as they glanced back at events which otherwise might have developed into little points of friction. With men this quality in Burke often turned a total stranger into a devoted admirer for life, and in an instant. These talents he did not consciously employ, and they were not at the root of his leadership genius. That root was the profound abstraction of faith—in himself, his fellow men, his Navy, and his mission. But going *to* people and anticipating and meeting problems were tools with which he worked instinctively, and they served him well.

The Captain met the Commodore as he came over *Claxton*'s rail and happily showed him the ship. Being the one, original, and only Heraldo Stout, the Captain had a number of little quirks and gimmicks tucked away here and there, and Burke was quick to respond to the slightly freewheeling but wholly efficient spirit of *Claxton*. He regarded thoughtfully the *Click with the Claxton* device painted on the face of the bridge, and he stopped stock still when he came to the quintuple torpedo tube mounts between the stacks. An abashed torpedoman, caught between wind and water by the sudden and totally unexpected appearance of his Captain accompanied by the Squadron Commodore himself, stood at embarrassed attention, a small can of enamel in one hand and a round pointed brush in the other.

"Carry on, son," said the Captain.

"What're you doing?" asked Burke curiously.

"Nothing much, sir. I was just painting a little decoration on these torp tubes to kind of set 'em off, you might say. I've about finished, sir," he added, still not at all sure that he wasn't in for a chewing out.

Arleigh Burke stepped closer, examined the art work, and threw back his head in uninhibited laughter. The design the boy had painted on the tube showed an Indian lad, naked save for a G-string and a beaded headband with feather, in the act of shooting an arrow into the bare and ample upturned rump of a character labeled "Tojo," just in case there should be any misconception. Certainly the picture was out of drawing. With the intuition of the on-deck mariner the artist had indicated the little Indian's phallus, ensconced in a sort of leather holster, as of a magnitude to grace a bull whale. But the humor and pugnacity of the thing, and the directness of its message were inescapable.

"You know, Stout," said the Commodore as they resumed their inspection, "that's something this Squadron needs. We need an insigne— a trademark that all the ships can wear and be proud of."

"Well, why not the Little Beaver, Commodore? I guess that's where the kid got his idea—from the comic strip character. The Good Lord knows these kids don't read anything but comic books when they can get 'em."

"It's good enough for me," said Burke. "We'll ask the other skippers about it the next time we all get together—maybe take a vote or something . . ."

The Little Beaver, with his bow, arrow, quiver, and phallic symbol of proportions to bar reproduction in any popular publication in the nation, soon afterward became the insigne of Destroyer Squadron 23. There is, today, other than the anchors and stars of Navy tradition, no device so universally recognized throughout the naval service as the Little Beaver. In formal reports the Squadron continued to be designated as DesRon-23, but in casual and even official discussions it was and is invariably referred to as "The Little Beavers." More—and this was a sociological phenomenon which probably was not lost on Arleigh Burke, although he never referred to it—the men of the eight Little Beaver ships, after Burke's assumption of command, quickly began identifying with the Squadron, the larger unit, rather than with their respective ships. This was new and surprising. Traditionally, in the Navy, the sailor identifies with his particular ship and his shipmates, and battles in which beer bottles flew have been fought in consequence. But in the Little Beavers under Burke it was different. Not only did the men identify with the Squadron but they gave it an intense loyalty beyond that customarily observed and, in time, they were to force the whole Navy to recognize the Little Beaver insigne as an exclusive mark of earned distinction.

At 1014 hours on the morning of Tuesday, 26th October, *Ausburne*, *Dyson*, *Spence*, *Claxton*, and *Foote* sortied with light cruisers *Cleveland* and *Denver* to play what turned out to be a static role in screening the diversionary landings on Choiseul and in the Treasuries. Task Group 39.3 moved in accordance with ComSoPac's Op-Plan 16A-43, and by 0400 on the morning of the 27th was in position at 07°—15′—00″ South; 155°—02′—00″ East. This placed them athwart the course of any enemy force coming down out of Rabaul, and the only friendly vessel they had to look out for was submarine *Guardfish*, en route Tulagi toward Cape Torokina. They could shoot at anything else. The night was dark with intermittent rain squalls, the sea calm, and the wind between force one and two from the southwest. Their patrol speed was 25 knots to minimize wake.

At 2300 on the previous night the ships had gone to general quarters and they were still at GQ when, at 0325 on the morning of the 27th, a bogey came in close and dropped float lights on *Ausburne*'s port beam and in her wake. The TBS speaker on *Ausburne*'s bridge crackled to life and the task force commander's voice was heard: "I'd rather we didn't open fire if it can be avoided, but I will not limit the discretion of the individual commanders. You are at liberty to use your best judgment." Seconds later *Foote* opened fire on the bogey but failed to register.

"Do you know what I think, Brute?" asked Arleigh Burke as he observed the futile air bursts and paced *Ausburne*'s bridge restlessly (he was always restless in combat but never careless). "I think that joker's just a snooper without any playmates within miles. Let's start a little maneuvering—just enough to keep him interested and curious. If we can suck him in maybe he won't tumble to what's going on to the eastward. It's worth a try, anyway."

Ausburne maneuvered as did the other ships of the formation. The snooper was intrigued, as Burke had hoped he would be, and hovered over and around them. He did not spy out the five transport groups making up toward the Treasury Island beaches. The landings were achieved much closer to the present time schedule than often is the case in such things. In relative terms casualties were not heavy although men died, men were wounded, and ships were sunk. The Elsie Item Gunboats took a beating, and LST-399 turned in a somewhat fabulous performance.

LST-399 grounded on Beach Orange One, Mono Island, exactly on schedule at 0735. Almost immediately she was taken under fire by several 80-mm mortars, two or more 30-mm mountain guns, and a well-covered and active Japanese pillbox located only 20 feet from her port bow door. Fires were started aboard but they were extinguished. The Japanese registered a direct hit on the breach of a 40-mm gun which was destroyed and three of its crew killed. During a momentary lull in the firing the doors were opened, but the first man off the ship was killed and the next two were dropped in their tracks by fire from the pillbox. The ship was buttoned up again.

At 0815 LST-399, still immobilized, asked permission to leave Beach Orange One. The answer came back at once: "*Permission not granted.*" What to do? The mortar and 30-mm fire had slacked off, but the fire from the pillbox was brisk and accurate, and it seemed obvious that troops could not debark from 399 against it.

A resourceful New Zealander supplied an audacious answer to the problem. Mounting a D-8 bulldozer he raised the great blade in front of him as a shield; then asked that the doors be opened. Awkwardly but undeviatingly the bulldozer lumbered toward the enemy pillbox, small caliber bullets ringing off its tempered steel blade like the clashing of a myriad tiny cymbals. At the last moment the New Zealander lowered his shield and, minutes later, he had plowed the pillbox and its seven occupants under the earth "tamping them down solidly all around" as the official report was to state.

LST-399 had other adventures and, finally, was forced to withdraw with 20 tons of cargo still aboard. During her retirement south she was subjected to air bombardment and suffered more casualties, but she lived to fight another day. Just before the retirement she sent one doctor and two corpsmen to join two other doctors already embarked in LST-485. During the 30 hours LST-485 was en route to Guadalcanal, this team, unsleeping, performed 15 major operations and administered 120 plasma and 50 dextrose injections. They left the Treasuries with 45 wounded on board. Only 5 died.

Of the larger ships *U.S.S. Cony* suffered the worst punishment. She was doing fighter-director duty when, at 1534, she took two bomb hits. Before it was over she lost Numbers 3, 4, and 5 5-inch guns; one 20-mm gun, and was without electrical power to fight her 40-mms. Her after engineroom was flooded, eight men were killed, many more wounded, and she had to retire from the engagement under tow of tug *Apache*.

At 0615 on the morning of the 27th the DDs and cruisers of Task Group 39.3 steamed to within 13 miles of the Treasuries and for a short time the officers watched through binoculars the activity going forward at the beaches. The sight was reassuring. Landing operations from the first echelon of transports were in full swing; the second and third transport groups were closing up; the fourth echelon was in view headed for its assigned position. While the enemy's reaction was violent, as had been expected, save on the beaches themselves it was limited to attacks from the air. By this time Allied fighter cover was on station and this problem was being dealt with. Neither the picket submarine keeping watch on Rabaul nor air scouts dispatched north reported any enemy surface forces in motion. The job of Task Group 39.3 had, therefore, been accomplished and in compliance with basic orders the ships retired toward Purvis at 30 knots on course 120 degrees true. They fought off a number of light air attacks, and secured from general quarters at 0917. At 1117 they passed Rendova; at 1500 the Russell Islands were abeam to port distant 4 miles, and at 1758 they passed through the nets at Purvis. *Ausburne, Claxton, Spence,* and *Foote* immediately moored either side of YO-164 and fueling was commenced. *Dyson* fueled at Marker Dog and at 1830 the group, just returned from battle, once more was placed on 2-hours' notice. They also received word that an ammunition barge was due at Purvis at 1000 the next morning, and plans immediately were set in motion to top off their ammo.

On *Claxton*'s bridge Heraldo Stout stood looking glumly down at the oil king and his helpers. Suddenly Stout's teeth clicked together, and his pipe fell out of his mouth. He'd bitten through the stem. "A hell of an ever-lovin' kind of operation *that* was!" stormed the Captain as he retrieved the operative portion of his briar. "No fun! No damned fun *AT* all!" He was talking about the mission to the Treasuries, not his broken pipe. Silently, utterly exhausted, officers and men who could be spared drifted off to their bunks, some shuffling through the necessary locomotion by instinct rather than by conscious thought. Aboard *Ausburne* the light burned almost until midnight in the Commodore's cabin. He was doing something perfectly normal for Arleigh Burke, but which most people would have considered absurd in the light of his responsibilities and the degree of his fatigue. The Commodore had recommended his communications officer, Lieutenant John "Stinky" Davis for a decoration. He hadn't told Davis, and he didn't mean to tell him—not just yet. But he was writing to Davis's mother and father, Stateside: "John is a splendid officer, and I have recommended him for a decoration. I don't know whether my recommendation will be complied with or not, so I haven't told him and I hope you won't, either. But I just want you to know that I have made the recommendation." Arleigh Burke signed, addressed, and sealed the letter. Then he shucked out of his scant clothing, sat on the edge of his bunk, and rolled heavily into it. The light in his cabin winked out. Save for the watch and those very special "mice" who handled oil, DesRon-23 was momentarily at peace with the world.

Rain, lashing over the anchorage in wind-whipped sheets, enfolded Purvis Bay on the morning of Thursday, 28th October, in an aqueous drapery of semi-opaque grey and near-zero visibility. Seemingly it came down not in drops but in slanting rods. The rainwater spread in a continuous thin film over decks, responsive to their pitch, and cascaded out of scuppers. Moisture formed in beads and droplets on surfaces shielded from the determined downpour, and seeped into ships as a primary burden of the air itself. Flags and pennants drooped sodden and lifeless from staffs and halyards and spun tiny threads of pure rainwater from their swollen corners. Here and there about the decks of the ships forlorn figures swathed about in foul-weather gear moved clumsily through the necessary on-deck chores. The whole prospect was muted, and seen from a distance of more than a very few yards all activity seemed fuzzy and to partake of the curious quality of slow motion. What a hell of a day to load ammo, reflected the Commodore of DesRon-23 as he gazed appraisingly out upon the dismal scene. Still and all, his captains had better be quick and thorough about it when the ammunition barge arrived. He probed his waking memory to recall the ammo allowances for the up-coming gunstrike. The figures which came into focus were 750 rounds of 6-inch .47-caliber high capacity for each cruiser, the first 200 rounds to be fired with flashless powder and the remainder with smokeless. Each cruiser he recalled also was allowed 600 rounds of 5-inch .38 anti-aircraft common, to be fired according to the same formula. The DDs, on the other hand, would fire counter-battery and it was hard to know how much ammo that might call for. They'd better take aboard all the "rocks" they could get their hands on; there was bound not to be enough in any case. Before turning away from the port in the door through which he was looking, Burke noticed that some bluejacket had left a swab blocking a drainpipe in consequence of which water stood inches deep on deck. He sighed. On such trivial things, he knew, the fate of men and ships and battles often turned . . .

The Commodore's appetite was not the least bit jittery in the face of what was fast developing into a tense strategic situation. Fresh eggs were scarce but *Ausburne*'s supply officer had managed to come up with some. In the privacy of his cabin Arleigh Burke packed away a solid breakfast of oatmeal, ham, eggs, toast and marmalade complemented by liberal libations of good old Navy "jamoke." Then he instructed his orderly to call away his boat, donned slicker and sou'wester, decided against boots after a moment's thought, and went topside. A half hour later a steward helped him out of this gear at the door of Admiral Merrill's suite aboard flagship *Montpelier*, and the two friends settled down to "thresh out a few kinks" as Merrill had suggested.

"I don't figure this Buka-Bonis-Shortlands bombardment mission's going to be particularly tough," said Burke.

"It all depends, Arleigh," Merrill replied. "The Jap has several 8-inch cruisers, a whole mess of destroyers, up to half a dozen attack transports, and plenty of men at Rabaul. He's bound to react to our Choiseul and Treasury landings. If he gets *really* het up we could run into a mess!"

"I figure we're *going* to run into a mess, Tip, but the way I see it, it'll be after the gunstrike, not during it. Koga's no fool. Neither is Samejima. They're going to wait to see which way the cat'll jump before committing a major task force."

"That may be," said the Admiral, "but I'll bet a cookie that, right now, they're gathering soldiers and transports to try to toss us off of Choiseul and out of the Treasuries. In any case I *hope* they are, because the stronger they react to those diversionary landings the less they'll have left to parry our real punch at Torokina. We've got to expect and be ready for just about anything from here on out."

"Of course. How about orders?"

"They're clear enough. We bombard enemy installations on Buka and Bonis starting at 0021 on D-Day. When that's over we run down to the Shortlands and shoot up Skunk Hollow, starting gunfire at 0631."

"After that . . . ?"

"After that, Arleigh, we stand off Vella La Vella waiting for the Jap to react to the bombardments and the Bougainville landings. If he sends a task force down to try to mess up those landings, we nail it."

"*That's* what I want to speak with you about, boss!" ejaculated Commodore Burke.

"Like how?"

"Tip, this morning I'm a salesman, and this is what I've got in my sample case . . ."

From an envelope Burke produced a sheaf of diagrams which he spread on the table. He then took time out to fill his pipe, light it, and tamp the glowing tobacco down with a matchbox. When the pipe was drawing satisfactorily he spoke around it and without releasing the grip of his teeth clenched on the bit.

"In my opinion we haven't been making the most of destroyers operating with cruiser task forces, Tip. I've got a one-two punch doctrine worked out with my boys and they understand it and are capable of executing it."

"I don't doubt that in the least, Arleigh. How does it work?"

"Simple! On contact with an enemy force DesDiv-45, which always is the leading Division, takes off instantly to mount a surprise torpedo attack. DesDiv-46 . . ."

"Just a minute, Arleigh," the Admiral interrupted. "You say '45' is always the leading Division. How come?"

"Aw, for God's sake, Tippy! Look, I've got a year's seniority over Austin. Isn't that worth a 10-degree advantage?"

Merrill burst into throaty laughter. "Sure—sure, Arleigh! I was just kidding! So what happens then?"

"Well, while I'm attacking, DesDiv-46 maneuvers into position to cover DesDiv-45 with gunfire if we are discovered by the enemy. Should that happen the fire of '46' is calculated to draw the fire of the enemy to that Division long enough to allow '45' to complete its attack. Once '45' has launched torpedoes, we haul out of the way and '46' maneuvers into a position to launch a second torpedo strike. This time we cover them the way they did us on the first go-round. Get it?"

"It sounds reasonable enough to me but, after all, you run your cans and how you fight them is your business. Why are we talking about all this?"

"I know, Tip . . . I know . . . but here's the point: with DDs positioned 6,000 yards ahead of the main body—and that's where we're usually stationed—they'll make contact by radar with an enemy force at between 20,000 and 25,000 yards and at about the same time that the cruisers do. The rate of change of range, Tip, with formations approaching each other may be between 600 and 1,700 yards a minute, depending upon their respective speeds. Now, before I fire torpedoes from DesDiv-45 I want to come to the reciprocal of the enemy's course, and get in closer than 6,000 yards if I can. That's the only way I can hope to achieve maximum results.

"As you'll recall, it takes a DD about 3 minutes to make a 180-degree turn with hard rudder. Aside from the obvious fact that TBS or visual traffic probably will betray our presence to the enemy and spoil the party if I have to wait for signalled permission from the Task Force Commander before I can take off with Division 45 to launch my torpedo attack, the chances are that the enemy will be long gone before I can get to the firing point and reverse course anyway." Burke looked at Merrill with wide blue eyes in which there flashed the flinty highlights of a zealot. He was leading up to the punch, and he was about to throw it.

"Well, what do you want from me, Arleigh?"

"*I want you to have faith in me and my boys,* Tip. I want you to have *enough* faith to let me get going on doctrine the moment I make enemy contact, and without first getting permission from you. I know it's hard, Tippy—but try . . . *please* try!"

"I *do* have faith in you, Arleigh, and in the situation we now find ourselves facing it seems to me your doctrine is exceptionally appropriate. Have you studied recent intelligence reports on Japanese torpedoes?"

"I haven't had time," said Burke, "and I don't have half the intelligence codes anyway. I've been looking for a staff officer who could take over that job and keep me informed, but I haven't found anybody. I've studied the Battle of Tassafaronga, though, if that's what you mean."

"Well, at least that'll help you understand the situation. We believe the Jap has a 24-inch torpedo with a range of better than 24,000 yards—15 miles, Arleigh!—and a payload double that of our 21-inch Mark XV. I believe they call it the 'Long Lance,' and that's a damned good name for it! In addition we have reliable reports that the Japanese cruisers have been equipped to carry as many as fifteen of these monsters!"

"I certainly didn't know that, Tip," said the now thoughtful Commodore of DesRon-23. "And our cruisers carry *no* torpedoes!"

"Arleigh, frankly I'm in a hell of a spot," continued the Admiral. "Our last recon photos show there are a minimum of two heavy cruisers, three light cruisers, and ten cans in the Japanese stable at Rabaul."

Burke nodded in dolorous acknowledgment and Merrill continued.

"That means they've got at least two ships throwing 8-inch salvos against our 6-inch. And, as you know very damned well, our 6-inch stuff will bounce right off the armor plate of their 8-inch cruisers at any kind of range. We'd have to be firing point-blank broadsides to come within a prayer of sinking them."

"So you plan to fight in close . . . ?"

"Of course I don't. They'd blow us out of water. Arleigh, the cruisers of Task Force 39 are just about all we've got left in this neck of the woods to cover the Bougainville landings and our drive northward. The Jap is dead certain to send a strong surface force down against us, once he's sure what's going on. We're trying to keep him confused, but he's bound to tumble. Now, if I try to close such a force to a point where my 6-inch guns will be effective Omori or whoever commands it either will tear me up with torpedoes or sink me with gunfire before I can do any good. Of course you must understand that if it was just a matter of this one job—one battle—I'd be inclined to take a chance, close him at best speed, and slug it out toe-to-toe. But I've got to save the few cruisers we've got left, and in the circumstances I just can't take avoidable risks."

"What do you plan, Tip?"

"If we *do* intercept an enemy surface force on the way to break up the landings at Torokina—and if he's there, we'll get him!—I've decided to try to fight a long-range action, at least out of his torpedo range although that will discount the effectiveness of my 6-inch. In such circumstances we'll have no chance of annihilating him, but we may turn him back. That should give us time to consolidate our beachheads, and it'll serve the immediate purpose of our mission."

"I gather, then," said Burke, "that I have your permission to initiate a torpedo attack upon enemy contact and without further specific authorization from you?"

"You have that permission, Arleigh, and we understand each other. Your DDs will be my only hope of effective hits at long range, and if your attack achieves any success at all it may well be decisive."

The two officers had coffee and talked a little longer but each had multiple duties waiting. When Arleigh Burke emerged on deck the rain had passed and the seascape was bathed in brilliant, washed sunlight. As he boarded *Ausburne* he ordered a signal calling all DesRon-23 Captains and senior officers to an immediate conference. Then he spoke casually to the young ensign who had the deck.

"Son, can you tell me the difference between a good officer and a poor one?"

The ensign stuttered, stammered, and finally delivered himself of a minutes-long dissertation on leadership qualities, aggressiveness (for he knew the Commodore's reputation), and technical proficiency. Burke heard him out in patience. Then he observed quietly, *"The difference between a good officer and a poor one is about 10 seconds, boy!* See that I'm called when the boats start to arrive."

At Truk, far north of Purvis Bay, a Japanese hawk was watching the American eagles as they gathered and sharpened beaks and talons for the inevitable combat to come. He was Admiral Mineichi Koga, Commander-in-Chief of the Japanese Imperial Navy combined fleets.

Koga, of impassive countenance, dark, and somewhat tall for his race, had not started out as one of the principal authors of the Japanese *Hakko Ichiu* scheme which means "bringing the eight corners of the world under one roof." That plan had been evolved by General Hideki Tojo and Admiral Isoroku Yamamoto, the top men of their respective services. Koga, of course, had striven mightily to achieve *Hakko Ichiu*, but at the beginning he had occupied a role sufficiently obscure to enable him to indulge a few personal caprices without attracting undue attention. One of these was a strong preference for the traditional kimono over the stiff uniform of the Westernized military, and he sought every opportunity, even on semi-formal occasions, to enjoy the loose comfort of the historic Japanese costume for men.

In the spring of 1943 fate, in the shape of sixteen U.S. fighter planes, catapulted Mineichi Koga into a top spot in the Imperial Japanese Navy. In mid-April a very interesting intelligence report reached Admirals Halsey and Nimitz. Yamamoto, then Japanese C-in-C at Rabaul and known to be a resourceful, intelligent, and determined naval commander, had decided to inspect the Jap defenses in the upper Solomons. The report was detailed and gave the date and time of Yamamoto's planned take-off and the schedule of his trip. Here was too promising an opportunity to be wasted. Permission was sought and secured from Washington to try to kill or capture this prize Japanese pigeon and when, at 0800 on the morning of 18th April, Yamamoto took off from Rabaul, an appropriate formation of sixteen U.S. planes also took off and headed for the same destination.

Yamamoto and his staff flew in two Bettys—Mitsubishi Zero Ones—protected by six Zekes—the Japanese Zero-Three one-engine fighter. They arrived over Buin on schedule at 0935, but so did the American formation. In a swift flash of wings and chatter of gunfire both Bettys were shot down while desperately trying to land, and top Admiral Yamamoto and his whole staff were dispatched to a rendezvous with their ancestors. Those in Nippon who knew were plunged into somber grief by this tragedy, but few were allowed to know for a long time. Yamamoto was considered irreplaceable as, in fact, he virtually was, and the Japanese did not acknowledge his death until many months after the event. Meanwhile Admiral Koga quietly took over the duties of C-in-C Combined Fleet, Imperial Japanese Navy.

On the afternoon of Thursday, 28th October, Admiral Mineichi Koga sat crosslegged on a mat at his Truk headquarters. Sitting in the group around him were three of his most trustworthy senior officers—Rear Admirals Sentaro Omori, Matsuji Ijuin, and Morikazu Osugi. They were all fighting Admirals on whom devolved command afloat. Present also was Admiral Tomoshige Samejima, in immediate command at Truk and next under Koga in the chain of command. A few staff members hovered in the background ready to produce facts or figures, charts, maps, or copies of reports. It was a command tenet of Koga's not to burden himself with detail and only to call for specific data when they were immediately pertinent. He opened the conference:

"Gentlemen, the enemy seems to be on the move."

"Ah, so!" agreed his confreres, nodding gravely.

"Admiral," continued Koga addressing Osugi who was junior in the group, "what is your thought?"

Osugi emitted a sibilant hiss and gave his opinion: "The enemy's operations thus far do not seem to me to be of importance, but I think they should be countered in the glorious tradition of our Navy."

"Admiral Ijuin . . . ?" Koga turned to the next senior.

"I feel that there should be a redeployment of our forces, especially from Bougainville, reinforced by strong formations from New Britain to drive the enemy into the sea. He does not seem to have made very substantial lodgments, but if he is allowed to build up his establishments on Choiseul and in the Treasuries they could prove embarrassing."

"Admiral Omori . . . ?"

"I find myself of two minds. I believe these developments should be watched very closely. At the same time I cannot help but feel that the enemy has not yet fully revealed his intentions. In the circumstances I favor watchful waiting."

"Admiral Samejima . . . ?"

"We know," said Samejima quietly, "that the enemy's surface forces, especially cruisers, have been sharply reduced in engagements fought in the fairly recent past. Our intelligence would seem to indicate that he has but one strong and effective cruiser task force left. There is no indication in our air reconnaissance reports that any such strong force participated in the recent landings. Splinter forces, maybe, but most of the preparation and support was left to his air arm.

"I conclude from this that we still have something more to hear. These assaults on Choiseul and the Treasury Islands could be simple diversions to draw us off balance so that we would find it difficult to meet a major thrust at another place. I agree with Ijuin that there might be a redeployment of our forces in the area to oppose these enemy moves, but I do not agree that troops in mass should be rushed south from Rabaul for the purpose. Let that wait awhile. Let the troops and transports be gathered and readied but, as Omori has said, I'm not yet sure that the enemy has revealed his basic plan, and I do not believe we should be frightened into action which we may quickly come to regret."

Koga clucked his tongue and a staff officer sprang to his side. "How many attack transports do we have at Rabaul?"

"Three there now, sir; two more en route and expected to arrive late tonight or early tomorrow morning."

"Have all five remain there until further orders, and alert five thousand troops to embark. Also prepare orders for assault forces to be organized in the Bougainville-Shortlands area to deal with the enemy on Choiseul and in the Treasuries."

"Instantly, Admiral!"

Koga turned once more to his conference. "Gentlemen, I thank you for your wise counsel. I am inclined to agree with Samejima and Omori that we should wait a reasonable time for the enemy to reveal his full intentions before we commit major formations. We shall, however, take precautionary steps while watching and waiting. You have heard my orders. Meanwhile, as you are my guests here at Truk, please accept warm sake and such other refreshment as I can offer you." The Admiral clapped his hands and the conference passed from a grim business to a mellow social mood.

At Purvis Bay the Captains of the Little Beavers were assembled aboard *Charlie Ausburne* and Arleigh Burke addressed them:

"I have very interesting news, fellows. We will sortie at 0200 on the morning of the 31st—a half hour before the cruiser formation—to mount our Buka-Bonis-Shortlands gunstrike. I know you've been expecting that information. The really *good* news is that, should we be lucky enough to make enemy contact, Admiral Merrill has approved our acting instantly on doctrine and without waiting to get permission from him at the time. You all know what that doctrine is so I won't go into it again except to remind you that destroyers will not—repeat, NOT—open gunfire ahead of the main body unless they themselves are under enemy gunfire. The whole basis of our doctrine is surprise, and I don't want any trigger-happy gunner lousing it up!

"You'll get your specific bombardment targets after we see how things are going. Our primary responsibility at the outset will be looking out for sneak Japanese surface formations, and firing counter-battery when the enemy opens up from the shore.

"I want to warn you now that should we find ourselves mixing it with an enemy surface force, I shall expect each of you to act with competent intelligence, and I shall issue a minimum of orders. I may maneuver without signal and if I do I shall expect you to follow me. After all, you should know how to handle your ships by now, and you should know what evolutions make sense in a battle, too. By the way, if I say 'up five!' I mean up 5 knots, not 5 revolutions. Now, has anybody got any problems?"

"I'm afraid I have, Commodore." It was habitually silent Commander Cavenagh, Captain of *Stanly*, who spoke.

"What's the trouble, Bob?"

"We've been having a hard time with our superheater tubes right along, sir. Now my Number 3 boiler's gone kaput, and my best speed is 31 knots."

"How'd it happen?"

"When our original tubes failed, Commodore, *Whitney* installed just ordinary tubes until the special replacements can get here from Pearl. They aren't here yet."

"Have you tried a full power run?"

"No, sir. I've hesitated to risk that."

"Well, this is no time for hesitation. Get under way early tomorrow morning, and give the old gal all she'll stand. If things are going to blow, let 'em blow. Better now than in battle. And if they don't blow, at least you'll know where you stand."

"Aye, sir!"

"Anything else?" Burke looked around. "You fellows sure you've got all the ammo you need?"

"I'm rollin' scuppers under with th' stuff," quipped Heraldo Stout. "Me, too," chimed in Ralph Lampman.

"Okeh, gentlemen," said the Commodore, rising. "This probably will be our last meeting before the gunstrike, and I don't have to remind you how important that mission is. If any problems arise that you feel you can't deal with, don't hesitate to come to me. That's what I'm here for. Otherwise I shall expect a very high level of performance from all of you."

The morning of 30th October could be said to have dawned at Purvis Bay only in a metaphorical sense. Great sheets of rain wrapped the ships about once more, and air activity in the immediate area was out of the question. But Arleigh Burke was due at a final Koli Point conference. In such circumstances it had become the custom for senior officers to use the fast little MTBs for transportation. The daring young MTB skippers always seemed able to make a proper landfall even in the thickest weather, and Burke personally found the MTB speed congenial. On this particular morning, while waiting for the MTB to nuzzle up against *Charlie Ausburne*'s ladder the Commodore had time only to glance quickly at a brief report from Bob Cavenagh. *Stanly*'s full power tests of the day before had proved successful, even with the inferior superheater tubes, and once more she was a member of the team capable of playing her full part. Burke thanked the special gods who have custody of things in boiler rooms as he tumbled aboard the MTB. The powerful engines pulsed, she sheered away from the destroyer, and started picking up speed as she threaded through the anchorage.

Admiral Merrill, the Captains and gunnery officers of the cruisers, Arleigh Burke, and other interested officers spent the morning poring over mosaics made from air reconnaissance photographs of the targets, collecting grid overlays to be used during the forthcoming bombardments, and discussing with photographic interpreters the latest air intelligence of targets in the Buka-Bonis and Shortlands areas. More than anything else the Commodore of DesRon-23 was worried about the navigational problems. Really, little or nothing was known about the offshore hazards in the Central and Northern Solomons. For a good many months now the survey ship *Pathfinder* had had her boats out making soundings in those portions of the islands under Allied control, but that was far short of the northern tip of Bougainville which was deep in enemy territory. *Charlie Ausburne*, Burke knew, would have the "honor" of leading this important cruiser task force through these virtually uncharted and reef-infested waters. An "honor" it might or might not be, but a tremendous responsibility it surely was. Hank Ereckson, *Ausburne*'s "exec" and navigator since Koenig had left in July, was at the conference and he examined the aerial photos both on and off shore with studious attention.

"What do you think, Ereck?" asked Burke who had little tolerance for incompetence but vast sympathy for a capable man with a really tough problem.

"I'll make it, Commodore," replied Ereckson quietly. "Don't worry."

It was typical of Burke that from that moment he dropped from his conscious mind the devastatingly difficult challenge of night navigation which lay ahead. Ereck had said he could handle it. Long ago Arleigh Burke had learned and had tried to sell to others the doctrine of faith in subordinates. Whether they could achieve it or not he didn't know, but *he* had achieved it. In less than 12 hours the fate of four United States cruisers and eight United States destroyers would be in the hands of this quiet little man named Ereckson. Arleigh Burke had observed the man intimately but briefly, and what he had observed he thought he could trust. He had faith, so he stopped worrying.

The conference over, the MTB took her party back to Purvis, and Commodore Arleigh Albert Burke was preparing to board his flagship when the young MTB skipper appeared at his elbow. The boy's name was Byron White and as a football college star and All-American he had earned the nickname "Whizzer White" by his dazzling distance dashes on the gridiron. But White had more than athletic prowess to offer. He was a Rhodes Scholar and impressive above the ears as well as below. His rank was Lieutenant, junior grade, and Burke had ridden with him many times out of Tulagi and regarded his quiet self-sufficiency with favor.

"Commodore, may I speak with you?"

"Of course, White. What's on your mind?"

"I'd like to sail with you, sir."

"And give up this pretty little thing?" Burke looked around at the neat and powerful little MTB.

"Yes, sir."

"Lieutenant," said the Commodore deliberately, "it so happens that there's a job open on my staff. I need an intelligence man—one who can get all the codes, read all the reports and dispatches, stay on top of the thing, and keep me informed about what's going on and, more important, what's probably *about* to go on. I don't have anything like time enough to do that myself."

"I'm sure I could do it, sir."

"Very well, come along . . ." Captain Burke placed his foot on the ladder to mount to *Ausburne*'s deck.

"But Commodore—what about my clothes . . . my gear . . . my orders . . . ?" Young Lieutenant White was suddenly thrown for a complete loss. Arleigh Burke once more turned to him and spoke patiently:

"Son, if those things worry you there's no place for you in my Squadron. In '23,' when there's a job to be done, we do it first and worry afterwards. I'm sorry . . ."

Whizzer White gulped. "But, Commodore . . . I'm sorry . . . I didn't understand . . ."

"Very well, come along then!" Burke mounted the ladder nor deigned to look behind him. But White was there. His second in command took the MTB back to Tulagi, and that's the last time Whizzer White was aboard her for a long time. At Burke's request Admiral Halsey confirmed Lieutenant White's transfer to DesRon-23, and in a very short time the young man was playing an important role on the Commodore's staff. White's omnivorous devouring of all sorts of traffic and his sagacity at interpretation gave Burke and the Little Beavers a considerable edge in anticipating events to come and measurably improved the efficiency of the Squadron. Also White turned out to be Burke's "No!" man. There were "Yes" men in plenty in the Solomons as elsewhere. Arleigh Burke was far too shrewd to countenance such a stooge. A "No!" man was far more to his taste, and Byron White often said "no" under circumstances which made the Commodore momentarily impatient. Usually the junior was right or at least had defensible logic on his side, and the two got on well together.

At 0200 on the dark morning of Sunday, 31st October, 1943, United States destroyer *Charles Ausburne* got her anchor and stood out of Purvis Bay. Silent on her bridge and taking no part in the evolution having once ordered it, stood Captain Arleigh Burke. Behind *Ausburne* sortied *Dyson, Stanly, Claxton, Spence, Thatcher, Converse,* and *Foote.* At long last DesRon-23, as a complete unit, was putting to sea against the enemy. Locked up in the Commodore's safe in his cabin was a copy of ComTaskForce-39's Op-Plan 3-43. It called for a simple gunstrike in the dark at Buka-Bonis followed by one in daylight at "Skunk Hollow," but Admiral Tomoshige Samejima, IJN, was making other plans —plans that would fructify in the vicious Battle of Empress Augusta Bay, and the deaths of many men now sailing in Squadron 23.

10

Gunstrike at Skunk Hollow

One hour and forty minutes after they had sortied from Purvis Bay the base course of *Task Force Merrill*, which was the designation used by the Office of Naval Intelligence for Task Force 39, was 270 degrees true, speed 20 knots. The twelve ships had something less than 24 hours of steaming ahead of them to cover the 537 airline miles between Port Purvis and Buka Island at the northern tip of Bougainville where they would unleash their first gunstrike. "Slipsticks" in engineering compartments and chartrooms had worked out the time-space-pressure-rpm formula. An average steam pressure of 525 pounds delivering an average of 369.9 revolutions per minute would get them to the site of their mission and still leave a prudent safety margin for navigational errors which must be anticipated in the circumstances.

In approaching his targets it pleased Admiral Merrill to avoid The Slot. This was largely to further the achievement of surprise which was regarded as of primary importance if it could be attained. For this reason the task force stood south of the Russells and the New Georgia complex. It was then the task force commander's intention to approach the vicinity of Simbo Island on a northerly heading, haul well to the west of the Treasuries, and then bear up for "Point George" on a course a bit north of west. "Point George" was a position on the chart at latitude 06°—39'—00" South; longitude 154°—25'—00" East. Upon reaching that point the formation would come to a 000-degree heading and continue up to 05°—21'—00" South. Here, approximately due west of Petat Island off the coast of Buka, they would turn east for 6 miles. This would bring them comfortably close to the Buka coast. They would then swing southeast to course 160 degrees true, roughly paralleling the island, and would mount their bombardment on that course as they traversed a leg approximately 9.6 miles long. The formation speed while the guns fired would be 20 knots. Their ETA "Point George" was 2040 on the night of the day of their

187

departure from Purvis. The turn toward Petat Island was scheduled for 2325. The turn southeast to the firing course would come at 2345, and the guns would speak at 0021 on the morning of Monday, 1st November. It was a brilliant challenge in precision navigating, station keeping, and split-knot formation steaming, and it had to be accomplished with all ships blacked out and amid total radio silence. In the event, all ETAs were to be made within a variation of less than 10 minutes, and the lad who led the speeding ships through black velvet darkness and overcast to the precise successive points for their course changes was Hank Ereckson, *Ausburne's* navigator and "exec." It was a performance which won him a merited "Well done!" from Arleigh Burke.

The order of steaming of the formation reflected the mission in hand rather than the conventional disposition of ships. At the outset Des-Div-45—*Ausburne, Dyson, Stanly,* and *Claxton,* steaming in that order, were in the van with a distance of 500 yards between ships, and *Claxton* 7,000 yards ahead of the guide cruiser, *Montpelier.* At a predetermined time *Stanly* would be detached to dash forward and take picket station 10 miles to the northwest of the leading cruiser, on the road to Rabaul. Her early warning of threatening enemy surface interference was relied upon.

The order of steaming of the cruiser line, with the ships at a distance of a thousand yards, was *Montpelier,* the flag, *Cleveland, Columbia,* and *Denver,* commanded respectively by Captains Robert G. Tobin, Andrew G. Shepard, Frank E. Beatty, and Robert P. Briscoe.

DesDiv-46, that often unhappy "off" Division held back on a 10-degree line of bearing in Burke's celebrated one-two punch formation and always in the position of trying to come to the party, was even worse off than usual this time, or so it seemed to Commodore Austin. The Division was split, *Spence* and *Thatcher* being positioned 3,000 yards astern of the last cruiser, *Denver,* with *Converse* and *Foote* being back another 1,500 yards behind *Thatcher,* the distance between DDs being the customary 500 yards. Thus disposed, the formation covered about 10 miles of ocean but this was to be tightened up to about 6 miles with the detachment of *Stanly* and the drawing together of the ships for the gunstrike.

Although Arleigh Burke had been Commodore of DesRon-23 for a short 10 days, already he had set his mark upon the ships and the men. For one thing, as *Task Force Merrill* steamed north, the destroyers of the formation maintained Condition One-Easy—a Burke innovation. The problem of fatigue was stark and dangerous. Condition One-Easy was designed to let as many of the men and officers as possible get as much rest as they could and still maintain necessary ship efficiency and alertness.

Actually, Condition One-Easy differed slightly in each ship depending upon the number and combination of experienced and competent officers and petty officers available. Under this Condition the engineering department stood a watch in two or even a watch in three if the ship was lucky enough to have a sufficiency of engineering personnel. This gave people 4 and sometimes 8 consecutive hours off duty, and did much to promote relaxed nerves and battle readiness. In the gunnery department key personnel manned the pointer and trainer stations, with one man on the phones. The rest could sleep at their stations dressed for battle, the watch being rotated every 2 or 4 hours. The same general arrangement fitted the torpedo battery.

Deck and bridge watches were almost invariably watch-and-watch— 4 hours on, 4 off. Communications and radar watches followed the same pattern except that station manning was so apportioned that each man had an extra hour off periodically. It was found impossible to maintain radar and sound alertness for more than 1 hour at a time, so the men rotated between these stations. The damage control people got what looked like the best break, being allowed to sleep at their stations save for a phone watch. However, since most of the commissary personnel were assigned to damage control when the ship was in a condition of alertness, and still had their regular duties to perform in feeding the ship's company, they probably did not benefit disproportionately from Condition One-Easy.

Another Burke innovation was his insistence that all hands, not just the officers, be as fully informed as possible on what the ship was doing, what she was expected to do, and why. Suggestions by bluejackets were welcomed by Arleigh Burke, and during his time in "23" he received and acted on a great number. One of the first things he did upon breaking his pennant in *Ausburne* was to have a special chair of his own design rigged inside the pilot house. It was a simple reclining affair made from canvas stretched on a frame of ¾-inch pipe and it was Burke's whim, when the ship went to general quarters at twilight each evening, to sit in this chair and dictate to his yeoman on the bridge how he would conduct naval engagements under varying circumstances. First he would postulate the enemy's strength and his own, then the relative positions of the formations, their missions, and the conditions obtaining. And then he would fight the battle. It was simply another example of Burke's reaching out to meet problems before they confronted him in the form of emergencies. What he was doing was trying to improve and fortify his instinctive action in battle, for it was his theory that all action in battle is basically instinctive. The more diversified battle problems he could invent and solve theoretically, the more reliable would be his instinct if he encountered such problems in reality and, most important, the quicker would be his recognition of them and the faster his specific action to meet them. The bridge watch aboard *Charlie Ausburne* came to look forward with great keenness to these imaginary naval conflicts, and from Brute Reynolds in his captain's seat forward of the binnacle to the lowliest bridge messenger they were all ears. Recognizing and appreciating their interest Burke frequently would interrupt his dictation to invite their solutions, complimenting astute contributions and patiently explaining the fallacies in those he considered less than optimum.

With almost the certainty of battle ahead—no responsible U.S. naval officer in the Solomons expected the Jap *not* to react violently to what we already had done to him and especially what we were then planning to do—sunset on Sunday, 31st October, found Arleigh Burke sitting in his special chair but concerned with very real and impending rather than imaginary fighting. The grim grey task force steamed silently at 29 knots on a course north of west. There had been reports indicating the possible presence of enemy submarines on their track, but as a DD's sound gear is not effective at anything like 29 knots, they'd ignored the reports and plowed ahead. "We might just as well forget about the stuff," Burke observed to Brute Reynolds. "If we're going to be hit, we'll be hit, and that's that."

The sky overhead was reasonably clear, but there were clouds on the horizon all around giving promise of an overcast night. Rain squalls were to be observed ahead to the northwest and heat lightning shimmered intermittently around the periphery of the full 360 degrees of their vision. However, as darkness descended, visibility still was good up to 6,000 yards and the sea was smooth with gentle rollers.

"Brute," began the Commodore, "let's check over these targets again."

"I know 'em by heart, Commodore. And as of right now *Ausburne* hasn't even got one!"

"Well, we sure as hell *will* have; don't worry about that! Let's see, now . . ."

From memory, for it was far too dark on the bridge to read from the Op-Plan, Burke began to recite the targets and the missions and responsibilities of the ships of the formation:

Two of the DDs, *Ausburne* leading the formation, and *Foote* bringing up the rear, had no assigned targets. *Ausburne*'s job was to be sure the ships avoided navigational hazards and, with *Foote*, to be especially alert to detect any surface movement which might signal the presence of an enemy afloat. The TFC had been warned that he might encounter Japanese PT boats in the area, and the head and tail DDs of the column were to keep a careful lookout for any such threat. The rest of the destroyers, at discretion after the cruisers opened up or unless the enemy discovered them and fired first, were to fire counter-battery in an effort to silence the enemy's fire against the cruisers while the latter went methodically about the primary job of destroying air strips and revetments, personnel and supply areas, and headquarters installations.

In the major work of destruction *Montpelier* was to take the Bou-gainville or Bonis side of Buka Strait, chopping up the air strip and the supply area to the west of it. *Cleveland* was given the air strip on Buka Island with its revetments as well as supply and personnel areas to the south and east of the field. *Columbia* had essentially the same targets as *Cleveland* save that she was to take care of the supply and personnel installation to the northwest of the field. *Denver* had been given an important mission but split targets. Her 6-inch battery would fire against the headquarters and supply and personnel areas north and northeast of the Buka airfield. Targets for her 5-inch battery were the air strips both at Buka and Bonis, and their revetments. Aboard every ship of the formation the targets were clearly revealed on photo mosaics compartmented by grid overlays for fire control, and two Black Cats had been promised as spotters for the cruiser fire. A night fighter—Corsair F-4-U2—also would be over the task force as a ges-ture toward keeping enemy snoopers at a distance, and *Columbia* was fighter-director ship. However, with the meteorological forecast indi-cating limited visibility over target as it did at the end of the second dog on the evening of 31st October, little really was expected of the night fighter.

Having ticked off the targets for the first bombardment and the role his ships were to play in its accomplishment, Arleigh Burke stretched out and chuckled comfortably. "Brute," he said, "you'd never guess what Tip Merrill said to me when we were going over this thing back at Koli Point."

"What was that, Commodore?"

"I asked him, 'Tip, when we get through heaving our rocks at Buka and Bonis, what do we do then?' He said, 'Arleigh, when that one's over we make a dignified retirement toward Skunk Hollow—*at 30 knots!*' Dignified, huh? At 30 knots! Some dignity!" Captain Reynolds joined the Squadron commander in an appreciative laugh, and a mess boy arrived on the bridge with a loaded tray under a clean white napkin.

"What've you got there, son?" asked the Commodore.

"Ham sandwiches, sah!"

"Ugh!" said Arleigh Burke, but he took one just the same and sat munching placidly as *Charlie Ausburne* knifed steadily along on her course toward "Point George." At the moment the Commodore wasn't thinking especially about Commander Robert W. Cavenagh, but Bob Cavenagh was thinking about the Commodore.

At 1504 that afternoon, with a saucy flirt of her tail and a seeming hunch of her shoulders as her stern bit deep, *Stanly* had peeled off and started a high-speed run toward her picket station 10 miles ahead and west of the task force. She was now on station. Standing impassively on the bridge Captain Cavenagh gazed ahead into the empty night and permitted himself mitigation of the monotony of his present duty in analytical reflection. Something had happened to the Squadron; something had happened to *Stanly*. There was a new spirit abroad. Two weeks ago the attitude of the men and officers alike had been a somewhat dogged "Let's get on with it." They'd been doing their job all right, he guessed, but there'd been no sparkle anywhere.

Now? Now it seemed different. God knew they were just as tired, just as exhausted, fine drawn like the twanging strings of a harp tuned to concert pitch. But, too, there was a new calm, a new confidence in the Squadron and in the ship. The flat resignation of "Let's get on with it" had been replaced by an irrefutable *"We're going to win this thing!"* Cavenagh had watched the change take place; he had felt it himself. From whence had it come?

Thus Bob Cavenagh approached the *mystique* which even so early was beginning to manifest itself in DesRon-23. He sought no easy answers, and he accepted no one answer. It was more complex than that. What part, he wondered, did Naval Academy training of officers play in the spirit which emerged in a ship and a naval unit? Not a great deal he concluded, as had Heraldo Stout and other of the Little Beaver skippers before him. Prior to *Stanly* Cavenagh had had an old four-piper. There had been very little Academy overlay in *that* ship, he reflected. Officers and men had come from all walks of life yet they'd been a can-do aggregation, and very keen. It had been the same in his old S-boat, too. Indoctrination at the "trade school" helped, of course, but it provided only a limited foundation for the operation of broader forces.

The war? Yes, certainly the war was a factor. The excitements and challenges of such a conflict as that in which they were engaged tended to crystallize and release strong spiritual drives in the best men. But the impact of the war wasn't new, either to men of *Stanly* or of Des-Ron-23. Yet there'd been a change—a *recent* change in them all. How about what he sometimes thought of as the "scend of the Navy"—the continuing flow of the spirit of the naval service handed on from one generation of officers and long-service men to the next? It was a very real thing, a compelling force deriving from tradition, patriotism, fraternity, and a fierce pride of service. It was, he concluded, of major importance. Thus nearly Bob Cavenagh approached the erudite philosophy of Hamberger, and the less complex formulizations of Gano. But still that wasn't the whole story and the skipper of *Stanly*, standing silent and reflective on his blacked-out bridge, well knew it.

In the Squadron and in the ship a new and electric quality—a sort of *character*—had emerged. It must, he finally decided, come from just one place: leadership at the Squadron level, and that meant the leadership of Arleigh Burke.

It was in such fashion that Bob Cavenagh, not one of the more forceful or dashing Little Beaver skippers, tiptoed toward participation in the *mystique* of DesRon-23. Like Hamberger, he did not perceive it as pristine, nor did he trouble to think of this force as a *mystique* either. To him it was an amalgam of faith, tradition, and fraternity. But there was no doubt in his mind of its potency, its indestructible reality, and that the man who had set it free to play its role in the affairs of the Squadron was Arleigh Albert Burke.

The surface of the sea around the ship and the heavens above her were empty of material things. *U.S.S. Stanly* stood on course . . .

At headquarters, Imperial Japanese Navy, Island of Truk, there was considerable confusion at the top although it was evidenced by no great bustling about. Since as early as noon Admiral Koga had been pondering intelligence of a United States Navy cruiser task force bound north. Where or how he got this intelligence so early never has been quite clear, for Admiral Merrill had been quite sure there had not been any enemy snoopers over his formation during daylight hours, but Koga had it and it disturbed him. With Admiral Samejima, sipping tea, he grappled with the problems which the news posed:

"Where do you suppose they're bound?"

Samejima shrugged. "The Treasuries . . . ?"

"That might be—but then, it might not. We have no word of transports with the formation. If the Americans planned to reinforce their beachheads they'd bring troops." *

"If we knew how strong their force was we'd know what to do," observed Samejima none too helpfully.

"I agree! The white bastards can't have a lot left, and if they'd just send most of it far enough up so we could get at it we could do something to make a lot of people in Tokyo happy!"

---

* As a matter of fact a fast second echelon transport force was, at that moment, coming up behind TF-39 at 14 knots, bound for our Treasury beaches, but the two forces were in no sense operating together.

"Ah, so!" agreed Samejima. "Omori and the others are at Rabaul, and they've got a lot of Eighth Fleet power there. Also the transports and men are waiting as you ordered. I could send them down to throw the enemy out of the Treasuries. It might be a good thing."

"No, Tomoshige," said Koga, "we'll wait! This may be too good a chance to risk spoiling by ill-considered action. For a long time I've been hoping for an opportunity to bring their one remaining cruiser task force to battle. If that can be managed we'll destroy it and start south again ourselves. Now that their big ships have ventured out I want to be very sure where I'll find them before I commit important forces."

"Well, maybe our air reconnaissance will turn up something."

"Ah, so!" said Koga. "Have you heard the latest from Tokyo?"

"Probably not," replied Samejima glumly.

"Those civilians! Those *damned* civilians!" burst out top Admiral Koga with a spitting hiss. "They're saying the war's *won*, and they're starting to slow down in the factories."

"No!" Samejima was incredulous and dismayed.

"That's not all," continued Koga. "Last week, in Ginza, the police actually had to break up a *victory* celebration!"

"M-m-m-m-m . . ." Admiral Samejima was far too wily to commit himself too positively in front of his chief, but the news induced a cold sensation at the pit of his stomach. He hoped it wasn't true. But it was.

At 2043 Brute Reynolds stepped into the double screened, lighted chartroom, quickly read the figures on a slip of paper which had been handed to him a moment before by Hank Ereckson, then returned to the bridge. "Commodore," he said, "we have arrived 'Point George.' "

"Very well," Burke told him. "Come right to course zero-zero-zero. How are we doing for time?"

"We're 3 minutes late, sir!" Although he tried not to show it, the note of pride in the Captain's voice was unmistakable.

"Brute, that is fine going indeed! Tip Merrill will want to give you the Congressional Medal of Honor, and so do I!"

"It's not my doing, sir," said Reynolds. "The Task Force Commander sets course and speed . . ."

"I know all about that!" replied Burke pugnaciously, "but we're out in front—we got here first, didn't we?" Captain Burke could be a wee mite illogical in his own right under certain circumstances. His pride in the precision job Ereckson was doing in leading the formation was enormous and, in his mind, it attached to all the ships of the Squadron.

Since 1947 the radar operators and the CIC men of *Task Force Merrill* had been busy with air bogies, but it was not until 2140, almost exactly an hour after the turn to a north heading, that a determined enemy snooper came in and spooked the task force. This plane was picked up on radar at a distance of 33 miles bearing 312 degrees true. He closed to within 5,000 yards, descended low enough to get a good look, then went winging away toward Rabaul and was lost on radar at 50 miles. It looked as though the snooper was going to take his report home personally, and Tip Merrill came on TBS:

"This is the Task Force Commander. I'm breaking radio silence to tell you what you all probably know by this time: we've been spooked. From now on all ships are free to fire at discretion at any bogey within a range of 6,000 yards. Of course this will compromise our secrecy, but that joker who just left us has taken care of that so don't worry about it. I might as well tell you now, too, that we've been monitoring a lot of enemy radio traffic during the last few hours, and it seems to concern this task force. Curiously, early enemy transmissions seem to have originated in the Treasuries although we don't quite understand what that means. We suspect the enemy knows we're bound for Buka, so from now on it's just 'good shooting' to you all, and God bless you!" Throughout the formation the loudspeakers subsided, the bridges fell silent once more, and *Task Force Merrill* stood on course . . .

At 2328 a small flurry of activity pulsed through the formation. On the point position and responsive to Ereck's calculations, *Charlie Ausburne* started swinging starboard toward course 090 degrees true— the run-in toward the Buka coast off the island of Petat. While the destroyer's head was still paying off Admiral Merrill once more came on TBS to announce that his calculations showed them to be at the turning point. At this crucial moment *Ausburne*'s TBS went out because of a relay failure, and Arleigh Burke could not receive the voice transmissions of the OTC. One of the transmissions he missed was Merrill's warning to the task force at 2336½: "*Confident we are expected! Be alert for traps!*"

Almost simultaneously with the Admiral's announcement that the time had come to change course, Roy Gano opened up on the flagship by blinker tube to state that *Dyson*'s navigator placed them opposite Yame Island rather than off Petat. This position proved to be correct; they'd overshot the mark by one mile; course was corrected. So far as the purposes of the gunstrike, now imminent, were concerned, the weather had "improved." The Fahrenheit temperature was 82 degrees. The wind was from the southeast at force two, and there were modest swells from the same direction. More importantly, the sky was overcast giving good dark cover.

If *Task Force Merrill*, steaming tensely toward what they still hoped might be a surprise blasting of the enemy within a few short minutes, seemed a forlorn formation in an empty ocean, such an impression was illusory. Behind them, steaming at 14 knots toward a slightly different target—Cape Torokina, on Empress Augusta Bay, Bougainville—came the punch with which we hoped to stagger and bewilder the Jap. This force, officially designated Main Body, Northern Force, was commanded by Commodore Lawrence F. Reifsnider, and was composed of eight transports, four cargo ships, seven destroyers, four destroyer minesweepers, and two fleet tugs. The force, which had the tremendous responsibility of making the first U.S. landings on Bougainville, was organized in three divisions. To avoid exciting enemy suspicion each division had originated at a different place, and only at 0740 that same morning had they rendezvoused 84 miles west of Guadalcanal and headed northwest toward target, a fully formed invasion armada.

TransDivAble, Captain Anton B. Anderson, included *President Jackson, President Adams, President Hayes*, and *George Clymer*. They were screened by DesDiv-9; Commander Edmund B. Taylor. They had left Guadalcanal on the night of 30th October.

TransDivBaker, Captain George B. Ashe, included *American Legion, Fuller, Crescent City*, and *Hunter Liggett*. They were screened by some ships of DesRon-45, Captain Ralph Earle, Jr., and had left Efate at noon on the 28th.

TransDivCharlie, Captain Henry E. Thornhill, was composed of *Alhena, Alchiba, Libra*, and *Titania*, screened by MineRon 2, Commander Wayne B. Loud. They had left Espiritu on the 28th.

It was the protection of this force by a surprise smashing of enemy air facilities at Buka and Bonis and in the Shortlands that was the immediate *raison d'etre* of Task Force 39. Thereafter the interception of an anticipated enemy surface attack on the transports at the landing sites would be the business of the task force, and would produce the interesting Battle of Empress Augusta Bay.

At 2338 *Charlie Ausburne*, her echo-ranging equipment sweeping 45 degrees on either bow and her fathometer constantly sounding to warn of shoal water, made her final turn to the firing course, which was 160 degrees true. At 0015 the next morning her TBS once more came back into service and Commodore Burke picked up fragments of a message from the Task Force Commander ordering all ships to fire on bogies if they came within range. Exactly 6 minutes later, at 0021, the cruiser line blazed into action and, as Merrill wrote in his battle report, "started pumping shell over the hills and far away."

From the vantage point of the open sea where the bombardment force steamed along at 20 knots, the immediate results of the gunstrike were spectacular. The Black Cats were over, and the Japanese had opened on them with anti-aircraft fire at 2356, but without result. Spotting for the cruisers the Cats reported their fire neatly zeroed in on all targets, and within minutes the foreshore was eerily silhouetted by huge fires raging in ammunition and supply dumps, plane-filled revetments, and the personnel and service buildings clustered about the air strips behind the hills. It appeared that a measure of surprise had been achieved, for it was several minutes before the cruiser fire was answered by a shore battery to the southeast. *Ausburne* silenced this battery and thereafter all van DDs fired brisk counter-battery. For the most part the enemy's fire was weak and erratic.

Stanly's orders had been to rejoin astern of *Foote* when the formation came to the firing course. Now, at 0028, while still some distance behind the formation but closing, *Stanly* picked up a surface contact at 3,000 yards. She reported, was ordered to attack, and roared into action with full radar control. The target built up speed to 28 knots, heading west. It was never clearly observed save on radar, but Bob Cavenagh thought it might have been a small destroyer. *Stanly* fired a half salvo of torpedoes, but observed no hits. A few minutes after she opened gunfire the target seemed to be enveloped in heavy black smoke. It was still smoking badly when it pulled out of range, Captain Cavenagh having decided against pursuit and in favor of rejoining the task force.

At the same time *Stanly* spotted her target, *Cleveland* picked up two surface contacts on radar, close aboard and moving at high speed. It seemed likely that these were PT boats whose torpedoes already had been fired, and *Cleveland* took evasive action. Meanwhile *Spence* charged toward the targets her 40-mm tracer etching lurid lines on the black velvet softness of the night. The targets turned away from *Spence* and very soon were lost on radar, merging with the shoreline.

At 0029 *Ausburne* turned to the retirement course, which was 220 degrees true, and as each ship reached that same point she ceased fire and turned away. *Stanly*, last in line, turned the point with some guns still shotted and, as was customary, requested and received permission to "unload through the muzzle"—a safer procedure than opening closed and primed breaches to withdraw the charges. For no special reason her gunnery officer chose a nearby island for a target, and cut loose. The Fourth of July effect which followed amazed him quite as much as it did those on other ships at the rear of the column. Out of the magician's hat *Stanly* had miraculously pulled an enemy ammo dump as a nuisance target, and the resulting pyrotechnical display was most gratifying to all hands.

By this time enemy air was over and a bogey up ahead of *Ausburne* was busily laying a flare path of white float lights across their course. Admiral Merrill was building up speed toward that "dignified" 30 knots he'd planned for retirement and hated to change course but decided he'd better do so. He ordered a 40-degree turn to the right at 0156, and a further turn of 30 degrees shortly thereafter. As they passed astern the flares were seen to be lying on a 140-degree true bearing and their obvious purpose was to point out the formation to additional enemy aircraft as they arrived on the scene. For the most part the U.S. ships were able to keep enemy air at a distance which robbed it of effective attack, but at 0200 one persistent fellow closed *Ausburne* from ahead and flew the length of the ship at masthead height, all of his guns winking viciously and spraying the ship's decks with a tattoo of snarling, ricocheting bullets. Brute Reynolds fishtailed "diligently," as he was to describe it later over a bottle of beer at the *Cloob des Slot*, and although *Charlie Ausburne* was pretty well shot up topside by small caliber stuff, she suffered no casualties. A moment later Heraldo Stout saw the plane crash out of control on his port beam, a victim either of *Ausburne's* or *Claxton's* antiaircraft.

As the formation stood south toward the far more dangerous gunstrike at Skunk Hollow, all hands were mustered to repair blast damage, clean batteries, and get up ammunition for the next phase of the mission. A check showed Admiral Merrill's favorite typewriter (he did much of his own typing) to have been the most important casualty. It had been demolished by an enemy shell which burst abreast of *Montpelier's* flag bridge just before she turned away from the firing course.

The high-speed retirement of the task force toward the Shortlands was marked by few incidents. Enemy air continued to harass the formation until 0209 but was kept at a respectful distance by accurate antiaircraft fire in volume or robbed of effectiveness by intricate maneuvering. *Stanly*, playing "Aunt Sally" at the tail end of the column, swooped back and forth looking for surface targets, and at 0128 picked up several by radar on a 330-degree true bearing, distant 6 miles. She went racing after them, guns pluming, and when she rejoined, Bob Cavenagh reported that he thought he had registered with his 5-inch battery. The targets disappeared from the radar screen before he'd turned back. At 0340 *Ausburne* picked up a numerous formation ahead which was quickly identified as the main body of the U.S. landing force headed for Empress Augusta Bay. Their ETA there was 0615, and the two formations swept silently past each other, port to port, unseen save by radar. At 0450 with the task force already nearing target, "*Foote*-the-Unfortunate" suddenly sheered sharply out of line to starboard, and *Stanly* plunged past her maintaining formation course and speed. Either blast damage or an unsuspected hit had ruptured a compartment in *Foote*; her fuel oil had become contaminated; she had to shut down both engines. It was no time, however, for *Task Force Merrill* to be diverted from its assigned mission, and all of the other ships stood on.

By 0456 *Foote* had her starboard engine back on the line. Two minutes later the port engine was back on the line and she was under way at 15 knots. On the bridge Governor Ramsay took the trouble philosophically. He'd seen a good bit of steaming in his day, and he knew those things happened. Within 11 minutes *Foote* had built up speed to 34 knots, but so fast was Task Force 39 knifing through the water toward target that *Foote* was unable to rejoin until 0620. When she did, she took station on *Converse,* and immediately found herself under fire from the shore batteries of the Shortlands.

Foote no longer was the flag of Division 46. Count Austin had broken his pennant in *Spence* some time before and at that moment, in his ever courtly way, was giving Captain Heinie Armstrong a hard time. For that matter the complaints of flagboat skippers always were the same. Destroyer Commodores, whether of Divisions or Squadrons, seemed to exhibit almost a phobia for monopolizing the PPI scopes, leaving their skippers to wring their hands and wonder what the hell was going on. At Empress Augusta Bay, however, the Count was to depart from this pattern and, at least briefly, try fighting his Division from CIC. The innovation helped produce a collision at 30 knots, and won him a thunderous black look from Arleigh Burke.

The plastering of the Shortlands was a punishing chore for *Task Force Merrill* and its component, DesRon-23. On one previous occasion, the night of 29–30th June, 1943, U.S. naval forces had attempted to blast Skunk Hollow. However, the conditions then were vastly different. The night was black, laced with violent thunderstorms, and visibility was zero. The shooting on both sides was unobserved and largely ineffective. A daytime bombardment was something else again. It was a strike under conditions of full visibility against an alerted enemy who was known to have plenty of firepower. On the face of it such conditions hardly could fail to be evocative of highly interesting developments.

The plan for the bombardment was complex and difficult. It was to be conducted at high speed, and on two courses. The first leg, on course 90 degrees true, would permit enfilading of the reverse slope of Poporang Island, the seaplane area, by indirect fire. It also would allow acceptable range coverage of the eastern ends of Shortland and Faisi Islands. The second leg, on course 50 degrees true, would permit direct fire and would bring Ballale Island with its airfield and ancillary installations within range of the cruiser 6-inch batteries. Target assignments were: *Montpelier,* Poporang Island; *Cleveland,* Faisi Island, with her 6-inch, and counter-battery with her 5-inch on Morgusaia and Poporang; *Columbia,* Korovo Island; *Denver,* the north shore of Kulitania Bay and Lofung Plantation. As at Buka-Bonis, the DDs were to fire counter-battery.

Salvo fire would be commenced simultaneously by the cruisers on signal, and in the absence of air observation, spotting would have to be by visually observed fall of shot.

In the event, the Jap did not wait for the signal which would have brought U.S. salvo fire plunging upon his installations. The sun rose at 0614. Exactly 5 minutes later a heavy battery on Shortland Island opened fire on *Charlie Ausburne,* and from that time forward it was a "Katie-bar-the-door" firefight. All ships of the formation maneuvered at high speed to try to neutralize the enemy's fire control solutions as fast as they were computed. It probably helped, but only a little, and certainly it contributed nothing to stabilizing the fire control of Task Force 39. On the other hand, the targets of the task force were much larger than the ships bombarding them, so some net advantage accrued to the ships.

By 0622 *Ausburne* had been straddled several times although not yet hit. "Those jokers are hell on deflection, but not so hot on range," growled Arleigh Burke. "Can't we hit 'em harder and faster, Brute?" The Captain relayed the word to his gunnery officer, Lieutenant John F. Briggs, Jr., who spoke to the battery and *Ausburne*'s rate of fire rose.

An early morning haze and low hanging gunsmoke made effective spotting almost impossible for the ships of the task force. They didn't know how much damage they were doing; they knew the enemy fire was much heavier than had been expected; the van DDs simply kept pumping out shell and hoping. At 0623 *Cleveland,* temporarily forsaking her assigned targets, was forced to fire counter-battery, and she was followed in this action a minute later by *Montpelier.* The other two cruisers were forced to join in counter-battery fire almost at once. At 0624 there was a notable slackening of the enemy fire which lasted until 0629 and probably reflected the switching of the cruiser fire to counter-battery. At 0629½ however a whole new group of enemy guns, positioned on the highest point of Morgusaia Island, unleashed fire of devastating volume against the formation, and within minutes the scheduled "orderly bombardment" had become pretty much a matter of every ship for herself.

Standing calmly on *Spence*'s shoreside bridge wing Heinie Armstrong watched the splashes of the Japanese shell walking toward him. "Hell, they're too short!" he yelled to Lieutenant B. W. Spore, USN, his "exec," who had just stepped in from the opposite wing of the bridge.

"I've got something interesting to show you, Captain!" shouted Spore cupping his hands to his mouth in order to be heard over the din of battle. "Take a look at the *other* side!" Spore led his captain to the opposite bridge wing, and within moments they both observed shell splashes. They, too, were being straddled, and in naval gunnery that usually is a prelude to being solidly hit.

"Well, let's get this can wiggling!" was Armstrong's immediate re-action—and *Spence* "went into her dance."

At 0631 an airburst sprayed *Ausburne's* fantail with steel fragments, and at 0636, with the formation now on the 50-degree course, the enemy 6-inch batteries once more got the range and straddled her. She started weaving violently through a curtain of bursting shell and, for a moment, even Arleigh Burke was nonplussed. "Brute," he said, "I simply don't understand it! Considering the volume of fire we're pouring on those fellows it just doesn't seem possible for them to sustain the fire they're sending our way."

"Well, they're sure as hell doing it, boss!" replied the dainty Reynolds, and if confirmation was needed it came between 0638 and 0643½, when the Commodore spotted eight "overs" and fourteen "shorts," none more than 1,500 yards off. He shook his head. No one had expected that kind of performance from the Jap!

Dyson had been straddled numerous times since 0634, and 2 minutes later *Montpelier* was very close to trouble. One shell passed between her stacks and landed less than 50 yards beyond the cruiser. Another landed in her wake about 50 yards astern, and an instant later a third landed only feet short of her port beam. This fire was from a 6-inch battery. At 0638 Roy Gano, standing loosely relaxed on the bridge and swaying instinctively with the heeling of the ship as she maneuvered, was almost lifted off the deck by a series of sharp detonations in quick succession. *Dyson* took a 6-inch shell in her bow above the water line; another cut her rigging; and three more explosions close aboard sent water foaming over her decks. Another near-hit caused shrapnel damage and five men were wounded, but the fighting efficiency of the ship was not impaired and she continued to "throw rocks."

The van DDs came to the retirement course—100 degrees true—at 0650 and, according to plan, broke off the engagement. The cruisers pegged their last shell at the enemy at 0657, and at 0700, with all ships retiring, hands were piped below for coffee and eggs. A friendly plane came over and informed the task force commander that large fires had been started behind the ridge on Poporang where the Jap had a sea-plane base, repair shops, hangars, and air defenses. This had been one of the Admiral's most important targets and the news was welcome. He knew, too, that they'd knocked out an undetermined number of shore guns of various calibers, but there were two 6-inch batteries which they hadn't been able to touch, and these continued to fire on *Task Force Merrill* until the ships were out of range. All in all, it had been a satisfying morning's work. But now the time had come to take stock and prepare to parry the swift enemy reaction which it was taken for granted must follow the two bombardments and the landings which, at that moment, were in progress at Cape Torokina.

While allowing wide latitude of action should contact be made with an enemy surface force, ComThirdFleet's orders to Admiral Merrill were specific in one particular. At the conclusion of the Shortlands bombardment Task Force 39 was to remain under way north of Vella La Vella prepared to perform two missions: (1) to intercept any enemy surface attempt to interfere with the landings; and (2) to cover withdrawal of the transports, which was scheduled to start at 1530 that afternoon, Monday, 1st November.

After the bombardment at Skunk Hollow Tip Merrill had two crucial problems—fuel, and ammunition—both centering in his destroyers. Although highly efficient as a fighting instrument the *Fletcher* class DD is not an economical ship fuel-wise. That problem had challenged Rosey Gillan and he had worked out her most frugal engine lashup and cruising speed, but combat called for full power and speeds upward from 30 knots. At such speeds fuel consumption in the *Fletcher* class reaches astronomical proportions.

These little vessels had now been constantly under way for 29 hours and had spent much of that time steaming at high speed. Also, they had expended prodigious quantities of ammunition. For example, on the way to Skunk Hollow and during the bombardment there, *Dyson* alone had fired 214 rounds of 5-inch .38 common, 440 rounds of 40-mm, and 1,065 rounds of 20-mm. Ammunition consumption in the other ships had been at least as great, and the DDs needed rearming. They did not have the capacity of the cruisers for carrying ample reserves of oil and ammo. With a battle almost a moral certainty in the immediate future Tip Merrill had to face these facts: So far as his DDs were concerned, what good was a battle unless they could get to it, and maneuver after they got there? And how could they fight a battle if they didn't have any "rocks" to throw?

The Admiral's decision was a hard one, but at 0725 he ordered Arleigh Burke to take Division 45 back to Hathorn Sound, refuel and rearm at top speed, and rejoin the task force off Vella La Vella at the earliest possible moment. However, to Burke's slight confusion, this order was belayed almost immediately after it was issued and before he'd had time to act upon it. What the Commodore didn't know was that, only moments after the order was issued, the TFC had received a dispatch from ComAirSols stating that one of his planes had spooked a Japanese force of four cruisers and six destroyers at latitude 05°—40'—00″ South; longitude 153°—30'—00″ East. This position was in the vicinity of Cape St. George, the entrance to Rabaul. The information of greatest interest to Admiral Merrill was that the enemy ships were reported on course 300 degrees true, speed 25 knots. This didn't look as though they were headed down toward Cape Torokina.

For several long minutes the task force commander pondered the implications of this intelligence. Then he took a resolute decision. He requested ComAirSols to maintain a special watch to detect any change of course by the enemy formation. Then he reinstated his order to Burke to return to Hathorn Sound to refuel and rearm. Hathorn was a rudimentary facility at the south end of Kula Gulf and accessible via Blackett Strait. It was only 108 miles away from their present position, and the Admiral knew it was the closest they'd be to fuel in the foreseeable future. He also knew that if any commander afloat could conduct a fueling operation and rejoin in record time, that officer's name probably was Arleigh Burke.

Merrill didn't dare detach the ships of DesDiv-46 simultaneously with those of "45" and leave his cruisers totally without a destroyer screen. Because of the nature of their recent evolutions, however, while *Ausburne, Dyson, Stanly,* and *Claxton* needed about 100,000 gallons each to top off, *Spence, Thatcher, Converse,* and *Foote* had burned less oil and were in relatively better shape, although still somewhat low. Division 45 departed at 0750 for Hathorn to fight what Arleigh Burke called "the battle for fuel." At the start the Commodore held the formation speed down to 25 knots to permit *Stanly* to come from the rear end of the column and join, which she did at 32 knots. Meanwhile *Task Force Merrill* altered course more to the eastward to skirt Vella La Vella, and for a few short hours the Task Force Commander was left in comparative peace with only the problem of trying to figure out the future when he couldn't even be sure he had a firm grip on the present moment.

On 1st November, 1943, the torrid sun of noon riding high over the North Central Solomons shone down upon a lot of little men desperately engaged in differing but not disparate activities. Stretching northwest from the bight of Empress Augusta Bay a double line of U.S. transports and cargo ships lay hove-to while small craft of all sorts shuttled between them and the beaches landing troops and supplies. There was a distance of 750 yards between ships, with an interval of 500 yards between the two files. The landings were being effected under intermittent air bombardment and torpedo plane attacks. These strikes by the enemy, partially parried by the planes from the carrier task force commanded by Rear Admiral Frederick C. Sherman and built around *Saratoga* and *Princeton,* several times drove the transports and cargo ships seaward, maneuvering radically. They returned doggedly to their stations however and although, by nightfall, 64 LCVPs and 22 LCMs were to end up forlorn and stranded derelicts—coffins for many gallant U.S. Marines—a lodgement on Bougainville was to be secured.

Up north at Imperial Japanese Navy Headquarters at Rabaul, Admiral Tomoshige Samejima was busy trying to fit together the pieces of a fascinating puzzle. He managed to do it all wrong, but the cruel realization of that fact was not to be his until he received the depressing news of a powerful Imperial task force slashed to pieces, part of it sunk, and the rest scattered to the four winds by Tip Merrill and Arleigh Burke's Little Beavers.

The day before, Admiral Koga, at Truk, had released strategic command to Samejima, who had flown to Rabaul. At their last conference Samejima had counseled action whereas Koga had still wanted to await the development of a clear picture of U.S. intentions. Once given his head, Samejima had immediately sent Admiral Omori to sea with a force of cruisers and destroyers. Although they must have been provocatively proximate at the time of the Buka-Bonis bombardment it was fated that Omori's force and Task Force 39 should not become aware of each other at that time. After a night of futile steaming Omori had turned back toward Rabaul, and it was his force which had been reported to Admiral Merrill early on the morning of 1st November, immediately after the gunstrike at Skunk Hollow, and had caused him to withdraw, temporarily, his refueling order to Burke.

Omori reached Rabaul at 1100 that Monday morning and immediately went into conference with Samejima. "Sentaro," said the senior Admiral genially, "this time we've *got* them!"

"Ah, so?"

"Look, this is the way it appears to me: there's only one U.S. cruiser task force left in the South Pacific. That task force bombarded Buka at midnight last night, and our installations in the Shortlands at dawn this morning. Then, doubtless, it steamed back up the Bougainville coast to protect the landings now in progress at Empress Augusta Bay. You've heard about all that?"

"Yes, I was notified of the bombardments and the landings. But why does that mean we shall be able to annihilate the enemy?"

"It's inevitable, Sentaro. Their cruisers and destroyers will pull out of Bougainville at dusk tonight. They've *got* to! All those ships must be low on fuel and ammunition, and the crews must be very fatigued after the work they've done. You'll see; they'll leave Empress Augusta Bay early this evening and retire south for rest and replenishment."

"Do we know for sure they're at Empress Augusta?"

"As a matter of fact, no. But I assume they are or soon will be. We'll be getting reports, of course."

"Ah, so!"

"Well, all this means that tonight is our great opportunity . . ."

"What do you want me to do, Tomoshige?"

"Primarily, get going as fast as you can. I'll give you Ijuin and Osugi. You'll have two heavy cruisers—the Americans don't have any so far as we know—two light cruisers, and six destroyers. In addition, five attack transports will be available. Get to Cape Torokina, smash any enemy ships you find there, land your troops, and throw the white bastards back into the sea. If you're *really* lucky you may catch their cruiser task force and tear it to pieces. That, of course, should be your principal mission should it prove possible."

Admiral Sentaro Omori, nobody's fool, and with plenty of hard naval fighting under his broad belt, permitted himself a reflective belch. "Perhaps," he conceded. "But I'd be a lot more comfortable without five transports to worry about. If I *do* intercept their task force I'll have to do some high speed maneuvering and hard fighting, and those things will just be in the way."

"You can always detach them and send them back on enemy contact, Sentaro. But time is the important factor. If you don't make it tonight the situation is bound to change, and it won't improve for us."

"Ah, so!" Dogged Omori lumbered to his feet, bowed stiffly, and waddled toward the door. Omori wasn't the world's brightest person but he was shrewd enough. New concepts dropped into his lap out of a clear sky and demanding prompt action were not to his liking. Especially, he didn't like the ambiguity of this mission—either to wipe out the enemy task force or to liquidate his beachheads on Bougainville, but hardly both. Omori was courageous and he had no fear of a fight, but those damned transports . . .

When Omori sortied at 1800 that evening he'd taken care of the transports in his own way. For some inexplicable reason they were late for the rendezvous with the main body. No one knew why . . . It might just possibly have been a confusion of orders reaching the transport commander from Admiral Omori's staff . . . In any case they were late, and time was the dominant factor. Hadn't Admiral Samejima himself said so? With a sigh of regret for the record, but also with a singular serenity of countenance under the circumstances, Sentaro Omori sailed South and left five fully loaded troop transports behind. Although they didn't know it, the little men of Nippon temporarily cooped up in those transports at Rabaul that night were among the Son of Heaven's more fortunate subjects. At least most of them subsequently had a chance to fight for their lives, which might not have been the case had they stood south with Omori.

At about the time the Japanese Admirals were holding their inter-

esting if inaccurate colloquy at Rabaul, Arleigh Burke, at the head
of Division 45, was storming through Blackett Strait toward nearby
Hathorn Sound, figuratively bawling his logistics message and making
the kind of luminous Navy legend which has only one part fact to fifty
parts humorous imagination, but endures. The Commodore's arrival at
Hathorn in a smother of spray and with a tempestuous demand for
instant and all-out service so he could get back to the expected battle,
gave birth to two reports one of which mightily amused Arleigh Burke
and the other of which embarrassed him. As usual, there was a crumb
of fact in each and both, embellished and presented as gospel, have since
reverberated around the world in song and story. Consider the simpler
phenomenon first:

It is customary, when a Navy ship returns to port, especially in war-
time, for the Captain to send a logistics message to competent authority
ashore. This is a routine statement of his logistic requirements—fuel,
ammunition, food—and usually is prepared for his signature by a
member of his staff. It may be transmitted in a variety of ways depending upon available facilities. At Hathorn Sound facilities were rudimentary in November, 1943, although there was a harbor voice circuit.
The concrete-hulled IX oiler lay anchored in the lee of Munda, and because of the erratic currents and occasional wind gusts at the anchorage, coming alongside her was a very tricky evolution. Blackett Strait
is relatively deep but narrow water; Arleigh Burke was in an almighty
hurry and, as has been indicated, he came snorting through the Strait
at high speed, the bows of his ships shooting iridescent fans of spray
high on either side, and the wakes foaming shoreward in tumultuous
breakers.

Upon approaching Hathorn through Blackett Strait it is certain
that Arleigh Burke sent his logistics message on before him. It was his
most vital preoccupation at the moment. It is also possible—although
the record is silent on this point—that he employed the harbor voice
circuit for this purpose in which case his voice or that of a delegated
officer may have boomed out from all TBS loud speakers activated in
the area at the moment. Further, transiting narrow Blackett Strait at
extremely high speed, as he did, it is conceivable that he may have used
the TBS voice circuit to warn slow and small harbor craft out of his
way. He himself had no precise recollection of this at war's end. However, the known facts, plus the obvious possibilities, plus Burke's colorful style (he was not eccentric and therefore not "colorful" in that
sense, but his dashing style compelled attention) spawned an interesting
story—but one which did not make the Commodore over-happy.

In the story the locus of the event was changed end-for-end. Instead
of happening at Hathorn Sound (where it conceivably *might* have
happened) it was reported as happening off Vella La Vella when Di-

vision 45 rejoined the task force after fueling. And the legend runs to the effect that the colorful Commodore and his four little ships came charging into the middle of *Task Force Merrill* thundering, *"Stand aside! Stand aside! I'm coming through at 34 knots!"*

Alas for a luminous legend, it never happened! Destroyers simply don't tell cruisers to get out of the way, and Destroyer Squadron Commodores don't dictate ship dispositions to Task Force Rear Admirals. Arleigh Burke rejoined at high speed, all right, but in doing so he reported well ahead of time to Admiral Merrill, and proceeded to his assigned station when ordered to do so. Burke was a thoroughgoing technician with a deep knowledge of his art, and it didn't make him happy to hear erroneous reports that he'd made himself conspicuous before his seniors, equals, and juniors in any such absurd fashion.

The second legend which arose out of the precipitate dash of Des-Div-45 through Blackett Strait on that memorable November morning was more factual and more humorous. It achieved expression in tinkling verse, became the subject of formal although tongue-in-cheek correspondence and memoranda on top Army and Navy letterheads, and was universally attributed to the Little Beavers because of their recognized bravura, despite the fact that another Squadron entirely was principally responsible.

The basic situation was provocative enough. The Army had a few troops stationed on Arundel Island at the entrance to Blackett Strait. As part of their sanitary program these soldiers had built Japanese-style privies on stilts at the water's edge. Destroyers, transiting the Strait at high speed, sent gigantic waves from their wakes racing shoreward, and these waves sometimes knocked over the not-too-well anchored privies, to the understandable confusion of soldier occupants of the moment.

Actually, it was Captain Roger W. Simpson's DesRon-12 which played this little game with enthusiasm. They painted the symbol of a palm-thatched privy on the bridges of the ships, and added a hashmark beneath it for every stilted structure knocked down by a DD's wake. Indeed, by January, 1944, things had gotten so bad that Commodore Simpson found it necessary to issue this order:

> *Unless emergency demands, vessels of this Squadron will not use speeds in excess of 25 knots in Blackett Strait. It has been observed that wakes from this speed give Army privies built over the water a good flushing without damaging them. A hashmark under the picture of a privy on the bridge for each one knocked down will be discontinued.*

On the anxious morning of Monday, 1st November, 1943, so far as Arleigh Burke was concerned, "emergency demanded" and he went busting through Blackett Strait hell for leather. He may have knocked down a whole file of privies or, again, he may not have. The significant point is this: within weeks of Burke's assumption of command the morale of the Gallant Squadron soared so high and the Squadron was regarded as so colorful and unmatchable by soldiers, sailors, and Marines alike, that despite its origin and long official history as an activity of DesRon-12, the chuckle-provoking "battle of the privies" invariably was attributed to DesRon-23 and has since been so attributed world-wide. It was just the natural kind of thing for the light-hearted, hard-fighting, don't-give-a-damn sailors of a Burke Squadron to do, and although he subsequently made several efforts to set the record straight and give credit where it was due, the peculiar aura of DesRon-23—part of the *mystique* shared in by officers and men alike—always has prevailed over the facts. The accolade for unerring range and deflection, and invincible purpose in the pursuit of privy-destroying will forever remain, erroneously, with DesRon-23.

According to the persistent legend it was a senior Admiral who collared Burke and roared *"Burke, if your ships don't stop knocking down those Godam privies, I'll have your stripes!"* Again, alas, it never happened! But even in the heat of the Solomons and amid the unconscionable pressures of jungle war a debonaire singer whose name, alas, has not been preserved for posterity, enshrined the business in these immortal lines (obviously penned from a point of most intimate vantage):

(With apologies to R. Kipling "The Young British Soldier")

When a soldier sits out here with the water lapping near
And dreams of pulley chains and apparatus,
He doesn't want to worry and he doesn't want to hurry,
And most surely doesn't want to get a wetass!

So any proposition that will introduce Marines
Can be naught but anathema to the soldiers in latrines,
And the aggravating splatter from any passing "can"
Will run him whacky-wacky; he'll forget that he's a man!

If "cans" must keep on running through Blackett's gory Strait
And they cannot make the passage unless the tide's in spate
'Twould be well to mind the moon's effect, and time dear nature's urge
To synchronize with ebbing tide, and get a better purge!

DD's high speed maneuvers should be in open water
And they shouldn't pass through Blackett Strait no faster than they
    orter,
But perfect peace will never be for any GI jerk
Who's subject to a sortie by 31-Knot-Burke!

The desperate speed which Arleigh Burke brought to the complicated evolution of refueling involved split-second maneuvering by the ships of the Division and saved, all in all, perhaps less than 10 minutes in the final completion of the job. Of what value are 10 measly minutes in the majestic sweep of history? It is a wise man who knows, and Arleigh Burke was a wise man. He well knew that battles sometimes are irretrievably won or lost by minutes, even by seconds, and when he'd told the young ensign that the difference between a good officer and a poor one was "about 10 seconds" he was not indulging in persiflage. He was stating what to him was a truism. That morning Burke knew that he had hard steaming ahead of him to rejoin the task force, and if the task force started north before he got there the chances of his catching it up in time would be remote. That would leave Tip Merrill in an extremely exposed position, and it might keep one Captain Arleigh Burke out of the first big action he'd smelled since coming to the South Pacific. Neither of those things, he resolved, must be allowed to happen.

DesDiv-45 slammed into Hathorn at 1115 hours. *Ausburne* and *Dyson*, both fully ready and with working parties on deck, went alongside the oiler at once and coupled up. Following tradition, *Stanly* and *Claxton* patrolled at the entrance on the lookout for submarines. The oil kings took over and, despite the tension and pressure, went about their jobs with an outward seeming almost of casualness. It was the professionals' mark of top efficiency; they wasted no moment, no movement. Arleigh Burke, not a calm man despite a patina of tranquility which he occasionally found it prudent to assume, paced the bridge, his cabin and, finally, as far aft as the fantail. It was with almost physical restraint that he kept himself from inquiring "How's the fueling going?" every 5 minutes. That, really, was Brute Reynolds' and Roy Gano's job, and the Commodore had no legitimate part in it unless things went wrong.

Standing off and on at the entrance to the anchorage Heraldo Stout, not a placid character and scorning to appear one, fumed and fretted. "What's the matter with those jackasses?" he snapped at his "exec."

"They're trying to get more capacity out of the pumps than there is in them, boss, is all," the "exec" told him.

"I know . . . but dammit, man . . ." Stout stamped away toward the opposite wing of the bridge. The "exec" snuffed in a good whiff of the Captain's sulphurous pipe, half buckled his knees in mock asphyxiation, and grimaced.

At 1235 *Claxton* and *Stanly* received a signal from the Commodore. They were to come in and moor alongside *Ausburne* and *Dyson*. The moment these two topped off they would pull out leaving their lines for *Claxton* and *Stanly*—maybe another minute saved. To hell with good standard manila lines now! Let the oil barge have 'em; let *anybody* have 'em. In Arleigh Burke's brain there burned but two words: *Fuel! Time!* Ammunition he'd forgotten; there was none for them at Hathorn.

At 1305 Roy Gano observed his fueling hoses clearing forward and aft, temporarily took over from his officer of the deck, and started barking orders in staccato succession and with only time enough between them for very smart execution. *"Single up your lines . . . let go aft . . . let go forward . . . all back, standard . . . indicate turns for 15 knots"* . . . *Dyson* withdrew smoothly from the oil barge. *Stanly* moved immediately into her place taking *Dyson*'s lines, hoses were connected, and life-giving fuel surged into her tanks. Meanwhile *Charlie Ausburne* had begun a similar routine, and within minutes *Claxton* had taken her place at the oil-soaked teats of the fuel cow.

Stanly, as picket DD during the run north, needed a bigger drink than the others. The time finally arrived when Arleigh Burke simply couldn't stand inaction any longer. At 1527 he took *Ausburne* and *Dyson* out of Kula Gulf at 15 knots, and messaged *Stanly* and *Claxton* to join at 32 knots as soon as they finished fueling. At the time the Commodore was not unaware that this might prove an unhandy expedient. *Stanly* had reported lethal gas fumes in one fireroom and the men on watch there had to work in oxygen masks. Also her improper superheater tubes were a constant threat. But with Arleigh Burke at that point it was a matter of getting into *some* sort of action or blowing his stack, and he elected to take the calculated risk.

Stanly and *Claxton* completed fueling at 1630, stood out of Kula Gulf, and managed to join *Ausburne* and *Dyson* by 1800. Shortly after quitting the gulf *Dyson* struck a submerged object and sustained damage which caused her to vibrate violently at high speed, but Captain Gano kept her to it and she held her station in the formation. Burke rang up all the knots he dared, and the ships raced through the gathering dusk.

"I think I know how we can save some time, Commodore," ventured Captain Reynolds.

"Now you're cooking on th' back burner, bub!" replied Burke airily, his tension fast dissipating under the meaningful hum of *Ausburne*'s singing hull. "How?"

"If we pass north and east of the Treasuries instead of south and west we'll save at least 6 miles. That's about 15 minutes."

The Commodore considered briefly before replying. He didn't want to hurt his flag skipper's feelings—didn't want to seem scornful of suggestions—but the notion was one he'd entertained a good while back and been forced to reject.

"Thanks for the idea, Brute," he said finally, "but I'm afraid to take that chance. It will be black dark by the time we get to the Treasuries area. We've got PT boats operating up there, and to a PT man in the dark one can looks like another. Likely we'd get a fanny full of torps before we got through. I want to save every minute we possibly can, but I'm afraid that's too dangerous an experiment to try. We'd better stand sufficiently far west to leave the Treasuries safely to starboard."

"Aye, sir," said Reynolds. Silence settled on the bridge. Steaming in "Dog" formation, each ship in line slightly offset from the one next ahead but on the same course, the DDs sliced onward into the darkening night.

11

The Battle of Empress Augusta Bay

Almost precisely to the minute when *Stanly* and *Claxton* joined Des-Div-45 arrowing north the commander of Task Force 31, Rear Admiral Wilkinson, gave the signal for the retirement of his transports and cargo ships from the Cape Torokina beaches. The operation had been costly; it had not proceeded according to schedule; its status was still precarious. Both personnel and matériel casualties had been heavy although dogged determination and inspiring courage finally had overcome the enemy's beach defenses. It was estimated that about half of his forces were killed. The remainder retired inland temporarily, and of the 14,321 Marines and naval personnel scheduled for landing by the first echelon of transports, all but the wounded were on the beach although an appreciable number constituted no threat to the enemy. They were dead.

The time schedule had been thrown hopelessly out of kilter. Careful rehearsals before the event had produced the optimistic estimate that both transports and cargo ships could be unloaded in approximately 4½ hours. This would have seen the operation concluded by about noon. These sanguine surmises, however, failed to anticipate that *American Legion* would spend 3 hours immobilized on a shoal, as she did, or that enemy air attacks would drive the ships temporarily from their beaches as they did, or that, in the words of Admiral Halsey, "the Torokina beaches are worse than anything we have previously encountered in the South Pacific." The net of all this was that, when the retirement signal was given, *Hunter Liggett*, *American Legion*, *Crescent City*, and *Alchiba* still had their decks and holds jam-packed with matériel and food.

Admiral Wilkinson had no intention of allowing these ships to take their precious cargoes back to Guadalcanal but they could perform no useful service off the Torokina beaches during the hours of darkness. They were ordered, therefore, to retire south until 2300 that night at which hour they would reverse course and return to Empress Augusta

Bay, prepared to complete the unloading at dawn. This force was designated Task Group 31.5.1 and Wilkinson requested Merrill to cover it during its return journey. Shortly after receiving this request Merrill got orders from ComSoPac to cover this force from the vicinity of Vella La Vella.

Almost as these dispositions were being made, however, they were altered by a message from plane Number 1 of Flight 33 which reported an enemy force of eight vessels at 04°—50′ South; 152°—40′ East, and announced that he was attacking. Admiral Halsey at once countermanded his earlier instructions to *Task Force Merrill* and ordered that formation to cover the four cargo ships from the west rather than the vicinity of Vella La Vella. He added that they should also be on the lookout for a U.S. minelaying group engaged in laying a mine field south of Cape Moltke, and due to retire south within a short time.

These were the antecedents which conditioned Arleigh Burke's considerable surprise when, at 2222, *Ausburne* made radar contact with a formation distant 15 miles to the northwest. It *had* to be Task Force 39—but where had the extra ships come from?

The Commodore soon was given the facts and ordered to take station on the starboard quarter of the transports. By 2234 TBS talk indicated that the transports were about to be detached, and Burke ordered Division 45 to steer well clear of the area of maneuver. At 2315 he had brought his Division to a position 6,000 yards astern of the cruiser column, and Division 46 was 6,000 yards ahead of the cruiser guide, *Montpelier*, on course 135 degrees true, speed 15 knots. By 2340 detachment of Task Group 31.5.1 was complete and Admiral Merrill brought his own force to cruising formation coming to course 270 degrees true by a turn of station units. By midnight he had altered course another 75 degrees northward, and Division 45 once more was in the van position 6,000 yards ahead of the guide, with Division 46 4,000 yards astern, station units on a line of bearing from *Montpelier*. Speed was increased to 20 knots, and all ships went to general quarters. *Task Force Merrill* was on the prowl, looking for an enemy who was pretty sure to show up, and certain to be an ugly customer when met.

Shortly after local midnight Plane 10 of Flight 24, and Plane 1 of Flight 23 sent the information for which Tip Merrill and Arleigh Burke hungered. The aircraft had located the Japanese task force at 05°—35′ South; 153°—26′ East; course 125 degrees true, speed 32 knots. Here was all the confirmation needed. Patently the enemy was headed for Empress Augusta Bay and in a great rush to get there. At 0100 on the morning of Tuesday, 2nd November, Admiral Merrill came on TBS and addressed all ships. First he summarized all plane reports received up until that time. This was a precautionary measure because not all ships "got the word" every time a report was received. Merrill knew that some of his skippers might have missed one or another of the plane messages and he wanted all hands to be fully informed.

"My calculation," continued the Admiral, "places the enemy approximately 83 miles away bearing 325 degrees true. Anybody find any fault with that conclusion?"

No one did, but Burke took the opportunity to supply the effective corollary of Merrill's figuring: "We should make contact at about 0230," he volunteered.

"Right you are, Arleigh—or maybe a little before that. I'm going to 28 knots."

Below decks throttlemen eased their great, polished valve wheels to the left, the beat of the propellers quickened, and Task Force 39 leaped forward through the night toward her unsuspecting adversary.

Standing almost due southeast through the thick night Rear Admiral Sentaro Omori, flying his flag in heavy cruiser *Myoko*, commanded a force with two fewer ships but tremendously more power than *Task Force Merrill*. And in addition to extra power he had extra professional help in the persons of Rear Admirals Matsuji Ijuin, who flew his flag in light cruiser *Sendai*, and Morikazu Osugi, with his flag in light cruiser *Agano*. Omori's ship disposition reflected the curious astigmatism which so often seemed to inhibit both the strategic and tactical vision of the Imperial Japanese Navy command in the sea war in the South Pacific. The ships were in a simple formation and not one designed to deal effectively with a United States battle formation of light cruisers and destroyers.

Omori's two heavy cruisers, *Myoko* and *Haguro*, steaming in that order, comprised the center column of a three column pattern. On their left steamed light cruiser *Sendai* followed by destroyers *Shigure*, *Samidare*, and *Shiratsuyu*, in that order. On Omori's right steamed light cruiser *Agano* followed by destroyers *Naganami*, *Hatsukaze*, and *Wakatsuki*, in that order.

Now, this was a good enough formation for what Omori expected to find in front of him. Over a period of time and through much bitter fighting the Allies had learned to identify certain somewhat baffling stigmata of command exhibited again and again by this Oriental enemy. In a high degree the Jap was courageous or fatalistic, whichever term may please the individual, and the number of senior Japanese officers who died fighting their ships was notable. On the other hand the Japanese commanders often exhibited a lack of resolution and the ability to exploit tactical advantages. This was dramatically evidenced at the Battle of Savo Island when Admiral Mikawa turned toward home at the instant when further attack would have assured him a victory double the magnitude of that he already had gained.

Finally, the Japanese staff work often was characterized by fuzziness and lack of clarity. Certainly, as he approached Empress Augusta Bay, Omori's mind was bemused by a good deal of wishful thinking. Originally, with Samejima, he had entertained the idea that he might find here the opportunity to destroy the one remaining U.S. cruiser task force in the area. Then the focus had shifted and he was urged to take troop-laden transports to reconquer the Bougainville beaches. In the event he'd managed to fall neatly between these two stools. He'd left the transports behind, thus discounting any chance of investing the beaches around Cape Torokina. On the other hand, by 0100 that Tuesday morning Admiral Omori had convinced himself that Samejima's guess about the retirement of the American cruiser task force for rest and replenishment had been right. Omori expected to encounter nothing more lethal than a handful of destroyers between him and the fat transports and cargo ships which he assumed were waiting at Cape Torokina. He'd made his ship dispositions in anticipation of smashing this puny screen, blasting the transports and cargo vessels to junk, and concluding with a leisurely annihilation of the U.S. Marines and their defenses ashore by the 8- and 6-inch gunfire of his cruisers supported by the DDs. It was a comfortable prospect for a complacent Admiral to contemplate, but had Omori been able to glimpse the opposite side of the coin he would have recoiled in shock, for he would have seen himself being relieved of command for his part in what was about to take place off Empress Augusta Bay.

At 0207 Arleigh Burke was brought up with a round turn when the task force commander messaged, "Will the Squadron Commodore please keep the destroyers closed up?"

The Commodore had thought his formation precisely on station but ordered an immediate check. It revealed that a radar operator, a reliable man skilled and competent but so drugged with the narcosis of fatigue and physical and nervous exhaustion as to resemble a zombie, had unconsciously shifted his range taking from the guide to another ship. In consequence Division 45 was only 4,000 yards ahead of the guide instead of 6,000 as ordered. Burke moved the formation ahead immediately but the radar operator was not censored. It was an error which, in the maneuver of battle, might easily have caused serious damage to a ship or ships. But the men of DesRon-23 and especially of Division 45 had given all they had; they were still doing so, and Burke knew it. Steaming, fighting and fueling they had all now been under well-nigh intolerable tension for 48 hours—from the moment of their sortie from Purvis at 0200 on the morning of Sunday, 31st October, until that present moment, 0215 on the morning of Tuesday, 2nd November.

Not knowing at what minute they might meet the enemy the ships were steaming in condition of readiness Able. Below decks pipes were blocked off into sections with a pump on each section. The engineering plant was completely split, Boilers 2 and 4 on the port side being compartmented from Boilers 1 and 3 on the starboard side by the pattern of their connections; all boilers were on the line, all connecting doors closed and dogged tight; blowers in the living spaces were off, and a maximum degree of water-tight integrity was in force. To men about to drop with weariness condition Able, long sustained, was pure murder. It seemed almost impossible—certainly not worth the effort—to follow the circuitous routes necessary to get from one part of the ship to another. In the boiler rooms watertenders sat hunkered down on the gratings watching their tubular glass gauges through red-rimmed eyes, and gulping salt tablets as though they were a specific for fatigue as well as helping to offset the debilitation of excessive humid heat. The temperature below soared; half-naked firemen found their fingers fumbling on the valves; sweat beaded the backs of their hairy hands and glistened in the stubble of their soggy beards. Chiefs and commissioned officers, hollow-eyed and silent, skipped from station to station checking. In a way unnecessary talk represented a dissipation of energy, and they had no energy to spare. On deck silent men at the guns and tube mounts licked their lips nervously and darted quick, questioning glances from beneath their battle helmets. Now and then their chalk-white eyeballs picked up flickering reflections from an occasional shimmer of heat lightning, and when that happened the eyes seemed monstrously enlarged, detached from faces, and floating eerily in space. The men were not frightened in the sense that amateurs might have' been frightened. They had all been under fire, were veterans, and had some small idea of what probably lay ahead. But they were terribly tense, terribly keyed up, terribly tired. And they longed for the first gun to fire, for that would send the adrenalin surging and, at least temporarily, divert their attention from their acute discomfort.

At 0219 *Ausburne* made a surface contact bearing 045 degrees true at 20,100 yards—12 miles. Although a formation of ships it was on the wrong bearing for the enemy and was quickly established as friendly through IFF. The ships proved to be the minelaying group returning from Cape Moltke and as *Renshaw*, leading the formation, approached the task force her Captain messaged, "I'm bringing my snooper with me!"

This was unhappy news for Tip Merrill. Behind him, to the southeast, were the still-loaded cargo vessels standing back toward Cape Torokina. Behind them, again, were eight empty transports standing toward Guadalcanal. Task Force 39 was the only thing on the surface of the sea between Omori and these prizes. At that moment, to delay detection until the last possible moment, Merrill was taking a calculated risk. The interception point which he had selected upon being apprised of Omori's advance, was much closer to the uncharted shoals around Empress Augusta Bay than was at all comfortable. Indeed, submarine reconnaissance had discovered one of these deadly shoals 17 miles to seaward. In skirting this dangerous area Merrill was deliberately sacrificing a measure of his room to turn away and maneuver to avoid the enemy torpedo attack which could reliably be expected as an early Japanese reaction on contact. The alternative, however, would have been to intercept Omori farther north and west. This would have demanded much higher speed of the task force on the way to meet the enemy, which in turn would greatly have increased the chance of detection from the air. Trying for a clear first shot at the Jap Merrill had elected the more dangerous course of holding to the eastward but now—here came a snooper anyway!

There was nothing Merrill could do about it so he stood on, Burke's Division 45 now ahead to starboard and Austin's Division 46 astern to port on a line of bearing of unit guides, speed reduced to 20 knots, to minimize wake. Tip Merrill didn't know it at the time but his colleagues the naval aviators already had drawn first blood. Also, although he couldn't have guessed it, the thing which, in a few short minutes would enable him to surprise Omori, was not Merrill's daring in keeping to the east, but the incorrect reports sent by two Japanese airmen, one of whom had spooked Task Force 39 an hour before without being discovered.

At 0130 a U.S. plane had planted a bomb in the superstructure of heavy cruiser *Haguro*. Unable, in the darkness, to determine whether he had hit or missed, the pilot reported only that he had bombed the Japanese formation. However the hit hurt *Haguro*, and Omori had been forced to reduce speed to 30 knots. Shortly after that a Jap scout plane had discovered Merrill's formation but had reported it as "one cruiser and three destroyers." That didn't bother Omori. Moments later another Japanese scout reported "a fleet of transports unloading in Empress Augusta Bay." These vessels were, in fact, minelayers *Reese*, *Gamble*, and *Sicard*, escorted by destroyer *Renshaw*. It was this force that Merrill had met retiring at 0219, and the snooper *Renshaw* reported she was "bringing with her" was the Jap who had erroneously reported the minelayers as transports unloading. He had not followed them as *Renshaw* feared however, so that *Task Force Merrill* still remained unreported in its proper dimension to the enemy.

The two erroneous reports from his scouts served only to confirm Rear Admiral Sentaro Omori's conviction that he had a turkey shoot ahead. He was racing toward Cape Torokina at best speed. Transports, unloading, awaited him there. Only one light cruiser and three destroyers barred the way. He would smash those into impotence with a few 8-inch salvos. Yes, he reflected as he drummed happily on the edge of the chart table with his pudgy fingers, Samejima had been right. This *was* a golden opportunity to teach the white bastards a lesson, and he was just the little boy who could do it, too!

The almost palpable quiet which sometimes prefaces impending chaos spread over the sea in the vicinity of 06°—20' South; 154°—10' East. The air temperature was 83 degrees, water temperature 86 degrees. At 29.85, the barometer was falling slowly. The sea was smooth with gentle swells from the southwest, and the wind was from the same quarter at force one. There was a new moon but it gave very little light, and the night was dark and overcast although brilliant stars occasionally could be glimpsed through broken spots in the low cloud cover. Intermittent rain squalls wheeled around the area, and there was enough heat lightning playing about to silhouette a ship for an instant now and then. This was unpleasant, but beyond the control of Rear Admirals.

Arleigh Burke stood, inwardly a knot of nerves but outwardly calm, at a forward window on *Charlie Ausburne*'s bridge. At last, as clocks turned 0231, came the word from Sugar George radar: "*Contact bearing 291 degrees true at 30,000 yards. Believe this is what we want!*"

The bearing was off *Ausburne*'s port bow; it had to be Omori!

Burke's action now was instinctive as he had known it would be. The collision course was 311 degrees and he put Division 45 on that course without a moment's hesitation. Following doctrine he did not increase speed, for that might have led to detection. Next he grabbed the TBS transmitter, pressed the button, and yelped, "Contact bearing two-nine-one, 30,000. *I'm heading in!*" He did not say "What are your orders?" or "By your leave." He said, simply, "*I'm heading in.*"

That moment—that fragment in the undeviating march of the seconds and the minutes and the hours which measure men's lives and establish fixed and immutable points for the orientation of their accomplishments in the broad tapestry of history—marked the first fulfillment of Arleigh Burke's doctrine of faith. Tip Merrill had accepted that doctrine. Division 45 suddenly became the pledge of the Admiral's faith, and dashed to the attack without formal release by higher authority. At long last the superb weapon which is the modern destroyer was ex-

ploiting fully its inherent offensive role with a cruiser task force. For
Arleigh Burke the moment was a joyous one. It was one which never can
be repeated in history for, while the doctrine of faith remains and is
indestructible, ships change and weapons change and tactics change.
The surprise naval attack is no longer a realistic probability.

Contact had been made at approximately 15 miles. Omori's Cruiser
Division 5 and Burke's Destroyer Division 45 were closing each other
at a combined speed of the order of 50 knots, and the Commodore estimated it would take him about 14 minutes to reach his torpedo-launch-
ing position. A man with an agile mind can do a good bit of thinking in
14 minutes and there was, in fact, a good bit of cerebration going forward on the bridges of all the ships of DesRon-23. The thoughts of
some of the skippers—Heinie Armstrong pacing *Spence*'s bridge, for
example—reflected the new ethos of the Squadron.

Spence was suffering from a shortage of radio operators and Captain Armstrong had not been able to keep abreast of the broader picture as had some of the others. However, within minutes of the contact
the Task Force Commander brought his ships to battle formation on a
000-degree heading, and Heinie realized that *this was it*. Could it be
said that he had a moment of panic? No. Captain Armstrong was at
times stern and regarded as something of a sundowner—an over-strict
disciplinarian—by a few of his colleagues, but he was not the panicking
type. Nevertheless he felt a twinge of concern now, and was impelled
to search his heart. Although he had studied war intensively and had
much experience behind him, Heinie Armstrong never had fought a
night naval battle. It was logical that command responsibilities should
be uppermost in his thoughts, and they ran thus:

> Well, HJA [he frequently identified himself in his thoughts by his
> initials], here you are up against the thing you've been reading about
> for years; a night action, and one that probably will turn into a general
> melee. [His anticipation of this development was to prove distressingly
> accurate.]
>
> You have over three hundred mothers' sons aboard this beautiful ship.
> What are you going to do about that responsibility?

The Captain had hardly posed the question when an acceptable answer, clear and unequivocal, formed in his mind. It was the fruit of
three factors—three forces. First was his indoctrination at the United
States Naval Academy. During those four golden years there had been
indelibly impressed upon his youthful and malleable mind the high concept of duty and individual responsibility as the alpha and omega of a
naval officer's functioning. He remembered his "Class A" and his so-
journ aboard the *Riena Mercedes*, and he was content with the lesson

learned. His second area of reference was the confirming experience and observation embedded in the pattern of his rise through the ranks to command. By both precept and practice he had consolidated his acceptance of duty as the paramount value. His third point of reference was his plainly perceived obligation to his fellows in DesRon-23 and their Commodore, Arleigh Burke. That obligation demanded just one thing of Heinie Armstrong and he knew it: the efficient exercise of the sum total of his technical talents and capabilities in fighting his ship and supporting his colleagues in the other ships of the Squadron. Maybe he hadn't felt that quite so strongly a month ago, but now it was a very real consideration. It constituted an important part of his recognition of the *mystique* of Destroyer Squadron 23. His individual responsibility for the lives of the men under his command was, he knew, important. But it was secondary to the demands of duty, and his duty now was to fight to the utmost without care for individual danger. So he put from his mind thoughts for the safety of the "three hundred mothers' sons" he had aboard for fear such thinking might affect his decisions in the battle ahead and, perchance, turn him however slightly from the stern path of duty. Heinie Armstrong did more than that. He'd noticed a young JA talker to CIC jabbering away in what plainly was compulsive fashion. The Captain warned the boy to steady down, but the kid simply couldn't. He continued spouting a well nigh unintelligible torrent of words. The skipper recognized the danger. An hysterical talker to CIC could easily turn a critical situation into a debacle, yet he had no trained replacement for the lad. Captain Henry J. Armstrong dealt with the problem immediately, directly, and in accordance with his high sense of duty. He stepped up to the talker and clipped him with a hard right to the jaw. The punch shocked the boy, but it had the desired effect. He calmed down, did a reliable job in combat, and later apologized to the Captain for losing his head and became one of Armstrong's most devoted admirers among the crew. Standing into battle *U.S.S. Spence* was a sound ship. She had every need to be to face the harrowing punishment which lay ahead of her.

On *Claxton*'s bridge the beatific expression on Heraldo Stout's broad and somewhat short face made him look like a Buddha with a mustache. With action at hand even his beloved pipe—by conscientious tolling of the skippers the only one in the Squadron that smelled worse than Ham Hamberger's—remained unlighted. "This is beautiful, just *beautiful!*" he murmured keeping his eyes on the faint flash of *Dyson*'s wake ahead. "Click with the *Claxton*" had been their private slogan, and Heraldo happily speculated that the time was at hand to do some A-Number-One, uptown-type clicking. *Claxton* was ready. *Claxton* was *always* ready. But even the bouncy Heraldo would have been aghast had he known that within a very short time his ship would get lost from the formation, blank *Stanly*'s fire, and for a few short thunderous moments concentrate on pouring shell into her own teammate, *Spence*. Man impatiently yearns to penetrate the future, but as often as not the veil which hides tomorrow is the merciful dispensation of a shielding Providence.

Responsive to training and experience, Arleigh Burke stood beside Brute Reynolds on *Ausburne*'s bridge and used the few minutes' grace of the run-in to review his orders and doctrine, making sure that no detail had been neglected. He was especially concerned about the torpedo settings. Doctrine called for a 1-degree spread, intermediate speed, and 6-foot depth. There were sound reasons for this combination. The Mark XV torps they were using had the heavy warheads which made them run slightly below the depth set on the indicator. All torpedo officers knew this and allowed for it in their settings but even if one forgot, the torps would have a fair chance of doing their job if set for 6 feet. There was, of course, the magnetic exploder but this mechanism had failed so often that Burke placed little reliance on it.

The intermediate speed was perhaps the most important of the three factors. The torpedoes could be set to run at any one of three speeds—high, intermediate, or low. The low speed was inappropriate for most situations. But at high speed it had been observed that the mechanical exploder mechanism often was crushed on impact and before functioning. This sad and sorry defect had broken the heart of more than one submarine skipper who had maneuvered his boat in for a close shot with torps set at high speed only to have them, their mechanical exploders crushed upon impact, bounce harmlessly off the hull of his intended victim. Burke wanted no such experience. Repeated experiments had convinced him that this did not happen when the Mark XV torpedo was fired at intermediate speed, and firing at that speed was gospel in DesRon-23. As for the 1-degree spread the Commodore was satisfied this offered the optimum chance of hits when attacking an enemy formation under way.

Studying the radar scope as the formations swept toward each other Arleigh Burke perceived the enemy's ship dispositions and was mildly surprised. There appeared to be three columns in a modified wedge formation with the right wing back, and the thing that arrested his attention was that this was not a strong battle formation. Even on radar he could distinguish larger from smaller ships. Instead of all cruisers being in the center column screened by the DDs, classic battle posture for both the Japanese and the Americans, Omori's center column was composed only of two cruisers and there appeared to be at least one cruiser in each of the flanking columns. This might have been

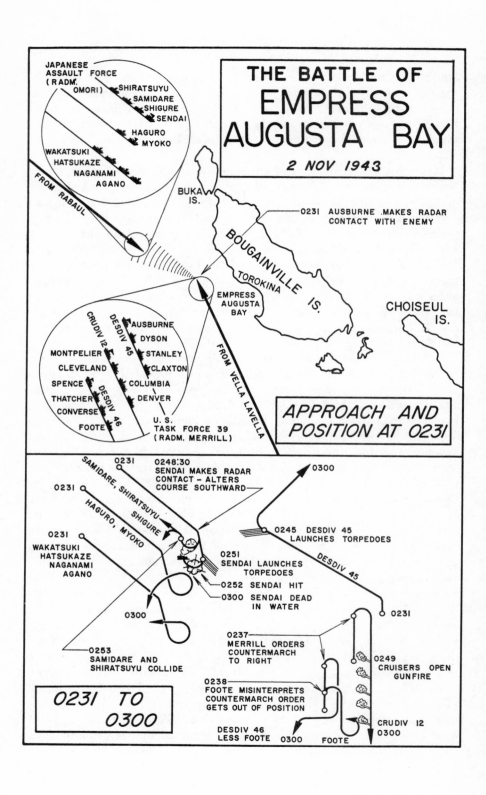

THE BATTLE OF EMPRESS AUGUSTA BAY

2 NOV 1943

JAPANESE ASSAULT FORCE (RADM. OMORI)

- SHIRATSUYU
- SAMIDARE
- SHIGURE
- SENDAI
- HAGURO
- MYOKO
- WAKATSUKI
- HATSUKAZE
- NAGANAMI
- AGANO

FROM RABAUL

BUKA IS.

BOUGAINVILLE IS.

TOROKINA

EMPRESS AUGUSTA BAY

CHOISEUL IS.

0231 AUSBURNE MAKES RADAR CONTACT WITH ENEMY

CRUDIV 12

DESDIV 45

- AUSBURNE
- DYSON
- STANLEY
- CLAXTON
- MONTPELIER
- CLEVELAND
- SPENCE
- THATCHER
- CONVERSE
- FOOTE
- COLUMBIA
- DENVER

DESDIV 46

FROM VELLA LAVELLA

U.S. TASK FORCE 39 (RADM. MERRILL)

APPROACH AND POSITION AT 0231

0231 TO 0300

0231

0248:30 SENDAI MAKES RADAR CONTACT – ALTERS COURSE SOUTHWARD

0300

0245 DESDIV 45 LAUNCHES TORPEDOES

0231 SAMIDARE, SHIRATSUYU

HAGURO, MYOKO SHIGURE

0251 SENDAI LAUNCHES TORPEDOES

0252 SENDAI HIT

0300 SENDAI DEAD IN WATER

DESDIV 45

0231

0231 WAKATSUKI HATSUKAZE NAGANAMI AGANO

0300

0237 MERRILL ORDERS COUNTERMARCH TO RIGHT

0249 CRUISERS OPEN GUNFIRE

0253 SAMIDARE AND SHIRATSUYU COLLIDE

0238 FOOTE MISINTERPRETS COUNTERMARCH ORDER GETS OUT OF POSITION

DESDIV 46 LESS FOOTE

0300 FOOTE

CRUDIV 12 0300

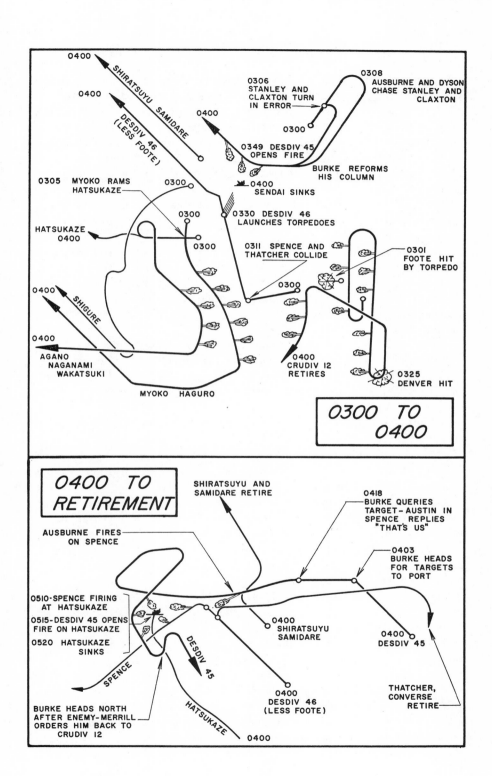

a handy formation from which to attack transports and that, of course, was what Omori thought he was soon to do. It was a weak pattern, however, from which to oppose a cruiser task force. Unable to detect any trap in the situation, the Commodore decided to fire torpedoes on the enemy's starboard bow and, if necessary, pass down between his leading and the center columns. It was an aggressive concept and would have placed *Ausburne, Dyson, Stanly*, and *Claxton* within point-blank range of heavy cruisers *Myoko* and *Haguro* to starboard as well as light cruiser *Agano* and her accompanying destroyers to port. Speed and maneuver, with very little room for the latter, would be Burke's only hopes for survival.

Without even knowing he was there, however, Admiral Omori took this initiative away from Captain Burke. At 0236, with the formations still some 18,000 yards apart, the Japanese Admiral altered course sufficiently far to his right to defeat Burke's intentions. So far as Omori was concerned it was a routine course correction. He was not yet aware of the presence of Division 45.

"Now what, Commodore?" asked Flag Skipper Reynolds.

"That's all right, Brute," Burke told him. "We'll fire on his port bow instead, and retire toward the north. After all, that's the direction he'll have to take if he hopes to get home, and maybe we'll get another crack at him."

"What if we tear up his port column but he drives in with the other two?"

"I've thought about that. We're firing only half salvos the first time. If he's got the guts to keep coming, we'll have torps enough left to give him a lot to think about."

While Division 45 made last-minute preparations for its attack significant events were taking place in *Task Force Merrill* behind it. At 0235 Admiral Merrill ordered Division 46 to mount a torpedo attack also. Immediately Heinie Armstrong was on TBS: "I have no targets on my screen!" A moment later Alston Ramsay in *Foote* echoed him: "Neither have I!"

"Very well," said the Admiral, "belay the torpedo attack." Two minutes later he issued a new order to the task force less Division 45: "*Execute to follow; turn one-eight.*"

This order proved to be a death warrant for a score of men in *Foote*-the-Unfortunate and very nearly cost the ship her life as well. In the oral command system used in the United States Navy, when the word "turn" precedes the numeral, the direction of the turn is to the right. When the numeral precedes the word "turn" the direction of the turn ordered is to the left. The numeral or numerals plus zero indicate the traverse of the turn in degrees. Thus Admiral Merrill, in ordering

"Turn one-eight," had called for a turn of his ships 180 degrees to the right which, of course, would reverse the direction of steaming of the formation. But the preface *"Execute to follow"* indicated that the order was preparatory and was not to be acted upon until the "execute" signal was given. For the moment, then, the steaming of the task force remained unaltered. Meanwhile a sinister technical state of affairs became operative.

A basic problem in the transmission of orders and other communications by TBS, especially in a numerous formation or in battle, was created by the fact that these transmissions usually were received through loud speakers or "squawk boxes" placed on the bridges and elsewhere in the ships. The cacophony which often developed when a multiplicity of messages was being transmitted not infrequently caused one ship or another to miss a message entirely; to misunderstand one received; or to receive only a fragment of a full transmission.

Some ships—Ham Hamberger pioneered this in *Converse*—mitigated the problem to some extent by a judicious separation of circuits and the installation of ear phones on the more important ones to screen out some of the confusion. Other ships, however, had not yet had time or equipment to effect this precaution.

It seems probable that this basic condition was in some measure responsible for what now took place in Task Force 39. Admiral Merrill had issued his *"Execute to follow; turn one-eight"* order at 0237, and in *Foote* that was the way the message had been received and logged. The order would bring the ships to a reverse course, each ship turning on her heel and, consequently, the order of steaming would be reversed also. Captain Ramsay did not receive any modification or qualification of that order. But there must have been either a qualification or a separate order addressed to the destroyers alone, although the preserved records do not show this. In any case 1 minute later, at 0238, Ramsay monitored the order *"Task Force Commander to Division 46: Execute your countermarch."*

The orders *"turn one-eight"* and *"countermarch"* were fundamentally different. Countermarch meant for the ships to maintain their order of steaming but to turn around a point as each ship reached it successively so that the formation, still in the original order of steaming, would be headed in a direction opposite to their original course. *"Turn one-eight"* meant that each ship turned in her place so that the order of steaming as well as the direction was reversed.

Captain Ramsay interpreted the countermarch *"execute"* as implementing the only order he had received which was *"turn one-eight."* He promptly swung his ship through a 180-degree arc to the right. Simultaneously, at the head of the column *Spence* turned but *Thatcher* and *Converse* continued on and turned only when they had reached the point where *Spence* had turned ahead of them. Thus *Foote* found herself far out of position, miles ahead of her column when she should have been astern of it. The "man nobody knew" immediately rang up flank speed, applied left hard rudder, circled around, and raced to regain formation position behind *Converse*. This *Foote* never achieved.

The action did not wait for *Foote*-the-Unfortunate to extricate herself from her dangerous dilemma. Off to the northwest *Charlie Ausburne* reached her torpedo-firing position at 0245, let go with a half salvo, turned nine and retired on a northeasterly course as Arleigh Burke reported to the Task Force Commander, *"My guppies are swimming!"* Aboard *Dyson* next in line Roy Gano stood impassive as they approached the firing point. A torpedoman fondled his pistol grip switch lovingly and when the torpedo officer gave the order *"Fire!"* squeezed the trigger with precision as the degree of spread was achieved and the selector switch turned by a mate to each successive torpedo. *Stanly* fired and turned, and then came *Claxton* with Heraldo Stout all but dancing a jig around a PPI scope. A half salvo was the Commodore's order, but once he'd gotten this close to the enemy a half salvo simply would not satisfy Heraldo. It was altogether too puny a gesture for Stout's taste. "There's a big ship out there—a cruiser!" he chortled a moment after the first barrage of torpedoes had leaped from *Claxton's* tubes. "Hell, fire the other half salvo! We can get that baby and I aim to do it!" *Claxton* fired her second half salvo and turned away. Having thus "clicked" she had no more torpedoes left, but there was an aching happiness in the heart of her bubbly little skipper. They'd surprised the enemy and they were going to do him in. Or so thought Heraldo Stout. This was what he'd been waiting for, and he savored every precious moment of it. Of one thing he was sure: Arleigh Burke might chew him out for a dereliction of duty, but he'd never oppose throwing too many rocks at the enemy. For the Commodore of DesRon-23 there just weren't too many rocks!

The torpedoes had an estimated run of 6 minutes to target. Rain squalls were sweeping the area at the moment and conditions seemed to Burke propitious for the infliction of some really crippling damage on the enemy. But Rear Admiral Sentaro Omori had a rudimentary sort of radar and at 0248.30, $3\frac{1}{2}$ minutes after the torps had left the tubes, his radar penetrated the cloak of darkness and showed him the symbols of the ships of Division 45. He knew instantly that they were destroyers and that torpedoes must be on their way.

The word which came to Arleigh Burke from CIC moments later almost broke his heart: "The enemy is altering course to the south."

All Burke could say to Reynolds was a husky, "My God, how do you like that!"

"That, Commodore," replied Reynolds drily, "is what comes of a Swede expecting to have the luck of the Irish!"

The battle which now blossomed 45 miles west of Empress Augusta Bay lasted more than 4 hours which is a long time as such things are measured. "Imbroglio" would be the most apt one-word description of it. During the fighting—and it was desperate—there were more misunderstandings, misinterpretations of signals, mistaken identifications of friend and foe, and misapprehensions of command intentions and orders than profaned any other night surface engagement in the South Pacific during World War II. With twenty-four ships maneuvering at high speed and firing as fast as shell could be got up and slammed home in gun breaches, so much happened all at one time over half a hundred square miles of ocean that the selection and pursuit of a chronological narrative thread is about as easy as picking 2 pounds of small dried peas out of 10 pounds of large buckshot while wearing boxing gloves.

Tip Merrill's fundamental strategy was to push Omori to the westward while keeping him at arm's length, thus preventing him from pinning Task Force 39 against the offshore reefs and shoals off Bougainville Island. Although the Admiral received Burke's triumphant announcement, *"My guppies are swimming!"* he also noted Omori's turn-away and rightly assumed that this would defeat the torpedo attack of Division 45. He guessed, also, that the presence of his cruisers was known to the enemy and he gave up any further serious attempt at surprise. Burke was speeding north trying to open to his maximum gun range of 10,000 yards, and Austin's Division 46 less *Foote* was on station with the cruisers. So at 0249, without waiting for Burke's torps to run to target, Merrill opened gunfire with his cruisers against Omori's northern column of *Sendai, Shigure, Samidare,* and *Shiratsuyu.*

From the first the radar-controlled fire of the U.S. light cruisers was extremely smart. The rate of fire was good and the 6-inch salvos walked right across the surface of the sea into light cruiser *Sendai.* She and her mates barely had time to fire a torpedo barrage, which they did, before *Sendai* was on the receiving end of a tempest of shell from her U.S. antagonists. One of her magazines exploded ripping out her guts and by 0252 she lay dead in the water although she continued to return Merrill's fire with vicious persistence.

Steaming in column behind *Sendai*, the Japanese DDs were thrown into a melee, and in addition to being damaged although not disabled by near-misses, *Samidare* and *Shiratsuyu* enjoyed a collision at high speed which sent them reeling off northwestward damaged and, for a short time, out of the battle. Burke's torpedoes had been due on target at 0251. Seeing *Sendai* and the enemy DDs blasted by Merrill's cruisers only 1 minute later, there was great jubilation in Division 45 where it was assumed their torps had done the damage. They had not. The Japanese turnaway had been effective and the twenty-five torpedoes scored a clean miss although that in no wise invalidated Burke's doctrine. It was simply the way the little ball bounced on that muggy morning.

Two minutes after Merrill opened fire Omori, in flagship *Myoko*, turned that heavy cruiser and her sister *Haguro* in a tight column loop to the left, firing steadily with his 8- and 6-inch batteries. The splashes from this firing fell consistently 2,000 to 3,000 yards short of target although accurate for deflection. Omori's shooting was to improve appreciably after he illuminated. He either didn't have the hookup for radar fire control or he didn't trust it, although Merrill relied entirely upon this device.

At 0256, with the battle now blazing all about her, *Foote*-the-Unfortunate cleared her own cruiser line and rolled her wheel down to catch up behind *Converse*. Unluckily for *Foote* Division 46 changed course to 255 degrees true at 0300 to stay clear of the fire of the U.S. cruisers and she was forced to alter course correspondingly in her panting effort to rejoin. This placed her squarely in Omori's torpedo water.

To the westward the Japanese were having their own troubles of maneuver. Swinging out of their loop at 0305, *Myoko* and *Haguro* went charging into the column led by light cruiser *Agano*, and 2 minutes later the lumbering *Myoko* speared into destroyer *Hatsukaze* forward, sliced through her hull as if the DD's plating had been so much prime Wisconsin cheese, and picked up part of her forward section which remained impaled on the bow of Omori's flagship.

While *Myoko* and *Hatsukaze* were flailing around, Merrill was holding to his southerly course. Now he ordered *"Turn one-eight"* in order to place his ships on a northerly heading—and up popped trouble for Arleigh Burke!

Merrill's TBS command *"Turn one-eight"* was read both by *Stanly* and *Claxton* at the rear of the Division 45 formation. Burke had a sharp, staccato delivery on TBS in marked contrast, for example, to Count Austin who went by the book and spoke slowly and enunciated deliberately. At the Battle of Empress Augusta Bay, however, there had not been time for the skippers of the Gallant Squadron to become familiar with Burke's distinctive and rapid TBS technique. A roaring crescendo of crashing gunfire smote ears on all sides until it threatened to produce a paralysis of the auditory senses, and in these confusing circumstances both Bob Cavenagh and Heraldo Stout thought the

"Turn one-eight" order had come from their own Commodore rather than the Task Force Commander, and that it applied to Division 45. Obedient to this second TBS misunderstanding within 30 minutes *Stanly* and *Claxton* spun around to starboard and went racing toward the U.S. cruiser formation.

This inadvertent tactic had the effect of taking Arleigh Burke and Division 45 out of the battle for almost a half hour. Not realizing that *Stanly* and *Claxton* had left him, and seeing two pips on his radar screen charging toward his own cruiser column, Burke feared that they might be enemy ships and promptly took off in hot pursuit. Fortunately identification was established before gunfire was exchanged, but it took Commodore Burke some 30 minutes to collect his wayward DDs, turn his Division, and head once more for the short-range fighting, the only kind of fighting at which his destroyers could be effective unless they found torpedo targets. He picked up *Samidare* and *Shiratsuyu* about 15 miles to the northwest and went plunging after them at 33 knots.

While this action was in progress the scene of the battle suddenly was transformed into a prospect of dazzling, diabolic beauty. Turning to his flag captain, Omori ordered "Offset your 5-inch battery from the firing solution and illuminate!" As this was done the cloak of almost impenetrable darkness was ripped from the ocean's surface by the superior pyrotechnics of the Japanese. Floating lazily overhead, brilliantly white and unwinking, each star shell seemed of the order of a million candlepower. The silhouettes of the U.S. ships—even their thread-like stays and spars—were etched stark black against the luminous sky above and behind them. It seemed as though some frightful garden of the devil himself, a garden replete with multicolored fountains and fantastic blossoms of fire, had sprung to life at the touch of a modern and mighty Merlin. Tall geysers of water flashing red, green, and gold leaped skyward from the bosom of the sea as Japanese shells splashed short or over, impregnating the ocean with their brightly colored spotting dyes. From *Cleveland* streamed livid lines of orange tracer, stenciling flat arcs of glowing color upon the unearthly pallor of the night as she fired against the *Sendai* column which still was Merrill's principal target. Something had happened to *Denver*'s Mark VIII radar; she could get no 6-inch spots and her rate of fire slowed. At the same time Omori's shooting improved miraculously now that his gunners could see their targets. Eight-inch salvo after 8-inch salvo plunged into the sea scant feet ahead of leading cruiser *Montpelier*, and the patterns of the shell splashes were disconcertingly small. Outwardly calm, Tippy Merrill stood on *Montpelier*'s bridge and drank in the raw beauty of the wild panorama for a fascinated minute. Already he had ordered counter-illumination but it was short, weak, and ineffective. At last he turned to Captain Robert G. Tobin, *Montpelier*'s commanding officer, who stood at his side:

"Bob, those guys over there can shoot all right. They've just been unlucky so far. But I guess the time has come to do something before we get clobbered. We'll make chemical and funnel smoke, and see how they like a little game of hide-and-seek."

Responsive to the Admiral's order, clouds of dense vapor soon were billowing from the funnels and smoke generators of the ships. The smoke hung suspended between the surface of the sea and the lowhanging clouds overhead, providing an insulating layer of bright opacity behind which Merrill tucked his cruisers. The vision of their radar eyes was in no wise dimmed by the protecting fog. The accuracy of Omori's heavy caliber fire was impaired but once having found the range his gunners continued to score frequent near-misses. A single one of the heavy 8-inch Japanese salvos landing aboard could tear any of Merrill's light cruisers to bits in an instant, and although hidden for the moment from the Japanese optics the U.S. cruiser force continued to walk intimately with death.

At 0301 *U.S.S. Foote* was under 25 degrees of left rudder, steadying from the swing she had made to the right to correct to the course of her Division which she was still striving to rejoin. With her polished shafts spinning at 374 rpms, she was tearing through the water at 34 knots. But 34 knots was not fast enough to dodge one of Omori's Long Lances which now reached out and cut her down.

The torpedo came down *Foote*'s starboard side at a shallow angle, and struck aft at the turn of the bilge. It is possible that she actually swung her stern into it. The detonation was tremendous and the damage devastating. Within seconds *Foote*-the-Unfortunate was substantially a derelict. Her mast whipped in a fore-and-aft direction describing an egg-shaped arc of about 10 feet maximum diameter at the top. A thick column of seawater shot up 75 feet, poised frozen to complete immobility for a fragment of a second at the peak of its perpendicular trajectory, and then crashed down on what was left of her afterdeck in a thunderous cascade which swept away men and fittings alike. H. S. Mix, a sailor stationed at the after 20-mm mount, was blown high into the air. With awful deliberation, as if caught and held in the lens of a slow-motion camera, his spread-eagled body cartwheeled forward toward the bridge over the after 5-inch guns and the after high 40-mms. The body bounced off the after stack, hit the gaff bending it double, and came to rest a bloody pulp on top of the after torpedo tubes.

The force of the explosion, exerted upward and outward, completely blew off three of *Foote*'s after compartments up to frame 192, her starboard propeller, and her rudder. The steering gear room, after crew's quarters, and ship's stores stowage compartment disappeared in an instant. Five more large compartments were opened to the sea. A 600-pound depth charge was blown into the damaged section on the port side at frame 194, but the safety wire and depth safety fork remained in position and the charge did not detonate.

Below, in the after 5-inch handling room and projectile stowage, all battens of shell and powder bins jumped out of their holders and shell and powder erupted from their receptacles in a deluge of steel and coarse granular explosive. Of the two men in this space, one escaped. The other was buried beneath the avalanche of plunging shell and powder, and his body was not found until divers eventually removed the ammunition from the flooded compartment. *Foote*'s main deck was badly buckled and her sides bulged out to a depth of 20 feet. Her after 5-inch gun was jammed in train and three of her 20-mms were blown overside along with her chemical smoke generators. The ship was lifted bodily upward and when she settled back her main deck was awash aft, she took a 4-degree port list, both engines were stopped cold, and she had lost all communications. Three enlisted men were dead on board; one officer and fifteen enlisted men either had been blown overside and forever lost or so atomized by the explosion that no trace of them ever was found. Two officers and fifteen enlisted men were wounded.

The fight to save *Foote*, directed by her Captain, Commander Alston Ramsay and her executive officer, Lieutenant Commander M. S. Schmidling, USN, was well worthy of the ethos of the Gallant Squadron at that moment being purified in the fining pot of desperate battle. Arleigh Burke had said he wouldn't leave a brave cripple, nor did he. Within minutes an unidentified destroyer appeared, steamed in a wide circle around *Foote* laying a thick chemical smoke screen which completely enveloped the stricken ship, and then steamed off. Burke still was fighting, and though he spared time to hide unhappy *Foote* from her enemies he could afford to do no more at the moment.

The wounded were collected by corpsmen and rescue parties and Lieutenant (jg) H. C. Moffitt (MC) USNR, *Foote*'s doctor, got to work on them at once. The ship was drawing 21 feet aft but only 6 feet forward, and Captain Ramsay knew he would have to shift weight if he hoped to save her. But first he had to get rid of some very dangerous cargo. The starboard depth charges, set on "very deep," had been blown overside but the port charges still were aboard. The pistols and boosters of these were pulled and a damage control party started jettisoning them. At 0304 while engaged in this task they heard and felt the starboard charges letting go in the depths below them.

At 0306 the Captain ordered the engines turned over. There followed a tremendous ripping and tearing sound accompanied by teeth-shaking vibration in the area of the after engine room, and the engines were hastily secured before they could pound what was left of the after end of the ship to pieces. Pumps were put on the flooded fuel tanks and at 0310 radio and radar circuits were restored and Ramsay reported the condition of his ship by TBS to Admiral Merrill. By 0312 the damage control party, which was virtually all hands, had three portable submersible pumps working on flooded compartments and 2 minutes later they got a handy billy on isolated compartment C-201-L. Fire and bilge pumps were put on the shaft alleys while hands turned to at the job of throwing overboard everything that was inflammable and shifting movable weight, including 5-inch ammunition, forward. Captain Ramsay, the man nobody knew and a lonely skipper indeed with his ship sore stricken and lying helpless at the very center of boisterous battle, didn't jettison his torpedoes. "We may get a shot at them yet," he told Schmidling grimly.

At 0308, with *Foote* out of the battle and fighting for her life against fire and the sea, Admiral Merrill ordered Count Austin to launch torpedoes against heavy cruisers *Myoko* and *Haguro* who were swinging down southeast and firing fast. In order to clear his own cruisers in the shortest possible time and gain a vantage point from which to attack the enemy, Commodore Austin brought his three remaining ships —*Spence*, *Thatcher*, and *Converse*—to a line of bearing formation and rang up 30 knots. Heinie Armstrong was on the bridge of flagship *Spence*, but Austin preferred at the moment to control his Division from CIC where, through radar, he had a picture of the broad scope of the battle although at the price of having only tenuous contact with the scene visible from his own bridge. Aboard *Spence* CIC was located two decks down from the bridge and the areas were not too conveniently accessible to each other.

Austin intended to bring his formation to a column of ships before launching torpedoes and at 0310, in anticipation of that evolution, he issued the preparatory order, *"Stand by to execute; turn nine!"*

At that moment, and for the third time in the battle, the TBS gremlins once more took command. On *Thatcher*'s bridge a seasoned old chief quartermaster "who could conn the ship as well as I could" as blunt and honest Ralph Lampman put it, had the wheel. What he heard over TBS and what Captain Lampman heard was simply an unequivocal *"Execute turn nine!"* They did not hear the qualifying *"stand by to."* The grizzled chief looked over at the man who puts his pants on one leg at a time, and raised a questioning eyebrow. The man who puts his pants on one leg at a time looked back and shrugged slightly. The chief rolled his wheel, and *Thatcher* swung 90 degrees to the right.

In less than 1 minute she was slicing along on a course that would take her crashing into nearby *Spence* dead amidships between the stacks!

Only the illumination thoughtfully provided by Admiral Omori saved *Spence* and *Thatcher* from desperate damage. Both skippers saw the danger at the same moment and both started turns to dodge. There was not time for an effective reduction of speed, although Lampman did back his engines full, in a futile gesture. Their turns brought the ships onto roughly parallel courses headed in opposite directions, but the centrifugal force of her careening turn gave *Thatcher* enough leeway to place her in a bow-on position dead ahead of *Spence*. Before anything further could be done sparks flew wildly into the night and the two ships made a "Chinese landing"—bow to bow—and raked each other from stem to stern as they plunged past at a combined speed of 60 knots.

Spence carried a handsome silver St. Christopher's medal affixed to her foremast and Heinie Armstrong surmised afterward that "the good saint must have been working overtime that morning." *Thatcher* suffered considerable structural damage. Her Number 3 40-mm clipping room was bashed in and her after starboard shaft was knocked out of line. She steamed on, however, and continued to fight. Aboard *Spence* the port motorwhaleboat was demolished and all of her starboard shaft bearings fell. She suffered superficial damage topside. Thinking quickly at the moment of impact elevating pointer D. E. Stephens elevated his gun thus saving it from serious damage. The fighting efficiency of the ship remained substantially unimpaired. By the time Count Austin gained the bridge to find out what the trouble was the ships had drawn apart and his torpedo attack against *Myoko* and *Haguro* had been relegated to the realm of things that might have been.

At this moment the battle stood upon the threshold of becoming the melee Merrill had feared and Armstrong had forecast. Behind their smoke breastworks *Montpelier*, *Cleveland*, *Colorado*, and *Denver* were steaming on a 000-degree heading, pumping out shell at the enemy's central and southern groups which were maneuvering to the southwest and replying briskly. Having collected *Stanly* and *Claxton*, Burke swung down from the north, then rounded sharply northwest after several targets which he had at ranges up to 24,000 yards. One of these was crippled *Sendai* and two of the others were destroyers *Samidare* and *Shiratsuyu* who were standing by her. Austin also saw this gaggle of targets and started racing north with *Spence*, *Thatcher*, and *Converse*. He didn't get far, however, before running into more trouble.

At 0320 *Spence* sustained damage from two near-misses, and took a solid hit from heavy cruiser *Myoko* in her starboard side at the junction of the mess hall, the bakers' living compartment, and the fuel tanks below. Again St. Christopher must have been on the job because the shell did not detonate but it ripped a 7-foot gash in her side 2 feet below the waterline. Here was a desperate job for *Spence*'s first lieutenant, sallow-complexioned Lieutenant R. B. Fox, USNR, and his assistant, Ensign N. R. Putnam, USNR. They turned to with the damage control party, stuffed the hole, which was long but not very wide, with bags of beans, and shored up the inside. Within a short time it seemed likely that the pumps could hold this situation, but another danger threatened. Division 46 had gone into the battle with only about 60,000 or 70,000 gallons of fuel oil per ship. Even under non-battle conditions that was a starvation ration for destroyers maneuvering at high speed. Now seawater rushing into *Spence* started contaminating her little remaining fuel, and for a time her afterdeck was awash. This latter condition threatened to silence her after 5-inch battery which needed ammunition stowed below. Two determined gunners met the crisis. Synchronizing their actions with the roll of the ship to minimize the amount of seawater admitted below, they flung open the hatch to the handling room, scrambled down, dogged the hatch above them, and started pushing up ammunition as fast as the hoist could handle it. Subsequently both men were awarded the Silver Star on recommendation of Captain Armstrong who said, in his nomination, that their deed "symbolized the spirit of *Spence*." However, although still racing north and "throwing rocks," the plucky little ship, portions of her fuel oil contaminated, fluttered on the brink of losing suction at any moment.*

At 0413 *Spence* finally wobbled from her place at the head of the column and although she later regained propulsion (almost to her own undoing!) Commodore Austin temporarily released tactical command of the remaining two ships of his Division to Ralph Lampman in *Thatcher*, he being senior captain.

Denver was a lucky ship on that thunderous morning. Between 0320 and 0325 she took three 8-inch hits from heavy cruisers *Myoko* and *Haguro*, each hit from a different salvo. Any one of these hits might have destroyed the lightly armored cruiser, but the god of battles ruled that none of these death warrants was to be executed. All three 8-inch shells were duds, and although *Denver* took a lot of water and Captain Briscoe was forced to sheer out of column on the disengaged side, he continued to fire and later was able to rejoin the formation. About

---

* In broad terms suction is used to supply fresh water to the boilers. This is converted into superheated steam, which passes through the tubes at a tremendous speed. The fire boxes are so hot that, if there is an interruption of this flow of steam, the tubes will melt. Lost suction, then, requires that all engines must be secured for as long as it may take to correct the situation. This is sometimes accomplished in minutes; on other occasions it may take from 4 to 6 hours.

this time, too, *Columbia* took a freak hit. The base plug from an 8-inch shell ripped through her plating above the waterline and ended harmlessly in the sail locker.

When *Samidare* and *Shiratsuyu* saw Burke bearing down on them from the southeast and Austin from the south those two DDs flipped their tails around and headed northwest with every pound of steam they had, leaving wounded *Sendai* to survive if she could. *Sendai* had regained some propulsion but was able to steam only in slow circles. She continued to fire heavy salvos, and was as dangerous as a wounded water buffalo. Both Burke's ships and Austin's were pounding along at speeds above computed full power, but neither Commodore knew where the other formation was. Austin was the first to gain a firing position on *Sendai* and the Count ordered a half torpedo salvo. The salvo was short by one torpedo however, because a malfunctioning firing key aboard *Converse* left one of her torps still in the tube. This rankled somewhat in the mind of perfectionist Ham Hamberger who, otherwise, fought a perfect battle. Division 46 did not wait to assay the effectiveness of her torpedo fire but raced on after Japanese destroyer targets.

Reaching *Sendai*'s vicinity at 0349 Arleigh Burke poured 5-inch shell into her at a range of 7,000 yards without reducing speed. When they had swept safely past Burke turned to Captain Reynolds. "You know, Brute, that was a big fellow, and she couldn't have been a light hulled ship either, considering the gun punishment we gave her without sinking her. She must be a cruiser. *But where th' hell is Division 46?* They must be low on fuel; we're all running out of ammo, and I don't like this business of not knowing where Austin is or what he's up to."

"Well, I'll tell you how I figure it, Commodore," replied the laconic Reynolds. "The Count, Heinie Armstrong, Ralph Lampman, and Ham Hamberger are all certain to do one thing. That's head for the enemy. I figure all we have to do is look around for a fight, head for it, and I dare say we'll pick 'em up!"

Reynolds was right as rain. Seeing two targets being engaged off his port beam Burke started for them at 0403, and by 0418 had closed the range to a handy 7,000 yards. Guessing that *Spence* was somewhere in the area he went on TBS and announced, "We have a target smoking badly at 7,000 yards and are about to open up." Instantly Austin's voice replied, "Oh, oh! Don't do it! *That's us!*"

Through this inadvertency either *Samidare* or *Shiratsuyu* survived the Battle of Empress Augusta Bay, for the smoking target was not *Spence* but one or the other of the Japanese DDs. *Spence* was in the vicinity but farther to the west.

Picking a new target Burke slowed to 24 knots and headed for it meanwhile reporting to Merrill, "There are a hell of a lot of ships of both nationalities in one tight little huddle on my port bow. If I can identify one as enemy we'll take care of him."

The Commodore's identifying technique chose that time to "throw a shoe." As Division 45 closed the target he asked his captains on TBS, "Does anybody doubt that guy ahead is an enemy?" There wasn't a peep out of the Little Beavers. "Okeh," said Burke happily, "let him have it!"

Within the next 60 seconds a dozen or more 5-inch projectiles slammed into the sea close aboard *Spence!* The action on her bridge was instantaneous. Heinie Armstrong turned on his battle lights and rang up all the knots *Spence* would do. Count Austin grabbed the TBS transmitter:

"We've just had another bad close miss," he said with the dignity of an English butler in the best Hollywood tradition. "I hope you're not shooting at us."

"Are you hit?" asked Burke anxiously.

"Negative," replied Austin, *"but they're not all here yet!"*

"Sorry," Burke told him with what has become a classic of Navy humor, "but you'll have to excuse the next four salvos. *They're already on their way!"*

Turning to Reynolds with a broad grin the Commodore concluded, "Well now, by God, at least we know where *Spence* is!"

Ordering *Thatcher* and *Converse* to join up, Burke swung to his right and for a time stalked a rain squall which appeared on his radar as an enemy ship. Realizing his error he picked another target and chased it briefly but the Japanese destroyer got up to 38 knots and the ships of DesRon-23 couldn't touch that pace. Swinging south once more, Battling Burke found *Spence* and *Hatsukaze* engaged in a blazing duel and once more the doughty Count was in trouble. At 0515 he messaged Burke, "I may be in a tight fight right now. We're almost out of ammunition."

"Hold on!" shouted Burke over TBS. "Hold on! I'm coming!"

Hatsukaze, wounded in her collision with *Myoko,* had been wandering around on the periphery of the battle and had blundered into *Spence.* The Japanese DD fought gamely but at 0515 the ships of Burke's formation opened on her and she lived but scant minutes thereafter. Blazing from stem to stern, her bow blown off and her bridge demolished, she rolled over and sank with all hands as dawn was flushing the East with pink radiance. Light cruiser *Sendai* had gone down at 0400, so that the U.S. bag of enemy ships sunk was two against none.

Unappeased while an enemy still floated, Burke turned north once more, this time at 25 knots so *Spence* could keep up, and messaged

Merrill, "I'm heading north. We left a guy on ice up there and I'd like to get him. Also there may be some other cripples, and we might pick up survivors from whom we can get good information."

It was a very pretty speech but Tip Merrill didn't buy the package. The surviving but badly battered Japanese forces were retiring. He knew that enemy air could be relied upon to jump him at any moment. *Foote* was in a very bad way, and Merrill was not unmindful of the cargo ships about to start unloading at Cape Torokina. So he replied, "Arleigh, this is Tip! For God's sake come home! We're lonesome!"

Reluctantly Burke turned his fighting formation toward the rendezvous, which was *Foote*'s position. *Stanly* advised the Commodore that she was having a tough time keeping up. Her boilers were leaking because of her intensive gunfire vibration, she was losing vacuum on her starboard engine, and the men in the engineroom still were wearing oxygen masks because of leaking lethal gases. Reflecting upon that news, and after a second cup of coffee, the Commodore felt better about the retirement which he recognized as tactically demanded. At Merrill's request, Burke sent Heraldo Stout dashing ahead to take *Foote* in tow, and upon arrival *Ausburne* and *Thatcher* took up escort positions flanking the cripple. Captain Ramsay mustered his ship's company on their stations, cast up his losses in dead and wounded, and reported to Merrill.

As the task force moved slowly off toward Purvis, Merrill's anticipation of an enemy air strike materialized with a vengeance. Radar scopes on all the ships blossomed with pips as though they had measles as approximately 100 Japanese planes tore south from Rabaul bent upon the destruction of Task Force 39. Only 15 U.S. planes arrived to oppose this air armada. *Foote* and her escorts were a good 10 miles behind the cruisers, but the Japanese airmen paid the cripple no attention, boring in for the bigger game ahead. Merrill threw his formation into a clockwise spin which he maintained while cutting loose with every gun he had. "It was an organized hell in which it was impossible to speak, hear, or even think," he reported afterward. "But we were happy to see the air full of enemy planes in a severe state of disrepair."

Task Force Merrill managed to beat off the air raid without important personnel casualties, and by 0720 they had come out of their anti-aircraft spin and once more were steaming south. Tip Merrill took that opportunity to send Arleigh Burke a message which is about tops in the Navy's restrained schedule of congratulations:

"Thanks for a job better than well done!"

"That's high praise indeed, Brute," observed Burke, "and from a mighty courageous commander."

"You deserve it, boss," said Reynolds.

"*We* may deserve it, Brute," Burke corrected him. "It's not me; it's the Squadron, and always will be."

At 0730 Navy tug *Sioux* took *Foote* in tow, and late on the afternoon of Wednesday, 3rd November, weary *Task Force Merrill* less *Claxton* who had been left behind to escort *Foote* and *Sioux* (all three were cheered to the echo upon arrival next day) passed into Purvis Bay and anchored. They had been constantly under way for 65 endless and consecutive hours. They had fought two intensive bombardments and one of the longest battles in the history of the South Pacific war. They had sunk two enemy ships, severely damaged several others, exacted almost a thousand enemy lives, and had fought off a massive air raid. They, themselves, had suffered relatively minor damage. Most important, they had been faithful to their high trust, keeping the enemy away from the transports, cargo ships, and still weak shore lodgments of the Marines at Cape Torokina. Officers and men alike were anaesthetized by fatigue. They groped their ways about the decks and up and down the ladders, the impelling signals from their brains seeming to come from so much hot oatmeal. Yet many of them couldn't sleep; not yet. Fueling commenced at once, and there were harbor watches to stand on deck and below . . .

Somewhat rested from the Battle of Empress Augusta Bay, Tip Merrill and Arleigh Burke sat in Pug's Pub in the Ironbottom Bay Club several afternoons later sipping beer and exchanging reminiscences.

"The Japs have got us skinned on pyrotechnics," observed Merrill.

"That they have!" assented Burke. "And their gun flashes were dimmer than ours, even with our best flashless powder."

"I thought their fire was accurate but slow," said Merrill.

"*Ausburne* maintained a salvo rate of 6 seconds there for a while, and *Thatcher*'s rate of salvo fire was 10 seconds," Burke told him. "I think we can do better than that."

"Your boys did very well, Arleigh."

"God bless 'em!" said Burke fervently. "You know, Tip, the thing that tickled me most was the seamanship those fellows showed handling their ships at high speed in battle. You and I both know that's the toughest kind of challenge, but they actually seemed to be enjoying it."

"We're both lucky they're all experienced destroyer sailors, Arleigh. You've given them a word of appreciation, of course?"

"I talked to them as soon as they were rested enough to understand what I had to say. You'll read what I told them in my battle report which should be on your desk by now. My remarks went about like this:

The Captains of Squadron 23 went out looking for trouble; they found it; they sank it; and then they looked for more. When a ship became lost, as some did, she simply headed for the enemy and continued to fight by herself. It is impossible for me to express the proud, paternal feeling I felt for you all during the heat of battle. There are many officers in the United States Navy who probably would have done as well had the opportunity been granted them. There are NO officers in the United States Navy who could have done better.

12

Their Finest Hour

~~~~~~

The potbellied bosun shoved his cap so far back on his head that it clung but precariously to its perch, leaned over, spread his fat fore-arms along the signal bridge rail aboard *U.S.S. Dyson*, knitted his strong fingers together knuckles upward, and gazed across the gently undulating waters of Hathorn Sound with an expression that was frankly contemptuous. He wore no shirt. The black belt holding up his dungarees was cinched in tight at the waist, and his ample sunburned belly bulged outward in folds of flesh which obscured his belt buckle and the top two buttons of his pants as well. After a moment he spat reflectively into the water 50 feet below and spoke out of the side of his mouth to the gunner, Pablo's ex-pal, who stood a deck below him:

"Brother! Get a load of *Spence* over there!"

The gunner looked across the anchorage at *U.S.S. Spence* moving slowly into position beside the fuel barge. "So what's the matter with *Spence*, 'Boats'?"

"Christ!" exclaimed the bosun in disgust. "She's got out more fenders than th' Presidential yacht!"

"That makes a difference?" queried the gunner.

"Sure," said the bosun with a sardonic sag of the left corner of his mouth. "Why do they need all those fenders just t' go alongside th' fuel barge? Didn't *Spence* go alongside *Thatcher* at 30 knots at Empress Augusta Bay—and nary a single fender between 'em?"

The gunner grinned his appreciative confirmation of the sarcasm. Having worked it off on a mate the bosun spat a final time as if to provide a proper strophe for his witticism, eased into an upright position for his backside ached with the pain of protruding hemorrhoids, and waddled off in quest of the doctor. He had borne this private cross with fortitude while they had been in the zone of immediately probable combat, which had been most of the time lately. Now the ship was on a generous 2-hours' notice and the bosun's best thought for using the time was to determine the effectiveness of professional treatment in resolving his painful problem.

The date was Wednesday, 24th November, 1943—the day before Thanksgiving—and the local time was straight up for noon. Since the Battle of Empress Augusta Bay, DesRon-23 had been continuously employed in the zone of combat around and north of Bougainville. Their primary responsibility was to support additional echelons of men and supplies which ComSoPac continued to pour into the U.S. positions on Bougainville to stiffen them. It was punishing duty without remission of constant demands for high speed steaming, beating off air attacks, anti-submarine screening, surface engagements and shore bombardments, all evolutions hyphenated by frantic refueling and re-arming.

On the morning of Monday, 8th November, DesRon-23 less *Foote* and *Thatcher*, had crept into Purvis Bay having returned from an exhausting combat mission climaxed by a particularly vicious enemy air attack which they had been able to fight off without serious casualties. Almost every man in the ships entertained a hope for just one thing: SLEEP. But nature laughed at these longings. At about 10 o'clock a tremendous tropical storm smote the anchorage, lashed the waters to frenzied fury, and raged for 2 shrieking, booming hours. The frail, arrowlike little ships plunged and bucked at their berths, rolled through an arc of 90 degrees port to starboard and starboard to port, and behaved like berserk leviathans in a mad marine nightmare. Extra chain was veered but still anchors dragged, and all vessels had to keep their engines turning slow ahead to avoid being swept high and dry on the beach. It would have been a first class test of seamanship for strong and fully rested sailors. For the tired men of DesRon-23 it was a sore trial indeed, but they managed to save their ships and survive. That afternoon higher authority detached *Foote* and *Thatcher* and they were ordered Stateside for repairs, *Foote* in tow of a tanker. *Thatcher* had been more seriously damaged than at first surmised, and the man who put his pants on one leg at a time and whose philosophy was to love his fellow men (even if he had to kill them!) didn't get back to the South Pacific for 4 months. Thus through the attrition of combat the Squadron was reduced to six operational ships.

On the afternoon of Wednesday, 10th November, the Squadron was operating with Task Force 39 when, at 1545, a lookout aboard *Spence* sighted what appeared to be a life raft with men aboard. Heinie Armstrong requested and received permission to investigate, and in a short while *Spence* eased up alongside the life raft, her captain leaning over the bridge wing rail and a man poised forward with a grapnel at the end of a light line, ready to snag the raft.

"I count seven men, Burns," said the Captain to Lieutenant Burns W. Spore, USN, from La Mesa, California, who had moved up to the job of executive officer. "They're Japs all right."

"I don't think they're dead either, Captain."

"They sure as hell aren't!" exploded Armstrong. "For Pete's sake, will you look at that . . ."

During the next 5 minutes the men of *Spence* watched in open-mouthed astonishment the enactment of a gruesome ritual which was typical of Oriental fatalism and the antithesis of Western mores. The seven Japanese on the raft appeared to be aviators and as *Spence* drifted gently toward them they had been feigning death, lying sprawled over their frail craft in grotesque postures. Realizing, however, that Captain Armstrong intended to bring the "bodies" and raft aboard to examine them for possible intelligence data the Japs suddenly came to life. The officer among them produced a 7.7-mm machine gun probably salvaged from their downed plane. Under his direction a sort of seagoing version of harakiri by gun instead of knife was enacted. In turn each man received the muzzle of the gun in his mouth. The officer pressed the trigger, the back of the man's head was blown out, and the body toppled overside to sink quickly but not too quickly for the ravenous sharks who churned and lashed the translucent water as it became marbled with the dirty brown stains of human blood. One Jap who did his own thinking seemed most reluctant to have his brains blown out, and made motions of resistance. He was seized by two of his comrades who held him securely while the officer dispatched him with a bullet and a grimace of distaste. Finally alone upon the raft, the officer addressed those on *Spence*'s bridge in Japanese. His farewell speech was brief and, of course, not understood by anybody aboard. Having delivered it he proceeded to blow his own brains out and his body followed those of his mates into the depths.

Although stunned by this intimate view of senseless slaughter the men of *Spence* soon found their amazement tempered by amusement. Upon investigation it was discovered that the Japanese airmen had left behind them on the raft all of their classified publications and their maps. Although *Spence* took no prisoners for interrogation she made a very good intelligence haul just the same.

By mid-November the below decks condition of almost all of the DDs was deplorable. They had been worked unmercifully and "engineering availability" was an euphemism to be found in the manuals but almost impossible of realistic attainment. *Stanly* had abiding boiler trouble which nothing seemed to remedy for long, and *Spence* badly needed a general overhaul. The pumping systems in all of the ships were in foul shape and ready to break down at any minute, but it had been decided to run them until they failed, in the face of the simple reality that there were no more DDs available to do the job that needed doing. In *Converse* chief engineer Lieutenant T. W. Ten Eyck had managed somehow to keep his propulsion plant reasonably close to concert pitch. He was a big fellow whose child bride was going to school Stateside. Through an amusing inadvertency Mrs. Ten Eyck's report card had been forwarded to Captain Hamberger, who in turn forwarded it to Lieutenant Ten Eyck "with endorsements"! In *Charlie Ausburne* versatile Lieutenant Otis Parker, USN, her mustang engineering officer, had his engines in better shape than most. Accordingly, on 11th November, Commodore Austin of the "off" Division transferred his pennant from *Spence* to *Converse*, the only other remaining ship of his bobtailed Division.

At 0455 on the morning of Saturday, 13th November, while Task Force 39 was covering the fourth echelon landing at Empress Augusta Bay [the Allies had 33,861 men and 23,137 tons of supplies and equipment ashore at that time] *Denver* was temporarily knocked out of the war by an aerial torpedo. The air attack was one of the heaviest ever fought off by the task force. One of *Denver*'s enginerooms was blasted to impotence by the hit, and *Stanly* stood by to take her in tow. It was discovered, however, that she could make about 5 knots on her remaining engine, and the tow was abandoned. With escort, *Denver* steamed slowly off toward Purvis with her dead and wounded.

In line with his energetic policy of striving constantly to improve the performance of the Squadron, Arleigh Burke called frequent conferences of the Captains during the brief hours when the ships were at Hathorn or Purvis. These were highly informal sessions at which all spoke their minds without reservation. Through them were developed and refined many subtle points of Squadron operating doctrine such as the determination that 500 yards distance between ships steaming in formation was the most efficient disposition of ships.*

Having grown enormously proud of and reliant upon the dashing perfection of ship handling and fighting efficiency which by this time distinguished the Little Beavers, Arleigh Burke several times suggested to higher authority that the Squadron was capable of executing a punitive mission deep in enemy territory and without the protection of their big brothers, the cruisers. This was audacious and heady stuff,

---

* "Distance" is the space between ships steaming one behind the other on the same course. "Interval" is the space between ships steaming parallel with each other on a line of bearing. The Captains of DesRon-23 had demonstrated to their own satisfaction that a distance of 500 yards enabled them to support each other and maneuver with maximum efficiency in battle, while at the same time providing adequate opportunity for a following ship to avoid collision with one immediately ahead should that vessel be hit or otherwise suffer sudden incapacity.

and from any other destroyer Squadron Commodore it might have seemed more of an impertinence than anything else. But the story of Burke's demonstration for the Admiral back at Pearl that his men could perform as they said they could was current in the Third Fleet, and the consistently high day-in-and-day-out accomplishments of Des-Ron-23 were well known to the high brass. In sober fact, they needed precious little urging, for they had not much to work with by way of fighting ships, and the number of holes which needed plugging seemed infinite. Thus it chanced that on Monday, 15th November, the Squadron got orders to proceed independently deep into enemy territory far beyond the arc of Allied air protection, there to destroy enemy surface units if encountered. If no enemy surface targets appeared, Commodore Burke was ordered to bombard once more the air installations which the Japanese were trying desperately to make operative once more on Buka Island, off the northwestern tip of Bougainville. It was the first time in the history of the South Pacific war that a Destroyer Squadron had been entrusted with such a dangerous and at the same time vitally important mission entirely on its own.

"Fellows," Burke told his Captains on the eve of departure, "let's face it: We're all tired out. Our best bet in the circumstances is to keep this thing as simple as possible. Enemy submarines are reported off Bougainville. His air snoopers are pretty sure to look for us close in along the coast where the echelons to Empress Augusta Bay are running. I'm going to try to fool 'em. We'll cut west to the 154th meridian, ride that meridian due north until we're abreast of Buka, then turn east and wait until we're right in among the reefs where we can really reach their distant shore installations before we begin our bombardment. On the last leg we'll hold our speed to 20 knots and maybe they won't know what it's all about until after we've opened up on 'em. In accordance with doctrine, we won't leave a cripple. If any ship is damaged the rest will stay with her and try to drag her home. Now let's check over some fire control data . . ."

The mission, which was in support of the fifth echelon to Empress Augusta Bay, was efficiently executed but it was far from being the simple affair which Arleigh Burke visualized. On the way to target, at 2145 on the night of the 16th, *Converse* made radar contact with a surfaced submarine and Commodore Austin sent his flagship plunging ahead to ram. Realizing that he wasn't going to make it in time he switched to gunfire, saw his bullets hit, and the enemy craft disappeared either sinking or diving. Subsequent evidence strongly indicated that the submarine was sunk, but the gunfire attracted enemy air. By 2300 the sky overhead was throbbing with the engine roar of Japanese bombers and, so far as DesRon-23 was concerned, the cat was in the cream jar. *Ausburne* took a near-miss that blew her bodily sideways, made her heel over dangerously, knocked down most of those on her bridge, and showered her decks with steel fragments. A check revealed no serious casualties however, and structural damage was confined to a series of large dents in her port side.

When the bombers finally withdrew, Burke had to ring up 25 knots to make his bombardment position on schedule. At 0100 on the morning of the 17th, the Squadron was jumped by a numerous formation of torpedo planes who mounted a well coordinated attack. By slamming their racing ships around like broncho busters, the talented ship handlers of DesRon-23 managed to make the torps miss, but the net of the thing was that they steamed toward Buka with their guns blazing an incessant symphony of warning. When they reached the bombardment position at 0418 Burke observed to Reynolds, "This is some surprise! Those fellows on shore know *who* we are, *what* we are, *where* we are, and what we're here for!"

The bombardment was completed by 0500. Despite heavy defensive fire from the enemy, the Squadron remained unscathed although they went in so close that they constantly had reef trouble. Spotting planes reported the gunstrike effective in setting fires and destroying Japanese shore installations, and Thursday afternoon, 18th November, found the ships once more anchored at Purvis and the skippers gathered at the *Cloob des Slot* holding their customary postmortem lubricated by a few bottles of Acme beer.

Technically they couldn't find much they'd done wrong but Heraldo Stout, in a mellow mood, pitched out a gambit that intrigued his colleagues. His suggestion was that if it had not been for the singular good luck which seemed invariably to attach to DesRon-23, the story might have been far different. "You fellows know darned well," he observed, "that the Japanese would have plastered th' ever-blue-eyed-lovin' out of any other Squadron of cans in this man's Navy who tried to do what we've just done."

"We *are* a lucky Squadron," assented Roy Gano. "I don't think I'm overly superstitious, but I know there are such things as lucky ships and lucky units."

For a minute or so, as the conversation drifted lazily along, Ham Hamberger puffed thoughtfully on his pipe and considered. Approaching the Squadron for the first time he had known that a simple but fundamental value would determine his attitude toward his colleagues and theirs toward him. All he'd need to know was "the cut of their jibs" —and now he knew. They were, each and every one of them, a sea-man in Hamberger's compound definition of that word. Thus he had long ago concluded that the Squadron was armed spiritually as well as technically, the one being at least as important as the other.

"I think, gentlemen," he observed when the conversation lulled, "that we probably make a good bit of our own luck through our general professional competence and attitude toward the job. We know what needs to be done, we're confident of our ability to do it, and Arleigh sees to it that we have both the incentive and the determination."

"I'll buy that!" replied Heraldo. "Speaking for myself, I have more confidence in this Squadron than I've ever had in a unit I sailed with before. While leadership is basic I think the fact that we've fought and drilled together so much and each has a pretty good idea of what the other fellow will do under any conditions has a lot to do with our luck. To coin a phrase, we're pretty good at marine equitation, and that helps."

"It does seem to be a lot more than just rabbit's foot stuff, and that's a fact," observed Brute Reynolds.

There was general agreement among the skippers. Thus closely and informally, as a group rather than individually, and on the eve of what was destined to be their most spectacular achievement did they approach to one aspect of the *mystique* which was the abstract sum of their virtues. DesRon-23 *was* a lucky Squadron and again and again they accomplished with seeming impunity combat missions the counterpart of which cost other Squadrons dearly. As they themselves perceived however, their luck was no legacy from leprechauns. It was the product of top technical skill in handling and fighting destroyers, implicit reliance upon each other which spelled teamwork of a high order, a measure of individual courage and stamina considerably above the average, and strong faith in their leadership and their mission.

On 24th November, with the Squadron once more moved up to Hathorn Sound, jovial Dr. Hollis Garrard, *Dyson*'s medico, was in the act of handing a thin box of suppositories to the potbellied bosun when both were startled by the insistent hooting of the ship's siren. The bosun emerged on deck to find "Roger," the recall signal, two-blocked at the signal yard and activity preparatory to getting under way going forward on the fo'c'sle head. The supply officer and a handful of men were aboard other ships or ashore. Captain Gano hoped they'd get back in time but he had no intention of waiting for anybody. The Squadron had received dispatch top priority orders the general import of which was to get gone from Hathorn Sound *but right now!* So sail they must and sail they would and if a ship was shorthanded that was just too bad.

When Burke sortied from Hathorn at 1405 that afternoon only five of his ships were operational. They were *Charles Ausburne, Dyson,*

Claxton, Converse, and *Spence. Foote* and *Thatcher* were en route to Pearl and then the Navy Yard at Bremerton, Washington, and *Stanly* was undergoing imperatively necessary engineering availability alongside *U.S.S. Whitney.* As was not unusual at the time and place the basic orders which sent Burke racing north told him nothing about what he was to look for or what he was to do. He was simply ordered to finish taking on oil at the earliest possible moment (through their own refinements the men of 23 had managed to clip about 30 minutes off the time required for refueling) and get under way for "Point Uncle," further information and instructions to follow. "Point Uncle" was an empty spot in the ocean at latitude 06°—47' South; longitude 154°—46' East, and was simply a relative point from which ship positions and movements could be visualized and controlled.

By 1730 the Squadron was rounding Vella La Vella, but there was some confusion back at Admiral Halsey's headquarters as to just how many ships Burke had with him. Because of this a staff officer messaged Burke, "Report ships with you, your speed, and ETA 'Point Uncle.' "

Burke's speed was only 31 knots, partly because some lubber had jammed a tube brush into a boiler tube aboard *Spence.* It had caused all sorts of complications and upon receiving his original orders Burke had asked Heinie Armstrong, "Do you want to go along, or do you want to stay back and get your boiler fixed up?" "Please, Arleigh," said Heinie, "we want to go!" "Okeh," said Burke. "With your plant cross-connected what do you figure you can do?" "Thirty-one knots," Heinie told him. "Very well," said Burke, "you may come along and our formation speed will be 31 knots." *

In consequence of *Spence*'s condition, when Burke reported the five ships in his formation and his ETA "Point Uncle" as 2200 that night, he added that his speed was 31 knots. Admiral Halsey knew the *Fletcher* class DDs were rated for 34 knots plus, and when the time came he used Burke's "modest" speed of 31 knots as the basis for a little joke.

The intelligence upon which the Squadron's orders were based was singularly interesting. Successive bombardments including the last gun-strike by DesRon-23 had kept the Japanese air facilities on Buka Island out of operation, and conditions indicated to Admiral J. Kusaka at Rabaul that the restoration of Buka as an active air base was unlikely in the immediate future. There were, however, some 700 Japanese air personnel on Buka including many irreplaceable specialists and technicians, and Kusaka wanted to get them back to Rabaul. This design

* Both Burke and Armstrong knew that in the circumstances a cross-connected plant was a technical violation. When in combat or expecting combat the Navy regulation was that a ship's propulsion plant must be "split" so that damage to one side would not affect the other. A cross-connected plant in such circumstances was vulnerable and against regulations.

harmonized perfectly with Japanese Army thinking. The generals anticipated a strike against Buka from the fast growing Allied Bougainville installations around Cape Torokina, and wanted to land about a thousand Japanese troops on Buka to meet this expected thrust. The upshot of these considerations was the activation of a Japanese fast destroyer transport mission which would, in one evolution, land the soldiers and evacuate the air personnel. The operation, scheduled for the night of 24–25th November, was reported in some detail to Halsey's headquarters and, in consequence, DesRon-23 was sent tearing toward Point Uncle on the afternoon of the 24th.

The Squadron was approaching the latitude of Treasury Island, a checkpoint for the ships using Purvis and Hathorn, when Lieutenant John H. "Stinky" Davis, Squadron communications officer, climbed the ladder to *Ausburne*'s bridge and handed Arleigh Burke a message from Admiral Halsey. The Commodore read the address: "*For 31-Knot-Burke.*" Then he threw back his head and shook with laughter.

It was a minute or so before Burke, wiping the tears of laughter from his eyes, could read the rest of the communication:

> *Get athwart the Buka-Rabaul evacuation line about 35 miles west of Buka. If no enemy contact by 0300 love [local time] 25th come south to refuel same place. If enemy contact you know what to do. For ComTaskForce 33: Get this word to your B-24s and Black Cats. Add a night fighter for Burke from 0330 to sunrise and give him day air cover.*

The Commodore immediately stepped to the chart table, picked up parallel rulers and dividers, and started stepping off distances and plotting courses and speeds. He interrupted this work a number of times to receive additional information from headquarters, and before his detailed planning was complete he was in possession of all the information available to Halsey concerning the Japanese intentions and the enemy force it now became Burke's duty to find and destroy. Not much information was available on the size or probable composition of the enemy DesRon-23 might expect to meet. It was assumed that Japanese destroyers would be used for this job, but there also were cruisers at Rabaul and it was quite possible that Kusaka would toss in a cruiser or two by way of making sure that this important mission was not molested.

By early evening, with his ships turning an average of 310 rpms on course 325 degrees true, Arleigh Burke was ready to announce his battle plans to his Captains and they and their senior officers were summoned to a conference via TBS. The Commodore first explained what the Japanese were up to, stated more or less rhetorically that the Squadron's job was to seek out and destroy the enemy, and concluded the first portion of his remarks with the observation, "Gentlemen, this is lovely work if you can get it—*and we've got it!*

"Now, fellows," Burke continued, "I've got a hunch the farther north and west we go on this deal the better off we'll be when we meet the Jap. We'll drive northwest, then, until we intersect the Buka-Rabaul route about 0130 tomorrow morning. If we get there earlier than that and thus have a little extra time we'll use it to get farther west. Then we'll come right a little and patrol athwart that line at 23 knots. By doing it that way, should we meet the enemy as I fervently hope we shall, we'll be coming from the direction of his own home base—the quarter he's least likely to look for us in—and if he does discover us he may confuse us with a formation of his own ships long enough for us to get in our surprise torpedo attack. Incidentally, you'd better turn on your IFF at 2245. I don't think it's likely we'll encounter anything friendly where we're going, but it may help keep us together.

"If we meet the enemy we will keep both Divisions on the same side of him to avoid such a melee as happened at Empress Augusta Bay, and so the supporting Division will be instantly ready to carry on the attack in case there are other enemy forces in the vicinity. We will attack immediately on contact. We will not withdraw while a ship floats and can fight. We will not abandon a cripple. Now, does everybody savvy this thing? Or has anyone any questions or suggestions? I don't want any confusion or misunderstanding this time. How about you, Heinie?"

"It sounds like good dope to me, Commodore. *Spence* will come to the party. I have no suggestions."

"Ham . . . ?"

"*Converse* is ready. As I understand your plan it's straight doctrine once contact is made, and I haven't any suggestions for improving that."

"Heraldo . . . ?"

"Check an' double check! *Claxton* will be there. No questions; no suggestions."

"Roy . . . ?"

"Just a minute, boss," replied Roy Gano lugubriously. "Major Smith is studying it."

"Who in blazes is Major Smith?" shot back Arleigh Burke. "Don't tell me you've got a stowaway in *Dyson!*"

"No, Commodore. *I'm* Major Smith. Don't you remember? General Grant used to have his dumbest officer, Major Smith, read all orders before they were issued. If Major Smith could understand an order, it was all right. But if Major Smith couldn't understand an order, it had to be rewritten. Well, now I think I grasp what you have in mind. *Dyson* will be in there pitching."

There was laughter all around the circuit. It was typical of light-hearted Roy Gano to pull some such jape as "Major Smith is studying it," but the other Captains knew there was nothing the matter with Commander Gano in the thinking department. He was far from being the dullest among them.

"Very well," said Arleigh Burke concluding the conference. "We have search planes, a Black Cat, and night fighters. There is nothing to be desired but an enemy contact."

Burke's Japanese opposite number was at that moment patrolling off Buka, and showing rather more impatience than popularly is associated with the Oriental temperament. He was Captain Kiyoto Kagawa, Imperial Japanese Navy, and he paced restlessly back and forth on the bridge of his flagship, destroyer *Onami*, occasionally stepping out on the bridge wing to squint for a moment at the dark, almost shapeless mass of destroyer *Makanami* patrolling several thousand yards off his port quarter.

"Why don't they hurry up!" he iterated irritably for the tenth time to his flag captain while looking at his wrist watch. "Yamashiro's been in there 2 hours now. At this rate it will take him all night to unload a few soldiers and pick up a few airmen! I *always* get stuck with this stupid kind of thing!" The echelon commander swung away from his respectful captive audience and resumed his pacing. Had he known that he would be dead before dawn he might have found more significant employment for his time and more pious preoccupation for his thoughts . . .

The force executing the mission of landing a thousand soldiers on Buka and picking up the 700 air personnel no longer needed there was composed of five new 2,000-ton destroyers which precisely matched Burke's force in number and size although they were a knot or two faster and probably in a better condition of maintenance because they had been operating out of a large base with ample repair facilities. Captain Kagawa was in over-all command of the echelon. The three transport destroyers, *Amigiri*, *Yugiri*, and *Uzuki*, were commanded by Captain Katsumori Yamashiro, who flew his flag in *Amigiri*. His was the job of exchanging the Army for the air personnel on Buka, and despite Kagawa's impatience as he patrolled monotonously off the harbor entrance, Yamashiro was getting on with it. Shifting nearly two thousand men between ships and shore installations is not an easy evolution, and it was full 2300 hours before Yamashiro cast off his last lines and stood out to join his escorts *Onami* and *Makanami*. The formation in two columns—*Onami* and *Makanami* steaming in that order farthest north, and *Amigiri,* *Yugiri,* and *Uzuki* steaming in that order in the southern column and several thousand yards astern of the other two DDs, set out for Rabaul at 25 knots.

As DesRon-23 stood deeper into enemy territory than any U.S. surface force had dared go since the beginning of the bitter Solomons campaign, a few routine messages pre-empted the attention of the Commodore. At about the time Kagawa was leaving Buka, Plane 1 of Flight 23 reported to Burke eight "boats" at 06°—22' South; 154°—45' East, course 108 degrees true, speed 35 knots. Ten minutes later the pilot reported two more "boats" in approximately the same area. As Arleigh Burke was well north of this position, and as identification of the "boats" was extremely doubtful, he ignored these reports. Along about midnight *Claxton* reported, "Have many bogies! Am tracking!" A minute later Captain Stout was back on TBS with the debonaire admission, "I'm sorry, but my bogies were a flock of seagulls!"

"Heraldo," Burke twitted him, "were those seagulls enemy or friendly?"

Seemingly trivial, the incident of the seagulls was revelatory of the relaxed confidence in their own skill and ability which the officers and men of the Squadron now shared. They *knew* they were good, and they dared the enemy to give them a chance to prove it. No longer did their unspoken fears whisper about the dark decks as they stood toward battle. No longer did they lick their lips nervously and fret for the first gun to fire and set them free from anxiety. They were seasoned fighting men with an awareness of their own strength and mission, and they faced combat with confidence and composure, marked neither by fear nor theatrical heroics. At the threshold of their finest hour they were the fulfillment of the high demands of Arleigh Burke's leadership, and the vindication of the Squadron *mystique* in which each man participated in his own private way, and to the extent of his own capacity for thinking and feeling.

At 0140, when DesRon-23 came to a 000-degree heading with Des-Div-46 on a 225-degree true line of bearing, "it was an ideal night for a nice quiet torpedo attack," as the Commodore expressed it. The night was very dark with no moon. The wind was from the east at force one and the sea, deeply breathing, presented a tranquil bosom of long, gentle rollers. The barometer stood at 29.86 inches; the air temperature was 85 degrees and the water a degree warmer. The sky was overcast with frequent rain squalls moving over the area, and visibility was about 3,000 yards with binoculars. Aboard *Claxton* the duty cook shoved his first batch of Thanksgiving turkeys into the pre-heated oven, checked the temperature control at 325 degrees, and turned to assembling the ingredients for pumpkin pie. He murmured a pious prayer that the

Squadron wouldn't open with the damned guns for a few hours, at least. Every time the guns fired his oven doors flew open and he had a hell of a time.

On *Converse*'s bridge her battle OOD had the duty. He was Ensign Ray Peet, USN, and Captain Hamberger always thought of him as a sort of little bantam rooster. Ray was very quiet of demeanor, quite short of stature, and dark almost to the point of swarthiness. When the guns began to slam he was a powerhouse of energy and acumen. Below decks engineers—throttlemen, watertenders, firemen, and all the rest of the goblins who inhabit those spaces vaguely fearsome to on-deck sailors—simmered and seasoned in their own distinctive aura compounded of the pungent smell of grease and the damp odor of hot steel. There were no sudden motions, no tenseness and, seemingly, no organization. But with the easy casualness of competence, where a man was needed, there a man was found. It was as simple as that.

Aboard *Charlie Ausburne* Brute Reynolds indulged in a moment of reflection. While being Flag Captain was not necessarily the happiest job in the world, what with this and that, he decided that at least he had two things to be thankful for. He wasn't going to misunderstand any of the Commodore's orders, because the Commodore would be at his elbow. And when action was joined the Captain could stay topside in God's free air, and not have to close himself up in some such claustrophobic cubicle as the forward 5-inch handling room. Never mind that there was no armor plate on the bridge to protect him. Never mind that he might run but he couldn't hide from the inquisitive trajectories of the searching shell. At least he'd have the comfortable feeling of space around him, and not the constrictive sense of the imprisoning walls of a steel box. The Brute didn't have any more claustrophobia than the next fellow, but in a fight he'd rather be topside and that's all there was to it. Run? The vagrant thought recurred to him and impinged briefly once more upon the sharp barbs of his brain. Of course he wouldn't run. Nobody would run. Long ago and far away beside the Severn River the Captains of the Gallant Squadron had learned not to run but to stand, and stand he knew they would though their decks dip beneath them and their mortal courses be cut short by the simple fact of their being where they were when they were. To stand was their tradition. The heritage of keeping faith had been bequeathed them by the generations of seamen and fighting men who had gone on before. The very names of their ships did honor to men who had stood and faced death and accepted it quite rationally that they might bear faith, and Brute Reynolds knew in his heart that neither he nor his colleagues could or would do less.

Out on a bridge wing of *Charlie Ausburne* Arleigh Burke spread his forearms along the teak rail, relaxed with the latent alertness of the cat, felt the warm wind flowing over his back and shoulders, and permitted himself a private and small sigh. How was Bobbie, he wondered. How was she weathering the dull erosions of civilian life amid the pressures and alarums of war? She was doing volunteer war work, he knew, and her frequent letters were calm and charged with a reflection of her quiet strength. Still and all, he'd been gone a long time now . . . Among all the hundreds of millions of human beings on this earth, he reflected, this one small woman was transcendentally dear to *him*. Nobody else would understand that. Nobody else really *could* understand it. But that's how it was. Of course they had their own communion which they shared secretly. Love could and love did span the thousands of miles which separated them. There were the little words, the special phrases with meaning for them and them alone, and of no significance for a censor. Freighted with their own tender messages never contemplated by dictionary definitions these flowed reassuringly between them. But for the demands of duty which always and throughout were his criteria of reference, he might be at her side now, giving her the courage and reassurance which, among all men, only he could give to Bobbie. For a brief moment snatched from the context of the scene in which he found himself, not as a naval officer but as a man, a husband, and a lover, Arleigh Burke allowed his thoughts to turn upon sentimental values to which he was no stranger.

At 0140 on that Thanksgiving morning of Thursday, 25th November, 1943, the Gallant Squadron, alert but relaxed, battle ready and unfearing, steamed slowly in search of its enemies.

Dyson, closely followed by *Spence* and *Claxton*, had the honor of first radar contact with Kagawa's formation. At 0141 Roy Gano messaged, "Please check bearing zero-eight-five, distance 22,000. We have two applegadgets * at zero-seven-five, distance 22,000."

Less than 1 minute later Heinie Armstrong reported, "We have two applegadgets at zero-seven-five, distance 22,000," and seconds after that Heraldo Stout crowed from *Claxton*'s position immediately behind *Charlie Ausburne*, "We have course 280, 20 knots for applegadgets. *Hello, DesRon-23! Hang on to your hats, boys, here we go!*"

On course 280 degrees true Kagawa's leading ships *Onami* and *Makanami* were headed almost due west, and for the moment these were the only two targets Burke could see on his radar screens. He instantly swung his Division to a collision course being careful to warn Count Austin, "Hold your Division back until you get your proper bearing

---

* "Applegadgets" was a code word sometimes although not always used to designate a surface contact whose status as friend or foe was unknown. Once the contact was identified as enemy the Little Beaver skippers were more apt to employ the word "target." However, the two words were used pretty much interchangeably in many actions.

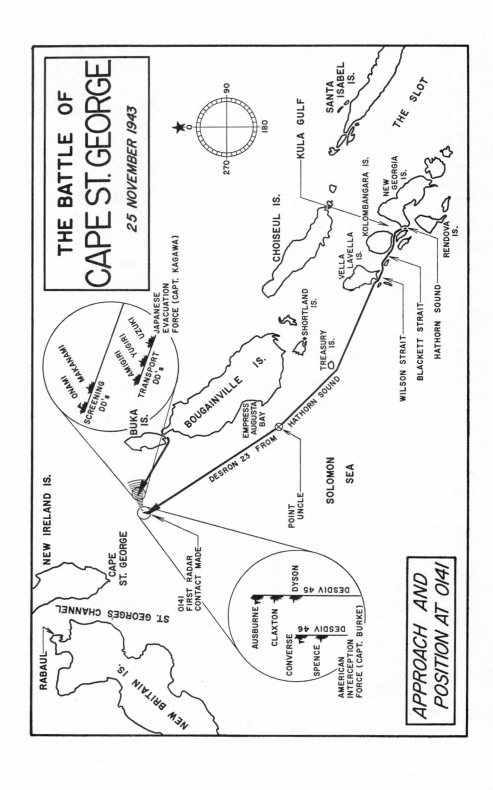

THE BATTLE OF
CAPE ST. GEORGE
25 NOVEMBER 1943

APPROACH AND
POSITION AT 0141

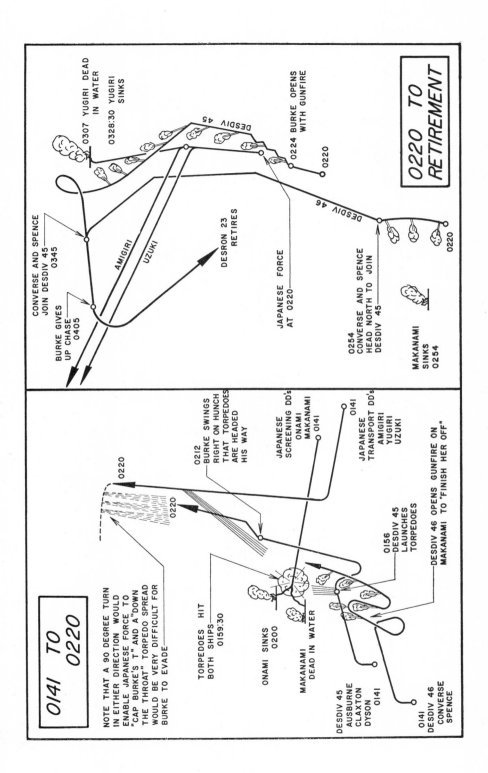

which is 225 degrees. *Commander Division 46 acknowledge.*" "*Wilco*," replied Austin with no great enthusiasm. Once more he saw himself being kept back on a line of bearing and for all immediately practical purposes out of the attack. He realized that according to Squadron doctrine his role was to cover Division 45's torpedo attack, but that didn't make him like the job any better. Indeed, for the next hour or so, Commander Bernard L. Austin tried every trick in the book to get *Converse* and *Spence* into the very center of the fast-moving battle, but Arleigh Burke frustrated his every gambit like a chess master toying with an eager novitiate.

While the Squadron still was in its turn toward the enemy Arleigh Burke messaged his headquarters, "Enemy vessels, strength unknown, at latitude 05°—16' South; longitude 153°—44' East. I am attacking. This is my first report this force."

At 0150, slicing toward his torpedo launching position, the Commodore messaged the Squadron, "We think he is on course 290 degrees, speed 20. We will fire on his port bow. We will fire to port—*I hope!*" This, again, was a warning to Austin to stay out of Burke's torpedo water should the Divisions become separated.

Burke's turn toward Kagawa brought Austin's Division on the starboard side of Division 45 which was now, therefore, between Division 46 and the still unsuspecting enemy. That was precisely where Burke wanted his "off" Division but The Count looked upon the whole ship-disposition scheme with a jaundiced eye, and at 0153.30 he made a bid to revise it more nearly to his heart's desire. "I suggest," he messaged Burke, "that I cross under your stern and cover your other side!" It was a cutey of a notion, but Burke wasn't buying: "Stay where you are!" he snapped in one of the shortest TBS transmissions of the battle. "Okeh," wailed Austin, "but this will keep me out of the show!" Burke didn't reply. He was busy issuing instructions that he didn't want to receive any more reports of bogies in the area. "This Squadron has too damned much to do now to bother with bogies," he observed.

Standing on *Ausburne*'s bridge, his feet braced well apart and his mind clicking with the complex calculations of relative courses and speeds and other fire control data demanding exact accommodation if his torpedo attack was to be effective, Arleigh Albert Burke shared with his Viking ancestors the lust for battle and for killing. Not that killing was for him an end in itself. Killing was a necessary but regrettable business demanded of him in order that his posterity might survive in freedom. In the discharge of that duty he stood ready, with his Captains and their crews, to pay the forfeit of his own life if need be. "*For it is better to perish in battle than to look upon the outrage of our altars and our nation . . .*"

At 0154 Burke ordered Division 45 to fire a half salvo of torps when the time came. At 0155 he ordered, *"Stand by to execute William"* [meaning to fire torpedoes]. A half minute later, as the few remaining seconds ticked through stop watches and the tension of stalking this as yet unsuspecting enemy mounted toward a peak almost insupportable, Stinky Davis came charging onto the bridge waving a dispatch. "What in hell is that?" demanded the Commodore, fully realizing that Davis must consider the message of supreme importance to press its delivery at this crucial moment. "It's a message from a B-24 about enemy ships in our immediate vicinity, sir," Davis replied. "Well, you can throw it overboard!" Burke thundered. "After all, *we* know where the enemy is now. Those guys upstairs are just a little bit late!"

By 0156 Burke was as close to the enemy as he dared go if he hoped to achieve surprise. Characteristically, in the last couple of hours he had conducted experiments with his own formations and had determined that in the conditions of visibility, wind and sea obtaining, the enemy probably would perceive his presence if he approached closer than 4,500 yards. Having closed to that distance, and with his angle on the bow 50 degrees—a perfect setup—he ordered, *"Execute William!"* Immediately afterward he ordered, "Turn nine," and rang up 30 knots to be clear of the enemy's torpedo water just in case the Japanese commander was playing a stealthy little game of his own.

As the ships of Division 45 fired and turned away, the blue flashes from their torpedo tubes seemed to Arleigh Burke as bright as so many clusters of diamonds catching the light of a noonday sun in Cartier's window. Would the enemy see—had the enemy seen . . . ? The next 210 seconds would tell the story, and for 31-Knot-Burke and his Little Beavers those seconds might have seemed aeons long save for a most interesting development. *Amigiri, Yugiri,* and *Uzuki,* all unknowing, were following along astern of Kagawa's column at a distance of 13,000 yards—a little over seven miles—and they suddenly registered on the radar screens of DesRon-23 at 0158, just 90 seconds before the torps were due to reach their targets.

Here was sport of arresting proportions, and Arleigh Burke let no barnacles attach themselves to his keels before plunging into it. There was no chance of a surprise torpedo attack upon these new targets. His first fifteen torps were due to detonate or reveal themselves by their wakes in passing at 0159.30 and it was certain all undamaged enemy ships would take evasive action immediately thereafter. Burke promptly swung Division 45 toward the new enemy, and at 0159 messaged Austin, "We have second target bearing east from us. Polish off the first targets fired on. Watch yourself now; don't get separated from one another, and don't get too far away. We're going after new targets."

Division 45 scarcely had steadied on the corrected course when they all felt a series of heavy concussions so closely spaced as to resemble the roll of thundering drums. The darkness behind them was ripped to shreds by broad sheets of flame leaping skyward hundreds of feet and raping the velvet blackness of the night with swift, insensate fury. Few aboard *Onami* including echelon commander Captain Kiyoto Kagawa knew more than a few moments of horror and of agony. Hissing upward from gigantic whirling spheres of blazing vapor at the base, thick fiery fingers 300 feet tall clawed spasmodically at the night for an awful 30 seconds. Then suddenly, at 0200 and as if someone had turned a switch, they disappeared. With them into oblivion went Imperial Japanese Navy destroyer *Onami*, her Captain, and her crew . . .

Moments after Burke's torpedoes hit, *Makanami* presented the aspect of a grotesque mirage. Her bow and stern appeared to be raised islands of billowing fire laced with dark patches of shapeless debris hurled high into the air by successive internal explosions. There was relatively little fire between bow and stern which gave the ship the appearance of having broken in half, but she had not. She floated stubbornly although not firing, and at 0202 Austin twitted Burke with the edged message, "I'm coming north to finish off what you didn't finish." "Keep your transmissions short, please!" snapped the Commodore.

In *Amigiri* Captain Katsumori Yamashiro showed no disposition whatever to pit his three DDs against the matching ships of Division 45. At the first sign of the U.S. force he wheeled by ship's turn movement to a course a little east of north and backed his throttles wide open. Burke streaked in behind him "with the safety valve tied down and his cap hung over the steam gauge" as the engineering saying has it, and for a few tense minutes the two formations greyhounded north in silence, the bows of the deep plunging ships flinging up great semicircular sheets of spume to be shredded on the wind and disappear in trailing veils of twinkling iridescence.

Could *Charlie Ausburne*, *Dyson*, and *Claxton* catch *Amigiri*, *Yugiri*, and *Uzuki?* That was a question bringing together for resolution such concrete values as boiler pressures and shaft revolutions per minute, and such imponderables as the art of seamanship and one of the hunches for which Arleigh Burke was famous. Yamashiro had a start of about 7 miles; the distance between his ships was 1,000 yards, and he was building up his speed rapidly from 31 knots. Burke called for "all the turns the engineers can make" and while waiting for time to resolve the mechanics of the chase and tell him whether he was gaining or losing, he sent his second report to Admiral Halsey:

> *Have made contact with two groups of enemy ships. The first group consisted of two ships destroyed by torpedo; the second group of three ships. I am attacking second group.*

At 0212, with the chase little more than 10 minutes old and the distance between formations indicating that the Japanese were slowly pulling away, Burke had a strong hunch that torpedoes were headed his way. It was a strong enough hunch to impel him to swing his formation sharply through a 45-degree turnaway to course 060 degrees true which they steered for 60 seconds before returning to their base course of 015 degrees true. While they were still steadying from their swing a thunderous detonation shook *Charlie Ausburne* and was followed by two more heavy explosions nearby. "Is our bow still there, Brute?" asked Burke looking forward anxiously. *Ausburne* still had her bow. The explosions were Yamashiro's torps blowing up in the heavy wake of Division 45. Burke's hunch and his radical turn had saved his ships.

By 0214 the Commodore of DesRon-23 was convinced not only that a stern chase is a long chase but that, in this instance, it was apt to be a losing one as well. "This is remarkable," he observed as much to himself as those standing with him on the bridge. "Here we are all lighted up and silhouetted by that blazing ship behind us, yet that monkey up ahead doesn't fire with guns."

"Maybe he has his decks crowded with personnel, sir," suggested Hank Ereckson, *Ausburne*'s "exec."

"Well," concluded Burke, "it doesn't look as though we're going to catch him unless we slow him down. We'll never reach him with torpedoes now, so let's see if we still know how to shoot." The Commodore pressed the TBS button and after a wondrously salty preface which certainly served to emphasize if not to clarify his intentions he ordered the ships of his Division: "Take station left echelon. We can't catch these rabbits, so we'll open fire as soon as you're in position. Our target is on course 005 degrees true, speed 31. *Claxton* and *Dyson* report when you are on echelon so we can open fire."

At 0220 Heraldo Stout reported *"On echelon and ready!"* and seconds later Roy Gano echoed him. At 0221 the Commodore ordered, "Stand by to execute DOG with guns," and at 0224 he followed this with the order, "Commence firing with guns. Start fishtailing—not too much; just enough to confuse the range." Instantly every ship in the Division began hurling 5-inch salvos at the scurrying enemy, and his reaction to being taken under fire was not long delayed. For a brief time Yamashiro confined himself to taking radical evasive action while returning the fire of Division 45. The Japanese salvos were well grouped, the patterns small and close aboard. Only the dexterous darting about resorted to by Reynolds, Gano and Stout enabled their ships to avoid crippling hits. The Japanese might be running but the sting in their tails was nonetheless lethal, and 2 inches of water sloshing around on *Claxton*'s bridge was an eloquent earnest of that fact. It was from enemy salvos straddling her continually and landing close ahead to toss up great gouts of sea water under which *Claxton* plunged as she tore along.

Despite Captain Katsumori Yamashiro's apparent desire to show a clean pair of heels, Arleigh Burke was, in fact, playing a sticky wicket and whether any of his Division captains grasped the realities or not, Burke was tactician enough to be fully aware of his danger. While the gun duel raged and pursued and pursuer alike became wreathed about with powder and stack smoke, 31-Knot-Burke watched intently for just one thing: a 90-degree turn either right or left by Yamashiro. Such a turn, he knew, could signal the beginning of the end for Division 45 of the Gallant Squadron.

The tactical threat Burke faced was this: A turn-nine or a nine-turn would place the fleeing Japanese destroyers on a course at a right angle to the course of *Ausburne, Dyson,* and *Claxton,* and constitute an effective capping of Burke's "T." *Amigiri, Yugiri,* and *Uzuki* had then only to fire a barrage of torpedoes practically down the throats of the U.S. ships which would be speeding to meet their own destruction. Masters of the Long Lance that they were, there was not apt to be much fumbling on the part of the Japanese if they undertook such a maneuver. Torpedo spreads, settings, and speeds could anticipate almost any countermove Burke might attempt, and whatever he did had more than a fair chance of being the wrong thing. In such circumstances the escape of the enemy would be almost a certainty, and the destruction of Division 45 a distinct possibility. It was not a happy prospect for Arleigh Burke. He could see some of his salvos registering on the Japanese DDs but the enemy did not slow down and he knew that as long as they had speed and time to maneuver they had the capability of giving him a sound thrashing.

On *Amigiri's* bridge Yamashiro studied the situation intently for a minute or two and then came to a quick decision. It was not to attempt to cap Burke's "T" as the Commodore feared, but rather to offer him a much more subtle gambit. Yamashiro's orders were issued quickly: "*Yugiri,* continue on course 350 degrees true. *Amigiri* and *Uzuki,* come left to course 305 degrees true by ship's turn movement." If the American commander wanted a fight, Yamashiro-san would separate his formation and invite Burke to continue the battle in a pattern of individual combat, ship against ship! Thus Arleigh Burke saw before him the enemy ships opening out like shoots from the main stalk of their base course, *Yugiri* continuing to race almost due north while *Amigiri* and *Uzuki* peeled off to the left on a course diverging 45 degrees from the original direction of their flight.

Burke watched this changing picture with narrowed eyes and grimly set jaw. The crescendo of battle roared around him. Aboard *Ausburne* there was a little trouble. Forward of the bridge the blasting fire of Number 2 5-inch gun shooting directly over Number 1, had blown the access hatch off Number 1 gun mount. Now, every time Number 2 gun fired, a long tongue of flame from the muzzle licked around the entrance to Number 1 mount and that space became choked with smoke, cordite fumes, and the lung-searing gases from Number 2 gun. The trainers and pointers and loaders and hot shell men continued to serve Number 1 until they dropped in their tracks, overcome. When that happened they were dragged out and others took their places. Brute Reynolds was fish-tailing *Ausburne* to bring her after battery to bear as often as possible, and she continued to fire a storm of shell.

In *Dyson*, gunnery officer Carl Sanders went methodically, quietly, and grimly about a job he'd been waiting for a long time. So they'd sunk him in old *"Vinny-Maru"* at the Battle of Savo Island, had they? Well, he'd fooled them. He'd lived to fight another day—*and this was the day*. His target was *Yugiri*. He had an instinctive felicity for fire control solutions. Every salvo he sent screaming through the night toward the enemy was propelled both by powder and a personal prayer for vengeance upon those who had cut down his beloved cruiser and cremated his comrades. He knew now a cold fury which made every alteration of elevation or train a memorial rite performed with dedicated skill and devotion toward the end that it might exact maximum retribution from the enemy. Nor were his prayers to be frustrated; *Yugiri* was feeling the lash of Carl Sanders' wrath.

In *Claxton* Captain Herald Franklin Stout was in heaven and his duty cook was in hell. The guns were shooting—*all* the guns were shooting—and the bouncy one was skittering his racing DD around with all the seeming abandon of an 8-year-old prancing about a May pole. Actually Heraldo was showing superlative seamanship, making maximum use of his own guns and never giving the enemy time to compute an effective firing solution. Seventeen years before, as he had expressed it, the curriculum and inflexible discipline of the United States Naval Academy had provided him with "the solid cake of necessary knowledge and information." Over it he had most certainly poured "the icing of his individual personality." But for him and for Reynolds and for Gano it was still "fundamentally the same pastry"—a confection compounded of almost flawless technical skill complementing a core of unshakable integrity and faith. The enemy was now being given a generous bite of this "cake," and Heraldo hoped it would be a big enough bite for him to choke on.

Below decks aboard *Claxton*, when the salvos slammed the boilers jumped 6 inches off their beds with the recoil and hot asbestos flaked

down like coarse snow from overhead pipes. In the galley a desperate
duty cook, nearsighted and wearing thick glasses, played a grim game
of his very own. The earthquake-like shocks of the guns recoiling upon
their glycerine-filled cylinders blasted his oven doors open in flapping
futility. The roll and plunge of the ship sent heroic-sized turkeys, slowly
acquiring the nut brown patina of perfect roasting, sliding and tumbling
end for end into remote corners. The cook, a mushgutted match for
the potbellied bosun and an irrefutable testament to his own culinary
talents, kept up the mad pace and chase until he was exhausted. Then
he turned out the fires, secured his galley, and relieved his lacerated
feelings by rushing on deck to scream imprecations at the four winds.
They paid him as little attention as did his busy mates at the guns.

Burke was feeling some concern about Division 46. The headlong pace
at which he was pounding north soon must place the Commodore beyond
TBS range with his "off" Division and he wanted to know where *Converse* and *Spence* were and what they were doing. At 0239 he messaged
Austin, "Have you finished your job and are you closing?"

"Negative!" came the reply. "Many explosions on target but he's still
afloat."

"*Sink him!*" demanded Burke. "And on your way up you should encounter a couple or three cripples. *Hope none of them is us!*"

31-Knot-Burke now faced a decision which racked his aggressive soul.
Would he play Yamashiro's game, or would he not? Superficially Captain Yamashiro's invitation to Captain Burke had about it the nice
punctilio of the *code duello*. A fair trial of strength and courage, ship
against ship—surely that was an honorable challenge? Arleigh Burke
wished with all his heart that it was, and had it been, he would have
accepted it instantly and with boisterous enthusiasm. One of his favorite
maxims was "ship against ship is a good battle in *any* language." In
the circumstances, however, this seemingly sporting ship-for-ship defi
had the deadly implications of the childhood jingle, "*Will you walk into
my parlor, said the spider to the fly . . . ?*" The fundamental values
which Burke knew he must resolve were these:

The chase had carried the ships of DesRon-23 far north and they
were very close to the principal Japanese base at Rabaul. There were
several strong air installations there. For that matter, there also were
enemy air installations behind Burke and between him and his own base
at Purvis. He was far beyond the range of Allied air protection, and he
could expect no friendly cover. Dawn was short hours away and at
dawn, if the Squadron stayed where it was and beyond a prayer of a
doubt, they could expect to be jumped by strong formations of bombers
and torpedo planes of which the enemy had ample numbers close by.
This in itself might be highly unpleasant but it need not be disastrous.

Fighter aircraft are trained to operate in teams of four, and so are destroyers. If he kept his Divisions together—five ships—Burke knew he had an even-Stephen chance of fighting off the air attacks and getting back home. But if he allowed his ships to separate and chase on diverging courses the scattering enemy ahead, no matter what their success against their individual targets (which would depend upon whether or not they could catch the Jap), dawn was certain to find the Squadron spread over many square miles of ocean. They would be unable to fight and maneuver as a unit for mutual protection. Instead, each ship would be a sitting duck to be pounced on at leisure by the Japanese hawks. On its face the invitation to slug it out ship-to-ship with the enemy was most alluring and almost irresistible to a man of Arleigh Burke's pugnacious temperament. Intrinsically, as Burke perceived, it was a booby trap and so, when "spider" Yamashiro hospitably invited "Will you walk into my parlor?," "fly" Burke had to decline pleading "other fish to fry."

The principal fish which 31-Knot-Burke now proceeded to fry was His Imperial Japanese Majesty's destroyer *Yugiri*, arrowing almost due north. Burke kept his formation together but ordered *Dyson* to fire on *Uzuki* while *Ausburne* and *Claxton* pounded *Yugiri*. With the calm of frigid fury Carl Sanders directed *Dyson*'s guns against the ordered target and started to register almost at once, although *Uzuki* continued to plow doggedly northwest. Arleigh Burke stepped out on *Charlie Ausburne*'s bridge wing, took a long look astern of him, and voiced a sibilant *phew-e-e-e!* "Brute," he said upon returning to the pilot house, "I was just out there looking right down the nozzles of *Claxton*'s guns. Heraldo's astern of us. He's shooting right over us, and he's paying us no mind whatever! It's a funny sort of feeling . . . just suppose . . ."

"Well, you want him to shoot don't you, boss?" asked the laconic Reynolds.

"I sure as hell do !" said Burke with a chuckle, "and he's doing it in style! I just hope he doesn't blow us out of water! But then, he's such an insouciant chap, even if he did sink us he'd manage to make a joke out of it !"

At 0247 Count Austin was once more knocking at the door with a plea to be freed from his onerous chore of sinking cripples and allowed to participate in the excitement of the chase. With courtly dignity his voice came over TBS: "We get a number of explosions and five fires on our target. Shall we continue, or join you?"

"*Sink him!*" rasped Arleigh Burke, his mellow mood banished. It was his conviction that an enemy ship surely at the bottom of the sea was a ship out of the war whereas a "possible" or a "probable" might be repaired to fight again. And it was his firm intention to see to it that

Makanami reached that conclusive destination if it took Austin all night. Truth to tell, *Converse* and *Spence* were doing a monumental job of shooting. In *Spence* ruddy-complexioned, fair-haired and slightly-built Lieutenant Arthur W. Bedell, USNR, from Albany, New York, her gunnery officer, sent salvo after salvo crashing into the target with a rhythmic cadence that had about it the awful implacability of time itself. Aboard *Converse* young tennis champion Hurley, who had performed most satisfactorily since wise Captain Hamberger gave him two vital jobs in order that he might accomplish one of them with distinction, achieved the incredible salvo interval of 3 seconds. Yet *Makanami*, blazing, exploding, and a funeral pyre for her people, refused to sink. Her hull was stout, her construction sound, and Bedell and Hurley were unfortunate in the placement of their shell. Not until 0254, 7 minutes after Austin had sensed that the end was close and inevitable, did *Makanami* disappear with her dead beneath the now deafening quiet surface of the sea.

"*One more rising sun has set!*" Austin messaged Burke. "*We are joining you now.*"

The 13 minutes between 0247 and 0300 were a form of crucifixion for Arleigh Burke. *Dyson* was pouring shell after *Uzuki* and thought she was scoring hits although the target didn't slow. *Claxton* and *Ausburne* were concentrating on *Yugiri* but with similarly disappointing results. Half beside himself with frustration, it seemed to the Commodore that the fire of all three ships had slackened and he messaged *Claxton* and *Dyson*, "*Please for Christ's sake continue to fire!*" Roy Gano replied at once, "Target out of range. We will close yours." "Get another target!" snapped Burke to *Dyson* and then, moments later and to both ships, "I simply don't understand why you're not firing to the north! That fellow's getting away!" "We're firing with all the guns that will bear," replied Stout. "Well, dammit," grumbled Burke, "*somebody* ought to be able to slow this target down!"

Having received Austin's report that he finally had sunk *Makanami* Burke ordered a TBS test to Division 46 and then messaged Austin, "Our targets are spreading out. We have one target on our port beam on course 310 degrees true. Please take care of him." The target was *Uzuki* and she was making knots, but Austin never received Burke's order. The test had been successful, but the order itself didn't get through and in consequence *Spence* and *Converse* came roaring north intent upon closing Division 45.

Steadfast in his determination to keep his Division together, Burke led *Ausburne*, *Dyson*, and *Claxton* jackrabbiting after *Yugiri*. Sealed in their mounts like crabs in shells the gunners continued to pump out their salvos. Their flashless powder had long since been used up and each time the batteries barked, blazing bulbous ribbons of orange flame burgeoned in the night like fat sparks from the anvils of Vulcan himself. The hot liners were beginning to protrude from the lips of the guns, and the lands and grooves stood starkly etched by flashes so close together that they gave the illusion of continuous light.

Burke had worked his speed up to 33 knots. Almost with awe in his voice he said to Reynolds, "That guy up ahead just *can't* take much more of the kind of punishment we're giving him, Brute."

"Well, don't look now, Boss, but I think he's slowing down," replied The Brute.

It was true, and by 0256 *Ausburne* had closed the range on *Yugiri* to 8,800 yards. Four minutes later, however, the Japanese destroyer seemed to get her second wind and went surging off, this time at 34 knots. Burke was not fooled. "That's just his dying gasp," the Commodore of DesRon-23 exulted. "That guy's number definitely has been posted!"

As the chase continued, Arleigh Burke took time to send his third report to the beach: "The gun battle continues. The enemy has scattered. Some may get away. These are tough babies to sink!"

In her last minutes of life *Yugiri* knew all the frantic desperation of a hare run to ground by a pack of relentless hounds. In just 90 seconds the symbols of her death were graved at evenly spaced intervals upon the endless dial of time by the stylus of destiny:

0305.30: *Speed 22 knots.*
0306: *Speed 10 knots.*
0306.30: *Speed 5 knots.*
0307: *Dead in the water.*

For 21½ minutes longer helpless, blazing *Yugiri* defied her executioners. At a range of 4,000 yards all ships of Division 45 poured shell into her, but she refused to sink. Burke countermarched and closed the range to 3,000 yards but the result was the same. "I guess you'll have to put a fish into her, Brute," he told Reynolds, but this time *Charlie Ausburne* couldn't oblige. Blast damage or near misses had fouled her torpedo battery and she couldn't fire. The Commodore then ordered Stout to administer the *coup de grace*, but belayed the order when *Yugiri* capsized to starboard. She continued to float, however, so *Dyson* came to bat at 0328, and fired torpedoes. At 0328.30, before *Dyson's* torps could run to target, *Yugiri* disappeared quietly beneath the surface of the tranquil sea, and Gano's torpedoes sailed silently over her as she descended into her grave. Arleigh Burke grabbed TBS and quipped to Gano, "*Roy, you must have fired those torpedoes at too much altitude!*" It was a grim jest but then—killing is a grim business . . .

31-Knot-Burke's anxiety to finish off *Yugiri* was spurred by the hope that he might still catch *Amigiri* and *Uzuki* although those vessels now were so far away that they no longer registered on his radar screens. Wheeling his Division to course 265 degrees true, he sent his fourth report to Admiral Halsey: "Have just sunk one enemy ship in latitude 04°—47'—30" South; longitude 153°—55'—30" East. Am pursuing others to the west. Will need a hell of a lot of air cover." He followed this 5 minutes later with a TBS transmission to Austin: "The two ships that escaped appeared to be on course 265. St. George's Channel is 265. *That is our course from now on!*"

Here, indeed, was daring with a 24-carat, king-sized capital "D"! At that moment Cape St. George, standing guard at the entrance to St. George's Channel, was less than 60 miles distant from Burke. A few miles up that channel, at Simpson Harbor, was Rabaul. In addition to the Japanese air installations at and contiguous to Rabaul, the latest U.S. air reconnaissance photos of the great base had disclosed the presence of several cruisers of the *Yubari* class, nine destroyers, a number of merchant ships, two oilers, and other ancillary craft. Dawn was only 2½ hours away, yet Arleigh Burke was streaking toward this hornet's nest in a bold effort to cut off *Amigiri* and *Uzuki!* It was the kind of thing that heroic fiction—sometimes very bad heroic fiction—is wrought on.

By 0345 *Spence* and *Converse* had closed to within 3 miles of Des-Div-45 and the Squadron steamed along, once more an effective unit of five ships. *Converse* had been on the receiving end of a dud torpedo, and had taken a shot of water in her fuel but young Ten Eyck played his pipes and valves with the virtuosity of an organist in the cathedral of the motion picture, and she kept her station. In *Spence* engineer officer Lieutenant J. A. Naylor, USN, had been bucking a tough job on three boilers throughout the operation but had managed to keep his ship at least within hailing distance of the others.

As the formation sped along Austin observed to Burke, "We saw three big explosions ahead when we were closing you."

"Sure," quipped the now happy and relaxed Commodore, "we did it to light your way."

"Thanks," replied Austin with over-elaborate courtesy. "As usual, you're most considerate!"

Originally Burke had intended to stand on their present course until 0415 but he was beginning to doubt that it would serve any purpose, and at 0356 he messaged the Squadron, "Does anybody think we can catch these babies?"

"It's getting to look as if they got away, unless we go right into Rabaul after them," replied Austin.

"Does your outfit have enough ammunition to go in after them?" asked Burke facetiously.

"*Affirmative!*" snapped Austin, happy to be able to say "yes" for a change, and joining in the spirit of bubbling banter which Burke himself had inaugurated.

"I don't have any ammo left up forward," chimed in Heraldo Stout happily. "We shot it all off! But I'm transferring some from the after end so we'll have guns firing on the bow when the planes come over at dawn."

"I don't think we can go much longer without refueling," said Austin seriously.

"Maybe we could refuel in Rabaul," joked Burke.

"Only trouble with that, Boss," objected Roy Gano with a deadpan voice, "is that the fuel connections might not fit!"

"Well," Heinie Armstrong told the company, "I'm almost out of fresh water, so if we keep on much longer I'm going to have to put beer in my boilers!"

"Oh, oh! Don't do that!" Burke told him. "We'll need that beer to celebrate when we get home. Put it on ice!"

"I think I see the tip of New Britain on my screen, Commodore," said Ham Hamberger.

"I've got it on my picture, too," confirmed Heraldo Stout.

"That's it, boys! It's right over there!" replied Burke.

"Mighty cozy! Mighty cozy!" concluded the imperturbable Heraldo. Of course the appearance of New Britain on the radar screens meant that they were practically in St. George's Channel.

"By the way, a happy Thanksgiving to you, Commodore," said Roy Gano seriously.

"And may you enjoy many more successful ones like this," added Austin with just a flick of accent on the word "more."

"I get it! I get it!" yelped Arleigh Burke happily. "*Stand by to turn one-eight and we'll head for the barn!*"

At 0405 on that Thanksgiving morning, having fought the nearest thing to a perfect naval battle produced by World War II, utterly destroyed three enemy ships, damaged at least one more, and exacted upward of 1,500 enemy lives with no loss to themselves, the triumphant Gallant Squadron set course for Treasury Island and home. With his puckish sense of humor sparking brightly now that the business of stalking and killing was put aside for a while, Burke messaged Admiral Halsey: "On this Thanksgiving Day we are to be thankful to ComAir-Sols for cover! At 0410 love, in latitude 04°—55′; longitude 153°—38′." Halsey replied:

> *31-Knot-Burke: Return to refuel at Purvis. Your Thanksgiving rendezvous with the enemy was a very excellent one, conceived by the Creator, and directed by Commander, Destroyer Squadron 23!*

The devious workings of the Oriental mind never were plumbed by U.S. naval men in the Solomons and Thursday, 25th November, 1943 provided just one more proof that trying to anticipate Japanese moves on what appeared a logical basis was apt to be an unrewarding exercise. DesRon-23, turning top knots and heading south at 6 o'clock dawn, was as inviting a target for enemy air attack as Kusaka could have hoped to find. But the air attack never came. Why it never came is one of the many mysteries still locked in the breasts of the officers who composed the Japanese high command at the time and place.

At 0643, 47 minutes ahead of schedule, the first of eight Lightnings appeared over the Squadron to escort it the rest of the way. Arleigh Burke and Brute Reynolds were enjoying coffee and ham sandwiches on *Ausburne*'s bridge. "You know, Brute," said Burke looking up, "never has the white star on a wing meant so much to tired sailors as the one on that Lightning!"

"Amen to that!" agreed Reynolds.

"And I'll tell you another thing," continued the Commodore. "When the Japanese make up their minds to run, they let nothing interfere with the carrying out of their decision!"

With air cover over, Arleigh Burke did two things: he sent a very private message to the beach about which even Brute Reynolds didn't know, then he permitted himself a few hours of rest. Like his Captains, he was now going on pure instinct, and he knew that wouldn't be good enough to meet the demands he'd have to face upon arrival Purvis.

Already famous when they'd left port 40 hours before, the officers and men of the Gallant Squadron sailed into Purvis Bay at 2200 on the night of Thursday, 25th November, to find themselves hoisted into the celebrity class. Not a man at Purvis but had followed their radio reports with breathless enthusiasm. In an unprecedented display of welcome and "Well done" the cruisers illuminated and manned the rails. Waves of cheers sped the tired little ships to their anchorages, but they were not yet quite ready for sleep. "Keep your ship trained for battle; keep your matériel ready for battle"—those were Burke's rules for the Squadron. And to be ready for battle they must refuel and rearm, and that they did before permitting themselves the rest they so desperately needed.

Midmorning of the next day found Captain DeWitt Clinton Ellis Hamberger, of *U.S.S. Converse* going quietly about a little plan of his own. He didn't know how the other skippers felt, but in *Converse* there was going to be a service of thanksgiving to an Almighty Providence for bringing them safely through the perils of the Battle of Cape St. George, as their latest victory has since become known to history. Arleigh Burke, however, deeply spiritual although a non-church goer, had anticipated Ham Hamberger and several other of the Captains who had the same idea. The private message the tired Commodore had sent ahead of him to Purvis Bay had arranged a thanksgiving service for the whole Squadron. Now, on the Commodore's orders, the bows of *Ausburne, Dyson,* and *Claxton* were drawn together and lashed temporarily. *Ausburne* was the center ship and on her fo'c'sle head appeared a wheezy portable organ whose pedals clacked and scraped against each other when pumped by the yeoman who sat at the keyboard. Beside the organ stood a young chaplain from one of the cruisers, hymnal and Bible in hand. Behind him ranged the choir—ebony and bronze for the most part, and recruited from the galleys of the ships. All the Captains of DesRon-23 were aboard, and officers and men of all the ships crowded forward aboard *Ausburne, Dyson,* and *Claxton* to participate in the service which was principally impressive in its simplicity.

The service was short. The padre knew his men and had a fitting feeling for the spirit of the occasion. He spoke briefly from the text, "These are they who have come out of great tribulation." His words were apt, but perhaps it was in the words of the closing hymn—*How Firm a Foundation*—that the spirit of the gathering and the Squadron found its truest expression. Hesitant and ragged at first, the measures slowly achieved cohesion and volume until, in the final stanza, both words and music rang out over the quiet harbor with the strength of conviction and the certitude of faith:

> *When through fiery trials thy pathway shall lie*
> *My grace, all-sufficient, shall be thy supply;*
> *The flame shall not hurt thee; I only design*
> *Thy dross to consume, and thy gold to refine.*

The promise of the hymn, given Christians centuries before by their God, summed up with startling aptness the *mystique* of the Gallant Squadron. Their pathway had, indeed, led through fiery trials. But their doctrine of faith had been their supply—faith in themselves, faith in their cause, and faith in their leadership. The flame had not hurt them. In the crucible of combat they had been drawn together; the dross of their uncertainty and hesitation had been consumed, and the gold of their true excellence refined.

No unit in the entire history of the United States Navy ever achieved such competence and such confidence in so short a time and in such magnificent measure as did the Gallant Squadron. Their victories in battle were great. Their victories in faith and dedication were greater. Well may Arleigh Burke say, with Lord Howard of Effingham, Admiral of the English Fleet in 1591:

God send us to sea in such company together again, when need is!

Postscript

~~~~~~

Although the Little Beavers went on to continued triumphs, fought until victory, and became the only United States Destroyer Squadron to win a Presidential Unit Citation and the right to wear the blue, yellow and red burgee signaling that honor, never did they or any other U.S. naval unit eclipse their record at the Battle of Cape St. George. Admiral Halsey called this battle "the Trafalgar of the Pacific," and it is studied to this day at the United States Naval War College and comparable institutions throughout the world as a classic and perfect battle.

As the war swept into other areas it became inevitable that DesRon-23 be detached from Task Force 39 and on Tuesday evening, 14th March, 1944 the officers of cruiser *Columbia* tendered a farewell reception to the officers of the Gallant Squadron. It was a merry occasion, made merrier by two *Columbia* officers who sang the following song especially written as a tribute to DesRon-23.*

DesRon-23

> Oh, the cruisers stay in Purvis Bay
> And bitch because it's hot.
> They sit on their butts wondering what's
> Happening up The Slot.
> Well, they'd find out quick if they stood a trick
> At the wheel of a good D D—e—e,
> And did some work with Captain Burke
> In DesRon-23.
> (chorus)
> Oh, DesRon-23, DesRon-23,
> Captain B. and his Little Beavers,
> DesRon-23!

* The verse was sung to the melody of "The Walloping Window Blind," the chorus to the melody of "Camptown Races."

267

Oh, the Jap tin cans they haven't a chance
Against this fighting crew.
They love to fight and they don't feel right
If they're not at all night G.Q.
Every Sunday morn at the break of dawn
In the O.D.'s log you'll see—e—e
"Under way at the break of day; DesRon-23!"
  (CHORUS)

Now these gallant ships were looking for Nips
A-steaming up the line,
When the Jap they found with their pants way down
Revealing their yellow behind.
Oh, they chased their ass from Buka Pass
Clear out of the Coral Sea—e—e . . .
If they'd had the fuel they'd have taken Rabaul,
Who? DesRon-23!

In the cruiser's paper, *The Columbia News*, appeared the following tribute to the Little Beavers from the entire Task Force:

HAPPY SAILING, CONQUERING BEAVERS!

Too often we have seen and heard of man's ingratitude, which has been likened to "a serpent's tooth" and "a flaming sword thrust through the heart." Lest the finger point at us, the officers and men of the *Columbia* want to express their sentiments on the eve of the departure of their faithful friends and team-mates, DesRon-23.

At a crucial period in this theater of war, Task Force 39 participated in a large part of the work and gave an outstanding performance. During this time the colorful "Beavers" set a pace in skill and fighting spirit which contributed materially to the defeat of the Japs in this area. In our mutual assignments, DesRon-23 has been an inspiration to the remainder of our fighting team and a "shot in the arm" to our combat confidence.

And so, goodbye and good luck to the fightingest destroyer Squadron in *any* Navy! May God bless each and every one of you, always.

Their Presidential Unit Citation, which covered only their gallant exploits under Arleigh Burke in the Solomons Campaign and not their subsequent victories, stated:

For extraordinary heroism in action against enemy Japanese forces during the Solomon Islands Campaign, from November 1, 1943 to February 23, 1944. Boldly penetrating submarine-infested waters during a period when Japanese naval and air power was at its height, Destroyer Squadron Twenty-Three operated in daring defiance of repeated attacks by hostile air groups, closing to the enemy's strongly fortified shores to carry out sustained bombardments against Japanese coastal defenses and render effective cover and fire support for the major invasion operations in that area. Commanded by forceful leaders and manned by aggressive, fearless crews, the ships of Squadron Twenty-Three coordinated as a superb fighting team; they countered the enemy's fierce aerial bombing attacks and destroyed or routed his planes; they intercepted his surface task forces, sank or damaged his warships by torpedo fire and prevented interference with our transports. The brilliant and heroic record achieved by Destroyer Squadron Twenty-Three is a distinctive tribute to the valiant fighting spirit of the individual units in this indomitable combat group and of each skilled and courageous ship's company.

Commodore Burke was not destined to lead the Gallant Squadron after the latter part of March, 1944. The Squadron went to Fast Carrier Task Force 38. The Commodore was detached and appointed Chief of Staff to Admiral Marc Mitscher, commanding Carrier Division 3. Although this appointment was another step along the path which was to lead Burke to the top job of Chief of Naval Operations, at the time he loathed the promotion and complained bitterly that somebody was "trying to railroad me out of these lovely destroyers." Before departing, and without mentioning his impending detachment, he sent a final message to the officers and men of DesRon-23:

> *No Squadron in any navy has won more battle honors in less time than the fighting, chasing Twenty-Third. There are no ships which have delivered more devastating blows to the enemy than those of this Squadron. Your heroic conduct and magnificent ability will make your families and your country proud of you. May God continue to bless you!*

When the day finally came Arleigh Burke stood facing Brute Reynolds aboard *Charlie Ausburne.* The Commodore's sennit-decorated and tassled chair stood on deck already hooked to the high line that stretched like an umbilical cord between the destroyer and carrier *Lexington,* and over which he was to be transferred. Burke and Reynolds exchanged photographs, and tears coursed unheeded down the cheeks of 31-Knot-Burke as he managed a farewell which he tried to make brusque to hide his emotion:

"I don't want any cheers, Brute. I'll always keep track of *Ausburne.* Tell the boys, if any of them ever is in Washington where I live, to look me up; they'll be welcome! Goodbye now—and for God's sake don't drop me in the drink when you transfer me by high line to the *Lex!*"

Index

The **Naval Institute Press** is the book-publishing arm of the U.S. Naval Institute, a private, nonprofit, membership society for sea service professionals and others who share an interest in naval and maritime affairs. Established in 1873 at the U.S. Naval Academy in Annapolis, Maryland, where its offices remain today, the Naval Institute has members worldwide.

Members of the Naval Institute support the education programs of the society and receive the influential monthly magazine *Proceedings* and discounts on fine nautical prints and on ship and aircraft photos. They also have access to the transcripts of the Institute's Oral History Program and get discounted admission to any of the Institute-sponsored seminars offered around the country.

The Naval Institute also publishes *Naval History* magazine. This colorful bimonthly is filled with entertaining and thought-provoking articles, first-person reminiscences, and dramatic art and photography. Members receive a discount on *Naval History* subscriptions.

The Naval Institute's book-publishing program, begun in 1898 with basic guides to naval practices, has broadened its scope in recent years to include books of more general interest. Now the Naval Institute Press publishes about 100 titles each year, ranging from how-to books on boating and navigation to battle histories, biographies, ship and aircraft guides, and novels. Institute members receive discounts of 20 to 50 percent on the Press's nearly 600 books in print.

Full-time students are eligible for special half-price membership rates. Life memberships are also available.

For a free catalog describing Naval Institute Press books currently available, and for further information about subscribing to *Naval History* magazine or about joining the U.S. Naval Institute, please write to:

Membership Department
U.S. Naval Institute
118 Maryland Avenue
Annapolis, MD 21402-5035

Telephone: (800) 233-8764
Fax: (410) 269-7940
Web address: www.usni.org